THE PUBLICATIONS
OF THE AMERICAN TRACT SOCIETY

VOLUME I

SOLID GROUND CHRISTIAN BOOKS
BIRMINGHAM, ALABAMA USA

THE PUBLICATIONS

OF THE

AMERICAN TRACT SOCIETY.

VOL. I.

"A very useful method of spreading the knowledge of religion is by distributing, or procuring to be distributed, such pious books, especially to the poorer sort, as are best suited to their capacities and circumstances. Much good may be done this way to considerable numbers at once, in a more acceptable manner, for a trifling expense." — ARCHBISHOP SECKER.

PUBLISHED BY THE

AMERICAN TRACT SOCIETY,

AND SOLD AT THEIR DEPOSITORY, NO. 150 NASSAU-STREET, NEAR THE CITY-HALL, NEW-YORK; AND BY AGENTS OF THE SOCIETY, ITS BRANCHES, AND AUXILIARIES, IN THE PRINCIPAL CITIES AND TOWNS IN THE UNITED STATES.

Solid Ground Christian Books
PO Box 660132
Vestavia Hills AL 35266
205-443-0311
sgcb@charter.net
www.solid-ground-books.com

The Publications of the American Tract Society
Volume I – Tracts 1 – 33

Published by the American Tract Society, New York

First Solid Ground Christian Books Edition Dec. 2007

Cover design by Borgo Design, Tuscaloosa, AL
Reach them at borgogirl@bellsouth.net

ISBN: 159925-0780

CONTENTS.

VOL. I.

No.		Page
1.	Address of the Executive Committee of the American Tract Society to the Christian Public	1
	Narratives illustrating the Usefulness of Tracts	13
2.	The Work of the Holy Spirit. By Rev. Robert Hall, A. M.	25
3.	A Friendly Visit to the House of Mourning. By Rev. Richard Cecil	41
4.	Without Holiness no Man shall see the Lord	73
5.	The Warning Voice	77
6.	Dialogue between a Traveller and Yourself	85
7.	The Happy Negro	89
	Praying Soldier	94
	Profligate Reclaimed	96
8.	On the Lord's Day	97
9.	The Dairyman's Daughter. By Rev. Legh Richmond	101
10.	The Shepherd of Salisbury Plain. By Mrs. Hannah More	129
11	'Tis all for the Best	153
12.	Profane Swearing	169
	The Swearer and Little Child	172
13.	To the Spectator of a Funeral	173
14.	The Poor Villager	177
15.	The Progress of Sin. By Rev. Andrew Fuller	185
	Suggestions of Rev. Dr. Witherspoon	191
16.	Pious Resolutions	193
17.	Parley the Porter. An Allegory. By Mrs. Hannah More	197
18.	Family Worship. By Philip Doddridge, D. D.	209
19.	Three Dialogues between a Minister and one of his Parishioners, on the true principles of Religion, and Salvation by Jesus Christ	221
20.	Remember the Sabbath Day, to keep it Holy	241
	Testimony of Sir Matthew Hale	243
21.	The Closet Companion; or a Help to Self-Examination	245
22.	Repentance and Happy Death of the Earl of Rochester	253
23.	God the Only Refuge	261
24.	On Keeping the Heart. By Rev. John Flavel	269
25.	The Evils of Excessive Drinking	281
	Scale of the Progress from Temperance to Intemperance. By Dr. Rush	288
26.	Sin no Trifle	289

CONTENTS.

No.		Page
27.	Parental Duties	293
	Parental Example	303
28.	Instruction of the Rising Generation in the principles of the Christian Religion, recommended	305
29.	To Children and Youth, on the Importance of Prayer. By Isaac Watts, D. D.	321
	Advice relating to Prayer. By the same Author	325
30.	Benevolence of God	329
31.	Divine Songs for Children. By Isaac Watts, D. D.	341
32.	Day of Judgment	361
33.	Redemption. By Joseph John Gurney	373

FIRST LINES OF HYMNS IN THIS VOLUME.

The Lord my pasture shall prepare	152
Sure there's a righteous God	168
Death, like an overflowing stream	176
Awak'd by Sinai's awful sound	184
'Tis a point I long to know	252
Show pity, Lord, O Lord, forgive	260
Hark, the voice of love and mercy	340
Lo! he comes—the King of glory	371
Day of Judgment, day of wonders	372
He dies! the Friend of sinners dies	404

No. 1.

THE ADDRESS
OF THE
EXECUTIVE COMMITTEE
OF THE
AMERICAN TRACT SOCIETY,
TO THE
CHRISTIAN PUBLIC.

PUBLISHED BY THE

AMERICAN TRACT SOCIETY,

150 NASSAU-STREET, NEW-YORK.

D Fanshaw, Printer.

ADDRESS

OF THE

EXECUTIVE COMMITTEE.

THE Executive Committee of the AMERICAN TRACT SOCIETY, by this document, beg the privilege of addressing the Christian community upon one of the most interesting subjects which has ever attracted the notice of those whose stations or whose character give them influence over the destiny of their fellow-men. In the month of March, 1825, incipient measures were adopted in the City of New-York, with the view of forming a Society, to be denominated the AMERICAN TRACT SOCIETY; the object of which should be, "to diffuse a knowledge of our Lord Jesus Christ as the Redeemer of sinners, and to promote the interest of vital godliness and sound morality, by the circulation of Religious Tracts, calculated to receive the approbation of all Evangelical Christians." Deference to the numerous existing Societies in the different States induced the original projectors of this design to invite a consultation of Delegates to be holden on the Tuesday preceding the Anniversary of the American Bible Society, in May then ensuing, for the purpose of maturing the enterprise, and giving existence and form to the Institution. At this consultation there were present a respectable number of Delegates, from various religious denominations, who, with the advice and assistance of other gentlemen of high consideration from different sections of the country, revised and agreed upon a Constitution to be submitted to a more public meeting on the following day, when the proceedings of the Convention were considered and sanctioned with a most delightful unanimity.

In making this presentation of their object to the friends of the Redeemer in the United States, and in venturing most respectfully to urge the claims of this institution to general patronage, the Committee feel that it is needless to exhibit, to any considerable extent, the superior advantages of that method of moral and religious instruction which is pursued by the distribution of Tracts. Though men are fallen by their iniquity, and are to be recovered from their apostacy and condemnation only through the redemption that is in Christ Jesus, and by the renewing of the Holy Ghost, yet does this method of mercy most distinctly recognise the use of means in the business of their salvation. Next to the Bible and the living Ministry, one of these means of light and salvation will be found to be short, plain, striking, entertaining, and instructive *Tracts*, exhibiting in writing some of the great and glorious truths of the Gospel. "The Word of Truth" is the great instrument of moral renovation. He who scatters it, scatters the seed of the Kingdom, and may look for the Harvest in God's own good time and way. A Tract may be perused at leisure; it may be consulted in the hour of retirement and solitude; it can be read in a little time; and though it may contain instruction important and weighty enough for the consideration of the sage, and yet simple enough to be accommodated to the taste and intelligence of a child, may be easily weighed and deposited in the memory. This method of instruction is peculiarly calculated for the poor, and is especially demanded by the poor of an extended population. It is a method by which the blessings of a religious education may, to no inconsiderable degree, be extended to the lower ranks of society with peculiar facility, and which, as a practical system, is already entitled to the claims of successful experiment. It is a means of doing good which is level to every capacity, and adapted to every condition. The man of low attainment in science, the mother, the child, the obscure in the meanest condition, can give away a Tract, and, perhaps, accompany it with a word of advice or admonition, with as much promise of success as a Missionary or an Apostle. A Minister may distribute Tracts among his people, and thus impress and extend his public instructions where impressions of his official duty would otherwise be lost, or never extended; and in this way he may double his usefulness, and devote two lives to his Master's glory instead of one. The teacher and the pupil, the parent and the child, the master and the servant, may become to each other the most effectual preachers, by the distribution of Tracts.

The traveller may scatter them along the roads and throughout the inns and cottages; and in return, the inns and cottages may spread them before the eye of the thoughtless traveller. Merchants may distribute them to ship-masters, and ship-masters to seamen; men of business may transmit them with every bale of goods, to the remote corners of the land and globe; and thus the infinitely important truths of the Gospel—truths by which it is the purpose of the God of Heaven to make men " wise to salvation"—like the diffusive light, may be emitted from numberless sources, and in every direction. All this may be done in the most inoffensive and inobtrusive way; with no magisterial authority; no claims of superior wisdom or goodness; and no alarm to human pride or frowardness. All this may be done, too, with no loss of time. " A Tract can be given away, and God's blessing asked upon it, in a moment." Aside from the influence of those institutions which involve no expense at all, in no way can so much probable good be effected at so little expense, as by the distribution of Tracts. A Tract which contains 15 *pages* can be published for a *single cent!* And when we recollect how long a single Tract may be preserved, by how many individuals and families it may be read, and when read by them, to how many others it may be lent, it is difficult to conceive of a way in which more good can be accomplished by a very small amount of means. As an auxiliary to other means of doing good, the distribution of Tracts also holds a distinguished place. In how many sick chambers, in how many meetings of anxious inquiry, in how many circles of wealth and prosperity, of fashion, folly, and vice, may these faithful witnesses be left to testify what otherwise never would be told. The language of every Missionary Society, either Domestic or Foreign, is, " A Missionary without a supply of Tracts is unprovided for his work; the press is the grand medium of communication in all parts of the missionary world." A Missionary at *Sumatra* writes—" I am fully of opinion that, among all nations not accustomed to books, the distribution of small Tracts, written in an easy style, or of single Gospels, is much more likely to do good than that of larger works. This opinion is strengthened by the experience and observation of every day." Nor are the preceding suggestions founded in mere theory, but warranted by facts.

The amount of good already achieved by the distribution of Tracts is incalculable. Much has been done, in this and other countries, to afford the most satisfactory evidence of their beneficial effects. The most interesting accounts accumulate upon us from every quarter where Tracts are circulated, either in Christian or Pagan lands, of their extended utility. It is impossible to recite them. Volumes might be profitably occupied with the most interesting narratives of this sort. There is not a week in which we have not striking accounts of their happy results. Some years ago, the author of the Tract called the *Dairyman's Daughter* is said to have received information of *three hundred conversions* by the instrumentality of that Tract. Of the labours of how many ministers of the Gospel can this be said, even though they have extended to very advanced age? Many revivals of religion this little Tract is known to have occasioned. The Tract called " *The Swearer's Prayer*" has been at least equally successful. More than twenty instances of conversion by the instrumentality of Tracts were reported, with their attending circumstances, to the Committee of one Society in the United States, during the year next preceding the formation of this Society, besides several revivals of religion occasioned, or greatly promoted, by that Society's publications. We are not ignorant of the alarming success with which Voltaire and his infidel associates on the continent of Europe, and elsewhere, proved the efficacy of this method of access to the common people, in producing one of the most terrible moral convulsions which have ever shaken the world. And we are not ignorant of the success of men of a different spirit, in those well-directed efforts in the cause of Tracts, by which the continent began to be enlightened and reformed in the days of the great Reformation.

But these laudable efforts, notwithstanding all they have achieved, have come short of the exigences of the world, and have, in no small degree, failed of their object, through a divided and partial operation. It has long been a doubtful point whether Christians of different denominations could unite their efforts beyond the single endeavour of distributing the Holy Scriptures " without note or comment." And yet the " body of Christ " is one. In all that pertains to the essential principles of Christianity, it cannot be otherwise than that there exists a union of affection and sentiment among all good men, by whatever name they may be called; and we are persuaded this harmony exists to a degree beyond the anticipations not only of the more vigilant and cautious, but of the more indulgent and liberal. All good men receive the Holy Scriptures as containing a complete and entire system of divine truth, by whose unerring standard every opinion is to be tried and decided. So long as they love the Bible, they cannot be at war with one another. And so long as they believe the truths of the Bible, are they united in their religious sentiments. We do not mean by this to become the abettors of that *modern liberality* which discovers no difference between the precious and the vile, and which consists in a virtual indifference to all religious opinions. To us it appears that the authority of the Divine Legislator extends to the understandings of men, as well as their conduct, and that they have no more right to believe what is false than to practise what is wrong. But we do believe that if good men beheld each other's goodness through a near medium, and one less obscured, they would be more under the direction of a reciprocated confidence, and their prejudices and fears would melt away before the benignant influence of holy love. And we do mean to affirm, that were there a more scrupulous regard to the infallible judgment of God, and a less scrupulous regard to the fallible judgment of men; if the rivalship of denomination were merged in the rivalship of benevolent enterprise; if the fear of God and the love of Jesus Christ; if a tender compassion for the salvation of sinners, and a tender affection toward all the friends of the Redeemer, were the paramount principles of action, chilling alienations would pass away, heart-burning suspicions would find no place, mutual criminations would be suppressed, more importance would be attached to the things in which we agree, and less to those in which we differ; there would be more of the soul of union; and while the enemies of our religion would be again constrained to bear the honourable testimony, " See how these Christians love one another," we ourselves should sing, " Behold how good and how pleasant it is for brethren to dwell together in unity!"

It is obvious that the only difficulty in forming a Tract Society upon these enlarged principles, lies in the doctrinal character of the Tracts to be circulated. On this subject the most full and liberal provision is made in the Constitution of the AMERICAN TRACT SOCIETY. The different denominations composing the Publishing Committee come to their work with the solemn and honest stipulation to be each the protector of his own peculiarities; and in this labour of mercy to publish and distribute such Tracts only as shall inculcate those great doctrines in which they all harmonize. Man's native sinfulness—the purity and obligation of the law of God—the true and proper Divinity of our Lord Jesus Christ—the necessity and reality of his atonement and sacrifice—the efficiency of the Holy Spirit in the work of renovation—the free and full offers of the Gospel, and the duty of men to accept it—the necessity of personal holiness—as well as an everlasting state of rewards and punishments beyond the grave—these are doctrines dear to our hearts, and constitute the basis of our union. And who does not see, that in the present state of our own country and the world, there is a wide sphere of successful operations, in simply diffusing these and other kindred truths in which we agree? It is hoped that the Publishing Committee, agreeably to the suggestion of the esteemed President of the Society, in his first official address, will " ever bear in mind the high responsibility of their office; and always feel that, as the eternal destinies of souls may hang upon their deliberations and measures, no Tract should ever be issued from the Depository of this Society which does not contain, should it find its way where a Bible was never seen, nor the Gospel ever heard, enough of Divine truth to guide the ignorant and inquiring sinner into the path of eternal life."

If in any instance we should hesitate about the terms in which any truth should be expressed, we may always be relieved from our embarrassment by resorting to the terms of the Bible, and adopting the very language of the spirit of all truth. The Committee cannot feel that this is a visionary enterprise. They no longer regard it as a doubtful experiment. On the most matured view of all the difficulties they can anticipate, they are persuaded that it is a practicable and high-born undertaking. The indications of Divine Providence have so manifestly led to it, that though they have all admitted some anxious speculations, they dare not hesitate. It is with deep-felt gratitude and delight that they have watched the superintendance of the Holy Spirit over this novel and hopeful attempt; and already do they indulge the expectation, that under the same refreshing influence, the riches of the harvest will correspond with the splendour of this early promise. Who can tell but the time is drawing near, when the different sections of the church of God on earth shall be " perfectly joined together in the same mind and the same judgment;" and that without either embracing or propagating error, or suppressing the truth, (and without withholding their censure from all who believe ".another Gospel,") they shall imbibe that amiable and conciliating temper whose attractive influence shall allure them to concentrated efforts in every labour of love? Who can tell but the present is an instance of harmony and co-operation which will prepare the way for other and more important instances, when in unity of faith and unity of spirit, no benevolent enterprise shall fail through the discordancy of Christians; and when in every cause that demands prompt and extended co-operation, the friends of the Redeemer shall know how to combine their energies against the common foe? Who will not say, " The Lord hasten it in his time!" "Thy watchmen shall lift up the voice; with the voice together shall they sing; for they shall see *eye to eye, when the Lord shall bring again Zion.*"

Peculiar advantages, it appears to the Committee, will result from the formation of a great Institution whose operations shall extend over our whole country, and, as far as practicable, even beyond its limits. The two-fold union of various local institutions, and of Christians of different denominations, all applying their powers in common direction, and uniting the concurrence and feeling of this free and enterprising nation, appears to be the only measure which can secure all the energy of operation that is needed. The world at large, the adjacent states of South America, the islands of the West Indies, and our own United States in particular, present a vast and inviting field for the exertions of a Society combining the efforts of the whole Christian community. Our own country contains a population of more than eleven millions, scattered over an extent of more than one million of square miles, every hour becoming a more numerous and more reading population. Four millions of this population consist of children; and under the operation of the system of Common Schools which is adopted in many of the states, aided by the influence of Sabbath Schools established in all, how comparatively easy is it to extend the power of moral and religious instruction, through the medium of Tracts, to these flourishing nurseries of the Church and the State. Should God lift his smile upon the Society, it will speak to the remoter corners of the globe. The purpose of its conductors is to publish Tracts in various languages, and to be heralds of Divine Mercy, not to our own population, only, or to the provinces of our Northern and Southern frontier, but to Eastern and Western Asia and the Southern Ocean. But how can this be accomplished without a more generous and undivided impulse? Every new Institution, also, of such character, exerts a happy influence on our national union, and is a new accession of the best and strongest affections of the human heart, gathered from the remotest parts of the land, to "lengthen the cords and strengthen the stakes" that bind together the body politic; so that, while public opinion maintains its existing ascendency, every new accession of diffusive benevolence will render it more and more difficult for the spirit of faction or usurpation to sever this cemented country. And so long as public opinion maintains its existing supremacy, who does not feel the immense importance of moulding it by a moral and religious influence, and of securing and augmenting our civil and political liberties by the most unconfined diffusion of the lights of science and religion throughout a community whose political existence depends on the intelligence, and, more especially, on the integrity of the people? We might add to these considerations that, should approved Tracts be supplied to the nation from one general establishment, one set of stereotype plates, and one set of engravings, one Board of Managers and Officers, and one centre of transportation, the economy of such a measure in all the expenditures and labours of the Society must be a powerful argument in favour of the union. Tracts are now exceedingly cheap, but the Committee are greatly deceived if the formation of the AMERICAN TRACT SOCIETY does not render them cheaper than they now are, and if the parent Depository is not able to supply the country at a lower rate than they can be supplied by the local Societies. And why should the establishment of a General Institution diminish the zeal of the local Societies? Are they not all moving forward from the desire of doing good, and under the paramount impulse to what is best? Has the National Bible Society diminished the zeal of the local Bible Societies? With the Divine blessing on the AMERICAN TRACT SOCIETY, the Committee have little doubt that a course will be pursued which, by augmenting the zeal of the whole, will augment the zeal of the parts; which, while it shall secure the confidence, will concentrate the unabated and increased efforts of the nation; and which, while it invigorates the heart, will pour its life-blood, with accelerated force, through every artery and vein.

The city of New-York, eminently distinguished by its natural and local advantages, its accumulating population and its increasing commercial prosperity and influence, seems destined, in the wisdom of Divine Providence, to become the centre of these extended operations. If the signs of the times call for a general Institution, where might we look for the seat of its operations, unless where there are greater facilities of ingress and egress, and more extended, constant, and direct intercommunications with foreign ports, and every part of our interior, than are to be found in any other locality in the nation? When the canals which are now in progress shall be completed, there will be a direct inland water communication between this port and every village of note in the extended country to the West of the Alleghany Mountains. Already one-third part of all the foreign goods brought into the United States are entered at this port, and here put up for merchants in every part of the Union. Merchants assemble here, and opportunities are constantly presented for sending Tracts, at a very small expense, and very frequently at no expense at all, to the remotest parts of the land, and of engaging the proper persons to use their influence in distributing them. And it is hoped that the increasing and well-directed zeal in Benevolent Institutions which has been manifested by our citizens for a few past years, and especially the interest which has recently been awakened in the Tract cause, affords the community some pledge of persevering exertion in this responsible work, which will be effectually redeemed. We are sensible that the eyes of good men in the country are directed towards us, and that they have a right to expect that every man engaged in this important business will do his duty.

The formation of the AMERICAN TRACT SOCIETY, therefore, in the city of New-York, we cannot but hope, is an event which will be regarded with interest by all the friends of our common Lord. This union forms a new era in the history of the American Churches; and the auspices under which it has been consummated are certainly of bright augury. We respectfully solicit the favour of the Christian community, not for our sakes, but his who "died for us and rose again." To Ministers and churches—to Societies already in existence, and to communities where Auxiliary Associations may be formed—to wealthy individuals whom God has made the stewards and almoners of his bounty—to benevolent males and females, we would affectionately and urgently say, *Come and help us*. The enterprise in which we are engaged, though among the most noiseless, may be ranked among the most noble exploits of the age in which we live. It cannot be carried forward without harmony of design and united perseverance and zeal; and "it is good to be zealously affected in a good thing." We feel justified in soliciting, for the object we pursue, your fixed and steady attention, your strong and ardent affections, your hearty and vigorous co-operation. There is great weight and influence in our design; and though there may be difficulties, and even dangers, in our way, we cherish sanguine expectations of the Divine favour and blessing.

We live, fellow-citizens, at an eventful period of the world. The purposes of God's mercy appear to be rapidly unfolding, and rapidly and surely advancing toward their final issue. New scenes are already opening upon the world and upon the Church; and the "enterprise to be achieved is the conversion of the world to its Redeeming God and King." In this vast and arduous enterprise no portion of mankind are bound to feel a deeper interest than the people of these United States. The state of our country is one of unparalleled prosperity. At peace among ourselves and with all nations, our population is becoming "as the sand which is by the sea, in multitude." Our industry and wealth are giving this favoured people a high elevation in the catalogue of nations. The light of science and the arts is diffusing its influence through every part of our growing Republic. Our plans of internal improvement and public utility are raising our dignity and glory in the view of future ages; and our happy religion, born of God, descended from Heaven, and dwelling in undisturbed security in this Western World, has already exerted its efficient power in forming here a people for his praise. The Committee indulge the hope that great multitudes in this happy portion of the globe will enrol their names among the patrons of this institution and the benefactors of mankind. They know that the enterprise in which they are engaged is one which cannot prosper, unless the God of all the earth control and prosper it. They earnestly solicit an interest in your prayers as well as your benefactions. To them it is a delightful thought that the cause is God's, and dependent absolutely on him. "*Not by might nor by power, but by my Spirit, saith the Lord of Hosts!*" This is their motto. We cannot hope too much from God. In the name of God alone they begin and go forward, confiding always in that divine guidance and favour, which in all their toil shall be invoked by prayer, and in all their success be honoured with thanksgiving.

NARRATIVES

ILLUSTRATING THE USEFULNESS OF RELIGIOUS TRACTS.

The following facts, communicated by persons who have been honoured as the instruments of doing much good by the distribution of Religious Tracts, will speak to the pious and feeling mind with peculiar force.

I consider it, says a pious, intelligent individual, one of the greatest enjoyments of my life, that I have been permitted to scatter so many thousands of these arrows of truth, in our own and other countries, by land and by sea. They have uniformly been received with apparent pleasure, and in many instances with great joy, and even with tears of gratitude. As I was but a *traveller*, I could only sow the seed, leaving it to future days to reveal the fruit. Yet, in some instances, immediate good was apparent. I gave a Tract to a female servant who was much alarmed in a thunder-storm, and accompanied it with some conversation. It made known to her the wrath of God revealed against her while continuing impenitent, and was the means, as there is reason to believe, of directing her to the only Refuge from the eternal storm that is coming on the ungodly. She continues, so far as man can judge, a sincere friend of Jesus.

I gave a few Tracts and a Testament to a young woman confined in a solitary cell in a jail. I had the pleasure of hearing afterward that there was reason to hope that they were blessed to the conversion of her soul.

When I reached the end of a long journey into a destitute part of the United States, I found that my Tracts were almost gone, and engaged a man to go on horseback, on Sabbath morning, and loan one Tract to each of thirty families in the neighbourhood, saying that he would take it the next Sabbath morning and lend them another.. One woman gave evidence of conversion in consequence of reading these Tracts.

To one poor old woman who could not read, and had been for years confined to her bed, I read that most excellent Tract, "*To the Aged.*" She could sit up in her bed;

and as I read, the tears streamed down her furrowed cheeks, and many an interruption did she make, to express her delight with the *feast* Providence was giving her. "*O !*" said she, "*I do bless God for sending you to me, and shall recollect you when I meet you in heaven; I know I shall.*" It was a precious season to me, and I trust to several others who could not read, but sat around, and heard the words of salvation.

I might add many interesting occurrences, but if there were no other advantage in distributing Religious Tracts, than its influence on the individual who scatters them, I would recommend to all never to travel without them. A hint from a friend suggested to me the duty of lifting my heart in prayer for a blessing on every Tract I delivered; and I never dared omit it. Thus, having the affections constantly elevated to God, "I seemed to be borne in the arms of my Saviour" as I journeyed onward; and I felt his strength enabling me to utter a word for Him whenever I had opportunity to speak to the person to whom a Tract was presented.

A Clergyman, several years ago, deposited in the store of a merchant in one of our large cities, a quantity of Tracts for sale. The merchant, supposing that the profits were for the Clergyman's personal benefit, disposed of the Tracts as he had opportunity, but took no interest in them himself; till one day curiosity led him to examine their contents. He soon found among them the *Shepherd of Salisbury Plain;* which its excellent author, Mrs. Hannah More, has mentioned as, in her judgment, the most useful of her publications. It found its way to his heart. He felt that he needed a religion which would render him happy in poverty and affliction. He sought and found. His partner in trade was influenced, by a Tract which he found in the same parcel, to attend to the things of religion, and consecrate himself to God. Both have since felt an unwavering attachment to the cause of Christ; have distributed thousands of Religious Tracts, and been efficient friends of Missions, Bible Societies, and all the Benevolent Institutions which God is now using to promote the kingdom of his dear Son.

A mutual friendship, writes the Lady of Rev. Dr. Henderson, at St. Petersburg, subsisted between Mr. Hender-

THE USEFULNESS OF TRACTS.

son and our excellent friend (Rev. Dr.) Paterson, in early life. The latter having finished his studies at Glasgow, was bent on labouring as a missionary in India. He sought a companion and fellow-labourer; and Mr. Henderson being willing to devote himself to the same work, they embarked together for Copenhagen, intending to proceed from that port. But war breaking out between England and Denmark, they were detained in that capital, and laboured in acquiring the language, translating and distributing Tracts, &c. It happened one day, as they were in the royal gardens, that Henderson gave a Tract (*The Great Question Answered. By Rev. Andrew Fuller*) to a young physician who passed by. He read it, and it made such an impression on his mind, that he wished to find who was the stranger that gave it to him. For this purpose he went to a patient, one of the Moravian Brethren, from whom he thought himself likely to obtain the information. This pious man rejoiced to find that such measures were taking to evangelize his countrymen, and rested not till he found out the abode of Paterson and his friend, and introduced himself to them. From this individual our young missionaries learned the deplorable state of *Iceland*, in respect to the distribution of the Scriptures, and a correspondence was entered into with the Bible Society for supplying its inhabitants. This laid the foundation for our two friends being engaged in the service of the Bible Society, and consequently for all the blessings that have flowed, are still flowing, and, no doubt, will yet more abundantly flow, from the Societies now existing in Denmark, Sweden, Russia, Iceland—I was going to add, by anticipation, Turkey, Persia, &c. &c.—See, my friend, what consequences may result from a *single Tract !*

You gave me a number of Tracts, writes a pious young Schoolmaster, among which was *The Swearer's Prayer*. I had in my school a boy who habitually made use of profane language. I made many efforts to reclaim him, by inflicting various punishments, but in vain. I directed all my scholars not to associate with him, on any occasion, lest he should corrupt them; and had almost determined to exclude him from the school. This enraged him so violently that I was at a loss what to do. One day, about twelve months since, while I was remonstrating with him, it occurred to me that to make him learn *The Swearer's Prayer* by heart, might have a good effect; I therefore gave it to him on Saturday to commit to memory. On the Monday following, he came to school with a dejected countenance, and I was convinced there was an outward sign of inward sorrow—his tongue faltered while repeating some of his task, and tears of contrition ran down his cheeks. I was affected very much at the sudden change in this boy, to see what the Lord can do by the simplest means. I asked his elder brother, lately, whether he had sworn since? He replied, " No;—*I think The Swearer's Prayer has cured him of swearing, and he has been more obedient to his parents since he got it than he ever was before.*" I can truly say that I have not a better behaved lad among my forty scholars than he has been during the last year.

I gave a Tract, says an Agent of a Tract Society in England, about two years since, to a poor black man, who had just landed from an American vessel, and was consulting with the rest of his crew how to spend the evening. After some consideration, they all decided upon their different pursuits except the poor black man, whom they left behind. Observing this, I went up to him, and asked him how it was he did not go with his brother seamen. He replied, "Oh, me poor man—me no money—me go on board and read de songs." "What, then," said I, " you can read?" "Oh, yes," was the answer. I then took from my pocket " *The Swearer's Prayer,*" and said, " perhaps you will read this, it will be something new to you." The Tract was accepted, and I saw nothing more of him until a few months since, when I was accosted in the street in the following manner:—" Tank you, Sir, for de book." " What book, my good fellow?" " De book of life dat you gave me two years ago." Not remembering ever to have given him a Bible, I still remained wondering; when the poor fellow exclaimed, " it was *De Swearer's Prayer;* and me did read it to all de crew, and not one of dem do swear now. Oh! it is de book of life!" I had some interesting conversation with him, and learned that his name was Alexander De Bows.

A gentleman of my congregation, says a clergyman in England, travelling to London by one of the stage-coaches, and distributing some Tracts by the way, at last said to the coachman, "I have not offered you any Tracts, but if you will read them, here are some for your acceptance," at the same time giving him seven or eight different Tracts, without any further conversation. About a year after, the same gentleman having occasion again to go to London, travelled in the same coach, and with the same coachman. Near the spot where he had formerly given him the Tracts, the coachman addressed him : "Sir, I believe you are the gentleman that some time ago gave me some Religious Tracts. I must be short, but I have reason to bless God for those Tracts; I would say more, if time permitted :" he added, "I have a wife that is a good woman, and I was her greatest persecutor; but now it is my greatest pleasure to go with her to the house of God."

In a late short journey, I was pleased with the manner in which some small publications I took with me were received by persons in many places. In some of them I stopped, and introduced the delivery with a short address, which I found often had a good effect. I now and then saw a tear start in the eye, and gratitude beam in the countenance. In most cases I exhorted the person to whom I presented a Tract, to read it with attention, and pray to God for a blessing. Once, in my way to ———, I passed a poor man employed in mending the road. I stopped my horse, and addressed him affectionately respecting the great concerns of his soul and eternity. I gave him a small Tract, and begged him to read it, and pray over it, which he promised to do. In a few days I returned the same way, and providentially met with the same poor man. I inquired whether he had read the little book I gave him. He began to weep, and humbly replied, "I have, sir, and thank you for it. I have learned what I did not know before, and what I hope I shall never forget."

About twelve months since, a person thus addressed me. "Sir, do you remember, about two years ago, giving some little books about religion to persons on the road to ——— ?" I replied, that I perfectly well recollected distributing some hundreds in that neighbourhood, about that time. "Yes, sir," said he, "and you called a poor man from the field, where he was working, and asked him if he could read; he said, No. You inquired if his children could read; he replied in the affirmative. You gave him some Tracts; he took them home; his children read them to him—the Lord blessed them to his soul. His eyes were enlightened, his heart affected, and his mind filled with sorrow. He sought retirement, poured out his soul before God, and became a new creature in Christ Jesus; has joined a church; and now, with his wife and children, appears to be following the Lamb." I was deeply impressed with this account, and intimated a wish to see him. He was soon informed of it, and sent to request that I would preach in the neighbourhood. I rode out accordingly, and preached at a farmer's house, where an aged woman had been for many years a cripple, and incapable of hearing the Gospel out of her own house. I continue to preach there to this day; and have every reason to believe that the old woman, aged eighty years, her son, the farmer, and one of their neighbours, are truly converted to God, through Jesus Christ our Lord. Such has been the blessed result of a few Tracts casually dispersed in the most barren parts of ———.

A pious and benevolent lady, who had been entrusted by the Committee of a Tract Society with a large number of their publications, writes thus: " It will be gratifying to the Committee to learn that the liberality with which they have permitted me to disperse their Tracts in this place has not been in vain. An evident blessing has accompanied their distribution. Through the medium of one of them, a soldier, in one of the regiments stationed here, marked among those who knew him as a most profane and wicked man, has been stopped in his career of iniquity, led to forsake the broad road in which he was walking, and enabled, it is hoped, to seek and find the narrow path which leads to everlasting life. His former wicked companions have in vain solicited him to return to their society; while those few of his comrades who are themselves religious, beholding the greatness of his change, exclaim, ' What hath God wrought! It is his work, and wonderful in our eyes!' "

Another soldier, it is hoped, has been truly awakened to a sense of his sinfulness, by reading in a Tract entitled " Short Sermons," the address on the text, *Without holiness no man shall see the Lord*. It was put into his hands when sick in the hospital, and by it he was convinced that he was, both by nature and practice, destitute of all holiness, and consequently without hope toward God. In considerable distress of mind he began to read his Bible, and there became acquainted with the gracious method of salvation it reveals. I have seen those who have conversed with him, and they have expressed themselves much pleased with his deep humility of mind, his earnest desire to walk worthy of his new and holy profession, as well as with the accounts they have heard of his general deportment.

A minister at —— writes thus: Some time since a friend of mine gave to a woman, who attends our church, a few Tracts to take home for her husband, who was about seventy years of age, and had grown gray in the service of sin; having not only neglected religion himself, but violently persecuted his wife for her attention to its important duties. He read the Tracts, and the happy result of their perusal was a deep conviction of sin, and concern for salvation. He lived just long enough to lay hold on eternal life, and to afford a pleasing testimony to the sincerity of his faith. After about six months' illness, he died in a full dependence upon the sacrifice of Christ for the justification of his soul in the sight of God; acknowledging, with almost his last breath, that he should have to bless God for ever for those who had been instrumental in the salvation of his immortal soul.

Another says: In distributing your Tracts, I gave one to a young woman in the village, who was very careless about the best things. She read it, and it was useful to her. A few days afterward she came to me in concern, saying she had laid the book in her window, and the casement being open, she supposed it had been blown by the wind into the road, and wished to have another, which I gave her. A short time after this, it appeared that her conjecture was true. The wind had blown the Tract into the road, where it was picked up by a young woman that was passing by at the time; and she had reason to hope the book had been very useful to her, by bringing her to attend regularly upon the means of grace, as well as producing a great change in her conduct.

As a man was passing through the town of A——, in M——, with a drove of cattle, on the Sabbath, a Tract was handed him, inculcating the duty of remembering the Sabbath-day, and keeping it holy. He determined that he would not read it, though he did not throw it away. When out of sight, he felt a curiosity to see what it contained, and began to read it. He soon began to feel the guilt and danger of profaning the Sabbath; and said to his companion, "Let us stop till the Sabbath is over." His companion refused. "Well," said he, "you may go on, but I shall stop." They both put up till the close of the Sabbath. But the man still felt the burden of a "wounded spirit;" and he found no relief till he submitted to Jesus. He is now a member of the church, and traces his first serious impressions to that Tract.

As a young man in P—— was about making a voyage at sea, his mother put into his trunk a parcel of Tracts. While on his voyage, curiosity led him to examine this little bundle. On opening it, his eye fastened on "*The Young Cottager.*" It arrested his attention, and he read it through; and there is reason to hope that it has left an impression on his mind which will *never* be effaced. He separated from his companions, and spent much of his time in reading, meditation, and prayer. He continued this course until his return; when he found that his relish for former pleasures was gone, and he was led to say, "I had rather be a door-keeper in the house of my God, than to dwell in the tents of wickedness." He has since made a public profession of religion; and relates, with humility and gratitude, the kindness of God in causing to be put into his trunk that little Tract.

The Tract entitled "*The Young Cottager,*" was handed by a little child to a young lady in B——. As she read it, an involuntary tear started from her eye, and offended with herself for being overcome by a Tract, she threw it down, and resolved to have nothing more to do with it. But she could not rest, and took it up again. She was again affected, even to tears, and angrily threw it down. But she could not rest then; she took it up again, and at length read it through. And an impression was fastened upon her mind which there is reason to believe will be eternal. "What!" said she, "can this poor cottager so bewail her sins, and I, who am ten-fold more guilty, feel no relentings?"

Days and weeks of anguish, on account of her sins, passed away; and she wandered in darkness, and saw no light. But at length a ray from the Sun of Righteousness broke in upon her, and she was brought out of darkness into marvellous light. For years she has now been engaged in seeking out the poor and destitute, and distributing among them Bibles and Religious Tracts; instructing them in Sabbath Schools, and exciting her acquaintance to greater and more systematical efforts for the salvation of men.

The Committee, says the report of a Tract Society in the United States, could tell you of a pious man passing a lowly cottage, solemnly impressed with his duty to enter and leave there the *Warning Voice;* and of his soon after hearing, in a distant part of the town, that the mother of the family was in anguish on account of her sins, unable to attend to her daily business, earnestly desirous to see the stranger whom God had thus made the instrument of awaking her from the slumber of death, that he might pray with her, and tell her what she must do to be saved;— of a carpenter that hewed his timber on the Sabbath, reformed by means of the Tract *On the Lord's Day;*—of a pious mechanic, on a sick bed, and, as he believed, about to depart, consoled and animated in view of the glory that awaited him, as described in the *Splendid Wedding;*— of a youth converted to God by means of a *Religious Card;*—of a pious young physician, who, at the time of a revival in college, heard them singing the words,

" Stop, poor sinner, stop, and think;"

which words he learned, when a child, from a Tract given him, and to which, through Divine mercy, he attributes all his desires and endeavours to promote the cause of Christ, and all his hopes of heaven.

They could tell you of a missionary, at the West, who read the History of *Dinah Doudney* all along as he travelled among the destitute, and found it opening a way to the heart and conscience of parents and children, many of whom, he has reason to think, will be benefited by that Tract to eternity;—of a father and a mother who neglected wholly the house of God, and made the Sabbath a day of recreation, convinced of their error and wickedness by the *Persuasive to Public Worship*, read to them on Saturday evening, found the next day with the assembly of God's people, and in one month after, trusting for pardon and salvation through the merits of the crucified Saviour;—of a mother who had been exceedingly depraved, even so much so as openly to blaspheme the name of her Maker, presented by her minister, who feared he should thus offend her, with the Tract, *Every Man the Friend or the Enemy of Christ.* And though detained from the house of God by the little children around her, and surrounded only by irreligious companions, to whom she dared not speak on the subject of religion, after many weeks of distress for her sins, visited the minister and his pious wife, and told them, that she had read the Tract given her, and believed he had selected it because he thought her the " enemy of God;" that her sins had appeared great to her, beyond description; none but God had known the anguish of her heart; but now she could " rejoice in the Lord, and joy in the God of her salvation." She has since united with the church, and does what she can to support and animate her minister in his labours of love.

They could tell you of a minister, who, when he first visited the parish where he is now settled, learned that the people had been seven years destitute of a pastor, obtained from the benevolent a quantity of Tracts, and went from house to house, distributing them, conversing on their contents, exchanging those read for others; and who found the Holy Spirit meeting them by his precious influences, and soon admitted twenty-six persons to the table of the Lord. " For this blessing," he says, " I can state my fullest conviction, that it was your Tracts which prepared the way."—They could tell of a pious female, in a country parish, who began to loan Tracts to the children around her, and in less than three months could say, " I must write a word to interest your feelings and engage your prayers for the large group of little Tract readers in our neighbourhood. Since I last wrote, as many as *seven* or *eight*, we hope, have begun to sing " Hosanna to the Son of David;" and nearly thirty present themselves at the anxious meetings which have lately been established, and appear deeply concerned for the salvation of their souls."

They could tell of the *Swearer's Prayer* given to the little daughter of a father who was a profane, wicked man.

laughed at the child for being pleased with so mean a present, and again indulged himself in blaspheming his Maker; but who at length took up the Tract, began to read it, and was affected almost to loud weeping, wondering he was out of hell; and now he and his wife are rejoicing in hope of mercy through the Redeemer.—They could tell of the Tract entitled *The Barren Fig Tree*, given to a little boy, whose father was fifty years old, and surrounded with a large family, all living in neglect of religion; and no sooner had the father begun to read it, than he thought it was written on purpose for him, and that the Lord had sent it to condemn him for his barren, irreligious life. His sins now rose up before him. He felt himself to be lost, and found peace only in applying to Christ by repentance and faith. And with him, three of his children became alarmed in view of their sins, and had no rest till, as is hoped, they rested on the Rock of Ages.

As I was passing a little brook in the country, says a merchant in P——, I observed a good-looking farmer beating his oxen unmercifully, and uttering at the same time awful imprecations. I alighted from my chaise, handed him the *Swearer's Prayer*, and went on my journey. Two years after, a stranger entered my counting-house, and said to me, with joy in his countenance, "How do you do?" I answered, "You are probably mistaken in the person, sir." "Did you never," said he, "give the *Swearer's Prayer* to a farmer who was whipping his oxen and swearing at them?" "I recollect the circumstance," said I—and observed his tears. "I have reason," said he, "to blush at the acknowledgment, but I am the man." Then taking my hand, he continued, "I am grateful that I have found my deliverer. I can never pay you. Take all my property, and every thing I have; and it shall all go, before I will part with that Tract which you so kindly placed in my hands, and which sunk deep into my soul. It was my salvation! it was my all! And you have not only sent salvation to my soul, but my wife, alarmed at my distress, was soon awakened to a sense of her duty; and my second daughter and eldest son are now joyful companions with us, in consequence of your giving me that little Tract.

The Tract entitled "*Without Holiness no man shall see*

the Lord," says an individual, who is exerting a most salutary and very extensive influence, especially for the spiritual welfare of the rising generation, was read to me by a friend who felt concerned for my eternal interest, and if I am not mistaken with regard to my hope in Jesus, it was the means of showing me my awful danger, and pointing me to the Saviour for mercy and eternal life. Not long after this, the same Tract was read at a prayer-meeting, and *about twelve or fifteen were deeply affected, and had no peace till they found it in Jesus. From that hour, the Spirit of God continued his gracious influences, and MORE THAN ONE HUNDRED were made the hopeful subjects of his sanctifying grace.*

In every district, says a Report of the Religious Tract Society of London, the Tracts have been gratefully received, and eagerly read. The pious distributors have been met with smiles, or followed with benedictions. They have often been casually accosted and recognised by individuals they had long forgotten, and have been reverenced as the bearers of a message from God, which, through his grace, they had not delivered in vain. This cannot appear surprising to any one who considers what a Tract really is. To the eye, it consists but of a few printed pages, without any pretensions to typographical beauty. To the understanding it is something infinitely more grand and venerable than the most splendid of merely human compositions. It contains " the words of eternal life." It is the Gospel in miniature. It concentrates the very essence of revelation, and presents, in a form the most simple, concise, and striking, the radical truths and precepts of Christianity. It is an admonition of human depravity, a proclamation of divine mercy, a summons to faith, repentance, and prayer, a remonstrance against sin, an exhortation to duty. Of such a nature are the publications which the Society would wish to disseminate over the earth: in the morning sowing the seed, and in the evening withholding not their hands, as they know not which shall prosper, or whether both may not prosper alike.

THE
WORK OF THE HOLY SPIRIT.

BY REV. ROBERT HALL, A. M.

The regeneration, and growth in holiness, of every Christian, are to be primarily attributed to the operation of the Holy Spirit. Without this, nothing can be done or attained, to any important purpose, in religion. Your candid attention is requested to a few hints respecting the means connected with the enjoyment of that blessed influence. The numerous cautions, warnings, and advices, with which the mention of this subject is joined in the Scriptures, are sufficient to show that the doctrine of which it treats is a practical doctrine, not designed to supersede the use of means, or the exercise of our rational powers, but rather to stimulate us to exertion, and teach us how to exert them aright. "If ye live in the Spirit, walk in the Spirit. Grieve not the Holy Spirit of God, whereby ye are sealed to the day of redemption."

The Spirit, we must remember, is a most free agent, and though he does not utterly forsake his work, he may be expected to withdraw himself, in a great measure, on being slighted, neglected, or opposed; and as our holiness and comfort depend entirely upon him, it is important for us to know what deportment is calculated to invite, and what to repel, his presence.

1. If we would wish for much of the presence of God by his Spirit, we should learn to *set a high value upon it*. The Lord seems to regulate his conduct by a rule, that of bestowing his richest favours where he knows they are most coveted, and will be most prized. The principle whence divine communications flow, is free, unmerited benignity; but in the mode of dispensing its fruits, it is worthy of the supreme Ruler to consult his own majesty, by withholding

a copious supply, till he has excited in the heart a profound estimation of his gifts.

No words are adequate to express the excellence and dignity of the gift of the Divine Spirit. While Solomon was dedicating the temple, his great soul appears to have been put into a rapture at the very idea, that he whom the heaven of heavens could not contain, should deign to dwell with man upon the earth. How much more should each of us be transported, when he finds the idea realized, by his own heart having become the seat of the divine presence. There are two considerations drawn from Scripture, which assist us in forming a conception of the magnitude of this blessing.

The first is, that it is the great promise of the Christian dispensation, and stands in nearly the same relation to us, that the coming of the Messiah did to pious Jews. They waited for the consolation of Israel in the birth of Christ; and now that that event is past, we are waiting, in a similar manner, for the promise of the Spirit, of which the church has hitherto enjoyed but the first fruits. To this, the Saviour after his resurrection pointed the expectation of his apostles, as emphatically the promise of the Father which they were to receive at the distance of a few days; and when it was accomplished at the day of Pentecost, we find Peter insisting on it as the most illustrious proof of his ascension, as well as the chief fruit that converts were to reap from their repentance and baptism. "Repent and be baptized," said he, "every one of you, in the name of Jesus Christ, for the remission of sins, and ye shall receive the gift of the Holy Ghost: for the promise (that is, the promise of the Spirit) is to you, and to your children, and to all that are afar off, even as many as the Lord our God shall call." The apostle Paul places it in a similar light, when he tells us, "Christ has redeemed us from the curse of the law, being made a curse for us, that the blessing of Abraham might come upon the Gentiles:" and in what that blessing consists, he informs us, by adding, "that we might receive the promise of the Spirit by faith." On this account, probably, he is styled the *Spirit of Promise, that is*, the Spirit so often promised; in the communication of whom, the promises of God so centre, that it may be considered as the sum and substance of all the promises.

Another consideration, which evinces the supreme importance of this gift, is, that, in the esteem of our Lord, it was more than a compensation to his disciples for the loss of his bodily presence; so much superior to it, that he tells them, it was expedient he should leave them, in order to make way for it: "If I go not away, the Comforter will not come unto you; but if I depart, I will send him unto you." Great as the advantages were, which they derived from his society, they yet remained in a state of minority; their views were contracted, their hearts full of earthly adhesions, and a degree of carnality and prejudice attended them, which it was the office of the Spirit only to remove. From his more ample and effectual teaching, a great increase of knowledge was to accrue, to qualify them for their work of bearing witness to Christ, and a powerful energy to go forth, which was to render their ministry, though in themselves so much inferior, far more successful than the personal ministry of our Lord. In consequence of his agency, the apostles were to become enlightened and intrepid, and the world convinced. "I have many things to say to you, but ye cannot bear them now. But when the Spirit of truth is come, he will lead you into all truth. He will convince the world of sin, of righteousness, and of judgment." Accordingly, after his descent, we find the apostles wonderfully transformed; an unction, a fervour, a boldness, marked their character, to which they had hitherto been strangers; and such conviction attended their preaching, that in a short time a great part of the world yielded to the weapons of their holy warfare. Nor is there any pretence for alleging that this communication was confined to miraculous gifts, since it is asserted to be that Spirit which should abide in them for ever, and by which the church should be distinguished from the world. He is styled, "The Spirit of truth, whom the world cannot receive, because it seeth him not, neither knoweth him:" but it is added, "Ye know him, for he dwelleth in you and shall be in you."

As we are indebted to the Spirit for the first formation of the divine life, so it is He alone who can maintain it, and render it strong and vigorous. It is his office to actuate the habits of grace where they are already planted; to hold our souls in life, and to "strengthen us that we may walk up and down in the name of the Lord." It is his office to present the mysteries of salvation, the truths which relate to the mediation of Christ and the riches of his grace, in so penetrating and transforming a manner, as to render them vital, operating principles, the food and the solace of our spirits. Without his agency, however intrinsically excellent, they will be to us mere dead speculation, an inert mass; it is only when they are animated by his breath, that they become spirit and life.

It is his office to afford that anointing by which we may know all things by a light which is not merely directive to the understanding, but which so shines upon the heart, as to give a relish of the sweetness of divine truth, and effectually produce a compliance with its dictates. It belongs to him " to seal us to the day of redemption," to put that mark and character upon us which distinguishes the children of God, as well as to afford a foretaste and an earnest of the future inheritance. " And hereby," saith an apostle, " we know that we are of God, by the Spirit which he hath given us." It is his office to subdue the corruption of our nature, not by leaving us inactive spectators of the combat, but by engaging us to a determined resistance to every sinful propensity, by teaching our hands to war, and our fingers to fight, so that the victory shall be ours, and the praise his. To help the infirmities of saints, who know not what to pray for as they ought, by making intercession for them " with groanings which cannot be uttered," is an important branch of his office. He kindles their desires, gives them a glimpse of the fulness of God, that all-comprehending good; and by exciting a relish of the beauties of holiness, and the ineffable pleasure which springs from nearness to God, disposes them to the fervent and effectual prayer, which availeth much. In short, as Christ is the way to the Father, so it is equally certain, that the Spirit is the fountain of all the light and strength which enable us to walk in that way. Lest it should be suspected that in ascribing so much to the agency of the Spirit, we diminish the obligations we owe to the Redeemer, it may not be improper to remark, that the tendency of what we have advanced, rightly understood, will be just the contrary; since the Scriptures constantly remind us, that the gift of the Holy Ghost is the fruit of his mediation, and the result of his death. It was his interposing as " Emmanuel, God with us," to repair the breach betwixt man and God, that prevailed upon the Father to communicate the Spirit to such as believe on him, and to intrust the whole agency of it to his hands. As the reward of his sufferings, he ascended on high, and received gifts for men; of which the right of bestowing the Spirit is the principal, that the Lord God might dwell among them. The donation, in every instance, through the successive periods of the church, looks back to the death of the Redeemer, as the root and principle whence it takes its rise, and consequently is calculated to enlarge our conceptions of his office and character, as the copiousness of the streams evinces the exuberance of the fountain. To him the Spirit was first given above measure; in him it resides as an inexhaustible spring to be imparted in the dispensation of his Gospel to every member of his mystical body, in pursuance of the purpose of his grace and the ends of his death. It is *his* Spirit; hence we read of " the supply of the Spirit of Christ Jesus;" not only by reason of the essential union which subsists between the persons of the Godhead, but because the right of bestowing it was ascertained to him in the covenant of redemption.

2. If we would wish to enjoy much of the light and influence of the Spirit, we must *seek it by fervent prayer.* There are peculiar encouragements held out in the word of God to this purpose. " Ask, and ye shall receive; seek, and ye shall find; knock, and it shall be opened unto you." To illustrate the readiness of our heavenly Father to bestow this blessing, our Lord borrows a comparison from the instinct of parental affection, which prompts a parent to give with alacrity good things to his children. He will not merely supply their wants, which benevolence might prompt him to do with respect to a stranger; but he will do it with feelings peculiar to the parental relation, and will experience as much pleasure in conferring, as the child in receiving, his favours. It is thus with our heavenly Father: He delights in exercising kindness to his children, and especially in promoting their spiritual welfare. He gives not merely with the liberality of a prince, but with the heart of a father. It is worth remarking, that in relating the preceding discourse, while one evangelist makes express mention of the Spirit, another speaks only of good things, intimating that the communications of the Spirit comprehend whatever is good. Other things may, or may not, be ultimately beneficial: they are either of a doubtful nature in themselves, or are rendered so by the propensity our corruption gives us to abuse them. But the influence of the Spirit, by its efficacy in subduing that corruption, must

be invariably beneficial : it is such an immediate emanation from God, the fountain of blessedness, that it can never fail of being intrinsically, essentially, and eternally good. It is also deserving our attention, that the injunction of seeking it by prayer is prefaced by a parable constructed on purpose to teach us the propriety of urging our suit with importunity. In imploring other gifts, (which we are at liberty to do with submission,) it is still a great point of duty to moderate our desires, and to be prepared for a disappointment, because, as we have already remarked, it is possible that the things we are seeking, may conduce neither to the glory of God nor to our ultimate benefit; " for who knoweth what is good for man, all the days of his vain life?" But when we present our requests for a larger measure of his grace, we labour under no such uncertainty, we may safely let forth all the ardour and vehemence of our spirits, since our desires are fixed upon what is the very knot and juncture, where the honour of God and the interests of his creatures are indissolubly united. Desires after grace are, in fact, desires after God; and how is it possible for them to be too vehement or intense, when directed to such an object? His gracious presence is not, like the limited goods of this life, fitted to a particular crisis, or adapted to a special exigency, in a fluctuating scene of things; it is equally suited to all times and seasons, the food of souls, the proper good of man, under every aspect of Providence, and every change of worlds. " My soul," said David, " panteth after God, yea, for the living God. My soul followeth hard after thee ; thy right hand upholdeth me." The most eminent effusions of the Spirit we read of in Scripture, were not only afforded to prayer, but appear to have taken place at the very time that exercise was performed. The descent of the Holy Ghost on the day of Pentecost, was while the disciples were with one accord in one place ; and after the imprisonment of Peter and John, who, being dismissed, went to their own company, " While they prayed, the place where they were assembled was shaken with a mighty wind, and they were all filled with the Holy Ghost."—When a new heart and a new spirit are promised in Ezekiel, it is added, " I will yet for this be inquired of by the house of Israel, to do it for them."

3. *Habitual dependance on divine influence* is an important duty. This may be considered as opposed to two

things; first, to depending on ourselves, to the neglect of divine agency; next, to despondency and distrust.

When the Holy Spirit has condescended to take the conduct of souls, it is unquestionably great presumption to enter upon duty in the same manner as if no such assistance were needed, or to be expected; and the result will be as with Samson, who said, "I will go forth and shake myself, as in times past; and he wist not that the Lord was departed from him." It is one thing to acknowledge a dependance on heavenly influence in speculation, and another thing so to realize and feel it, as to say from the heart, "I will go in the strength of the Lord God." A mere assent to the proposition, that the Spirit must concur in the production of every great work, (an assent not easily withheld without rejecting the Scriptures,) falls very short of the practical homage due from feeble worms to so great an Agent; and a most solemn and explicit acknowledgment of entire dependance may reasonably be expected. When you engage in prayer, or in any other duty, endeavour to enter upon it with a serious and deliberate recollection of your need of the Spirit. Let the consciousness of your weakness and insufficiency for every good work, be a sentiment rendered familiar to your minds, and deeply impressed on your hearts.

But while we recommend this, there is another extreme against which we think it our duty to guard you, and that is, a disposition to despondency and distrust. We are most ready to acknowledge that the assistance you need is free and gratuitous, neither given to our deservings, nor flowing from any connexion subsisting betwixt our endeavours and the exertion of divine agency. The Spirit of God is a free Spirit; and it is impossible to conceive how either faith or prayer should have an intrinsic efficacy in drawing down influence from heaven. There is, however, a connexion established by divine vouchsafement, which entitles believers to expect, in the use of means, such measures of gracious assistance, as are requisite to sustain and support them in their religious course. The Spirit is spoken of as the matter of promise to which every christian is encouraged to look: "The promise is to you and to your children, and to all that are afar off, even to as many as the Lord our God shall call." Agreeably to this, it is represented as the express purpose of Christ's becoming a curse for us, that the "promise of the Spirit might come on the Gentiles through faith." The same expectation is justified by the Saviour's own declaration, when on the last and great day of the feast he stood and cried, " If any man thirst, let him come unto me and drink, for he that believeth on me, out of his belly shall flow rivers of living water: this," says the Evangelist, " he spake of the Spirit, which they that believe on him should receive."

The readiness of the Holy Spirit, to communicate himself to true believers, is also evinced by the tenor of evangelical precepts: " Be ye strong in the Lord, and in the power of his might." To command a person to be strong, seems strange and unusual language, but it is sufficiently explained when we reflect, that a portion of spiritual power is ready to be communicated to those who duly seek it. " Be ye filled with the Spirit," which is the exhortation of the same apostle, takes it for granted that a copious supply is at hand, sufficient to satisfy the desires of the saints. We are at a loss to account for such precepts, without supposing an established connexion betwixt the condition of believers and the further communication of divine influence. To the same purport, Paul speaks with apostolic authority, " This, I say, walk in the Spirit, and ye shall not fulfil the lusts of the flesh;" and Jude inculcates the duty of praying in the Holy Ghost, which would be strange if no assistance were to be obtained; and as prayer is a duty of daily occurrence, the injunction implies that it is ready to be imparted to christians, not by fits and starts, or at distant intervals, but in a stated, regular course.

For this reason, when we hear christians complaining of the habitual withdrawment of the divine presence, we are under the necessity of ascribing it to their own fault: not that we mean to deny there is much of sovereignty in this affair, or that " the Spirit, like the wind, bloweth where it listeth." But it should be remembered, we are now adverting to the situation of real believers, who are entitled to the promise; and though it is probable that there is much of sovereignty exercised even with respect to *them*, we apprehend it rather concerns those influences which are consolatory, than such as are sanctifying; for, though there is a degree of satisfaction intermingled with every exercise of genuine piety, yet it is manifest that some influences of the Spirit tend more immediately to comfort, others to purification By some we are engaged in the fixed contemplation of objects which exist out of ourselves, the perfections of God, the excellency of Christ, the admirable constitution of the Gospel, accompanied with a delightful conviction of a personal interest in whatever comes under our view; the natural food of which is "joy unspeakable and full of glory." By others we are more immediately impressed with a lasting sense of our extreme unworthiness, and made to mourn over remaining corruption, and the criminal defects inherent in our best services.

In the midst of such exercises, it is possible that hope may languish, and comfort be reduced to a low ebb, yet the divine life may still be advancing, and the soul growing in humility, deadness to the world, and the mortification of her own will, as the sap during winter retires to the root of the plant, ready to ascend and produce verdure and beauty on the return of spring. This is the will of God, even our sanctification; and though he delights in comforting his people at proper seasons, he is much less intent on this, than on promoting their spiritual improvement, to which, in their state of discipline, every thing is made subservient. Let us not then confound the decay of consolation with the decay of piety, nor imagine we can want the aids necessary to prevent the latter, unless we have forfeited them by presumption, negligence, and sloth. Whenever christians sensibly decline in religion, they ought to charge themselves with the guilt of having grieved the Spirit; they should take the alarm, repent, and do their first works; they are suffering under the rebukes of that paternal justice which God exercises in his own family. Such a measure of gracious assistance in the use of means, as is requisite for their comfortable walk with God, being by the tenor of the new covenant *ascertained* to real christians, to find it withheld, should engage them in deep searchings of heart, and make them fear lest, " a promise being left them of entering into rest, they should appear to come short of it." But this leads us to observe, in the last place, that.

4. If we wish to enjoy the light of the Spirit, we must take care to *maintain a deportment suited to the character of that Divine Agent.* When the apostle exhorts us not to grieve the Spirit of God, by which we are sealed to the day of redempiton, it is forcibly implied, that he is susceptible of offence, and that to offend him involves heinous in-

gratitude and folly: *ingratitude*—for what a requital is this for being sealed to the day of redemption! and *folly*—inasmuch as we may fitly say on this, as Paul did on a different occasion, "Who is he that maketh us glad, but the same that is made sorry by us?" Have we any other comforter when he is withdrawn? Can a single ray of light visit us in his absence, or can we be safe for a moment without his guidance and support? If the immense and infinite Spirit, by a mysterious condescension, deigns to undertake the conduct of a worm, ought it not to yield the most implicit submission? The appropriate duty owing to a faithful and experienced guide, is a ready compliance with his dictates; and how much more may this be expected, when the disparity betwixt the parties in question is no less than infinite. The language of the Holy Spirit, in describing the conduct of the ancient Israelites, is awfully monitory to professors in every age, "They rebelled, and vexed his Holy Spirit; therefore he turned to be their enemy, and fought against them." As we wish to avoid whatever is more curious than useful, we shall not stay to inquire precisely on what occasions, or to what extent, the Spirit is capable of being resisted: it may be sufficient to observe, it is evident from melancholy experience, that it is very possible to neglect what is the obvious tendency of his motions, which is invariably to produce universal holiness. "The fruit of the Spirit is love, joy, peace, long-suffering, goodness, meekness, gentleness, temperance, faith." Whatever is contrary to these, involves an opposition to the Spirit, and is directly calculated to quench his sacred influence.

From his descending on Christ in the form of a dove, as well as from many express declarations of Scripture, we may with certainty conclude the indulgence of all the irascible and malignant passions to be peculiarly repugnant to his nature; and it is remarkable, that the injunction of not grieving the Holy Spirit is immediately followed by a particular caution against cherishing such dispositions: "Let all bitterness, and wrath, and anger, and clamour, and evil speaking, be put away from you, with all malice. And be ye kind one to another, tender-hearted, forgiving one another, even as God for Christ's sake hath forgiven you." Have you not found by experience, that the indulgence of the former has destroyed that self-recollection and composure, which are so essential to devotion? Vindictive passions surround the soul with a sort of turbulent atmosphere, than which nothing can be conceived more opposite to that calm and holy light in which the blessed Spirit loves to dwell. The indulgence of sensual lusts, or of whatever enslaves the soul to the appetites of the body, in violation of the rules of sobriety and chastity, it seems almost unnecessary to add, must have a direct tendency to quench his sacred influences; wherever such desires prevail, they war against the soul, immerse it in carnality, and utterly indispose it to every thing spiritual and heavenly. "That which is born of the Spirit, is spirit;" it bears a resemblance to its Author, in being a spiritual production, which requires to be nourished by divine meditation, by pure and holy thoughts.

If you wish to live in the fellowship of the Spirit, you must guard with no less care against the encroachments of worldly-mindedness, recollecting we are christians just as far as our treasure and our hearts are planted in heaven, and no further A heart overcharged with the cares of this world, is as much disqualified for converse with God, and for walking in the Spirit, as it would be by surfeiting and drunkenness; to which, by their tendency to intoxicate and stupify, they bear a great resemblance.

How many, by an immoderate attachment to wealth, and by being determined at all events to become rich, " have fallen into divers foolish and hurtful lusts, and pierced themselves through with many sorrows!" and where the result has not been so signally disastrous, a visible languor in religion has ensued, the friendship of serious christians has been shunned, and the public ordinances of religion attended with little fruit or advantage. As it is the design of the Spirit in his sacred visitations to form us for an habitual converse with spiritual and eternal objects, nothing can tend more directly to counteract it, than to bury our souls in earth; it is as impossible for the eye of the mind as for that of the body to look opposite ways at once; nor can we aim supremely at " the things which are seen and temporal," but by losing sight of those " which are unseen and eternal."

But though a general attention to the duties of piety and virtue, and a careful avoidance of the sins opposed to these, are certainly included in a becoming deportment to the Holy Spirit, perhaps it is not *all* that is included. The children of God are characterized in Scripture by their being " led by the Spirit :" *led*—evidently not impelled, nor driven forward in a headlong course, without choice or design ; but, being, by the constitution of their nature, rational and intelligent, and by the influence of grace rendered spiritual, they are disposed to obey at a touch, and to comply with the gentler insinuations of divine grace ; they are ready to take that precise impression which corresponds with the mind and purpose of the Spirit. You are aware of what consequence it is in worldly concerns to embrace opportunities, and to improve critical seasons ; and thus, in the things of the Spirit, there are times peculiarly favourable, moments of happy visitation, where much more may be done towards the advancement of our spiritual interest than usual. There are gales of the Spirit, unexpected influences of light and power, which no assiduity in the means of grace can command, but which it is a great point of wisdom to improve. If the husbandman is attentive to the vicissitudes of weather, and the face of the sky, that he may be prepared to take the full benefit of every gleam of sunshine, and every falling shower, how much more alert and attentive should we be in watching for those influences from above, which are necessary to ripen and mature a far more precious crop ! As the natural consequence of being long under the guidance of another, is a quick perception of his meaning, so that we can meet his wishes before they are verbally expressed ; something of this ready discernment, accompanied with instant compliance, may reasonably be expected from those who profess to be habitually led by the Spirit. " The *secret* of the Lord is with them that fear him." Psalm xxv. 14.

The design of his operation is in one view invariably the same—the production of holiness ; but the branches of which that consists, and the exercises of mind which are rendered subservient to it, are various ; and he who is intent on walking in the Spirit, will be careful to fall in with that train of thought, and cherish that cast of reflection, to which he is especially invited. For want of more docility in this respect, it is probable, we have often sustained loss. Permit us here to suggest two or three heads of inquiry. You have sometimes felt a peculiar seriousness of mind, the delusive glare of worldly objects has faded away, or become dim before your eyes, and death and eternity, appearing at the door, have filled the whole field of vision. Have you improved such seasons for fixing those maxims, and establishing those practical conclusions, which may produce an habitual sobriety of mind, when things appear under a different aspect? You have sometimes found, instead of a reluctance to pray, a powerful impulse to that exercise, so that you felt as if you could do nothing else. Have you always complied with these motions, and suffered nothing but the claims of absolute necessity to divert you from pouring out your hearts at a throne of grace? The Spirit is said to make intercession for saints, with groanings which cannot be uttered; when you have felt those ineffable longings after God, have you indulged them to the utmost? Have you spread every sail, launched forth into the deep of the divine perfections and promises, and possessed yourselves, as much as possible, of the fulness of God? There are moments when the conscience of a good man is more tender, has a nicer and more discriminating touch, than usual; the evil of sin in general, and of his own in particular, appears in a more clear and piercing light. Have you availed yourselves of such seasons as these for searching into "the chambers of imagery," and while you detected greater and greater abominations, been at pains to bring them out and slay them before the Lord? Have such visitations effected something towards the mortification of sin? Or have they been suffered to expire in mere ineffectual resolutions? The fruits which godly sorrow produced in the Corinthians are thus beautifully portrayed: "What carefulness it wrought in you, yea, what clearing of yourselves, yea, what indignation, yea, what fear, yea, what vehement desire, yea, what revenge!" There are moments in the experience of a good man, when he feels a more than ordinary softness of mind; the frost of selfishness dissolves, and his heart flows forth in love to God and his fellow-creatures. How careful should we be to cherish such a frame, and to embrace the opportunity of subduing resentments, and of healing those scars and wounds which it is scarcely possible to avoid in passing through this unquiet world.

There is a holy skill in turning the several parts of christian experience to account, analagous to what the votaries of the world display in the improvement of every conjuncture from which it is possible to derive emolument; and though the end they propose is mean and contemptible, the steadiness with which they pursue it, and their dexterity in the choice of means, deserve imitation. In these respects "they are wiser in their generation than the children of light."

Do not allow yourselves to indulge in religious sloth, or to give way to the solicitations of the tempter, from a confidence in the safety of your state, or in your spiritual immunities as christians.—The habitual prevalence of such a disposition will afford a much stronger proof of insincerity than any arguments which can be adduced for the contrary; and admitting your pretensions to piety to be ever so valid, a little reflection may convince you, that a careless and negligent course will lay you open to the severest rebukes. "You only have I known," says the Lord by the prophet, "of all the families of the earth; therefore will I punish you for all your iniquities."

Remember, dear brethren, we profess a peculiar relation to God as his children, his witnesses, his people, his temple; the character of that glorious Being, and of his religion, will be contemplated by the world, chiefly through the medium of our spirit and conduct, which ought to display, as in a mirror, the virtues of Him who " hath called you out of darkness into his marvellous light." It is strictly appropriate to the subject of our present meditations to remind you that you are " temples." "For ye," says the apostle, " are the temples of the living God, as God hath said, I will dwell in them, and walk in them, and I will be their God, and they shall be my people." What purity, sanctity, and dignity, may be expected in persons who bear such a character! A christian should look upon himself as something sacred and devoted, so that what involves but an ordinary degree of criminality in others, in him partakes of the nature of sacrilege; what is a breach of trust in others, is in him the profanation of a temple. Let us, dear brethren, watch and pray, that nothing may be allowed a place in our hearts, that is not suitable to the residence of the holy and blessed God. Finally, " having such great and precious promises, dearly beloved, let us cleanse ourselves from all filthiness of flesh and spirit, perfecting holiness in the fear of the Lord."

Having thus endeavoured to lay before you the most likely methods of obtaining the communications of the Spirit, as well as to show the great importance of this gift, we might now dismiss the subject, were we not desirous of first guarding you against a dangerous mistake. The mistake to which we refer, is that of taking conviction for conversion, certain impressions of the guilt and danger of sin made upon the conscience, for the saving operations of the Spirit. These convictions are important: it is highly desirable and necessary to have a settled persuasion of the established connexion betwixt sin and punishment, and, as a natural consequence, to feel uneasiness and alarm, in proportion as we have reason to believe our sins are yet unpardoned. Until we see ourselves *lost*, we shall never truly come to Christ for salvation. Until we feel our malady, and dread its consequences, we shall never have recourse to the Physician, or be willing to comply with his prescription. We adjure you, therefore, as you value your eternal interests, not to trifle with convictions, or to endeavour to wear off religious concern and uneasiness by the vanities of life and the stupefactions of pleasure. Regard and cherish them as the sacred visitations of Heaven; look upon them as mercifully designed to rouse and awaken you from a fatal stupor. They are often the harbingers of mercy. Wherever the Spirit of God is in reality, he will convince of sin; but conviction is produced in thousands who still remain destitute of saving grace.—That influence of the Spirit, by which a *change of heart* is effected, is essentially different from that distress and alarm which may be resolved into the exercise of mere natural conscience. For a man to be convinced that he is a sinner, and to tremble at the apprehension of wrath to come, is certainly something very distinct from becoming a new creature. Real christians have not only perceived their danger, but have fled for refuge; have not only been less or more troubled with a sense of guilt, but, in consequence of coming to Christ, have found rest for their souls. On a review of your past life, you perceive innumerable transgressions, it may be, and are perfectly convinced that you have been " walking according to the course of this world, according to the prince of the power of the air, the spirit that now worketh in the children of disobedience." So far it is well; your apprehensions are just and well founded, and your situation more replete with danger than you have ever conceived it to be. Do not, however, rest here. Let the views you entertain excite you the more earnestly to press into the kingdom of God. Let them engage you to a more diligent use of the means of grace ; and, above all, let them lead you to fix your hope and trust on the Redeemer, whose blood alone can cleanse you from sin, and whose intercession is able to save, " to the uttermost, all that come unto God by him." Apply to him with humble faith and ardent prayer, and though you may be tempted to cherish doubts of the extent of his power and grace, say with him of old, " Lord, I believe, help thou my unbelief." Lay aside, as far as possible, every other concern ; postpone your attention to every other object, till you have reason to believe you have obtained mercy, and are renewed in the spirit of your mind. Address the throne of Grace with unceasing importunity, remembering who hath said, " Ask, and ye shall receive ; seek, and ye shall find. Him that cometh unto me I will in nowise cast out." In all your addresses to God, make use of the name and intercession of Christ, plead the efficacy of his blood, and the encouragement he hath offered sinners, in his Gospel, to return to God. Keep a continual watch over your words, thoughts, and actions : keep your heart with all diligence. Guard with the utmost care against levity and sloth, two most dangerous snares to the souls of men.

If you ask how you may know whether you are partakers of the special grace of God; we reply, This will be best ascertained by its fruits. When you feel a fixed hatred of sin, an intense thirst after holiness and perfection, and a delight in the word and ways of God ; when you are habitually disposed to dwell on the thoughts of Christ and heaven ; when the Saviour appears unspeakably precious, as " the Pearl of great price," and you are habitually ready to part with every thing for his sake, you may be certain that you are born of God. These are the fruits of the Spirit, which sufficiently demonstrate the influence and presence of that blessed Agent. Till you have experienced effects of this kind, you are in a wretched state, though surrounded with all the brightest earthly prospects, because you are estranged from God, and exposed to his eternal wrath and displeasure.

No. 3.

A FRIENDLY VISIT

TO THE

HOUSE OF MOURNING.

BY REV. RICHARD CECIL, LONDON.

Your present affliction, my dear friend, demands something more than the usual forms of condolence. Sorrow which, like yours, cannot be prevented, may yet be *alleviated* and *improved*. This is my design in addressing you, and if I seem to intrude upon your retirement, let my motive be my apology. Having felt how much "better it is to go to the house of mourning than to the house of feasting;" having received my best *lessons, companions*, and even *comforts*, in it, I would administer from my little stock of experience; and while I thus endeavor to assist your meditations, shall rejoice if I may contribute, though but a mite, to your comfort.

Were I, indeed, acquainted with the peculiar circumstances of your loss, I should employ particular considerations; but my present address can have only a *general* aim, which is to acquaint the heart, at a favorable moment, with its grand concerns; to give it a serious impression when *softened*, and a heavenly direction when *moved*. Let us, therefore, sit down humbly together in this house of mourning. If "the heart of the wise be found" here, your experience, I hope, will prove that here also it is *formed;* and let us calmly contemplate some momentous objects intimately connected with it, and viewed with peculiar advantage from it.

Our GOD is the first of these objects: with him we seldom form any close acquaintance till we meet him in trouble. He commands silence now, that he may be heard; and removes intervening objects, that he may be seen. A Sovereign Disposer appears, who, as *Lord of all*, has only resumed what he lent; whose will is the law of his creatures, and who expressly declares his will in the present affliction. We should seriously consider that all allowed repugnance to the determinations of his government, however made known to us, is sin; and that every wish to alter the appointments of his wisdom is folly: *we know not what we ask.* When God discovers himself in any matter, those who know him "will keep silence before him." "Shall he that contendeth with the Almighty instruct him?" How just was the reply of Job, "Behold, I am vile! what shall I answer thee? I will lay my hand upon my mouth."

This silent submission under trying dispensations is variously exemplified, as well as inculcated, in the Scriptures. An awful instance of sin and sorrow occurs in the family of Aaron: his sons disregarded a divine appointment, and "there went out fire from the Lord and devoured them; but Aaron held his peace." Eli, in similar circumstances, silenced his heart with this single but sufficient consideration, "It is the Lord." David, under a stroke which he declares consumed him, observes, "I was dumb, I opened not my mouth, because thou didst it." And Job, when stripped of every comfort, blessed the name of him who "took away" as well as "gave." Whatever be the nature of your calamity, may it be attended with such an humble and childlike spirit as these possessed!

But the Sovereign Disposer is also the Compassionate Father. Among other instances of his tenderness, you may have observed the peculiar supports he affords under peculiar trials. Let us mark and acknowledge the hand which mingles mercy with judgment, and alleviation with distress. The parents I have just mentioned lost their children under circumstances far more distressing than yours; the desire of your eyes (if not the idol of your heart) was, perhaps, almost a stranger; you strove hard to detain it, but He who took the young children into his arms and blessed them, took yours; and, taking it, seemed to say "What I do thou knowest not now, but thou shalt know hereafter;" patiently "suffer this little one to come unto me, for of such is my kingdom." Is not this infinitely better than any thing you could do for it? Could you say to it, if it had lived, thou shalt "weep no more, the days of thy mourning are ended?" Could you show it any thing in this world like "the glory of God and of the Lamb?" Could you raise it to any honor here like "receiving a crown of life?" The voice of the "Father of mercies and the God of all comfort" speaks as distinctly in the death, as in the birth of an infant.

Is it a *pious friend* that has just yielded up his breath? The same voice seems to say, Turn from him, or rather turn from his *clay*, his faded *garment*. "He" himself "is taken from the evil to come; he is entered into peace."

When the able *minister*, the exemplary *parent*, or the faithful *partner* is removed, consternation often seizes the circle which they blessed. We are so stunned by the sudden blow, or occupied with the distressing circumstances, that we scarcely can hear God saying, "Fear not, I, even I, am he that comforteth you: I, your Father, am yet alive: I gave you your departed friend; I sent every benefit which was conveyed through him; trust me for blessings yet in store; trust me with him and with yourselves."

Whatever notions one who lives *without God in the world* may form of dying, *we* should learn from his word to regard the departure of the just merely as a *translation;* a change in which nothing is lost which is really valuable. As surely as we "believe that Jesus died and rose again," so surely do we believe that "them also which sleep in Jesus, will God bring with him." Taught of God, we should view losses, sickness, pain, and death, but as the several trying stages by which a good man, like Joseph, is conducted from a *tent* to a *court:* *sin* his disorder; ***Christ*** his physician; *pain* his medicine; the ***Bible*** his support; the *grave* his bed; and *death* itself an angel expressly sent to release the wornout laborer, or crown the faithful soldier. "I heard a voice from heaven saying unto me, Write, Blessed are the dead which die in the Lord from henceforth: Yea, saith the Spirit, that they may rest from their labors; and their works do follow them."

But admitting the state of your departed friend to be doubtful, yet, in all cases that are really so, let us cultivate honorable thoughts of God; let us remember the FAITHFUL CREATOR. Righteousness is his throne, though clouds surround it. Whatever he has left *obscure* we may safely leave him to explain. Let us recollect, that amidst innumerable obscurities he has made things *clear* in proportion as they are *important;* and therefore repeatedly urges it upon our conscience, that the door of duty is still open to us, that it is awful to stand before it *unresolved,* that we must trust him to-day, and that to-morrow he will equally remove our conjectures and our complaints.

Perhaps you are ready to reply, "I have heard many such things," and "I also could speak as you do, if your soul were in my soul's stead;" but my heart and my expectations are so crushed by this blow, that I can hear nothing but, "Thy bruise is incurable, and thy wound grievous; thou hast no healing medicines."

Beware, however, of falling into their sin, who "limited the Holy One of Israel." There is a charge continually brought against man, that, in his troubles, the source and the resource are equally forgotten. "Though affliction cometh not forth of the dust," yet "none saith, Where is God my Maker, who giveth songs in the night?" Endeavor then, in extremities, to recollect an ALL-SUFFICIENT Friend—a very present HELP in trouble. He at least may add, as he does in the passage just alluded to, "I will restore health unto thee, and I will heal thee of thy wounds, saith the Lord." Cannot the voice which rebuked a tempestuous sea calm our troubled spirits? Is his hand shortened at all, that he cannot bless our latter end, like Job's, more than the beginning? Is it not the Lord "that maketh poor and maketh rich, that bringeth low and lifteth up?" Many, whose hearts have been desolate like yours, while they have looked "around," have at length "looked UP-WARD unto him, and been lightened." A single promise has afforded them not only relief, but strong consolation.

Let us therefore, my dear friend, "turn again to this strong hold, as prisoners of hope." Let us look to *Abraham's* God, and his encouragement is ours: "Fear not; I am GOD ALMIGHTY:" as if he had said, "I am all-sufficient in all cases; I am enough; 'able to do exceeding abundantly above all that you ask or think.' I have taken away thy *gourd*, but doest thou well to be angry? Have I left nothing for thankfulness? This world cannot be your *home*, nor its objects your *consolation:* they are all too poor for the soul of man. 'Look unto me, and be saved;' 'acquaint thyself with me, and be at peace;' 'follow me, and you shall not walk in darkness, but have the light of life.' However dark and distressing the present state of things may appear, 'commit thy fatherless children to my care, I will preserve them alive; and let thy widows trust in me.'"

Still the beloved object is gone, and your heart follows it. You can scarcely receive counsel from infinite Wisdom, or comfort from Omnipotence. To every fresh encouragement you are ready to reply, "Wilt thou show wonders to the dead? Shall the dead arise and praise thee? Shall thy loving-kindness be declared in the grave, or thy faithfulness in destruction?" His word repeatedly assures you they shall, and that "all that are in the graves shall hear his voice;" but it informs you also, that he can do abundantly more for the living than merely restore their dead friends, or revive their fainting spirits; it teaches you that he can sanctify the separation, that he can give a divine life to the survivor, "though dead in trespasses and sins," and inseparably unite both to his kingdom. If the Comforter could make up for the loss of *Christ's* bodily presence; yea, make it even *expedient* that HE *should go away;* how much more can he supply the place of every creature!

May this COMFORTER, writing his word in your mind, help you to say, with a confidence highly honorable to himself and his Gospel, "My poor perishing gourd is, indeed, withered a day before I expected it; but God is left, 'a father to the fatherless, a husband to the widow;' and now, Lord, what wait I for? Truly my hope is in thee.' 'Though the fig-tree shall not blossom, neither shall fruit be in the vine, yet I will rejoice in the LORD, I will joy in the GOD OF MY SALVATION.'"

Once more; let us endeavor, at such seasons as these, to recognize a GRACIOUS MONITOR. Whenever the Lord *strikes,* he *speaks.* Let us listen, at such a time as this, with humble attention, yet with holy confidence, for it is the voice of a *Friend,* a wonderful *Counsellor.* Let us, with the prophet, resolve to ascend the tower of observation, and observe " what he will say unto us, and what we shall answer when we are reproved." If with him we thus watch our dispensation, " at the end," like his, " it shall speak."

And is it not, my afflicted friend, an infinite mercy, if God by *any* means, even by his minister *death,* will arrest the attention of him who has slighted every other minister? What patience! what long-suffering! to take such a one apart, bring him from noise and occupation into the secret and silent chamber; speak to his heart, and seal the most important truths on it by the most affecting impressions! Is it not saying, " How shall I give thee up, Ephraim? How shall I make thee as Admah?" Certain it is, that questions which before only reached the ear, often now, like barbed arrows, remain fixed in the conscience; conscience, no longer stifled, discovers the CONTENDER, and, trembling before him, cries, " Thou hast chastised me, and I was chastised as a bullock unaccustomed to the yoke: turn thou me and I shall be turned, for thou art the Lord my God."

This, I say, is often the case; and if, instead of flying for relief to every object but God, you are brought humbly to his feet, with patient submission, serious inquiry, fervent prayer, holy resolution, and firm reliance; if, in a word, by the severest stroke, the *enchantment* is also broken, your soul " escaped as a bird out of the snare of the fowler," and returned to its proper REST, what reason will you have to say,

" Those we call *wretched,* are a chosen band.—
Amid my list of blessings infinite,
Stand this the foremost, *that my heart has bled.*
For *all* I bless Thee—most for the *severe;*
Her death—*my own* at hand——."

OUR PROSPECTS, as the inhabitants of a present **and future** world, should also be considered from this house **of** sorrow. Many suppose that they can best contemplate the *present* world by crowding the "house of mirth;" their whole deportment, however, shows that it makes them too giddy for serious observation: "having eyes, they see not."

Look at the deceased, and contemplate present things. His days a *hand-breadth;* his beauty consumed; his cares and pleasures a *dream;* his years a *tale;* his strength *labor and sorrow.* So soon is the whole *cut off and fled*, that we cannot help repeating with the psalmist, "*Verily, every* man at his *best* estate is *altogether* VANITY," "a vapor that appeareth for a little time and then vanisheth away."

Few, perhaps, reflect, when they follow a friend to his grave, that life itself exhibits little more than a funeral procession, where friend follows friend, weeping to-day, and wept for to-morrow. While we are talking of one, another passes: we are alarmed, but behold a third! Let us then hear the voice of God calling us, though in an unexpected way, "to commune with our heart and be still;" to know, "at least in this our day of visitation, the things which belong to our peace."

It is at such seasons as these that we more clearly detect the lies of life: it is in the house of mourning that what the Scripture calls *lying vanities* lie peculiarly naked and exposed. Let us here examine what so lately dazzled us. What now is the "purple and fine linen" that caught our eye? What is it to fare sumptuously only for a *day?* Who is he that cries, "Soul, thou hast much goods laid up for many years, take thine ease, eat, drink, and be merry?" I trust you now feel the deep misery and utter ruin of that dying creature, who can say nothing better to his soul than *this.* You can scarcely help crying out, "What sottishness, what madness this, in a moment so interesting as life, with a prospect so awful as eternity!"

The truth is, God speaks variously and incessantly to man, respecting his prospects both present and future; but present things seize his heart, blind his eyes, stupify his conscience, and carry him away captive. Now "affliction is God speaking louder," and striving with the heart of man; crying, as he has lately in your house, "Arise and depart, this is not your rest."

By thus rending the veils which men try to throw over a dying state, the most careless are often so roused that they seem to awake and recover themselves; they appear, for a time at least, to become "wise," to "understand these things," and seriously to "consider their latter end." May this salutary impression, my dear friend, never be worn from *your* mind, but lead you habitually to look from this fading to that abiding prospect which is to be found only in the ETERNAL WORLD.

Be this the language of your heart: "Let the gay laugh; let the despisers 'wonder and perish;' with such prospects before me, I must be serious. He that cannot lie has revealed the *terrors* as well as the glories of a future state: he speaks of 'a worm that dieth not, and a fire that is not quenched,' as well as of 'fullness of joy and pleasures for evermore.' I must not, I dare not shut my eyes against these awful realities. I will not sacrifice my soul to a jest, nor miss the single opportunity afforded me for its salvation. He that calls for my whole heart is worthy of it; while the things which have hitherto engrossed it, though they cannot *satisfy*, I find they can *ruin* it; 'I will therefore arise and go to my Father,' to my Savior, who has promised to 'cast out none that come unto him.' Yea, doubtless, I 'count all things but loss that I may be found in him,' the true ARK, the only REFUGE which God has provided for perishing sinners."

Here then, my afflicted, but I hope instructed friend, let us study the heavenly science of gaining by *losses*, and rising by *depressions*. Leaving the wilderness, like Moses, let us ascend the mount of Scriptural discovery, and survey a prospect of which his was but a shadow. Let us look from vicissitude and desolation to what alone is "incorruptible, undefiled, and that fadeth not away;" and in the house of affliction and death let us contemplate "a house not made with hands, eternal in the heavens." How refreshing to look from a family bereft of its companions and comforts to "Mount Zion, the city of the living God, the heavenly Jerusalem; to an innumerable company of angels; and to the general assembly and church of the first-born which are written in heaven!" the only family which cannot be divided; the only friendship which shall not disappoint our warmest expectation.

"Glorious as this prospect is," perhaps you are ready to reply, "I have been long in the habit of viewing it very indistinctly. My attention has been so fixed on one below, that I live looking *into* the grave rather than *beyond* it. My spirits are so broken, my heart so wounded, and my eyes so dim with watching and weeping, that I can hardly read what is before me, or recollect what I read. If serious reflection composes me for a few moments, I soon relapse, and seem to lose sight of every support. I indeed severely feel what you say concerning the *present* life, but I view the glories of the *future* like a starving creature, who, looking through the gate of the wealthy, surveys a plenty which but increases his anguish."

There is, however, this difference at least between your cases; the plenty which *you* see is *yours*, if you are really willing to accept it. You never received a gift which was so freely bestowed, or so suited to your necessity, as that " gift of God, which is eternal life through Jesus Christ."

To prepare the heart for the reception of this treasure, as a God of order, he is pleased to use a system of means; one of which I hope he is now employing for your soul's health. I love to indulge hope, for affliction is a seed-time; and let me freely inquire, since God has called you aside, has spoken so emphatically, and you have had leisure for serious meditation, do not the provisions of the Gospel appear new, sufficient, and exactly suited to your case? Do you not mark that gold which the thief cannot steal, that foundation which no tempest can shake, that life over which death hath no power, and that peace which the world can neither give nor take away? Does not the religion of JESUS, that is so forgotten and degraded among men, stand forward now as the *one thing needful?* Does not his friendship appear now to be " that better part which shall not be taken away," and which alone can help in extremities? In the wreck of human affairs, indeed, it is that God often makes his truth appear, and causes his Gospel, like a plank thrown out to the perishing mariner, to be properly known and prized.

In health and ease, ingenious speculations may amuse and satisfy us; but I think you now feel with me, that when he " takes away the desires of our eyes with a stroke," we need a support the world cannot afford. " I faint," says the wounded soul: " I want an Almighty arm to lean on now; yea, a very tender and compassionate one too· one like that of the Son of man. I need a 'merciful and faithful Highpriest, who, having been tempted, knows how to succor the tempted:' that man of sorrows, that brother born for adversity, who, being *acquainted with grief*, can enter into my case and commune with me in all the peculiarities of my distress. I now need one, who can quiet me on his own breast, and speak to me with his own voice, 'Weep not, the child is not dead, but sleepeth.' 'Weep not,' thou afflicted, tossed with the tempest; 'when thou passest through the waters I will be with thee.' It is true, this is the land of death, but 'I am the resurrection and the life;' this is, indeed, a 'dry and thirsty land where no water is;' but I 'will lead you to fountains of living water. I will wipe away all tears from your eyes.'"

You are ready, perhaps, to say, "O that I knew where I might find him; but religion has been with me rather a case of necessity than the high privilege of communing with such a comforter. I feel the misery of living at such a distance from my heavenly Friend, especially at this time, but want liberty to approach nearer. Could I indeed repose on the bosom you just mentioned; but, alas! my understanding is clouded, my faith weak, sense strong, and Satan busy in filling my thoughts with false notions, difficulties and doubts, respecting a future state and the efficacy of prayer. Though I see very gracious proposals made to returning sinners, I tremble to venture; death itself reminds me of transgression. My thoughts fly every where but to God."

We readily acknowledge that among other views of death it should be regarded as the "wages of sin." It is also natural for convinced sinners to tremble before a Judge who charges even angels with folly. But while the Christian, as a penitent, looks upon him whom he has pierced, *and mourns;* as a believer, he looks to him who was wounded for transgression, and *hopes.* He finds it as desperate to doubt the *remedy*, as to deny the *disorder.* Having formerly rushed headlong with the *presumptuous,* he now fears perishing with the *fearful* and *unbelieving.* He sees an atonement of God's own providing; he pleads, upon God's own authority, the merit of that blood "which cleanseth from all sin," and by thus receiving the "record which God gives of his Son, he sets his seal to it that God is true."

Is this, my dear friend, in any degree your case? Fearful, wandering, and wounded as your heart is, does it yet discover a resting-place? Instead of wishing to evade the charge of manifold sins and wickedness committed by thought, word, and deed, against the Divine Majesty; is the remembrance of them grievous, and the burden of them intolerable? Do you sincerely desire to be freed from this burden, and to enter into the glorious liberty of the children of God, that heavenly communion and rest which has been mentioned?" "Behold the Lamb of God which taketh away the sin of the world!" "Behold him exalted to be a Prince and a Savior, to give repentance and forgiveness of sins!" Come to him as a sinner, and touch with humble confidence, but the "hem of his garment," and you "shall be made whole." Wait upon him, and you shall obtain both strength and liberty; "for if the Son make you free, you shall be free indeed."

But I must not pass by a temptation to which you are exposed, in reference to *your approaches to God.* You will, perhaps, too readily object, 'Here it is that I sink; I prayed earnestly for the life of the deceased; I thought at one time I saw signs of a recovery; but the event makes me fear that I was not heard, and that I have NO FRIEND left now in earth or heaven.' A little consideration will, I hope, show you your mistake, and prove that a petition may be graciously accepted, when its particular object is not granted. Did not our LORD declare that his Father heard him always? Are we not told that when "in the days of his flesh he had offered up prayers, with strong crying and tears, unto him that was able to save him from death, he was HEARD in that he feared?" But consider how he was heard: certainly not by having the cup *taken away,* (a cup at which human nature, however perfect, must recoil,) but in being accepted when he prayed, in being supported while he drank it, and in victoriously accomplishing his grand design through drinking it to the very dregs.

To come nearer to our own condition, we find PAUL going to CHRIST for deliverance from some severe trial, which he calls a *thorn in the flesh:* he tells us that he also was heard, and in the same way as his Master; not by being released from suffering, but by receiving something more honorable and advantageous; namely, that *grace* which not only supports a believer through his trials, but puts a healing virtue into them.

Far removed from the holy resignation of our Master, we too much resemble, in our prayers, the impatience of our children. I remember, when a sick one of mine had some medicine to take, he called loudly to me to come and assist him against those who were endeavoring to force it down: he, probably, wondered at my refusing to relieve him; but the little sufferer did not consider, though often told, that he was not to be helped in that way; he did not recollect that, while I tenderly felt his cry, the very compassion I felt for him, and the desire I had to relieve him, kept me from taking away the bitter draught.

The truth is, (and it is a truth frequently told us,) that our heavenly Father always sends his children the things they ask, or better things. He answers their petitions in *kind*, or in *kindness*. But while we think only of our *ease*, he consults our *profit*; we are urgent about the *body*, he about the *soul*; we call for present *comfort*, he considers our everlasting *rest*; and therefore, when he sends not the very things we ask, he hears us by sending greater "than we can ask or think."

Is *any*, therefore, *afflicted? let him pray*—not only in the public sanctuary, or in the retired closet, but let him consider that there is a "new and living way, consecrated through the vail" of a Redeemer's human nature, from every scene of retirement or action to a MERCY SEAT; where he "satisfies the longing soul," and fills the "hungry soul with goodness," especially "such as sit in darkness and the shadow of death."

Is it not a time of need with you? Endeavor, at his command, to approach with a holy confidence for the "supply of all your need, according to his riches in glory," and at this time particularly, for the illumination and comfort of his Holy Spirit. He whom you supplicate, not only *invites*, but *reasons* with you. "If ye, being evil, know how to give good gifts unto your children, how much more shall your heavenly Father give the Holy Spirit to them that ask him?"

The religion of education and custom obtains, more or less, every where; but serious, vital, spiritual religion, is a *case of necessity* with us all. We summon our forces, we ransack our stores, we "spend our money for that which is not bread, and our labor for that which satisfieth not;"

we look every way, and call to every thing, till each in return loudly replies, " It is not in me." Well, indeed, will it be, if, after all our fruitless efforts, we are brought to feel that the provisions of the Gospel are the only *bread* for a hungry soul, the only *balm* for a wounded heart.

However foreign, my dear friend, these truths were from your consideration when we first sat down together, if it shall please Him, " who commanded the light to shine out of darkness," to shine into your heart, and effectually discover the *exceeding riches of his grace* in these provisions; then, though *you* sit weeping over your loss, we are assured, from unquestionable authority, that angels are rejoicing for your unspeakable gain. We are certain, also, that not only every *real* friend will cry, " this day is salvation come to the house" where we lately wept; but that, drying your tears, you yourself will be compelled to express your grateful sense of the correction you now deplore, and sing with a companion and fellow-proficient in the school of affliction :

> Father, I bless thy gentle hand;
>   How kind was thy chastising rod,
> That forc'd my conscience to a stand,
>   And brought my wandering soul to God !
>
> Foolish and vain, I went astray,
>   Ere I had felt thy scourges, Lord;
> I left my guide—I lost my way;
>   But now I love and keep thy word.

And here suffer me to drop a word or two respecting

OUR COMPANIONS in the house of mourning. Society is peculiarly pleasant when we are benighted on a journey; and especially that of a citizen of the place to which we are going. It is encouraging to travel with those who are convinced that, if " they are chastened of the Lord, it is that they should not be condemned with the world."

" Go thy way forth by the footsteps of the flock;" for in this house they all have left the prints of their feet. Here stood Jacob weeping over his beloved Rachel; and here Aaron deplored his sons. Here we trace the steps of David going up to his chamber, and crying with a loud voice, "Would to God I had died for thee, O Absalom, my son! my son!" and the steps of Ezekiel, who, forbidden to cry, silently resigned "the desire of his eyes to the stroke." But enumeration is vain; hither came all the sons of God, the only begotten not excepted, for JESUS himself stood and "wept" at the grave of a friend.

With such company, is it not far "better to go to the house of mourning than to the house of feasting?" I knew one of these, "a man who had seen affliction by a rod" like yours; a man who walked and wept in solitude, but with no expectation of being overheard. There is something sacred in grief, and we cannot listen to its effusions with too much candor; great candor, indeed, is here required, but, if afforded, it may procure you at least a *companion* as you pass through this vale of tears.

[CECIL'S PRIVATE REFLECTIONS.]

' * * * * * * * "Set thee up way-marks;" I desire here to set them up, and to record the severest of my visitations in the house of my pilgrimage. Lord, prepare me for the next!

' I perceive I could not have properly sympathised with a friend in a similar case before this stroke. I could not have *understood* it.

' I have, at times, so felt the importance of eternal things, that I thought the loss of any present comfort would be tolerable; but I had no idea how much depended on being *ready* when the Son of man came in such a providence.

' I feel I now stand in the right position to see the *world* and the *word;* they both appear under aspects entirely new.

' When I find "my joys packed up and gone," my heart slain, the delight of my eyes taken away; when I recollect who is gone before her, who is following, and what remains for the world to offer; my heart cries, "I loathe it, I would not live alway;" I thank God that *I* am also to go.

' I perceive I did not know how much my life was bound up in the life of a creature; when *she* went, nothing seemed left; one is not; and the rest seem a few thin and scattered remains.

' And yet how much better for my lamb to be suddenly housed, to slip unexpectedly into the fold to which I was conducting her, than remain exposed here! perhaps become a victim!

'I cried, "O Lord, spare my child!" he did; but not as I meant; he snatched it from danger, and took it to his own home.

'I have often prayed, "Lord, soften my heart! humble my pride! destroy my levity!" I knew enough of his way to fear the *means;* and he has, in mercy toward me, regarded my *soul* more than my feelings.

'I prayed earnestly for her life, duty compelled me to say, "*Thy will be done;*" but I *meant* nothing.

'O my God, how long hast thou come *seeking fruit on this tree!* how much hast thou done to cultivate it! Shall it remain fruitless? shall it be cut down after all?

'My passions forged impressions that she would live; but I now plainly perceive I am called to regard *God*, and not *impressions*.

'I have been long like one in a fever, attended at times with a strong delirium: I begged hard that I might not be bled, but he meant a cure, and pierced my heart.

'O how slender, how brittle the thread on which hang all my earthly joys!

'I wish ever to be asking, "Am I ready, should he send again, and take *** or *** or myself?" Setting my house in order will not make death approach sooner: but, that it would render his coming much *easier*, I feel by sad experience.

'When I pass by the blaze of dissipation and intemperance, I feel a moment's relief. I say to my heart, "Be still;" at least she is not left to follow these *ignes fatui:* how much better is even the grave for my T——!

'It is vain for me to wish, as I have done, to leave the world and go to my Father, that I might inquire into the whole of the case: the reasons, the steps, the issue, &c. In a short time I shall; but he says enough *now*, if I have ears to hear.

'In the mean time, help me, O my God and Father, to recollect that I received this drop of earthly comfort from a spring which still remains! help me to feel that nothing *essential* is altered! "for with thee is the fountain of life:" part of myself is already gone to thee, help what remains to follow!' *

If this humble attempt to improve your affliction has been attended with any success, you will readily admit a few concluding hints with respect to

OUR DUTY in such circumstances. And one of the first and principal duties of the state is, as has been expressed, to ACKNOWLEDGE GOD in it. It was charged upon some, that they "returned not to him that smote them, nor sought the Lord" in their distress. On the contrary, the clear apprehension Job had of a Divine hand in his afflictions, is as instructive as his patience under them. While grief "rent his mantle," faith fell down and worshipped: "The Lord gave, the Lord hath taken away, blessed be the name of the Lord." Let us learn from him never to lose sight of the *Author* by an undue regard to the mere *circumstances* of our loss. We may think and speak of the symptoms and stages of the late removal; of the physicians, of the remedies, &c. in their supposed right or wrong application; but not so as to forget that an unerring Providence presided over the whole, yea, actually *conducted* every part on reasons as righteous as inscrutable.

Whatever may appear to *us* peculiar in the sick chamber, the whole was but God's intended method of removing one who had lived his *full*, his *appointed* time. "Seeing his days are determined, the number of his months are with thee: thou hast appointed him his bounds which he cannot pass." Instead of fixing our attention upon means and creatures, of which we know very little, let us turn to Him who wrought by these instruments, and merely effected his own determinations by them. "Cease from man, for wherein is he to be accounted of?" Let not the creature hide the Creator, nor present things prove the fatal screen of the future; but, in every occurrence, mark the great Cause, "of whom, and through whom, and to whom are all things;" who numbereth the *very hairs of our head*, and without whom even a "sparrow falls not to the ground."

While others, therefore, are wandering without an object, and bereaved without a comforter, yea, are going to their worst enemy for relief, let us endeavor to say, with Peter, "Lord, to whom shall we go" but to "THEE?" Consider the great Physician as now proposing a most serious question to your conscience, "Wilt thou be made whole?" May the language of your heart be that of the Apostle: "If by any means:" then, though seemingly swallowed up of this grief, like Jonah, you shall find a resource *in* it, and finally be preserved *by* it." This dart, like that which once pierced an imposthume in battle, shall bring health with its wounds: and you shall be enabled, with many that are gone before you, to say, "The Lord hath chastened me sore: but he hath not given me over unto death."

Duty also directs you to MODERATE YOUR GRIEF. Our heavenly Father, who "knows our frame, and remembers that we are but dust," allows us to mourn when he afflicts us; he often, in his providence, calls us to it, and charges us to "weep with them that weep;" but he admonishes us also of a danger on each hand: "My son, despise not thou the chastening of the Lord, nor faint when thou art rebuked of him." If we seriously profess Christianity, our very profession implies not only a subjection to our Lord's will, but that we have special resources in our affliction, several of which have been already named: that, among other of our privileges, there is "a peace from God which passeth all understanding, to keep our hearts and minds" through life and death; and that we have many reasons for "not sorrowing as others who have no hope." Beside which, Christians have a post of honor to maintain, an "high calling" to demonstrate and commend: we shall, like the pilot in the storm, be brought to our principles; and, "as sorrowful yet always rejoicing," should prove that we have them not now to learn.

There is such a thing as nursing and cherishing our grief, employing a "busy meddling memory to muster up past endearments" and personate a vast variety of tender and heart-rending circumstances. There is a tearing open the wound afresh by images and remembrances, and thereby multiplying those pangs which constitute the very bitterness of death itself. Our melancholy exceedingly affects this voluntary torture; it seeks expedients, and will listen to the most unjust and aggravated accusations which can approach a tender conscience respecting the deceased. But conscience should rather be concerned to repress such a disposition. It is a temptation. It desperately strives to retain what God has determined to remove: in some cases it seeks to penetrate an abyss he forbids even conjecture to explore: and while it unfits the mourner for the pressing duties of his station, it leads to that "sorrow of the world which worketh death" to his body, soul, and Christian character. How different and superior the sentiments of David! "His servants said unto him, What thing is this that thou hast done? thou didst fast and weep for the child while it was alive, but when the child was dead thou didst rise and eat bread. And he said, While the child was yet alive, I fasted and wept: for I said, Who can tell whether God will be gracious to me, that the child may live; but now he is dead, wherefore should I fast? can I bring him back again? I SHALL GO TO HIM, BUT HE SHALL NOT RETURN TO ME."

Present circumstances also admonish you to KNOW YOUR OPPORTUNITY, and to improve this season as peculiarly favorable for spiritual advancement. Your heart is now soft, its fascinations withdrawn, and the call loud and affecting; endeavor, therefore, to take the benefit of a remedy you feel to be so expensive.

If, in a sense, "smitten friends are angels sent on errands full of love," instead of weeping over their tombs, let us listen to the voice which properly arises from them; especially if it be our privilege to bury one, who, like Abel, "being dead, yet speaketh," and who would be ready to say to his mourners, "Weep not for me, but for yourselves and for your children!" "I have fought the good fight, I have finished my course, I have kept the faith," and received my crown. I cannot now come to weep with you, but you may ascend and rejoice with me, where there is "no more death, neither sorrow, nor crying, for the former things are passed away." If you truly love me, prepare to follow me. If you earnestly wish to see me again, seek not the living among the dead, but arise and become "a follower of them who through faith and patience inherit the promises." Take that heavenly lamp which "shineth as a light in a dark place;" walk humbly by it, "till the day dawn and the day-star arise in your heart." Haste, my beloved, toward the things which eye hath not seen; and, ere the eternal day break, and the present shadows flee away, "run with patience the race set before you, looking unto Jesus." How will my cup overflow to meet you among those who daily come hither "out of great tribulation;" and having "washed their robes in the blood of the Lamb, serve him day and night in his temple!"

Embrace every method God has recommended for maintaining communion with him, and obtaining relief from him: the various ordinances of his house, the encouragements of his word, the society of his children, and especially prayer. Often speak to Him who "seeth in secret," "and is nigh unto all that call upon him," though, with the woman of Canaan, you can only say, "Lord, help me." You have both a command and a promise, "Call upon me in the day of trouble, I will deliver thee, and thou shalt glorify me." Christ encourages no one to advance on the ground of his own *strength*, any more than on that of his own *desert:* he is as jealous of the power of his arm as of the merit of his blood. He admitted infirmity and misery to be presented as a *complaint*, but never as an *objection*.

Again, that you may seek cheerfully this assistance, REGARD YOUR ENCOURAGEMENTS. What hath God not done in order to commend his love? By every expression of tender concern, he, in the person of a *man of sorrows*, invites the guilty, the weary, the trembling and the tempted to come unto him, assuring them that he will neither "break the bruised reed nor quench the smoking flax." May he meet you at this time, my dear friend, with consolations which none but himself can afford; and then, at the very grave, shall that saying be brought to pass, "death is swallowed up in victory."

To conclude: the late event solemnly repeats the charge, "BE YE ALSO READY." Your friend is gone: your following is certain; it may be sudden; it may be next. But should it take place this night, and find you provided with nothing better for the change than the miserable subterfuges of the profane, or the scarcely less miserable supports of the formal, what an alarm, if you are not left to the most affecting delusion or stupidity, will it occasion! What an awful transition to pass from the SAVIOR to the JUDGE! without love to him, without even an acquaintance with him; unwilling, unreconciled, unrenewed!—and to him who has so often invited you, warned you, and at times affected your conscience with the truths we have been considering! What a subject for eternal reflection: "You would not come to him that you might have life!"

God forbid that this should be *your* case. I only suppose it, lest it should; and it is too common to render the supposition improper. From such a danger we cannot be too secure; and therefore, having lately seen how soon " the night cometh, when no man can work," let us seek *to-day*, in the redemption which is in Christ Jesus, that peace and safety which you must be conscious can never be found OUT of it, and which it may be too late to seek to-morrow.

Some things belonging to our important change are wisely hid from us; nothing, however, is more plain than that it is *near*, and therefore demands our most serious attention: that it is finally " decisive," and therefore warns us to watch against those errors which eternity cannot rectify; and that the hour is *uncertain*, and therefore calls us to stand prepared. With our *loins girded* and our *lights burning*, may we thus wait for our Lord!

Impressed with such views, I have often wished to take the afflicted by the hand and lead them to a resource their passions have obscured. I have wished them to see that the Christian hope is then most alive and full of immortality when every other hope perishes: these wishes, and the request of a friend, (who was solicitous to obtain something of this kind more compendious than he had yet seen,) have drawn from me some imperfect hints. Imperfect, however, as they are, like a few words presented by the road's side to the eye of a weary traveler, they may afford you some present direction and relief. And should He, who is pleased to employ the feeblest means in his greatest work, conduct you by them though but a single step on your way toward a *morning without clouds*—a *house* without *mourning*—the service of your affectionate friend will obtain a high reward.

END.

NO. 4.

WITHOUT HOLINESS
NO MAN SHALL SEE THE LORD.

A SOLEMN declaration! The unchangeable God hath made it. Shall not then the unholy sinner see the Lord? See him indeed the sinner must, when he cometh with clouds. Every eye shall then behold him, and all unholy hearts will fear and tremble. But to behold the Lord in peace—to see his face and live, will be, to the sinner, for ever impossible. Impenitent and unholy, he is under condemnation—a prisoner to offended justice. The wrath of God abideth on him. He that believeth not, is condemned already. The wages of sin is death.

It is naturally impossible for the sinner to see God in peace, while sinful principles and tempers reign within him. There is no agreement between sin and holiness. The heart must be pleased with the character, government, and service of God, before it can be happy in God himself. The sinner dislikes God and his holy requisitions. He is pursuing interests and pleasures which God hath forbidden. He will not have God to reign over him. Such opposition of character and views will keep the soul at an infinite remove from the presence and enjoyment of God.

Sin cherished in the soul will fill it with darkness—will exclude the light of God's countenance and the tokens of his favor. The sinner, with his unholy heart and carnal affections, cannot approach the throne of grace. He has no interest there. He is a stranger—an alien—an enemy, by wicked works. He has no access to God—no communion with him—no settled peace of conscience—no preparation for a holy heaven. When flesh and heart begin to fail, and the sinner feels himself drawn irresistibly towards death and judgment—whither will he look? Will he raise his eyes to heaven? Alas! how unavailing! He never sought the friendship of God: and now God is not his friend. As he was far from God in life, now God is far from him. Darkness and gloom brood over his mind, and shut out the light of heaven.

Conscious guilt and fearful forebodings anticipate the wrath of God.

Besides, the heavenly world, with all its glory and felicity, would be a place of torment to an unholy mind. Should the sinner, with his unholy heart and character, be admitted into the regions of the blessed, what would he find, suited to his desires and reigning temper of his heart? He would find the character and taste of every being totally opposite to his own. He would find every employment of heaven holy and spiritual, and opposed to his inclinations. He would find himself perfectly alone—no one to associate with him among all the millions of the heavenly world. He would feel himself unfit for the society of the blessed. A sight of the glory of Jehovah would fill his soul with unutterable pain, and wake within him the worm that never dies. Covered with pollution, and filled with conscious guilt, he would shrink from the place, and cover himself in the dark abodes of hell, rather than endure the light, the purity, and the joys of heaven.

Reader, let me entreat you to consider, as a dying, accountable creature, the momentous truth before us. Do you not wish to know what is necessary, to see God in peace? and what you must be, to enjoy his favor, and be happy for ever? This is, of all concerns, the first and greatest. Whatever interests you have in the world, depend upon it, they are far less important than being of the temper and character necessary to the favor and friendship of your Maker. God has expressly assured us, that without holiness, we cannot see his face and live. It is a point irreversibly determined. Deceive not yourself, then, with the vain hope of being blessed in his favor, without holiness of heart and life. Has God declared, that holiness is indispensable to the enjoyment of him, here and hereafter? and can you be indifferent, whether you have this all-important qualification for heaven, or are yet in your sins—whether you are travelling the narrow road to life, or the broad road to death? Can you trifle with heaven and hell? Is it a small thing whether you be doomed to the lake of fire, or dwell for ever in the Paradise of God? When these heavens shall be on fire, and these elements shall melt with fervent heat—

when the voice of the archangel and the trump of God shall sound the general alarm, and call the world to judgment; then, O dreadful to declare, then will trembling sinners call to the rocks and mountains to fall on them, and hide them from the sight of their offended Judge. No one can then be indifferent. All hearts which are not holy, and not fixed on God, will then be filled with consternation and dismay.

This dreadful day will surely come: are you prepared for its amazing solemnities? Be faithful to yourself. Now is a blessed season for grace; to-morrow it may be past for ever. Ask, then, without delay, the momentous question—Have *I* that holiness, without which I cannot see the Lord? Does the love of God dwell in my heart? Are my affections placed on things above? Am I conformed to the image of God? Do I delight in his holy service? Do I heartily repent of sin? Have I the spirit of Christ, and am I reconciled unto God by his atoning blood? Reader, you have made these inquiries; let conscience now answer them as in the presence of God. Are you indeed penitent and heavenly-minded, pardoned by the blood, and renewed by the Spirit of the Lord Jesus? Or, on the contrary, does not your conscience bring the melancholy report, that you are yet in your sins—without God and without hope in the world? This, then, is your conclusion. The testimony of your conscience is, that you are destitute of holy love to God, and of saving faith in Jesus; and consequently that you are condemned already. Dreadful condition! Awake, O sinner, from your security in sin, and behold your threatening danger. You have no preparation for the hour of death, nor for standing before your eternal Judge. You have no qualifications for heavenly blessedness—no temper for the holy praises of eternity. nor for dwelling in the presence of a holy God and Savior. With your present character, you must be shut out of heaven; for no impenitent, unsanctified, unholy heart, can be admitted there; and without supreme love to God, and delight in his praises, the heavenly world would be a place of pain and torment to the soul

Wherever the sinner, in the future world, is, he must **be wretched** His opposition of heart to God, his unholy temper, and love of sinful pleasures, will constitute the prime ingredients of hell. Consider, I beseech you, how criminal you are in the sight of your Maker and Redeemer, while your heart is at variance with him, and refuses to love and serve him. He demands your love. You will not have him to reign over you. But who hath hardened himself against God, and prospered? You are perishing in sin, and yet refuse the Almighty arm stretched out for your relief. Consider the awful guilt of rejecting God's eternal Son, and of setting at nought the messages of his grace. How can you escape, if you neglect so great salvation? Let not, I pray you, the pleasures, and gains, and pursuits of this world, divert your attention from the danger which threatens you, while impenitent and unholy. The end of your present course is the second death—the punishment of hell. If, after this solemn warning, you remain stupid, impenitent, and forgetful of God, you will not only run the hazard of losing your soul, but will awfully aggravate your final condemnation. We must look forward with fearful apprehensions of seeing your death-bed a place of terror and remorse, and of hearing you take up the bitter lamentation—the harvest is past, the summer is ended, and I am not saved. We must look forward to the great and dreadful day, and see you a trembling criminal, on the left hand of your offended Judge, ready to hear the irreversible sentence, " Depart from me, ye cursed, into everlasting fire." O prevent a doom so dreadful, while God is on the throne of mercy, and entreats you to come unto him and live. O come and bow before a gracious God, and with deep repentance sue for pardon through the blood of Jesus. Fly to the Savior, make the Judge your friend. Behold he cometh! Prepare to meet your God. *Without holiness, ye cannot see the Lord.*

PUBLISHED BY THE
AMERICAN TRACT SOCIETY,

And sold at their Depository, No. 150 Nassau-street, near the City-Hall, New-York; and by Agents of the Society, its Branches, and Auxiliaries, in the principal cities and towns in the United States.

NO. 5.

THE WARNING VOICE.

Mount Sinai.

This little book is addressed to you on the weighty and everlasting interests of your soul. You see that people all around you are dying; and you know that you too must die, and be fixed in a state that is unchangeable. Is it not then a question of great importance for you to put to yourself, "Have I any solid ground of hope that I shall go to heaven when I die? or have I not rather awful reason to fear that I shall sink down to hell, and there lift up my eyes in everlasting torments?" If you live and die in sin, this must be your portion. Attend therefore with seriousness to the following considerations:

1. While living in sin *you are in imminent danger!* You would pity the poor man who was thoughtless and unconcerned on the brink of some frightful precipice; but the precipice on the edge of which *you* are standing is infinitely more tremendous. You would reckon him a madman who, for one short hour of pleasure, would expose himself to misery for all future time; but *you* are more inexcusable, who, for pleasures of sin which are but for a season, are venturing upon a miserable eternity.

A warning voice from God's word now sounds in your ear, *except a man be born again, he cannot see the king-*

dom of God; a voice uttered by that Savior who will shortly be your judge; and if you should then be found a stranger to this new birth, it would be better for you had you never been born; for he will say to you, "Depart, ye cursed, into everlasting fire." Were you now to think of these things, as becomes men that have never-dying souls, they would ever be uppermost in your mind; you would think of them when at labor in the field, when at work in the shop, or when busy in the house. How happy would it be for you, if an abiding sense of them should drive you to Christ, the strong hold, as a prisoner of hope! But if you determine to banish these thoughts because they make you uneasy, and go on dreaming of happiness over the pit of destruction, be assured your delusion cannot last long. Soon DEATH will tear the bandage from your eyes; and O, what sights will you then see! what sounds will you then hear! what anguish will you then feel! You that could not bear to *hear* of hell, how will you *endure* the fire that shall never be quenched?

Perhaps you now take the name of God in vain, and call for damnation on your soul. Alas! you have never considered what damnation is, or you would not trifle with it upon your tongue. Perhaps you profane the Sabbath. Instead of attending upon the worship of God, you spend the day in a tavern, or in idleness, or in your worldly calling, or in visiting, or receiving visits. Perhaps you live in the indulgence of forbidden lusts, which drown men in perdition. These sins harden the heart, stupify the conscience, and bring upon those that commit them swift destruction. God says of such, "They shall have their portion in the lake of fire and brimstone, which is the second death."

But consider, however free you are from gross immorality, what is your *true character* in the sight of Him who looketh on the *heart.* Be not deceived. Delusion here is fatal. Whatever form of holiness you have, while a stranger to conversion, you are destitute of the reality of religion, and notwithstanding all your fair appearances, are an ungodly man.

For the discovery of yourself, consider the following marks and evidences of an ungodly man; and in contrast, the marks of one that is truly godly; and may the Lord help you to examine yourself as in the sight of God!

An ungodly man places his chief happiness in *this world*. Here is his chief treasure; and where his treasure is, there his heart will be also. If his farm flourishes, or his trade increases, or he lives a little better than his poor neighbors, he thinks himself happy, and like the rich man in the Gospel, says to his soul, "Soul, thou hast much goods laid up for many years, take thine ease, eat, drink, and be merry." Reader, is this your case? Is your soul bound to the earth? If it is, be assured, as if a voice from heaven had proclaimed it, you are in an unconverted state an enemy of God; for "if any man love the world, the love of the Father is not in him," "he is an enemy of God."

On the other hand, a truly godly man is enlightened to see the utter vanity, and insufficiency, and emptiness of this present world. He knows it can never make him happy; and therefore, while many are saying, "Who will show us any earthly good?" his language is, "Lord, lift thou up the light of thy countenance upon me, and it shall put gladness into my heart, more than when their corn and wine are increased." Nothing less can satisfy him than the favor of God, which is life, and his loving kindness, which is better than life. He had rather be a poor man, a persecuted man, with the favor of God, than have all the riches of the world without it.

An ungodly man is one who does not delight in the *service of God*. There are many who never attend upon public worship; or, if they do it, it is only out of custom, and they are heartily glad when it is over. Unless they have some pleasure to pursue, or some worldly business to promote, they count the Sabbath-day the longest in all the week; and say, "What a weariness is it!" As to more retired worship, either in the family or in the closet, in that they take no delight. They know that God is their enemy, and they feel an aversion to his company. But a godly man loves the place where God's honor dwelleth. He says, "I was glad when they said unto me, Let us go up to the house of the Lord." He goes to the house of God hungering and thirsting after living bread and living waters; and he has found there some of the happiest moments of his life. Nor can he live without secret prayer; and when he has been pouring out his heart to God he has experienced some of the foretastes of heaven, some of the beginnings of glory.

An ungodly man is one who pays no regard to the *souls* of his children. If they are strong and healthy, and he can provide food and clothing for them, and they thrive in the world, that is all he cares for. But as to their souls, he does not trouble himself about them. So far as he is concerned, they are left to grow up in sin, and in ignorance of God and Christ; strangers to the Gospel, even in a Christian land. Surely those who have no concern about the spiritual and eternal interests of their children must be ungodly parents.

On the contrary, a truly godly man makes the souls of his children a principal concern. He tries to impress their minds with a deep sense of their misery and guilt, of the corruption of their hearts and the depravity of their lives, of their need of the Gospel, and of the excellent and suitable blessings it contains—blessings that will make them rich in the favor of God, not only in this world, but also in eternity. He had rather see his children good than great; rather see them pressing after the kingdom of glory than possessed of the most powerful kingdom upon earth.

Now, reader, if you discern your own picture in the marks which have been given of an ungodly man; if, in the description which has been drawn, you see your own likeness, know then that you are in a state of *the greatest danger*, " in the gall of bitterness and in the bonds of iniquity;" and that there is but a step between you and everlasting burnings! O then FLEE, FLEE FROM THE WRATH TO COME. The avenger of blood pursues you. The judge, even now, standeth at the door; and in a very little time, without deep repentance and turning to God through Christ, you will cry out in torment, without a drop of water to cool your tongue.

II. While you are living in sin, and are a stranger to God and Christ, *you know nothing of true and real happiness.* It is utterly impossible, in the very nature of things, that there can be real peace and happiness in the ways of sin. A prophet has declared, " There is no peace, saith my God, to the wicked." Have not you often found the truth of these words in your own melancholy experience? Have not you often felt the most dreadful pangs of conscience, and fearful forebodings of eternal misery? What could this be but the gnawings of that worm that never dieth, the beginnings of that fire which shall never be quenched? You try to banish the thoughts of death and judgment. You fly to company, to vain amusements, or the cares of this world to stifle the voice of conscience. Why do you strive to stifle her voice? Alas! it is because you know that conscience witnesses against you. But though you endeavor to drown her voice, yet you know that now and then she speaks in a tone of terror. And is this the happiness you promise yourself in the ways of sin?

You have already made the dreadful experiment, that there is no real happiness to be found in the ways of sin; try then what the ways of Christ will produce, and you will find these words fulfilled in your own happy experience, " Great peace have they that love thy law." Instances unnumbered might be readily produced, which would show the power of religion to support and solace the mind under the heaviest trials, and to inspire the soul with peace and triumph in the dying hour. No such instances can be found in all the registers of sin. O that you would then be convinced that you can never experience happiness till your peace is made with God through Christ.

III. While living in sin, *the great God is your enemy.* And, O man or woman, youth or child, whoever you are, if God be against you, all things are against you; this world is but your prison till the day of wrath, when you will be brought out, like a felon, to everlasting punishment. Your own conscience now tells you that God is your enemy, because you know you are a rebel against him, though he has been doing you good ever since you were born. Yea, your actions testify against you; for they say, " I will not have him to reign over me."

Now to have God for your enemy, how dreadful! Far better have all the men in the world, yea, all the devils in hell, to your enemies, than the blessed God. The weight of his arm you cannot endure, and from his vengeance you cannot escape. O you will find it a fearful thing to fall into the hands of the living God! Then neither pious friends nor godly ministers can help you.

Then you will remember this "Warning Voice;" and it will add to your anguish that you turned a deaf ear to the counsel that is now given you.

IV. In a very little time *death, judgment, and eternity will overtake you.* O what haste is death making! There is no post so swift, no messenger so sure; and when he comes, then of all your unjust gains, for which you have sold your soul and salvation, and of all your sinful pleasures, nothing will remain but the heavy reckoning and the bitter remembrance. Yes, you must stand before the judgment-seat of Christ. You must there give an account to him of your stewardship, of your time, your talents, and privileges; and why you employed them for sinful pleasure and profit, and not for his glory. And when he shall say, "Did I send you into the world only to get wealth, and to forget your immortal soul? Did I appoint my Sabbaths to be profaned by you; and give you my word only to be neglected? Did I give you my laws and commandments only to be trampled upon? Did I not send my faithful ministers to set before you the blessings which my grace provided for the chief of sinners? And still, notwithstanding all this, did you not harden your heart, and go on in the way of your own evil thoughts?"—when the awful judge shall put these questions, what answer will you be able to give? Will you not be speechless with confusion and self-conviction? And will not your heart sink within you when you shall hear him pronounce the awful sentence, "Depart, ye cursed, into everlasting fire, prepared for the devil and his angels."

There is an energy in the word *eternity* which deserves to be seriously thought of; and which you will begin to know the meaning of whenever this slender veil of flesh is removed, and eternal things in all their grandeur and importance burst upon your sight. If God were to impress this thought upon your mind, it would put an effectual stop to your present course of folly.

V. Miserable as your present state is, *the Gospel of Christ points out a way of escape.* There is a *great* salvation provided by a *great* Savior, and accomplished by *great* means. This salvation is free for all that are willing heartily and with true penitence to receive it. Do not think of trying to make yourselves worthy of this salvation, or of making yourselves clean before you go to him for cleansing. You may as well bid a sick man heal himself before he apply to a physician.

O that you would listen to these glad tidings with a heart warm with love to that God who has been pleased to manifest such a display of his love to a lost world, as to " give his only-begotten Son, that whosoever believeth in him might not perish, but have everlasting life." He sent him *to die,* that you might *live*—to be made a *curse* for you, that you might be *delivered from the curse* of that law which you have broken. There is free and full pardon offered in the Gospel to every one that will but come unto God by Jesus Christ, however vile your past life may have been, and however great a sense you may now have of your transgressions. And such has been the energy of this doctrine of free forgiveness for the greatest offenders, that it has influenced drunkards to become sober, unclean persons to become chaste, fraudulent persons to become honest, and those who have long been under the power of darkness to become fellow-citizens of the saints, and of the household of God.

O consider that the God of mercy condescends to entreat you to attend to the things that belong to your everlasting peace, before they are for ever hidden from your eyes;—and that the compassionate Redeemer, who gave his life to redeem sinners from everlasting destruction, speaks to them in the most gracious language, " Come unto me, all ye that labor and are heavy laden, and I will give you rest;" and he tells you for your encouragement, that " whoever cometh, he will in no wise cast out;" and he moreover assures you, that though you have long resisted his grace, *there is yet room* in his heart for you. Yea, notwithstanding he is now exalted to the throne of infinite glory, he sees you, he observes you, as you are reading these lines. He observes the effect they have upon you. And will you, *can* you bear the thought of rejecting him, and neglecting the grace that is now held up to you? O consider that there will be no possibility of escaping if you neglect so great salvation!

Consider also, that your conversion and salvation will give joy to all the good. Such know that in their Father's house is bread enough and to spare, and that in their Father's heart are infinite compassions. They know you never can be happy, till, as a returning prodigal, you come to him; and they would think their happiness greatly increased by promoting yours.

Reflect upon the privileges those enjoy who with their whole heart have, like Mary, chosen *the one thing needful*. They are in possession of that good part which shall never be taken from them. The promises of God are all theirs. All the blessings of life are theirs, and all the afflictions of life work for their good; whether life, or death, or things present, or things to come; all are theirs, for they are Christ's, and Christ is God's. They are now heirs of glory. They are looking for that eternal kingdom which they will for ever possess. And is not this enough to excite your earnest desires that *you* may be a partaker of all this bliss? Come then to Christ. Cast yourself upon his mercy. He will reject none who trust in him. He will hear the prayer of the penitent. His holy Spirit will soften your hard heart, change your corrupt affections, and mold and form you into his own blessed image.

Go to him for strength to resist your own corruptions, the insinuations of wicked companions, and the temptations of the devil. Resolve, like the faithful servant of God of old, *Let others do what they will, as for me, I will serve the Lord.*

PUBLISHED BY THE
AMERICAN TRACT SOCIETY,

And sold at their Depository, No. 150 Nassau-street, near the City-Hall, New-York; and by Agents of the Society, its Branches, and Auxiliaries, in the principal cities and towns in the United States.

NO. 6

THE ONE THING NEEDFUL.

A DIALOGUE.

Traveler. Pray, friend, will you give me leave to ask you a question or two?

Yourself. With all my heart, Sir, as many as you please.

Tr. Of what religion are you?

You. Of what religion, Sir? the same as my neighbors.

Tr. And pray what religion is that?

You. Why the same as our fathers' before us.

Tr. I should be glad to know what that was?

You. You ask very odd questions. I never thought much about religion. I go to church now and then, and pay every man his own. That's all I know about it.

Tr. I am very sorry you know no more about religion than that. It is right that you should go to church, and pay every man his due; but much more is necessary, if you would be happy when you die.

You. Sir, I hope to be saved as well as others, and should be glad to be put in the right way if I am wrong. I am no scholar, nor have I had time to mind religion much.

Tr. It may be your ignorance arises rather from want of inclination than from want of time. It is not necessary, in order to salvation, that you be a great scholar; but absolutely necessary that you be *born again*.

You. *Born again!* Sir, *born again!* Pray what do you mean?

Tr. I mean that no man can be saved whose *heart* is not changed by grace, and himself thus made a *new creature*.

You. I don't understand you. This is a *new doctrine* to me. Excuse me, Sir if I ask what religion you are of, for I have heard of many false prophets.

Tr. I am a Christian and a Protestant. I believe no doctrines but those of the Bible.

You. Pray tell me if there is any thing in my Bible about being born again?

Tr. Yes, a great deal. Our blessed Lord said to Nicodemus, "Verily, verily, I say unto thee, except a man be *born again*, he cannot see the kingdom of God." "Except a man be *born of water and of the Spirit*, he cannot enter into the kingdom of God." John, 3: 3. and 2. "Being *born again*," says St. Peter, "not of corruptible seed, but of incorruptible, by the word of God, which liveth and abideth for ever." 1 Pet. 1: 23. St. John, speaking of those who believe in the Lord Jesus Christ, says, "Which were *born*, not of blood, nor of the will of the flesh, nor of the will of man, but *of God*." John, 1: 13. And again, "Whosoever is *born of God* doth not commit sin; for his seed remaineth in him, and he cannot sin, because he is *born of God*." 1 John, 3: 9. "Whosoever believeth that Jesus is the Christ, is *born of God*." 1 John, 5: 1.

You. Well, Sir, this is all very good; I remember it now in my Bible.

Tr. But, my friend, as you find that a man cannot be saved except he be *born again*, are *you* born again?

You. Why, Sir, as to that, I hope so.

Tr. Pray *why* do you hope so? what evidence have you?

You. I was baptized. I am honest and industrious, and live in peace with my neighbors. I am neither a profane swearer, a drunkard, nor a Sabbath-breaker, and have done no harm to any one.

Tr. But observe, my friend, it is by the *new birth*, not by *baptism*, nor by any *works of righteousness which we have done*, (Titus, 3: 5.) that we are made children of grace. It is when this *new birth* takes place, when we are *born again*, that, as the Scripture says, *old things pass away, and all things become new.* 2 Cor. 5: 17.

You. Sir, I should be glad to hear more of this matter. I confess I have been very careless and ignorant; will you please to tell me *what it is to be born again?*

Tr. To be born again implies, first, a discovery that you are a poor, lost *sinner;* which will make you deeply concerned about your soul. Hitherto, by your own account you have felt easy and secure, you have been satisfied with having as much religion as your neighbors, or rather with none at all. Now, a new creature is convinced that the care of the soul is the *one thing needful;* and that it would be dreadful to gain the whole world at the expense of losing the soul.

You. If this be the case, I am all wrong, for I have minded my body more than my soul. But go on.

Tr. The new creature will habitually *pray.* Prayer is his breath. A true Christian can no more live without prayer, than without breathing. As soon as Paul was converted, he prayed; and so will every soul that is born again. The whole want not a physician, but the sick do; and they will look to Christ for healing. But none truly desire to be saved till they feel that they are lost.

You. Alas! I scarcely ever pray. Too often I lie down and rise up like a beast. Lord teach me to pray!

Tr. Again, a true Christian sees the *odious nature of sin*, and abhors himself on account of it. The infinitely holy law of God condemns a man for one wrong action, or thought; for, as the apostle says, "Whosoever shall offend in one point, is guilty of all." James, 2: 10. And "Cursed is every one that continueth not in all things written in the book of the law to do them." Gal. 3. 10. The least offender is therefore liable to God's wrath in hell for ever.

You. I know I am a sinner and at times have been concerned about it, especially when I was sick, or in great danger. At such times I was afraid of going to hell; but my fears soon wore off. Now I see I have awful reason to be afraid. *God be merciful to me!*

Tr. The true Christian *looks to Christ*, and to him alone for deliverance from the wrath to come. When the distressed jailer asked St. Paul what he must do to be saved, he was directed to "*believe on the Lord Jesus Christ.*"

You. Pray, Sir, what is it to believe? I have often heard of faith, and used to think I was a believer, but never knew what faith is.

Tr. Faith includes two things. First, a believing of the *truths and doctrines* of the Gospel, especially those that respect the person of Christ as God-man, and what he did and suffered in our stead. And secondly, *trusting in Christ,* and relying on him alone for salvation, under an affecting sense of our own unworthiness and guilt.

You. But, Sir, does not this trust in Christ make people careless about good works?

Tr. By no means; for good works are the fruits of faith; and if faith be *true,* it always *works by love.*

You. Have you any thing more to add?

Tr. Yes, a true Christian is *holy;* for "*without holiness no man can see the Lord.*" He cannot live in sin, for he hates it, and is dead to it. He cannot be a drunkard, but will wholly avoid strong drink for fear of temptation. He cannot be a swearer, for he now loves and fears God. He cannot be dishonest, for now he loves his neighbor as himself. He cannot be unchaste, for God has given him a clean heart. He cannot be a Sabbath-breaker, for the delight of his soul is to employ the Sabbath wholly in religion. Thus you see that faith produces good works.

You. All this is right; and I wish from my heart I was as you say. Pray tell me how I may become so?

Tr. Consider prayerfully *what you need.* You need a heart to love the great God supremely: and can you refuse to love Him who is infinitely amiable? You need a heart to confess and forsake all sin: and are you too *proud* to comply, or such a *slave* that you cannot quit sin? You need an interest in Christ: and will you not now come to him, who, though Lord of all worlds, has once *died* for sinners? O hesitate no longer. Say heartily, "I cannot live without God, without Christ, without hope." "*Lord I believe; help thou mine unbelief.*"

PUBLISHED BY THE AMERICAN TRACT SOCIETY.

THE HAPPY NEGRO.

By the late Ambrose Serle, Esq. England.

We knew not how to part.—*See page* 4.

Every day's observation convinces me that the children of God are made so by his own special grace, and that all means are equally effectual with him whenever he is pleased to employ them for conversion.

Being called some years ago to visit the United States. I was walking by myself over a considerable plantation, amused with its husbandry and comparing it with that of my own country, when I came within a little distance of a middle-aged Negro who was tilling the ground. I felt a strong inclination, unusual with me, to converse with him. After asking him some little questions about his work, which he answered very sensibly, I wished him to tell me whether his state of slavery was not disagreeable to him, and whether he would not gladly exchange it for his liberty. "Massa," said he, looking seriously upon me, "I have a wife and children; my Massa take care of them, and I have no care to provide any thing; I have a good Massa who teach me to read; and I read good book that makes me happy." I am glad, replied I to hear you say so; and pray what is the good book you read? "The Bible, Massa, God's own book." Do you understand, friend, as well as read this book? for many can read the words well who cannot get hold of the true and good sense. "O Massa," says he, "I read the book much before I understand: but at last I felt pain in my heart; I found things in the book that cut me to pieces." Ah, says I, and what things were they? "Why, Massa, I found that I had a bad heart, Massa, a very bad heart indeed; I felt pain that God would destroy me, because I was wicked, and done nothing as I should do. God was holy, and I was very vile and naughty; I could have nothing from him but fire and brimstone in hell." In short, he entered into a full account of his convictions of sin, (which were indeed as deep and piercing as almost any I had ever heard of,) and what Scriptures came to his mind which he had read, that both probed to the bottom of his sinful heart and were made the means of light and comfort to his soul.

I then inquired of him what ministry or means he made use of, and found that his master was an honest, plain sort of man, who had taught his slaves to read, but who had not, however, conversed with this negro upon the state of his soul. I asked him likewise how he got comfort under all this trial? "O Massa," says he, "it was Christ gave me comfort by his dear word. He bade me come unto him and he would give me rest, for I was very weary and heavy laden. And here he went through a line of precious texts, showing, by his artless comment upon them as he went along, what great things God had done in the course of some years for his soul.

Being rather more acquainted with doctrinal truths and the analogy of the Bible than he had been, or, in his situation, could easily be, I had a mind to try how far a simple, untutored experience, graciously given without the usual means, could carry a man from some speculative errors. I therefore asked him some questions about the merit of works, the justification of a sinner, the power of grace, and the like. I own I was as much astonished as I admired the sweet spirit and simplicity of his answers, with the heavenly wisdom that God had put into the mind of this Negro. His discourse, flowing merely from the richness of grace, with a tenderness and expression far "beyond the reach of art," perfectly charmed me. On the other hand, my entering into all his feelings, together with an account to him that thus and thus the Lord in his mercy dealt with all his children, and had dealt with me, drew streams of joyful tears down his black face, so that we looked upon each other and talked with that inexpressible glow of christian affection that made me more than ever believe, what I have often too thoughtlessly professed to believe, *the communion of saints.* I shall never forget how the poor excellent creature seemed to hang upon my lips, and to eat my very words, when I enlarged upon the love of Christ to poor sinners, the free bounty and tender mercy of God, the frequent and delightful sense he gives of his presence, the faith he bestows in his promises, the victories this faith is enabled to get over trials and temptations, the joy and peace in believing, the hope in life and death, and the glorious expectation of immortality. To have taken off his eager, delighted, animated air and manner would have been a master-piece for a Reynolds. He had never heard such discourse, nor found the opportunity of hearing it before. He seemed like a man who had been thrown into a new world, and at length had found company. Though my conversation lasted at least two or three hours, I scarcely ever enjoyed the happy swiftness of time so sweetly in all my life. We knew not how to part. He would accompany me as far as he might; and I felt, on my side, such a delight in the artless, savory, solid, unaffected experience of this dear soul, that I could have been glad to see him often then, or to see his like at any time now; but my situation rendered it impossible. I therefore took an affectionate adieu with an ardor equal to the warmest and the most ancient friendship; telling him that neither the color of his body nor the condition of his present life, could prevent him from being my dear brother in our dear Savior; and that though we must part now, never to see each other again in this world, I had no doubt of our having another joyful meeting in our Father's house, where we should live together, and love one another, throughout a long and happy eternity. "Amen, Amen, my dear Massa; God bless you, and poor me too, for ever and ever." If I had been an angel from heaven he could not have received me with more evident delight than he did; nor could I have considered him with a more sympathetic regard if he had been a long known Christian of the good old sort, grown up into my affections in the course of many years.

Happy world, if all were Christians! or at least happy Christians, if they showed more of this brotherly love to each other in the world! None can deny that so it ought to be. O that every one who names the name of Christ, and believes himself to be a member of his undivided body, would pray for faith and love to make him a consistent follower of Jesus.

Blessed Lord! Fountain of life and love! send forth the Spirit of thy Son into my heart, and into the hearts of all my brethren; that, waving all mean and selfish distinctions, we may first love thee above all things, and then each other for thy sake, with a pure heart, fervently. Subdue animosities and all the separating corruptions of the flesh, and let us consider ourselves as *brethren, fellow-heirs* of the grace of life, persons who shall pass an eternity together; as parts of each other, and *members, holy* Jesus, *of thy body, thy flesh, and thy bones.* Even so let it be, for thy glory, and for our present and eternal consolation through thy grace!

How happily does this narrative illustrate the blessed reality of VITAL RELIGION! Christians of every age and nation have all spoken, in spite of their several peculiarities, one common language of the heart about God and Christ, sin and holiness, time and eternity: their religious hopes and fears, their joys and their sorrows, have been the same. As on the day of Pentecost the truth of the Gospel was proved by the fact that *one person* spoke many languages, so has it been verified in all ages since by the fact that *many persons*, of every kindred, nation, tongue and people to whom the Gospel has come, have spoken *one* language.

PUBLISHED BY THE AMERICAN TRACT SOCIETY.
150 Nassau-street, New-York.

No. 8.

ON THE LORD'S DAY.

Permit a friend respectfully and affectionately to remind you of a divine law, too much forgotten by many, perhaps by you—REMEMBER THE SABBATH DAY TO KEEP IT HOLY.

This is the command of God; "the God in whose hand our breath is, and whose are all our ways;" the God who gives us all our time, and who allows us six days out of seven for worldly concerns. "Six days shalt thou labor and do all thy work; but the seventh day is the Sabbath of the Lord thy God." He claims this day as his own. And can you refuse so just a claim? He has *hallowed* this day; he has reserved it for his own service; he has ordained that from the beginning of the world to the end of it, the children of men should employ the sacred hours in holy acts of private or public worship.

Say now, are you not solemnly bound to obey the heavenly command? Consider how *necessary* and *reasonable* the appointment! It is necessary, were it only to give suitable rest to the bodies of man and beast. Without this merciful institution, how many would have allowed neither themselves nor their servants proper seasons of repose! If there were no Sabbaths in a nation, there would soon be no religion; and what then would become of the interests of morality? The merciful God appoints a Sabbath for your good. It is *for your sake* that he requires it to be kept holy. He seeks your good, your everlasting good, and for this purpose he has not only *hallowed* this day, but has also *blessed* it. It is a day of special grace. The King of heaven, sitting on the throne of mercy, gives audience on this best of days to the assembled subjects of this gracious empire. Millions of happy spirits now in heaven will bless God to all eternity for the spiritual blessings in Christ Jesus, which, when on earth, they received on this happy day; and thousands now on their way to glory, find it good for them to draw near to God, and justly esteem "a day in his courts better than a thousand." So that you are an enemy to yourself, if you profane this day. If you love your own soul, why will you lose the opportunity of being happy?

If you study *only your present good*, you will keep the Sabbath. God honors them that honor him. Many have found that a Sabbath, well spent, is followed by a prosperous week; for it is "the blessing of the Lord that maketh rich;" and how can you expect this blessing if you disobey him? Lord Chief Justice Hale made the following observation:—"I have found that a due observing the duty of the Lord's day, has ever joined to it a blessing upon the rest of my time; and the week that has been so begun, has been blessed and prosperous to me. And on the other hand, when I have been negligent of the duties of this day, the rest of the week has been unsuccessful and unhappy to my secular employment."

And has not God frequently manifested *his anger against Sabbath breakers?* How many have perished in the midst of their amusements, and been suddenly called to the bar of God while engaged in actual rebellion against him! How many lovers of pleasure have been known, whose dying agonies have been awfully increased by the sad remembrance of the manner in which they spent their former Sabbaths! And how many unhappy criminals have in their last moments ascribed their ruin to this sin! Beware of a vice so dangerous in its tendency, so fatal in its consequences; for if you forsake God, he may justly forsake you, and then you are undone for ever.

Do you hope to be happy in *heaven* when you leave this world? I know you do. But consider how the saints in glory are employed. They keep perpetual Sabbath, and the worship of God is their constant delight. But how can you reasonably hope for heaven, unless your heart is formed, through grace, for its holy employments? and how could you enjoy an eternal Sabbath, if you now turn your back upon God's worship, or say of the Sabbath "What a weariness is it?"

As you estimate *the favor of God*—as you value your immortal soul—let the time past suffice to have rebelled against your Maker. Rebel no longer. Now say, "Lord, it is enough. I have fought against thee too long. Forgive my sins for Christ's sake, and give me grace to consecrate all my powers to thee." No more let worldly business or vain amusements engross these holy hours. You must not rob God; the day is all his own. Let it be a whole day—a day as long as others. Say not, what harm is there in taking a little amusement after divine service? Think a moment, and you will perceive the harm. Why should you erase the impressions of holy things as soon as they are made? Is not *retirement* as necessary as public worship? Improve then the leisure of the Sabbath. Retire and read your Bible. Converse with God in prayer. Converse with your own heart. Converse with good books. And above all, be concerned that the Gospel which you hear may have its saving effect on your own heart. Have you heard of Christ and salvation by him? Let it be your chief concern to "be found in him;" not trusting to your own works of righteousness, but to the righteousness he has brought in, and which is "to and upon all them that believe."

Have you heard of the natural state of man as a sinner? Apply this to yourself, and be humbled in the dust of humiliation. Have you been told from the word of God, that, "except a man be born again, he cannot see the kingdom of God?" Go humbly, and with a heart broken for sin, pray for the Holy Spirit in all his gracious influences, that you may be sanctified throughout. Has some holy temper, or moral duty, been recommended to you from the pulpit? Endeavor to fix the necessity and beauty of it in your mind, that so you may bring it into habitual exercise. This is the way to keep a christian Sabbath; and thus proceeding in the fear of God, you may humbly hope for God's blessing in the present world, and in the world to come.

On the morning of the Sabbath let your reflections be such as these: "This day is to be kept *holy* to the Lord; no trifles must be talked of, no needless work or world-business, no play or diversion attended to; but Christ and his salvation only be thought of. Before the next Lord's day I may be in *eternity*, and be fixed in heaven or hell for ever. Let me then spend this day as if I were sure it would be my last. I am going where prayer is wont to be made; Lord, teach me to pray in the faith of the Gospel, with reverence, humility, earnestness of desire after the light of thy countenance, and confidence of finding mercy through the blood of Jesus. May I 'sing with the Spirit, and with the understanding also;' feeling in my heart what I sing with my lips, and rejoicing in the free love of Christ to guilty men, to me a sinner. O may I hear with seriousness, receive the truth in the love of it, and lay it to my heart; remembering, that by the word my soul must be profited and saved, or else be judged and condemned. John, 3 : 18. O God of all grace, let not this day be spent in vain, for the sake of my precious soul, and for the glory of thy holy name, through Jesus Christ."

Blessed is the man that keepeth the Sabbath from polluting it. Isaiah, 56 : 2.

Accept, candid reader, this friendly admonition, flowing from a sincere desire for your benefit. Give it a second reading; and may God, whose cause and glory, together with your best interests, are pleaded in this Tract, be pleased to give it his blessing, for Christ's sake!

PUBLISHED BY THE
AMERICAN TRACT SOCIETY.

No. 9

THE DAIRYMAN'S DAUGHTER.

AN AUTHENTIC NARRATIVE—ABRIDGED.

BY REV. LEGH RICHMOND,
RECTOR OF TURVEY, BEDFORDSHIRE, ENGLAND.

Thoughts of death, eternity, and salvation, inspired by the sight of a house where a dying believer lay, filled my own mind, and I doubt not, that of my companion also.—*See page* 20.

It is a delightful employment to trace and discover the operations of divine grace, as they are manifested in the dispositions and lives of God's real children. It is peculiarly gratifying to observe how frequently among the poorer classes of mankind, the sunshine of mercy beams upon the heart, and bears witness to the image of Christ which the Spirit of God has impressed thereupon. Among such, the sincerity and simplicity of the christian character appear unencumbered by those fetters to spirituality of mind and conversation which too often prove a great hinderance to those who live in the higher ranks. Many are the difficulties which riches, polished society, worldly importance, and high connexions throw in the way of religious profession. Happy indeed it is, (and some such happy instances I know,) where grace has so strikingly supported its conflict with natural pride, self-importance, the allurements of luxury, ease, and worldly opinions, that the noble and mighty appear adorned with genuine poverty of spirit, self-denial, humble-mindedness, and deep spirituality of heart.

But, in general, if we want to see religion in its purest character, we must look for it among the poor of this world, who are rich in faith. How often is the poor man's cottage the palace of God! Many of us can truly declare, that we have there learned our most valuable lessons of faith and hope, and there witnessed the most striking demonstrations of the wisdom, power, and goodness of God.

The character which the present narrative is designed to introduce to the notice of my readers, is given *from real life and circumstance.* I first became acquainted with the Dairyman's Daughter by the reception of a letter, a part of which I transcribe from the original, now before me.

"Rev. Sir—I take the liberty to write to you. Pray excuse me, for I have never spoken to you. But I once heard you preach at ——— church. I believe you are a faithful preacher, to warn sinners to flee from the wrath that will be revealed against all those that live in sin, and die impenitent.

"I was much rejoiced to hear of those marks of love and affection which you showed to that poor soldier of the S. D. militia. Surely the love of Christ sent you to that poor man; may that love ever dwell richly in you by faith. May it constrain you to seek the wandering souls of men with the fervent desire to spend and be spent for his glory.

"Sir, be fervent in prayer with God for the conviction and conversion of sinners. He has promised to answer the prayer of faith, that is put up in his Son's name. 'Ask what you will, and it shall be granted you.' Through faith in Christ we rejoice in hope, and look up in expectation of that time drawing near, when all shall know and fear the Lord, and when a nation shall be born in a day.

"What a happy time, when Christ's kingdom shall come! Then shall 'his will be done on earth, as it is in heaven.' Men shall be daily fed with the manna of his love, and delight themselves in the Lord all the day long.

"Sir, I began to write this on Sunday, being detained from attending on public worship. My dear and only sister, living as a servant with Mrs. ———, was so ill that I came here to attend in her place, and on her. But now she is no more.

"She expressed a desire to receive the Lord's supper, and commemorate his precious death and sufferings. I told her, as well as I was able, what it was to receive Christ into her heart; but as her weakness of body increased, she did not mention it again. She seemed quite resigned before she died. I do hope she has gone from a world of death and sin, to be with God for ever.

"My sister expressed a wish that you might bury her. The minister of our parish, whither she will be carried, cannot come. She died on Tuesday morning, and will be buried on Friday or Saturday, (whichever is most convenient to you,) at three o'clock in the afternoon. Please to send an answer by the bearer, to let me know whether you can comply with this request.

"From your unworthy servant,
"Elizabeth W———e."

I was much struck with the simple and earnest strain of devotion which the letter breathed. It was but indifferently written and spelt; but this the rather tended to endear the hitherto unknown writer, as it seemed characteristic of the union of humbleness of station with eminence of piety. I felt quite thankful that I was favored with a correspondent of this description; the more so, as such characters were, at that time, very rare in the neighborhood. As soon as it was read, I inquired who was the bearer of it.

"He is waiting at the outside of the gate, Sir," was the reply.

I went out to speak to him; and saw a venerable old man, whose long hoary hair and deeply wrinkled countenance commanded more than common respect. He was resting his arm and head upon the gate, the tears were streaming down his cheeks. On my approach, he made a low bow, and said,

"Sir, I have brought you a letter from my daughter; but I fear you will think us very bold in asking you to take so much trouble."

"By no means," I replied; "I shall be truly glad to oblige you and any of your family in this matter.

I desired him to come into the house, and then said, "What is your occupation?"

"Sir, I have lived most of my days in a little cottage, six miles from here. I have rented a few acres of ground and kept a few cows, which, in addition to my day labour, has been my means of supporting and bringing up my family."

"What family have you?"

"A wife, now getting very aged and helpless; two sons and one daughter; for my other poor dear child is just departed out of this wicked world."

"I hope, for a better."

"I hope so too; poor thing, she did not use to take to such good ways as her sister; but I do believe that her sister's manner of talking with her before she died, was the means of saving her soul. What a mercy it is to have such a child as mine is! I never thought about my own soul seriously till she, poor girl, begged and prayed me to flee from the wrath to come."

"How old are you?"

"Turned seventy, and my wife is older; we are getting old and almost past our labour; but our daughter has left a good place, where she lived in service, on purpose to come home and take care of us and our little dairy. And a dear, dutiful, affectionate girl she is."

"Was she always so?"

"No, Sir; when she was very young, she was all for the world, and pleasure, and dress, and company. Indeed we were all very ignorant, and thought, if we took care for this life, and wronged nobody, we should be sure to go to heaven at last. My daughters were both wilful, and, like ourselves, were strangers to the ways of God and the word of his grace. But the eldest of them went out to service; and some years ago she heard a sermon preached; and from that time she became quite an altered creature. She began to read the Bible, and became quite sober and steady. The first time she came home afterwards to see us, she brought us a guinea which she had saved from her wages, and said, as we were getting old, she was sure we should want help: adding, that she did not wish to spend it in fine clothes, as she used to do, only to feed pride and vanity. She would rather show gratitude to her dear father and mother; and this, she said, because Christ had shown such mercy to her

"We wondered to hear her talk, and took great delight in her company, for her temper and behavior were so humble and kind, she seemed so desirous to do us good both in soul and body, and was so different from what we had ever seen her before, that, careless and ignorant as we had been, we began to think there must be something real in religion, or it never could alter a person so much in a little time.

"Her younger sister, poor soul, used to laugh and ridicule her at that time, and said her head was turned with her new ways. 'No, sister,' she would say, 'not my *head*, but I hope my *heart* is turned from the love of sin to the love of God. I wish you may one day see, as I do, the danger and vanity of your present condition.'

"Her poor sister would reply, 'I do not want to hear any of your preaching: I am no worse than other people, and that is enough for me.'—'Well, sister,' Elizabeth would say, 'If you will not hear me, you cannot hinder me from praying for you, which I do with all my heart.'

"And now, Sir, I believe those prayers are answered. For when her sister was taken ill, Elizabeth went to wait in her place and take care of her. She said a great deal to her about her soul; and the poor girl began to be so deeply affected, and sensible of her past sin, and so thankful for her sister's kind behavior, that it gave her great hopes indeed for her sake. When my wife and I went to see her as she lay sick, she told us how grieved and ashamed she was of her past state; but said, she had a hope, through grace, that her dear sister's Savior would be her Savior too; for she saw her own sinfulness, felt her own helplessness, and only wished to cast herself upon Christ as her hope and salvation.

"And now, Sir, she is gone, and I hope and think her sister's prayers for her conversion to God have been answered. The Lord grant the same, for her poor father and mother's sake likewise."

This conversation was a very pleasing commentary upon the letter which I had received, and made me anxious both to comply with the request, and to become acquainted with the writer. I promised the good old Dairyman I would attend the funeral on Friday, at the appointed hour; and after some more conversation respecting his own state under the present trial, he went away.

He was a reverend old man; his furrowed cheeks, white locks, weeping eyes, bent shoulders, and feeble gait, were characteristic of the old pilgrim; and as he slowly departed, supported by a stick, which seemed to have been the companion of many a long year, a train of reflections occurred, which I retrace with emotion and pleasure.

At the appointed hour, I arrived at the church; and after a little while, was summoned to meet at the church-yard gate a very decent funeral procession. The aged parents, the brother and the sister, with other relatives, formed an affecting group. I was struck with the humble, pious, and pleasing countenance of the young woman from whom I received the letter: it bore the marks of great seriousness without affectation, and of much serenity mingled with a glow of devotion.

A circumstance occurred during the burial service, which I think it right to mention.

A man of the village, who had hitherto been of a very careless and even profligate character, came into the church through mere curiosity, and with no better purpose than that of a vacant gazing at the ceremony. He came likewise to the grave; and during the burial service his mind received a deep, serious conviction of his sin and danger, through some of the expressions contained therein. It was an impression that never wore off, but gradually ripened into the most satisfactory evidence of an entire change, of which I had many and long continued proofs. He always referred to the burial service, and to some particular sentences of it, as the clearly ascertained instrument of bringing him, through grace, to the knowledge of the truth.

The day was therefore one to be remembered. Remembered let it be by those who love to hear " the short and simple annals of the poor."

Was there not a manifest and happy connexion between the circumstances that providentially brought the serious and the careless to the same grave on that day together? How much do *they* lose, who neglect to trace the leadings of God in providence, as links in the chain of his eternal purpose of redemption and grace!

" While infidels may scoff, let us adore.'

After the service was concluded, I had a short conversation with the good old couple and their daughter Her aspect and address were highly interesting. I promised to visit their cottage; and from that time became well acquainted with them. Let us bless the God of the poor, and pray continually that the poor may become rich in faith, and the rich be made poor in spirit.

A sweet solemnity often possesses the mind, while retracing past intercourse with departed friends. How much is this increased, when they were such as lived and died in the Lord! The remembrance of former scenes and conversations with those who, we believe, are now enjoying the uninterrupted happiness of a better world, fills the heart with pleasing sadness, and animates the soul with the hopeful anticipation of a day, when the glory of the Lord shall be revealed in the assembling of all his children together, never more to be separated. Whether they were rich or poor, while on earth, it is a matter of trifling consequence; the valuable part of their character is, that they are now kings and priests unto God. In the number of departed believers, with whom I once loved to converse on the grace and glory of the kingdom of God, was the Dairyman's Daughter. I propose now to give some further account of her, and hope it may be useful to every reader.

A few days after the funeral of the younger sister, I rode over to visit the family in their own cottage. The principal part of the road lay through retired, narrow lanes, beautifully over-arched with groves of nut and other trees, which screened the traveller from the rays of the sun, and afforded many interesting objects for admiration, in the beautiful flowers, shrubs, and young trees, which grew upon the high banks on each side of the road Many grotesque rocks, with little streams of water occasionally breaking out of them, varied the recluse scenery, and produced a new, romantic, and pleasing effect.

Here and there, the more distant and rich prospect beyond appeared through gaps and hollow places on the road-side. Lofty hills, with navy signal-posts, obelisks, and light-houses on their summits, appeared at these intervals: rich corn-fields were also visible through some of the open places; and now and then, when the road ascended any hill, the sea, with ships at various distances, opened delightfully upon me. But, for the most part, shady seclusion, and beauties of a more minute and confined nature, gave a character to the journey, and invited contemplation.

What do not *they* lose, who are strangers to serious meditation on the wonders and beauties of created nature! How gloriously the God of creation shines in his works! Not a tree, or leaf, or flower; not a bird, or insect, but proclaims in glowing language, "God made me."

As I approached the village where the good old Dairyman dwelt, I observed him in a little field, driving a few cows before him towards a yard and hovel which adjoined his cottage. I advanced very near him, without his observing me, for his sight was dim. On my calling out to him, he started at the sound of my voice, but with much gladness of countenance welcomed me, saying—"Bless your heart, Sir, I am very glad you are come; we have looked for you every day this week."

The cottage-door opened, and the daughter came out, followed by her aged and infirm mother. The sight of me naturally brought to recollection the grave at which we had before met. Tears of affection mingled with the smile of satisfaction with which I was received by these worthy cottagers. I dismounted, and was conducted through a very neat little garden, part of which was shaded by two large, overspreading elm-trees, to the house. Decency and cleanliness were manifest within and without.

This, thought I, is a fit residence for piety, peace, and contentment. May I learn a fresh lesson in each, through the blessing of God on this visit.

"Sir," said the daughter, "we are not worthy that you should come under our roof. We take it very kind that you should come so far to see us."

"My Master," I replied, "came a great deal farther to visit us, poor sinners. He left the bosom of his Father, aid aside his glory, and came down to this lower world on a visit of mercy and love; and ought not we, if we profess to follow him, to bear each other's infirmities, and go about doing good as he did?"

The old man was now coming in, and joined his wife and daughter in giving me a cordial welcome. Our conversation soon turned to the late loss they had sustained; and the pious and sensible disposition of the daughter was peculiarly manifested, as well in what she said to her parents, as in what she said to me. I was struck with the good sense and agreeable manner which accompanied her expressions of devotedness to God, and love to Christ for the great mercies which he had bestowed upon her. She seemed anxious to improve the opportunity of my visit to the best purpose for her own and her parents' sake; yet there was nothing of unbecoming forwardness, no self-consequence or conceitedness, in her behavior. She united the firmness and earnestness of the Christian with the modesty of the female and the dutifulness of the daughter. It was impossible to be in her company, and not observe how truly her temper and conversation adorned the evangelical principles which she professed.

I soon discovered how eager and how successful also she had been in her endeavors to bring her father and mother to the knowledge and experience of the truth. This is a lovely circumstance in the character of a young Christian. If it hath pleased God, in the free dispensations of his mercy, to call the child by his grace, while the parent remains still in ignorance and sin, how great is the duty of that child to do what is possible for the conversion of those to whom it owes its birth! Happy is it when the ties of grace sanctify those of nature!

This aged couple evidently looked upon and spoke of their daughter as their teacher and admonisher in divine things, while they received from her every token of filial submission and obedience, testified by continual endeavors to serve and assist them to the utmost in the little concerns of the household.

The religion of this young woman was of a highly spiritual character, and of no ordinary attainment. Her views of the divine plan in saving the sinner, were clear and scriptural. She spoke much of the joys and sorrows which, in the course of her religious progress, she had experienced; but she was fully sensible that there is far more in real religion than mere occasional transition from one frame of mind and spirit to another. She believed that the experimental acquaintance of the heart with God, principally consisted in so living upon Christ by faith, as to seek to live like him by love. She knew that the love of God toward the sinner, and the path of duty prescribed to the sinner, are both of an unchangeable nature. In a believing dependence on the one, and an affectionate walk in the other, she sought and found "the peace of God which passeth all understanding;" "for so he giveth his beloved rest."

She had read but few books besides her Bible; but these few were excellent in their kind, and she spoke of their contents as one who knew their value. In addition to a Bible and Common Prayer-Book, "Doddridge's Rise and Progress," "Romaine's Life, Walk, and Triumph of Faith," "Bunyan's Pilgrim," "Alleine's Alarm," "Baxter's Saints' Everlasting Rest," a hymn-book, and a few Tracts, composed her library.

I observed in her countenance a pale and delicate look, which I afterwards found to be a presage of consumption; and the idea then occurred to me that she would not live many years. In fact, it pleased God to take her hence about a year and a half after I first saw her.

Time passed on swiftly with this little interesting family; and after having partaken of some plain and wholesome refreshment, and enjoyed a few hours' conversation with them, I found it was necessary for me to return homewards.

"I thank you, Sir," said the daughter, "for your christian kindness to me and my friends. I believe the blessing of the Lord has attended your visit, and I hope I have experienced it to be so. My dear father and mother will, I am sure, remember it, and I rejoice in an opportunity, which we have never before enjoyed, of seeing a serious minister under this roof. My Savior has been abundantly good to me in plucking me 'as a brand from the burning,' and showing me the way of life and peace: and I hope it is my heart's desire to live to his glory. But I long to see these dear friends enjoy the comfort and power of religion also."

"I think it evident," I replied, "that the promise is fulfilled in their case: 'It shall come to pass, that at evening time it shall be light.'"

"I believe it,' she said, "and praise God for the blessed hope."

"Thank him too that you have been the happy instrument of bringing them to the light."

"I do, Sir; yet when I think of my own unworthiness and insufficiency, I rejoice with trembling."

"Sir," said the good old man, "I am sure the Lord will reward you for this kindness. Pray for us, that, old as we are, and sinners as we have been, yet he would have mercy upon us at the eleventh hour. Poor Betsey strives hard for our sakes, both in body and soul; she works hard all day to save us trouble, and I fear has not strength to support all she does; and then she talks to us, and reads to us, and prays for us, that we may be saved from the wrath to come. Indeed, Sir, she's a rare child to us.'

" Peace be to you, and all that belong to you."

" Amen, and thank you, dear Sir," was echoed from each tongue.

Thus we parted for that time. My returning meditations were sweet, and, I hope, profitable. Many other visits were afterwards made by me to this peaceful cottage, and I always found increasing reason to thank God for the intercourse I enjoyed.

I soon perceived that the health of the daughter was rapidly on the decline. The pale wasting consumption, which is the Lord's instrument for removing so many thousands every year from the land of the living, made hasty strides on her constitution. The hollow eye, the distressing cough, and the often too flattering red on the cheek, foretold the approach of death.

I have often thought what a field for usefulness and affectionate attention on the part of ministers and christian friends, is opened by the frequent attacks and lingering progress of *consumptive* illness. How many such precious opportunities are daily lost, where Providence seems in so marked a way to afford time and space for serious and godly instruction! Of how many may it be said, "The way of peace have they not known;" for not one friend came nigh, to warn them to "flee from the wrath to come."

But the Dairyman's Daughter was happily made acquainted with the things which belonged to her everlasting peace, before the present disease had taken root in her constitution. In my visit to her, I might be said rather to receive information than to impart it. Her mind was abundantly stored with divine truths, and her conversation was truly edifying. The recollection of it still produces a thankful sensation in my heart.

I one day received a short note to the following effect·

Dear Sir,

I should be very glad, if your convenience will allow, that you would come and see a poor unworthy sinner: my hour-glass is nearly run out, but I hope I can see Christ to be precious to my soul. Your conversation has often been blessed to me, and I now feel the need of it more than ever. My father and mother send their duty to you.

From your obedient and unworthy servant,

ELIZABETH W———.

I obeyed the summons that same afternoon. On my arrival at the Dairyman's cottage, his wife opened the door. The tears streamed down her cheek, as she silently shook her head. Her heart was full. She tried to speak, but could not. I took her by the hand, and said,

"My good friend, all is right, and as the Lord of wisdom and mercy directs."

"Oh! my Betsy, my dear girl, is so bad, Sir: what shall I do without her?—I thought I should have gone first to the grave, but ———"

"But the Lord sees good, that, before you die yourself, you should behold your child safe home to glory. Is there no mercy in this?"

"Oh! dear Sir, I am very old, and very weak; and she is a dear child, the staff and prop of a poor old creature, as I am."

As I advanced, I saw Elizabeth sitting by the fire-side, supported in an arm-chair by pillows, with every mark of rapid decline and approaching death. She appeared to me within three or four weeks at the farthest from her end. A sweet smile of friendly complacency enlightened her pale countenance, as she said,

"This is very kind indeed, Sir, to come so soon after I sent to you. You find me daily wasting away, and I cannot have long to continue here. My flesh and my heart fail, but God is the strength of my weak heart, and I trust will be my portion for ever."

The conversation which follows was occasionally interrupted by her cough and want of breath. Her tone of voice was clear, though feeble; her manner solemn and collected; and her eye, though more dim than formerly, by no means wanting in liveliness as she spoke. I had frequently admired the superior language in which she expressed her ideas, as well as the scriptural consistency with which she communicated her thoughts. She had a good natural understanding; and grace, as is generally the case, had much improved it. On the present occasion I could not help thinking she was peculiarly favored. The whole strength of grace and nature seemed to be in full exercise.

After taking my seat between the daughter and the mother, (the latter fixing her fond eyes upon her child with great anxiety while we were conversing,) I said to Elizabeth,

"I hope you enjoy a sense of the divine presence, and can rest all upon him who has 'been with thee,' and has kept 'thee in all places whither thou hast gone,' and will bring thee into 'the land of pure delights, where saints immortal reign.'"

"Sir, I think I can. My mind has lately been sometimes clouded, but I believe it has been partly owing to the great weakness and suffering of my bodily frame, and partly to the envy of my spiritual enemy, who wants to persuade me that Christ has no love for me, and that I have been a self-deceiver."

"And do you give way to his suggestions? Can you doubt, amidst such numerous tokens of past and present mercy?"

"No, Sir, I mostly am enabled to preserve a clear evidence of his love. I do not wish to add to my other sins that of denying his manifest goodness to my soul. I would acknowledge it to his praise and glory."

"What is your present view of the state in which you were before he called you by his grace?"

"Sir, I was a proud, thoughtless girl; fond of dress and finery; I loved the world and the things that are in the world; I lived in service among worldly people, and never had the happiness of being in a family where worship was regarded, and the souls of the servants cared for, either by master or mistress. I went once on a Sunday to church, more to see and be seen, than to pray, or hear the word of God. I thought I was quite good enough to be saved, and disliked and often laughed at religious people. I was in great darkness; I knew nothing of the way of salvation; I never prayed, nor was sensible of the awful danger of a prayerless state. I wished to maintain the character of a good servant, and was much lifted up whenever I met with applause. I was tolerably moral and decent in my conduct, from motives of carnal and worldly policy; but I was a stranger to God and Christ; I neglected my soul; and had I died in such a state, hell must, and would justly, have been my portion."

"How long is it since you heard the sermon which you hope, through God's blessing, effected your conversion?"

"About five years ago."

"How was it brought about?"

"It was reported that a Mr. ———, who was detained by contrary winds from embarking on board a ship, as chaplain, to a distant part of the world, was to preach at ——— church. Many advised me not to go, for fear he should turn my head; as they said he held strange notions. But curiosity, and an opportunity of appearing in a new gown, which I was very proud of, induced me to ask leave to go. Indeed, Sir, I had no better motives than vanity and curiosity. Yet thus it pleased the Lord to order it for his own glory.

"I accordingly went to church, and saw a great crowd of people collected together. I often think of the contrary states of my mind during the former and latter part of the service. For a while, regardless of the worship of God, I looked around me, and was anxious to attract notice myself. My dress, like that of too many gay, vain and silly girls, was much above my station, and very different from that which becomes a humble sinner, who has a modest sense of propriety and decency. The state of my mind was visible enough from the foolish finery of my apparel.

"At length the clergyman gave out his text: 'Be ye clothed with humility.' He drew a comparison between the clothing of the body and that of the soul. At a very early part of his discourse, I began to feel ashamed of my passion for fine dressing and apparel; but when he came to describe the garment of salvation with which a Christian is clothed, I felt a powerful discovery of the nakedness of my own soul. I saw that I had neither the humility mentioned in the text, nor any one part of the true christian character. I looked at my gay dress, and blushed for shame on account of my pride. I looked at the minister, and he seemed to be as a messenger sent from heaven to open my eyes. I looked at the congregation, and wondered whether any one else felt as I did. I looked at my heart, and it appeared full of iniquity. I trembled as he spoke, and yet I felt a great drawing of heart to the words he uttered.

"He opened the riches of divine grace in God's method of saving the sinner. I was astonished at what I had been doing all the days of my life. He described the meek, lowly, and humble example of Christ; I felt proud, lofty, vain, and self-consequential. He represented Christ as 'Wisdom;' I felt my ignorance. He held him forth as 'Righteousness;' I was convinced of my own guilt. He proved him to be 'Sanctification;' I saw my corruption. He proclaimed him as 'Redemption;' I felt my slavery to sin, and my captivity to Satan. He concluded with an animated address to sinners, in which he exhorted them to flee from the wrath to come, to cast off the love of outward ornaments, to put on Christ, and be clothed with true humility.

"From that hour I never lost sight of the value of my soul and the danger of a sinful state. I inwardly blessed God for the sermon, although my mind was in a state of great confusion.

"The preacher had brought forward the ruling passion of my heart, which was pride in outward dress; and by the grace of God it was made instrumental to the awakening of my soul. Happy, Sir, would it be, if many a poor girl, like myself, were turned from the love of outward adorning and putting on of fine apparel, to seek that which is not corruptible, even the ornament of a meek and quiet spirit, which is in the sight of God of great price.

"The greater part of the congregation, unused to such faithful and scriptural sermons, disliked and complained of the severity of the preacher; while a few, as I afterwards found, like myself, were deeply affected, and earnestly wished to hear him again. But he preached there no more.

"From that time I was led, through a course of private prayer, reading, and meditation, to see my lost estate as a sinner, and the great mercy of God, through Jesus

Christ, in raising sinful dust and ashes to a share in the glorious happiness of heaven. And oh! Sir, what a Savior have I found! He is more than I could ask or desire. In his fulness I have found all that my poverty could need; in his bosom I have found a resting-place from all sin and sorrow; in his word I have found strength against doubt and unbelief."

"Were you not soon convinced," said I, "that your salvation must be an act of entire grace on the part of God, wholly independent of your own previous works or deservings?"

"Dear Sir, what were my works before I heard that sermon, but evil, carnal, selfish, and ungodly? The thoughts of my heart, from my youth upward, were only evil, and that continually. And my deservings, what were they, but the deservings of a fallen, depraved, careless soul, that regards neither law nor Gospel? Yes, Sir, I immediately saw that, if ever I were saved, it must be by the free mercy of God, and that the whole praise and honor of the work would be his from first to last."

"What change did you perceive in yourself with respect to the world?"

"It appeared all vanity and vexation of spirit. I found it necessary to my peace of mind to 'come out from among them and be separate.' I gave myself to prayer; and many a precious hour of secret delight I enjoyed in communion with God. Often I mourned over my sins, and sometimes had a great conflict through unbelief, fear, temptation to return back again to my old ways, and a variety of difficulties which lay in my way. But he who loved me with an everlasting love, drew me by his loving kindness, showed me the way of peace, gradually strengthened me in my resolutions of leading a new life, and taught me that, while without him I could do nothing, I yet might do all things through his strength.'

"Did you not find many difficulties in your situation, owing to your change of principle and practice?"

"Yes, Sir, every day of my life. I was laughed at by some, scolded at by others, scorned by enemies, and pitied by friends. I was called hypocrite, saint, false deceiver, and many more names, which were meant to render me hateful in the sight of the world. But I esteemed the reproach of the cross an honor. I forgave and prayed for my persecutors, and remembered how very lately I had acted the same part toward others myself. I thought also that Christ endured the contradiction of sinners; and, as the disciple is not above his Master, I was glad to be in any way conformed to his sufferings."

"Did you not then feel for your relatives at home?"

"Yes, that I did indeed, Sir; they were never out of my thoughts. I prayed continually for them, and had a longing desire to do them good. In particular I felt for my father and mother, as they were getting into years, and were very ignorant and dark in matters of religion."

"Ay," interrupted her mother, sobbing, "ignorant and dark, sinful and miserable we were, till this dear Betsy—this dear Betsy—this dear child, Sir, brought Christ Jesus home to her poor father and mother's house."

"No, dearest mother, say rather, Christ Jesus brought your poor daughter home to tell you what he had done for her soul, and I hope, to do the same for yours."

At this moment the Dairyman came in with two pails of milk hanging from the yoke on his shoulders. He had stood behind the half-opened door for a few minutes, and heard the last sentences spoken by his wife and daughter.

"Blessing and mercy upon her," said he, "it is very true; she would leave a good place of service on purpose to live with us, that she might help us both in soul and body. Sir, don't she look very ill? I think, Sir, we shan't have her here long."

"Leave that to the Lord," said Elizabeth. "All our times are in his hand, and happy it is that they are. I am willing to go; are not you willing, my father, to part with me into *his* hands, who gave me to you at first?"

"Ask me any question in the world but that," said the weeping father.

"I know," said she, "you wish me to be happy."

"I do, I do," answered he: "let the Lord do with you and us as best pleases him."

I then asked her, on what her present consolations

chiefly depended, in the prospect of approaching death.

"Entirely, Sir, on my view of Christ. When I look at myself, many sins, infirmities, and imperfections, cloud the image of Christ which I want to see in my own heart. But when I look at the Savior himself, he is altogether lovely; there is not one spot in his countenance, nor one cloud over all his perfections.

"I think of his coming in the flesh, and it reconciles me to the sufferings of the body; for he had them as well as I. I think of his temptations, and believe that he is able to succor me when I am tempted. Then I think of his cross, and learn to bear my own. I reflect on his death, and long to die unto sin, so that it may no longer have dominion over me. I sometimes think on his resurrection, and trust that he has given me a part in it, for I feel that my affections are set upon things above. Chiefly I take comfort in thinking of him as at the right hand of the Father, pleading my cause, and rendering acceptable even my feeble prayers, both for myself and, as I hope, for my dear friends.

"These are the views which, through mercy, I have of my Savior's goodness; and they have made me wish and strive in my poor way to serve him, to give myself up to him, and to labor to do my duty in that state of life into which it has pleased him to call me.

"A thousand times I should have fallen and fainted, if he had not upheld me. I feel that I am nothing without him. He is all in all.

"Just so far as I can cast my care upon him, I find strength to do his will. May he give me grace to trust him to the last moment! I do not fear death, because I believe he has taken away its sting. And oh! what happiness beyond!—Tell me, Sir, whether you think I am right. I hope I am under no delusion. I dare not look for my hope at any thing short of the entire fulness of Christ. When I ask my own heart a question, I am afraid to trust it, for it is treacherous, and has often deceived me. But when I ask Christ, he answers me with promises that strengthen and refresh me, and leave me no room to doubt his power and will to save. I am in his hands, and would remain there; and I do believe that he will never leave nor forsake me, but will perfect the thing that concerns me. He loved me and gave himself for me, and I believe that his gifts and calling are without repentance. In this hope I live, in this I wish to die."

I looked around me as she was speaking, and thought, "Surely this is none other than the house of God, and the gate of heaven." Every thing appeared neat, cleanly, and interesting. The afternoon had been rather overcast with dark clouds, but just now the setting sun shone brightly and rather suddenly into the room. It was reflected from three or four rows of bright pewter plates and white earthen-ware arranged on shelves against the wall: it also gave brilliancy to a few prints of sacred subjects that hung there also, and served for monitors or the birth, baptism, crucifixion, and resurrection of Christ. A large map of Jerusalem, and a hieroglyphic of "the old and new man," completed the decorations on that side of the room. Clean as was the white-washed wall, it was not cleaner than the rest of the place and its furniture. Seldom had the sun enlightened a house where cleanliness and general neatness (those sure attendants of pious and decent poverty) were more conspicuous.

This gleam of setting sunshine was emblematical of the bright and serene close of this young Christian's departing season. One ray happened to be reflected from a little looking-glass upon the face of the young woman. Amidst her pallid and decaying features there appeared a calm resignation, triumphant confidence, unaffected humility, and tender anxiety, which fully declared the feelings of her heart.

Some further affectionate conversation, and a short prayer, closed this interview.

As I rode home by departing day-light, tranquillity characterized the scene. The gentle lowing of cattle, the bleating of sheep just penned in their folds, the humming of the insects of the night, the distant murmurs of the sea, the last notes of the birds of day, and the first warblings of the nightingale, broke upon the ear, and served rather to increase than lessen the peaceful serenity of the evening, and its corresponding effects on my own mind. It invited and cherished just such meditations as my visit had already inspired. Natural scenery, when viewed in a christian mirror, frequently affords very beautiful illustrations of divine truth. We are highly favored, when we can enjoy them, and at the same time draw near to God in them.

Soon after this, I received a hasty summons, to inform me that my young friend was dying. It was brought by a soldier, whose countenance bespoke seriousness, good sense, and piety.

"I am sent, Sir, by the father and mother of Elizabeth W———, at her own particular request, to say how much they all wish to see you. She is going *home*, Sir, very fast indeed."

"Have you known her long?" I replied.

"About a month, Sir; I love to visit the sick, and hearing of her case from a serious person who lives close by our camp, I went to see her. I bless God that ever I did go. Her conversation has been very profitable to me."

"I rejoice," said I, "to see in you, as I trust, *a brother soldier*. Though we differ in our outward regimentals, I hope we serve under the same spiritual Captain. I will go with you."

My horse was soon ready. My military companion walked by my side, and gratified me with very sensible and pious conversation. He related some remarkable testimonies of the excellent disposition of the Dairyman's Daughter, as they appeared from some recent intercourse which he had had with her.

"She is a bright diamond, Sir," said the soldier, "and will soon shine brighter than any diamond upon earth."

Conversation beguiled the distance, and shortened the apparent time of our journey, till we were nearly arrived at the Dairyman's cottage.

As we approached it, we became silent. Thoughts of death, eternity, and salvation, inspired by the sight of a house where a dying believer lay, filled my own mind, and, I doubt not, that of my companion also.

No living object yet appeared, except the Dairyman's dog, keeping a kind of mute watch at the door; for he did not, as formerly, bark at my approach. He seemed to partake so far of the feelings appropriate to the circumstances of the family, as not to wish to give a hasty or painful alarm. He came forward to the little wicket-gate, then looked back at the house-door, as if conscious there was sorrow within. It was as if he wanted to say

"Tread softly over the threshold, as you enter the house of mourning; for my master's heart is full of grief."

A solemn serenity appeared to surround the whole place. It was only interrupted by the breeze passing through the large elm-trees which stood near the house, which my imagination indulged itself in thinking were plaintive sighs of sorrow. I gently opened the door; no one appeared, and all was still silent. The soldier followed; we came to the foot of the stairs.

"They are come," said a voice, which I knew to be the father's; "they are come."

He appeared at the top; I gave him my hand, and said nothing. On entering the room above, I saw the aged mother and her son supporting the much-loved daughter and sister; the son's wife sat weeping in a window-seat with a child on her lap; two or three persons attended in the room to discharge any office which friendship or necessity might require.

I sat down by the bedside. The mother could not weep, but now and then sighed deeply, as she alternately looked at Elizabeth and at me. The big tear rolled down the brother's cheek, and testified an affectionate regard. The good old man stood at the foot of the bed, leaning upon the post, and unable to take his eyes off the child from whom he was so soon to part.

Elizabeth's eyes were closed, and as yet she perceived me not. But over her face, though pale, sunk, and hollow, the peace of God, which passeth all understanding, had cast a triumphant calm.

The soldier, after a short pause, silently reached out his Bible toward me, pointing with his finger at 1 Cor. 15: 55, 56, 58. I then broke silence by reading the passage, "O death, where is thy sting? O grave, where is thy victory? The sting of death is sin, and the strength of sin is the law. But thanks be to God, which giveth us the victory, through our Lord Jesus Christ."

At the sound of these words her eyes opened, and something like a ray of divine light beamed on her countenance, as she said, 'Victory, victory! through our Lord Jesus Christ."

She relapsed again, taking no further notice of any one present.

"God be praised for the triumph of faith," I said.

"Amen," replied the soldier.

The Dairyman's uplifted eye showed that the Amen was in his heart, though his tongue failed to utter it.

A short struggling for breath took place in the dying young woman, which was soon over, and then I said to her,

"My dear friend, do you not feel that you are supported?"

"The Lord deals very gently with me," she replied.

"Are not his promises now very precious to you?"

"They are all yea and amen in Christ Jesus."

"Are you in much bodily pain?"

"So little that I almost forget it!"

"How good the Lord is!"

"And how unworthy am I!"

"You are going to see him as he is."

"I think......I hope......I believe that I am."

She again fell into a short slumber.

Looking at her mother, I said, "What a mercy to have a child so near heaven as yours is!"

"And what a mercy," she replied in broken accents, "if her poor old mother might but follow her there! But, Sir, it is so hard to part—"

"I hope through grace by faith you will soon meet, to part no more; it will be but a little while."

"Sir," said the Dairyman, "that thought supports me, and the Lord's goodness makes me feel more reconciled than I was."

"Father....mother,...." said the reviving daughter, "he is good to me....trust him, praise him evermore."

"Sir," added she in a faint voice, "I want to thank you for your kindness to me....I want to ask a favor;......you buried my sister....will you do the same for me?"

"All shall be as you wish, if God permit," I replied.

"Thank you, Sir, thank you....I have another favor to ask....When I am gone, remember my father and mother. They are old, but I hope the good work is begun in their souls....My prayers are heard....Pray come and see them ....I cannot speak much, but I want to speak, for their sakes.....Sir, remember them."—

The aged parents now sighed and sobbed aloud, uttering broken sentences, and gained some relief by such an expression of their feelings.

At length I said to Elizabeth, "do you experience any doubts or temptations on the subject of your safety?"

"No, Sir; the Lord deals very gently with me, and gives me peace."

"What are your views of the dark valley of death, now that you are passing through it?"

"It is *not* dark."

'Why so?"

"My Lord is *there*, and he is my light and my salvation."

' Have you any fears of more bodily suffering?"

"The Lord deals so gently with me, I can trust him '

Something of a convulsion came on. When it was past, she said again and again,

"The Lord deals very gently with me. Lord, I am thine, save me...Blessed Jesus...Precious Savior... His blood cleanseth from all sin....Who shall separate?....His name is Wonderful....Thanks be to God....He giveth us the victory....I, even I, am saved....O grace, mercy, and wonder—Lord, receive my spirit.

Dear Sir....Dear father, mother, friends, I am going... but all is well, well, well——————."

She relapsed again—We knelt down to prayer—The Lord was in the midst of us, and blessed us.

She did not again revive while I remained, nor ever speak any more words which could be understood. She slumbered for about ten hours, and at last sweetly fell asleep in the arms of the Lord, who had dealt so gently with her.

I left the house an hour after she had ceased to speak. I pressed her hand as I was taking leave, and said, "Christ is the resurrection and the life."

She gently returned the pressure, but could neither open her eyes nor utter a reply. I never had witnessed a scene so impressive as this before. It completely filled my imagination as I returned home.

"Farewell," thought I, "dear friend, till the morning of an eternal day shall renew our personal intercourse. Thou wast a brand plucked from the burning, that thou mightest become a star shining in the firmament of glory. I have seen thy light, and thy good works, and I will therefore glorify our Father which is in heaven. I have seen in thy example, what it is to be a sinner freely saved by grace. I have learned from thee, as in a living mirror, *who* it is, that begins, continues, and ends the work of faith and love. Jesus is all in all; he will and shall be glorified. He won the crown, and alone deserves to wear it. May no one attempt to rob him of his glory; he saves, and saves to the uttermost. Farewell, dear sister in the Lord. Thy flesh and thy heart may fail; but God is the strength of thy heart, and shall be thy portion for ever."

I was soon called to attend the funeral of my friend, who breathed her last shortly after my visit. Many pleasing yet melancholy thoughts were connected with the fulfilment of this task. I retraced the numerous and important conversations which I had held with her. But these could now no longer be held on earth. I reflected on the interesting and improving nature of Christian friendships, whether formed in palaces or in cottages; and felt thankful that I had so long enjoyed that privilege with the subject of this memorial. I indulged a sigh, for a moment, on thinking that I could no longer hear the great truths of Christianity uttered by one who had drunk so deep of the waters of life. But the rising murmur was checked by the animating thought, "She is gone to eternal rest—could I wish to bring her back to this vale of tears?"

As I travelled onward to the house where lay her remains in solemn preparation for the grave, the first sound of a tolling bell struck my ear. It proceeded from a village church in the valley directly beneath the ridge of a high hill, over which I had taken my way—it was poor Elizabeth's funeral knell. It was a solemn sound, but it seemed to proclaim at once the blessedness of the dead who die in the Lord, and the necessity of the living pondering these things, and laying them to heart.

On entering the cottage, I found that several christian friends, from different parts of the neighborhood, had assembled together to show their last tribute of esteem and regard to the memory of the Dairyman's Daughter.

I was requested to go into the chamber where the relatives and a few other friends were gone to take a last look at the remains of Elizabeth.

If there be a moment when Christ and salvation, death, judgment, heaven, and hell, appear more than ever to be momentous subjects of meditation, it is that which brings us to the side of a coffin containing the body of a departed believer.

Elizabeth's features were altered, but much of her likeness remained. Her father and mother sat at the head, her brother at the foot of the coffin, manifesting their deep and unfeigned sorrow. The weakness and infirmity of old age added a character to the parents' grief, which called for much tenderness and compassion.

A remarkably decent-looking woman, who had the management of the few simple though solemn ceremonies which the case required, advanced towards me, saying,

"Sir, this is rather a sight of joy than of sorrow. Our dear friend Elizabeth finds it to be so, I have no doubt. She is beyond all sorrow Do you not think she is, Sir?"

"After what I have known, and seen, and heard," I replied, "I feel the fullest assurance, that while her body remains here, her soul is with her Savior in Paradise. She loved him *here*, and *there* she enjoys the pleasures which are at his right hand for evermore."

"Mercy, mercy upon a poor old creature almost broken down with age and grief, what shall I do? Betsey's gone—my daughter's dead. Oh! my child, I shall never see thee more! God be merciful to me a sinner!" sobbed out the poor mother.

"That last prayer, my dear good woman," said I, "will bring you together again. It is a cry that has brought thousands to glory. It brought your daughter thither, and I hope it will bring you there likewise. He will in no wise cast out any that come to him."

"My dear," said the Dairyman, breaking the long silence he had maintained, "let us trust God with our child, and let us trust him with our ownselves. The Lord gave, and the Lord has taken away; blessed be the name of the Lord! We are old, and can have but a little farther to travel in our journey, and then"—he could say no more.

The soldier before mentioned reached a Bible into my hand, and said, "Perhaps, Sir, you would not object to reading a chapter before we go to the church."

I did so; it was the fourteenth of the book of Job. A sweet tranquillity prevailed while I read it. Each minute that was spent in this funeral-chamber, seemed to be valuable. I made a few observations on the chapter, and connected them with the case of our departed sister.

"I am but a poor soldier," said our military friend, "and have nothing of this world's goods beyond my daily subsistence; but I would not exchange my hope of salvation in the next world, for all that this world could bestow without it. What is wealth without grace? Blessed be God, as I march about from one quarter to another, I still find the Lord wherever I go; and thanks be to his holy name, he is here to-day in the midst of this company of the living and the dead. I feel that it is good to be here."

Some other persons present began to take a part in the conversation, in the course of which the life and experience of the Dairyman's Daughter were brought forward in a very interesting manner; each friend had something to relate in testimony of her gracious disposition. One distant relative, a young woman under twenty, who had hitherto been a very light and trifling character, appeared to be remarkably impressed by the conversation of that day; and I have since had ground to believe that divine grace then began to influence her in the choice of that better part, which shall not be taken from her.

What a contrast does such a scene as this exhibit, when compared with the dull, formal, unedifying, and often indecent manner in which funeral parties assemble in the house of death!

But the time for departure to the church was now at hand. I went to take my last look at the deceased. There was much written on her countenance: she had evidently departed with a smile. It still remained, and spoke the tranquillity of her departing soul. According to the custom of the place, she was decorated with leaves and flowers in the coffin: these indeed were fading flowers, but they reminded me of that Paradise whose flowers are immortal, and where her never-dying soul is at rest.

I remembered the last words which I had heard her speak, and was instantly struck with the happy thought, that "death was indeed swallowed up in victory."

As I slowly retired, I said inwardly, "Peace, my honored sister, to *thy* memory, and to *my* soul, till we meet in a better world."

In a little time the procession formed; it was rendered the more interesting by the consideration of so many that followed the coffin being persons of truly serious and spiritual character.

After we had advanced about a hundred yards, my meditation was unexpectedly and most agreeably interrupted by the friends, who followed the family, beginning to sing a funeral Psalm. Nothing could be more sweet or solemn. The well-known effect of the open air in softening and blending the sounds of music was here peculiarly felt. The road through which we passed was beautiful and romantic: it lay at the foot of a hill, which occasionally re-echoed the voices of the singers, and seemed to give faint replies to the sound of the mourners. The funeral knell was distinctly heard from the church tower, and greatly increased the effect which this simple and becoming service produced.

I cannot describe the state of my own mind as peculiarly connected with the solemn singing. I never witnessed a similar instance before or since. I was reminded of elder times and ancient piety. I wished the practice more frequent. It seems well calculated to excite and cherish devotion and religious affection.

We at length arrived at the church. The service was heard with deep and affectionate attention. When we came to the grave, the hymn which Elizabeth had selected, was sung. All was devout, simple, decent, animating. We committed our dear friend's body to the grave, in full hope of a joyful resurrection from the dead.

Thus was the vail of separation drawn for a season. She is departed and no more seen. But she *will* be seen at the right hand of her Redeemer at the last day; and will again appear to his glory, a miracle of grace and a monument of mercy.

My reader, rich or poor, shall you and I appear there likewise? Are we " clothed with humility," and arrayed in the wedding-garment of a Redeemer's righteousness? Are we turned from idols to serve the living God? Are we sensible of our own emptiness, flying to a Savior's fulness to obtain grace and strength? Do we live in him, and of him, and by him, and with him? Is he our all in all? Are we "lost and found?" "dead and alive again?"

My *poor* reader, the Dairyman's Daughter was a *poor* girl, and the child of a *poor* man. Herein thou resemblest her: but dost thou resemble *her*, as she resembled Christ? Art thou made *rich* by faith? Hast thou a crown laid up for thee? Is thine heart set upon heavenly riches? If not, read this story once more, and then pray earnestly for like precious faith. If, through grace, thou dost love and serve the Redeemer that saved the Dairyman's Daughter, grace, peace, and mercy be with thee. The lines are fallen unto thee in pleasant places: thou hast a goodly heritage. Press forward in duty, and wait upon the Lord, possessing thy soul in holy patience. Thou hast just been with me to the grave of a departed believer. Now "go thy way till the end be; for thou shalt rest, and stand in thy lot at the end of the days." Dan. 12:13.

NOTE. The mother died about six months after her daughter and I have good reason to believe that God was merciful to her, and took her to himself. May every converted child thus labor and pray for the salvation of their unconverted parents. The father continued for some time after her, and adorned his old age with a walk and conversation becoming the Gospel. I cannot doubt that the daughter and both her parents are now met together in "the land of pure delights, where saints immortal reign."

No. 10.

THE SHEPHERD OF SALISBURY PLAIN.

BY MRS. HANNAH MORE.

"Look here, father; only see how much I have got to-day!"—*Page 7*

PUBLISHED BY THE
AMERICAN TRACT SOCIETY,
150 NASSAU-STREET, NEW-YORK.

D. Fanshaw, Printer.

THE SHEPHERD

OF

SALISBURY PLAIN.

Mr. Johnson, a very worthy, charitable gentleman, was travelling some time ago across one of those vast plains, which are well known in Wiltshire. It was a fine summer's evening, and he rode slowly, that he might have leisure to admire God in the works of his creation. For this gentleman was of opinion, that a walk or a ride was as proper a time as any to think about good things: for which reason, on such occasions, he seldom thought so much about his money, or his trade, or public news, as at other times, that he might with more ease and satisfaction enjoy the pious thoughts, which the visible works of the great Maker of heaven and earth are intended to raise in the mind.

His attention was all of a sudden called off by the barking of a Shepherd's dog, and looking up he spied one of those little huts, which are here and there to be seen on those great Downs; and near it was the Shepherd himself, busily employed with his dog in collecting together his vast flock of sheep. As he drew nearer, he perceived him to be a clean, well looking, poor man, near fifty years of age. His coat, though at first it had probably been of one dark colour, had been in a long course of years so often patched with different sorts of cloth, that it was now become hard to say which had been the original colour. But this, while it gave plain proof of the Shepherd's poverty, equally proved the exceeding neatness, industry, and good management of his wife. His stockings no less proved her good housewifery, for they were entirely covered with darns of different coloured worsted, but had not a hole in them; and his shirt, though nearly as coarse as the sails of a ship, was as white as the drifted snow, and was neatly mended where time had either made a rent or worn it thin. This furnishes a rule of judging, by which one will seldom be deceived. If I meet with a labourer hedging, ditching, or mending the high ways, with his stockings and shirt tight and whole, however mean and bad his other garments are, I have seldom failed, on visiting his cottage, to find that also clean and well ordered, and his wife notable, and worthy of encouragement. Whereas a poor woman, who will be lying a bed, or gossipping with her neighbours, when she ought to be fitting out her husband in a cleanly manner, will seldom be found to be very good in other respects.

This was not the case with our Shepherd; and Mr. Johnson was not more struck with the decency of his mean and frugal dress, than with his open, honest countenance, which bore strong marks of health, cheerfulness, and spirit.

Mr. Johnson, who was on a journey, and somewhat fearful, from the appearance of the sky, that rain was at no great distance, accosted the Shepherd with asking what sort of weather he thought it would be on the morrow. 'It will be such weather as pleases me,' answered the Shepherd. Though the answer was delivered in the mildest and civilest tone that could be imagined, the gentleman thought the words themselves rather rude and surly, and asked him how that could be? 'Because,' replied the Shepherd, 'it will be such weather as shall please God, and whatever pleases him always pleases me.'

Mr. Johnson, who delighted in good men and good things, was very well satisfied with his reply. For he justly thought, that though a hypocrite may easily contrive to appear better than he really is to a stranger, and that no one should be too soon trusted, merely for having a few good words in his mouth; yet as he knew that " out of the abundance of the heart the mouth speaketh," he always accustomed himself to judge favourably of those, who had a serious deportment and solid manner of speaking. It looks as if it proceeded from a good habit, said he, and though I may now and then be deceived by it, yet it has not often happened to me to be so. Whereas, if a man accosts me with an idle, dissolute, vulgar, indecent, or profane expression, I have never been deceived in him, but have generally on inquiry found his character to be as bad, as his language gave me room to expect.

He entered into conversation with the Shepherd in the

following manner: 'Yours is a troublesome life, honest friend,' said he. 'To be sure, Sir,' replied the Shepherd, ' 'tis not a very lazy life; but 'tis not near so toilsome as that which my great MASTER led for my sake; and he had every state and condition of life at his choice, and chose a hard one, while I only submit to the lot that is appointed me.' 'You are exposed to great cold and heat,' said the gentleman. 'True, Sir,' said the Shepherd; 'but then I am not exposed to great temptations; and so throwing one thing against another, God is pleased to contrive to make things more equal than we poor, ignorant, short-sighted creatures are apt to think. David was happier when he kept his father's sheep on such a plain as this, and was employed in singing some of his own Psalms, perhaps, than ever he was when he became king of Israel and Judah. And I dare say, we should never have had some of the most beautiful texts in all those fine Psalms, if he had not been a Shepherd, which enabled him to make so many fine comparisons and similitudes, as one may say, from country life, flocks of sheep, hills and vallies, and fountains of water.'

'You think then,' said the gentleman, ' that a laborious life is a happy one.' 'I do, Sir, and more so especially as it exposes a man to fewer sins. If king Saul had continued a poor, laborious man to the end of his days, he might have lived happy and honest, and died a natural death in his bed at last, which you know, Sir, was more than he did. But I speak with reverence; for it was divine Providence overruled all that, you know, Sir, and I do not presume to make comparisons. Besides, Sir, my employment has been particularly honoured. Moses was a Shepherd in the plains of Midian. It was to " Shepherds keeping their flocks by night," that the angels appeared in Bethlehem, to tell the best news, the gladdest tidings, that ever were revealed to poor, sinful men; often and often has the thought warmed my poor heart in the coldest night, and filled me with more joy and thankfulness than the best supper could have done.'

Here the Shepherd stopped, for he began to feel that he had made too free, and had talked too long. But Mr. Johnson was so well pleased with what he said, and with the cheerful, contented manner in which he said it, that he desired him to go on freely, for that it was a pleasure to him to meet with a plain man, who without any kind of learning but what he had got from the Bible, was able to talk so well on a subject, in which all men, high and low, rich and poor, are equally concerned.

'Indeed I am afraid I make too bold, Sir, for it better becomes me to listen to such a gentleman as you seem to be, than to talk in my poor way; but, as I was saying, Sir, I wonder all working men do not derive as great joy and delight, as I do, in thinking how God has honoured poverty! Oh! Sir, what great, or rich, or mighty men have had such honour put on them, or their condition, as Shepherds, Tent-makers, Fishermen, and Carpenters have had?'

'My honest friend,' said the gentleman, 'I perceive you are well acquainted with scripture.' 'Yes, Sir, pretty well, blessed be God! Through his mercy I learnt to read, when I was a little boy; though reading was not so common when I was a child, as I am told, through the goodness of Providence, and the generosity of the rich, it is likely to become now-a-days. I believe there is no day, for the last thirty years, that I have not peeped at my Bible. If we can't find time to read a chapter, I defy any man to say he can't find time to read a verse; and a single text, Sir, well followed, and put in practice every day, would make no bad figure at the year's end; three hundred and sixty-five texts, without the loss of a moment's time, would make a pretty stock, a little golden treasury, as one may say, from new year's day to new year's day; and if children were brought up to it, they would come to look for their texts as naturally as they do for their breakfast. No labouring man, 'tis true, has so much leisure as a Shepherd; for while the flock is feeding, I am obliged to be still, and at such times I can now and then tap a shoe for my children or myself, which is a great saving to us: and while I am doing that, I repeat a bit of a chapter, which makes the time pass pleasantly in this wild, solitary place. I can say the best part of the Bible by heart; I believe I should not say the best part, for every part is good, but I mean the greatest part. I have led but a lonely life, and have often had but little to eat; but my Bible has been meat, drink, and company to me, as I may say; and when want and trouble have come upon me, I don't know what I should have done indeed, Sir, if I had not had the promises of this book for my stay and support.'

'You have had great difficulties then,' said Mr. Johnson. 'Why as to that, Sir, not more than neighbours' fare; I have but little cause to complain, and much to be thankful; but I have had some struggles, as I will leave you to judge. I have a wife and eight children, whom I bred up in that little cottage, which you see under the hill about half a mile off.' 'What, that with the smoke coming out of the chimney?' said the gentleman. 'Oh no, Sir,' replied the Shepherd, smiling, 'we have seldom smoke in the evening, for we have little to cook, and firing is very dear in these parts. 'Tis that cottage which you see on the left hand of the church, near that little tuft of hawthorns.' 'What, that hovel with only one room above and below, with scarcely any chimney? How is it possible you can live there with such a family?' 'O! it is very possible and very certain too,' cried the Shepherd. 'How many better men have been worse lodged! How many good Christians have perished in prisons and dungeons, in comparison of which my cottage is a palace! The house is very well, Sir, and if the rain did not sometimes beat down upon us through the thatch, when we are a-bed, I should not desire a better; for I have health, peace, and liberty, and no man maketh me afraid.'

'Well, I will certainly call upon you before it be long; but how can you contrive to lodge so many children?' 'We do the best we can, Sir. My poor wife is a very sickly woman, or we should always have done tolerably well. There are no gentry in the parish, so that she has not met with any great assistance in her sickness. The good curate of the parish, who lives in that pretty parsonage in the valley, is very willing, but not very able to assist us on these trying occasions, for he has little enough for himself, and a large family into the bargain. Yet he does what he can, and more than many rich men do, and more than he can well afford. Besides that, his prayers and good advice we are always sure of, and we are truly thankful for that; for a man must give, you know, Sir, according to what he hath, and not according to what he hath not.'

'Are you in any distress, at present?' said Mr. Johnson

' No, Sir, thank God,' replied the Shepherd. ' I get my shilling a day, and most of my children will soon be able to earn something; for we have only three under five years old.' ' Only!' said the gentleman; ' that is a heavy burden.' ' Not at all; God fits the back to it. Though my wife is not able to do any out of door work, yet she breeds up her children to such habits of industry, that our little maids, before they are six years old, can first get a halfpenny, and then a penny a day, by knitting. The boys who are too little to do hard work, get a trifle by keeping the birds off the corn; for this the farmers will give them a penny or two pence, and now and then a bit of bread and cheese into the bargain. When the season of crow keeping is over, then they glean, or pick stones; any thing is better than idleness, Sir; and if they did not get a farthing by it, I would make them do it just the same, for the sake of giving them early habits of labour.

' So you see, Sir, I am not so badly off as many are; nay, if it were not that it cost me so much in 'potecary's stuff for my poor wife, I should reckon myself well off: nay, I do reckon myself well off: for, blessed be God, he has granted her life to my prayers, and I would work myself to a 'natomy, and live on one meal a day, to add one comfort to her valuable life. Indeed I have often done the last, and thought it no great matter neither.'

While they were in this part of the discourse, a fine, plump, cherry-cheek little girl ran up out of breath, with a smile on her young happy face, and without taking any notice of the gentleman, cried out with great joy, ' Look here, father, only see how much I have got to-day!' Mr. Johnson was much struck with her simplicity, but puzzled to know what was the occasion of this great joy. On looking at her, he perceived a small quantity of coarse wool, some of which had found its way through the holes of her clean, but scanty and ragged, woollen apron. The father said, ' this has been a successful day indeed, Molly, but don't you see the gentleman?' Molly now made a low courtesy down to the very ground; while Mr. Johnson inquired into the cause of the mutual satisfaction which both father and daughter had expressed at the unusual good fortune of the day.

' Sir,' said the Shepherd, ' poverty is a great sharper er of the wits. My wife and I cannot endure to see our children (poor as they are) without shoes and stockings, not only on account of the pinching cold, which cramps their poor little limbs, but because it degrades and debases them; and poor people who have but little regard to appearance, will seldom be found to have any great regard to honesty and goodness: I don't say this is always the case; but I am sure it is so too often. Now shoes and stockings being very dear, we never could afford to get them without a little contrivance. I must show you how I manage about the shoes, when you condescend to call at our cottage, Sir: as to stockings, this is one way we take to help to get them. My young ones, who are too little to do much work, sometimes wander at odd hours over the hills for the chance of finding what little wool the sheep may drop when they rub themselves, as they are apt to do, against the bushes.* These scattered bits of wool the children pick up out of the brambles, which I see have torn sad holes in Molly's apron to-day; they carry this wool home, and when they have got a pretty parcel together, their mother cards it; for she can sit and card in the chimney corner, when she is not able to wash or work about house. The biggest girl then spins it: it does very well for us without dying, for poor people must not stand for the colour of their stockings. After this, our little boys knit it for themselves, while they are employed in crow-keeping in the fields, and after they get home at night. As for the knitting the girls and their mother do, that is chiefly for sale, which helps to pay our rent.'

Mr. Johnson lifted up his eyes in silent astonishment at the shifts which honest poverty can make, rather than beg or steal; and was surprised to think how many ways of subsisting there are, which those who live at their ease, little suspect. He secretly resolved to be more attentive to his own petty expenses, than he had hitherto been; and to be more watchful that nothing was wasted in his family.

But to return to the Shepherd. Mr. Johnson told him, that as he must needs be at his friend's house who lived many miles off, that night, he could not, as he wished to do, make a visit to his cottage at present. 'But I will certainly do it,' said he, 'on my return, for I long to see your wife and

* This piece of frugal industry is not imaginary, but a real fact, as is the character of the Shepherd, and his uncommon knowledge of the Scriptures.

her nice little family, and to be an eye witness of her neatness and good management.' The poor man's tears started into his eyes on hearing the commendation bestowed on his wife; and wiping them off with the sleeve of his coat, for he was not worth a handkerchief in the world, he said, 'Oh, Sir, you just now, I am afraid, called me a humble man, but indeed I am a very proud one.' 'Proud!' exclaimed Mr. Johnson, 'I hope not; pride is a great sin, and as the poor are liable to it, as well as the rich, so good a man as you seem to be, ought to guard against it.' 'Sir,' said he, 'you are right but I am not proud of myself; God knows I have nothing to be proud of. I am a poor sinner; but indeed, Sir, I am proud of my wife; she is not only the most tidy, notable woman on the plain, but she is the kindest wife and mother, and the most contented, thankful Christian that I know. Last year I thought I should have lost her in a violent fit of the rheumatism, caught by going to work too soon after her lying in, I fear; for 'tis but a bleak, coldish place, as you may see, Sir, in winter; and sometimes the snow lies so long under the hill, that I can hardly make myself a path to get out and buy a few necessaries in the next village; and we are afraid to send out the children, for fear they would be lost when the snow is deep. So, as I was saying, the poor soul was very bad indeed, and for several weeks lost the use of all her limbs except her hands; a merciful Providence spared her the use of these, so that when she could not turn in her bed, she could contrive to patch a rag or two for her family. She was always saying, had it not been for the great goodness of God, she might have had her hands lame, as well as her feet, or the palsy instead of the rheumatism, and then she could have done nothing—but nobody had so many mercies as she had.

'I will not tell you what we suffered during the bitter weather, Sir; but my wife's faith and patience during that trying time, were as good a lesson to me, as any sermon I could hear; and yet Mr. Jenkins gave us very comfortable ones too, that helped to keep up my spirits.

'One Sunday afternoon, when my wife was at the worst, as I was coming out of church, (for I went one part of the day, and my eldest daughter the other, so my poor wife was never left alone;) as I was coming out of church, I say, Mr. Jenkins the minister called out to me, and asked me how my wife did, saying, he had been kept from coming to see her by the deep fall of snow; and indeed from the parsonage house to my hovel it was quite impossible. . I gave him all the particulars he asked, and I am afraid a good many more, for my heart was quite full. He kindly gave me a shilling, and said he would certainly try to pick out his way, and come and see her in a day or two.

'While he was talking to me, a plain, farmer-looking gentleman, in boots, who stood by, listened to all I said, but seemed to take no notice. It was Mr. Jenkins' wife's father, who was come to pass the Christmas-holidays at the parsonage house. I had always heard him spoken of as a plain, frugal man, who lived close himself, but was remarked to give away more than any of his show-a-way neighbours.

'Well; I went home with great spirits at this seasonable and unexpected supply; for we had tapped our last sixpence, and there was little work to be had, on account of the weather. I told my wife I had not come back empty-handed. No, I dare say not, says she, you have been serving a Master "who filleth the hungry with good things, though he sendeth the rich empty away." True, Mary, said I, we seldom fail to get good spiritual food from Mr. Jenkins, but to-day he has kindly supplied our bodily wants. She was more thankful, when I showed her the shilling, than I dare say some of you great people are when they get a hundred pounds.'

Mr. Johnson's heart smote him, when he heard such a value set upon a shilling; surely, said he to himself, I will never waste another; but he said nothing to the Shepherd, who thus pursued his story.

'Next morning, before I went out, I sent part of the money to buy a little ale and brown sugar, to put into her water gruel; which you know, Sir, made it nice and nourishing. I went out to cleave wood in a farm yard, for there was no standing out on the plain, after such a snow as had fallen in the night. I went with a lighter heart than usual, because I had left my poor wife a little better, and comfortably supplied for this day, and I now resolved more than ever, to trust God for the supplies of the next. When I came back at night, my wife fell a crying as soon as she saw me. This, I own, I thought but a bad return for the blessings she had so lately received, and so I told her. O, said she, it is too much, we are too rich; I am now frightened, not lest we should have no portion in this world, but for fear we should have our whole portion in it. Look here, John! So saying she uncovered the bed whereon she lay, and showed me two warm, thick, new blankets. I could not believe my own eyes, Sir, because, when I went out in the morning I had left her with no other covering than our little old blue rug. I was still more amazed when she put half a crown into my hand, telling me she had had a visit from Mr. Jenkins and Mr. Jones, the latter of whom had bestowed all these good things upon us. Thus, Sir, have our lives been crowned with mercies. My wife got about again, and I do believe, under Providence, it was owing to these comforts; for the rheumatism, Sir, without blankets by night and flannel by day, is but a baddish job, especially to people who have but little or no fire. She will always be a weakly body; but thank God, her soul prospers, and is in health. But I beg your pardon, Sir, for talking on at this rate.' 'Not at all, not at all,' said Mr. Johnson; 'I am much pleased with your story; you shall certainly see me in a few days. Good night.' So saying, he slipped a crown into his hand and rode off. Surely, said the Shepherd, "*goodness and mercy have followed me all the days of my life,*" as he gave the money to his wife when he got home at night.

As to Mr. Johnson, he found abundant matter for his thoughts during the rest of his journey. On the whole he was more disposed to envy than to pity the Shepherd. I have seldom seen, said he, so happy a man. It is a sort of happiness which the world could not give, and which I plainly see, it has not been able to take away. This must be the true spirit of religion. I see more and more, that true goodness is not merely a thing of words and opinions, but a living principle brought into every common action of a man's life. What else could have supported this poor couple under every bitter trial of want and sickness? No, my honest Shepherd, I do not pity, but I respect and even honour thee; and I will visit thy poor hovel on my return to Salisbury, with as much pleasure as I am now going to the house of my friend.

If Mr. Johnson keeps his word in sending me the account of his visit to the Shepherd's cottage, I shall be very glad to entertain my readers with it

PART II.

I am willing to hope, that my readers will not be sorry to hear some farther particulars of their old acquaintance, *The Shepherd of Salisbury Plain.* They will call to mind, that at the end of the first part he was returning home, full of gratitude for the favours he had received from Mr. Johnson, whom we left pursuing his journey, after having promised to make a visit to the Shepherd's cottage.

Mr. Johnson, after having passed some time with his friend, set out on his return to Salisbury, and on the Saturday evening reached a very small inn, a mile or two distant from the Shepherd's village; for he never travelled on a Sunday. He went next morning to the church nearest the house where he had passed the night; and after taking such refreshment as he could get at that house, he walked on to find out the Shepherd's cottage. His reason for visiting him on Sunday was chiefly because he supposed it to be the only day which the Shepherd's employment allowed him to pass at home with his family; and as Mr. Johnson had been struck with his talk, he thought it would be neither unpleasant nor unprofitable to observe how a man, who carried such an appearance of piety, spent his Sunday; for, though he was so low in the world, this gentleman was not above entering very closely into his character, of which he thought he should be able to form a better judgment, by seeing whether his practice at home kept pace with his profession abroad. For it is not so much by observing how people talk, as how they live, that we ought to judge of their characters.

After a pleasant walk, Mr. Johnson got within sight of the cottage, to which he was directed by the clump of hawthorns and the broken chimney. He wished to take the family by surprise; and walking gently up to the house, he stood a while to listen. The door being half open, he saw the Shepherd, (who looked so respectable in his Sunday coat, that he should hardly have known him,) **his wife** and their numerous family drawing round their little table, which was covered with a clean, though very **coarse cloth.** There stood on it a large dish of potatoes, a brown pitcher, and a piece of coarse loaf. The wife and children stood in silent attention, while the Shepherd, with uplifted hands and eyes, devoutly begged the blessing of Heaven on their homely fare. Mr. Johnson could not help sighing to reflect, that he had sometimes seen better dinners eaten with less appearance of thankfulness.

The Shepherd and his wife then sat down with great seeming cheerfulness, but the children stood; and while the mother was helping them, little fresh coloured Molly, who had picked the wool from the bushes with so much delight, cried out, 'Father, I wish I was big enough to say grace, I am sure I should say it very heartily to-day, for I was thinking, what must *poor* people do, who have no salt to their potatoes; and do but look, our dish is quite full.' That is the true way of thinking, Molly, said the father; in whatever concerns bodily wants, and bodily comforts, it is our duty to compare our own lot with the lot of those who are worse off, and this will keep us thankful. On the other hand, whenever we are tempted to set up our own wisdom or goodness, we must compare ourselves with those who are wiser and better, and that will keep us humble. Molly was now so hungry, and found the potatoes so good, that she had no time to make any more remarks; but was devouring her dinner very heartily, when the barking of the great dog drew her attention from her trencher to the door, and spying the stranger, she cried out, 'Look, father, see here, is not that the good gentleman?' Mr. Johnson, finding himself discovered, immediately walked in, and was heartily welcomed by the honest Shepherd, who told his wife, that this was the gentleman to whom they were so much obliged.

The good woman began, as some very neat people are rather too apt to do, with making many apologies, that her house was not cleaner, and that things were not in fitter order to receive such a gentleman. Mr. Johnson, however, on looking round, could discover nothing but the most perfect neatness. The trenchers on which they were eating were almost as white as their linen; and, notwithstanding the number and smallness of the children, there was not the least appearance of dirt or litter. The furniture was very simple and poor, hardly indeed amounting to bare necessaries. It consisted of four brown wooden chairs, which, by constant rubbing, were become as bright as a looking-glass;

an iron pot and kettle; a poor old grate, which scarcely held a handful of coal, and out of which the little fire that had been in it appeared to have been taken as soon as it had answered the end for which it had been lighted, that of boiling their potatoes. Over the chimney stood an old fashioned broad bright candlestick, and a still brighter spit; it was pretty clear that this last was kept rather for ornament than use. An old carved elbow-chair, and a chest of the same date, which stood in the corner, were considered as the most valuable part of the Shepherd's goods, having been in his family for three generations. But all these were lightly esteemed by him, in comparison of another possession, which, added to the above, made up the whole of what he had inherited from his father; and which last he would not have parted with, if no other could have been had, for a king's ransom; this was a large old Bible, which lay on the window-seat, neatly covered with brown cloth, variously patched. This sacred book was most reverently preserved from dog's ears, dirt, and every other injury, but such as time and much use had made it suffer, in spite of care. On the clean white walls were pasted a Hymn on the Crucifixion of our Saviour, a print of the Prodigal Son, the Shepherd's Hymn, a New History of a true Book, and Patient Joe.

After the first salutations were over, Mr. Johnson said, that if they would go on quietly with their dinner, he would sit down. Though a good deal ashamed, they thought it more respectful to obey the gentleman, who, having cast his eye on their slender provisions, gently rebuked the Shepherd for not having indulged himself, as it was Sunday, with a morsel of bacon to relish his potatoes. The Shepherd said nothing, but poor Mary coloured and hung down her head, saying, 'indeed, Sir, it is not my fault, I did beg my husband to allow himself a bit of meat to-day out of your honour's bounty; but he was too good to do it, and it is all for my sake.'—The Shepherd seemed unwilling to come to an explanation, but Mr. Johnson desired Mary to go on. So she continued, ' you must know, Sir, that both of us, next to a sin, dread a debt, and indeed in some cases, a debt is a sin, but with all our care and pains we have never been able quite to pay off the doctor's bill for that bad fit of rheumatism, which I had last winter. Now, when you were pleased to give my husband that kind present the other day, I heartily desired him to buy a bit of meat for Sunday, as I said before, that he might have a little refreshment out of your kindness. But he answered, 'Mary, it is never out of my mind long together, that we still owe a few shillings to the doctor (and, thank God, it was all we did owe in the world.)—Now if I carry him this money directly, it will not only show him our honesty and our good will, but it will be an encouragement to him to come to you another time, in case you should be taken once more in such a bad fit; for I must own,' added my poor husband, 'that the thought of your being so terribly ill, without any help, is the only misfortune that I want courage to face.''

Here the grateful woman's tears ran down so fast that she could not go on. She wiped them with the corner of her apron, and humbly begged pardon for making so free. 'Indeed, Sir,' said the Shepherd, ' though my wife is full as unwilling to be in debt as myself, yet I could hardly prevail on her to consent to my paying this money just then, because, she said, it was hard I should not have a taste of the gentleman's bounty myself. But for once, Sir, I would have my own way. For you must know, as I pass the best part of my time alone, tending my sheep, 'tis a great point with me, Sir, to get comfortable matter for my own thoughts; so that 'tis rather self-interest in me, to allow myself no pleasures and no practices that won't bear thinking on over and over. For when one is a good deal alone, you know, Sir, all one's bad deeds do so rush in upon one, as I may say, and so torment one, that there is no true comfort to be had, but in keeping clear of wrong doings and false pleasures; and that I suppose may be one reason why so many folks hate to stay a bit by themselves. But, as I was saying, when I came to think the matter over on the hill yonder, said I to myself, a good dinner is a good thing, I grant, and yet it will be but cold comfort to me a week after, to be able to say—to be sure I had a nice shoulder of mutton last Sunday for dinner, thanks to the good gentleman, but then I am in debt—I *had* a rare dinner, that's certain, but the pleasure of that has long been over, and the debt still remains—I have spent the crown, and now if my poor wife should be taken in one of those fits again, die she must, unless God work a miracle to prevent it, for I can get no help for her. This thought settled all; and I set off directly and paid the crown to the doctor with as much cheerfulness as I could have felt on sitting down to the fattest shoulder of mutton that was ever roasted. And if I was contented at the time, think how much more happy I have been at the remembrance! O Sir, there are no pleasures worth the name, but such as bring no plague or penitence after them.' Mr. Johnson was satisfied with the Shepherd's reasons; and agreed, that though a good dinner was not to be despised, yet it was not worthy to be compared with a *contented mind, which* (as the Proverb truly says) *is a continual feast.* 'But come,' said the good gentleman, 'what have we got in this brown mug?' 'As good water,' said the Shepherd, 'as any in the king's dominions. I have heard of countries beyond sea, in which there is no wholesome water; nay, I have been myself in a great town not far off, where they are obliged to buy all the water they get, while a good Providence sends to my very door a spring as clear and fine as Jacob's well. When I am tempted to repine that I have often no other drink, I call to mind, that it was nothing better than a cup of cold water which the woman of Samaria drew for the greatest guest that ever visited this world.'

'Very well,' replied Mr. Johnson; 'but as your honesty has made you prefer a poor meal to being in debt, I will at least send and get something for you to drink. I saw a little public house just by the church, as I came along. Let that little rosy faced fellow fetch a mug of beer.'

So saying he looked full at the boy, who did not offer to stir; but cast an eye at his father, to know what he was to do. 'Sir,' said the Shepherd, 'I hope we shall not appear ungrateful, if we seem to refuse your favour; my little boy would, I am sure, fly to serve you on any other occasion. But, good Sir, it is Sunday, and should any of my family be seen at a publick house on a Sabbath-day, it would be a much greater grief to me than to drink water all my life. I am often talking against these doings to others! and if I should say one thing and do another, you can't think what an advantage it would give many of my neighbours over me, who would be glad enough to report, that they caught the Shepherd's son at the ale-house, without explaining how it happened. Christians, you know, Sir, must be doubly watchful, or they will not only bring disgrace on them selves, but, what is much worse, on that holy name by which they are called.'

'Are you not a little too cautious, my honest friend?' said Mr. Johnson. 'I humbly ask your pardon, Sir,' replied the Shepherd, 'if I think that impossible. In my poor notion, I no more understand how a man can be too cautious, than how he can be too strong, or too healthy.'

'You are right, indeed,' said Mr. Johnson, 'as a general principle, but this struck me as a very small thing.' 'Sir,' said the Shepherd, 'I am afraid you will think me very bold, but you encourage me to speak out.' ' 'Tis what I wish,' said the gentleman.—' Then, Sir,' resumed the Shepherd, ' I doubt if, where there is a temptation to do wrong, any thing can be called small; that is, in short, if there is any such thing as a small wilful sin. A poor man, like me, is seldom called out to do great things, so that it is not by a few striking deeds his character can be judged by his neighbours, but by the little round of daily customs he allows himself in.'—While they were thus talking, the children, who had stood very quietly behind, and had not stirred a foot, now began to scamper about all at once, and in a moment ran to the window-seat to pick up their little old hats. Mr. Johnson looked surprised at this disturbance; the Shepherd asked his pardon, telling him it was the sound of the church bell, which had been the cause of their rudeness; for their mother had brought them up with such a fear of being too late for church, that it was but who could catch the first stroke of the bell, and be first ready. He had always taught them to think that nothing was more indecent than to get into church after it was begun; for as the service opened with an exhortation to repentance, and a confession of sin, it looked very presumptuous not to be ready to join in it; it looked as if people did not feel themselves to be sinners. And though such as lived at a great distance might plead difference of clocks as an excuse, yet those who lived within the sound of the bell could pretend neither ignorance nor mistake.

Mary and her children set forward. Mr. Johnson and the Shepherd followed, taking care to talk the whole way on such subjects as might fit them for the solemn duties of the place to which they were going. ' I have often been sorry to observe,' said Mr. Johnson, ' that many, who are reckoned decent, good kind of people, and who would on no account neglect going to church, yet seem to care but little in what frame or temper of mind they go thither. They will talk of their worldly concerns till they get within the door, and then take them up again the very minute the sermon is over, which makes me ready to fear they lay too much stress on the mere form of going to a place of worship. Now, for my part, I always find that it requires a little time to bring my mind into a state fit to do any *common* business well, much more this great and most necessary business of all.' ' Yes, Sir,' said the Shepherd, ' and then I think, too, how busy I should be in preparing my mind, if I was going into the presence of a great gentleman, or a lord, or a king ; and shall the King of kings be treated with less respect? Besides, one likes to see people feel as if going to church was a thing of choice and pleasure, as well as a duty, and that they were as desirous not to be the last there, as they would be if they were going to a feast or a fair.'

After service, Mr. Jenkins, the clergyman, who was well acquainted with the character of Mr. Johnson, and had a great respect for him, accosted him with much civility; expressing his concern that he could not enjoy just now so much of his conversation as he wished, as he was obliged to visit a sick person at a distance, but hoped to have a little talk with him before he left the village. As they walked along together, Mr. Johnson made such inquiries about the Shepherd as served to confirm him in the high opinion he entertained of his piety, good sense, industry, and self-denial. They parted, the clergyman promising to call in at the cottage on his way home.

The Shepherd, who took it for granted that Mr. Johnson was gone to the parsonage, walked home with his wife and children, and was beginning in his usual way to catechise and instruct his family, when Mr. Johnson came in, and insisted that the Shepherd should go on with his instructions just as if he were not there.—This gentleman, who was very desirous of being useful to his own servants and workmen in the way of religious instruction, was sometimes sorry to find, that though he took a good deal of pains, they did not now and then quite understand him; for though his meaning was very good, his language was not always very plain; and though the *things* he said were not hard to be understood, yet the *words* were, especially to such as were very ignorant. And he now began to find out, that if people were ever so wise and good, yet if they had not a simple, agreeable, and familiar way of expressing themselves, some of their plain hearers would not be much the better for them. For this reason he was not above listening to the plain, humble way, in which this honest man taught his family; for though he knew that he himself had many advantages over the Shepherd, had more learning, and could teach him many things; yet he was not too proud to learn, even of so poor a man, in any point where he thought the Shepherd might have the advantage of him.

This gentleman was much pleased with the knowledge and piety he discovered in the answers of the children; and desired the Shepherd to tell him, how he contrived to keep up a sense of divine things in his own mind and in that of his family, with so little leisure and so little reading. 'O, as to that, Sir,' said the Shepherd, 'we do not read much except in one book, to be sure, but by hearty prayer for God's blessing on the use of that book, what little knowledge is needful seems to come of course, as it were; and my chief study has been to bring the fruits of the Sunday reading into the week's business, and to keep up the same sense of God in the heart, when the Bible is in the cupboard, as when it is in the hand. In short, to apply what I read in the book to what I meet with in the field.'

'I don't quite understand you,' said Mr. Johnson.—'Sir,' replied the Shepherd, 'I have but a poor gift at conveying these things to others, though I have much comfort from them in my own mind; but I am sure that the most ignorant and hard working people, who are in earnest about their salvation, may help to keep up devout thoughts and good affections during the week, though they have hardly any time to look at a book.—And it will help them to keep out bad thoughts, too, which is no small matter. But then they must know the Bible; they must have read the word of God: that is a kind of stock in trade for a Christian to set up with; and it is this which makes me so diligent in teaching it to my children, and even in storing their memories with psalms and chapters. This is a great help to a poor hard working man, who will scarcely meet with any thing, but what he may turn to some good account. If one lives in the fear and love of God, almost every thing one sees abroad will teach one to adore his power and goodness, and bring to mind some text of scripture, which shall fill the heart with thankfulness and the mouth with praise. When I look upwards, *the heavens declare the glory of God ;* and shall I be silent and ungrateful ? If I look round and see the vallies standing thick with corn, how can I help blessing that Power, *who giveth me all things richly to enjoy ?* I may learn gratitude from the beasts of the field, for the *ox knoweth his owner, and the ass his master's crib ;* and shall a Christian not know, shall a Christian not consider what great things God has done for him ? I, who am a Shepherd, endeavour to fill my soul with a constant remembrance of that good Shepherd, who *feedeth me in green pastures, and maketh me to lie down beside the still waters, and whose rod and staff comfort me.*'

'You are happy,' said Mr. Johnson, 'in this retired life, by which you escape the corruptions of the world.' 'Sir,' said the Shepherd, 'I do not escape the corruptions of my own evil nature. Even there, on that wild solitary hill, I can find out that my heart is prone to evil thoughts. I suppose, Sir, that different states have different temptations. You great folks that live in the world, perhaps, are exposed to some, of which such a poor man as I am, knows nothing. But to one who leads a lonely life like me, evil thoughts are a chief besetting sin ; and I can no more withstand these without the grace of God, than a rich gentleman can withstand the snares of evil company without the same grace. And I feel that I stand in need of God's help continually, and if he should give me up to my own evil heart, I should be lost.'

Mr. Johnson approved of the Shepherd's sincerity, for he had always observed, that where there was no humility, and no watchfulness against sin, there was no religion ; and he said, that the man, who did not feel himself to be a sinner, in his opinion, could not be a Christian.

Just as they were in this part of their discourse, Mr. Jenkins, the clergyman, came in. After the usual salutations, he said, 'Well, Shepherd, I wish you joy: I know you will be sorry to gain any advantage by the death of a neighbour; but old Wilson, my clerk, was so infirm, and, I trust, so well prepared, that there is no reason to be sorry for his death. I have been to pray by him, but he died while I staid. I have always intended you should succeed to his place; 'tis no great matter of profit, but every little is something.'

'No great matter! Sir,' cried the Shepherd; 'indeed it is a great matter to me; 'twill more than pay my rent. Blessed be God for all his goodness.' Mary said nothing, but lifted up her eyes, full of tears, in silent gratitude.

'I am glad of this little circumstance,' said Mr. Jenkins, 'not only for your sake, but for the sake of the office itself. I so heartily reverence every religious institution, that I would never have even the *Amen* added to the excellent prayers of our church by vain or profane lips; and, if it depended on me, there should be no such thing in the land as an idle, drunken, or irreligious parish clerk. Sorry I am to say, that this matter is not always sufficiently attended to, and that I know some of a very different character.'

Mr. Johnson now inquired of the clergyman, whether there were many children in the parish. 'More than you would expect,' replied he, 'from the seeming smallness of it, but there are some little hamlets which you do not see.'

'I think,' returned Mr. Johnson, 'I recollect that in the conversation I had with the Shepherd on the hill yonder, he told me you had no Sunday-school.' 'I am sorry to say we have none,' said the minister; 'I do what I can to remedy this misfortune by public catechising; but having two or three churches to serve, I cannot give so much time as I wish to private instruction; and having a large family of my own, and no assistance from others, I have never been able to establish a school.'

'There is an excellent institution in London,' said Mr. Johnson, 'called the Sunday-School Society, which kindly gives books and other helps, on the application of such pious ministers as stand in need of their aid, and which, I am sure, would have assisted you; but, I think, we shall be able to do something ourselves. —'Shepherd,' continued he, 'if I were a king, and had it in my power to make you a rich and a great man, with a word speaking, I would not do it. Those who are raised by some sudden stroke, much above the station in which divine Providence had placed them, seldom turn out good or very happy. I have never had any great things in my power, but as far as I have been able, I have always been glad to assist the worthy; I have, however, never attempted or desired to set any poor man much above his natural condition; but it is a pleasure to me to lend him such assistance as may make that condition more easy to himself, and to put him in a way which shall call him to the performance of more duties than perhaps he could have performed without my help, and of performing them in a better manner.—What rent do you pay for this cottage?'

'Fifty shillings a year, Sir.'

'It is in a sad, tattered condition: is there not a better to be had in the village?'

'That in which the poor clerk lived,' said the clergyman, 'is not only more tight and whole, but has two decent chambers, and a very large, light kitchen.' 'That will be very convenient,' replied Mr. Johnson; 'pray what is the rent?' 'I think,' said the shepherd, 'poor neighbour Wilson gave somewhere about four pounds a year, or it might be guineas.' 'Very well,' said Mr. Johnson, 'and what will the clerk's place be worth, think you?' 'About three pounds,' was the answer.

'Now,' continued Mr. Johnson, 'my plan is, that the Shepherd should take that house immediately; for as the poor man is dead, there will be no need of waiting till quarter day, if I make up the difference.' 'True, Sir,' said Mr. Jenkins, 'and I am sure my wife's father, whom I expect to-morrow, will willingly assist a little towards buying some of the clerk's old goods. And the sooner they remove, the better, for poor Mary caught that bad rheumatism by sleeping under a leaky thatch.' The Shepherd was too much moved to speak, and Mary could hardly sob out, 'O, Sir, you are too good; indeed this house will do very well.' 'It may do very well for you and your poor children, Mary,' said Mr. Johnson, gravely, 'but it will not do for a school; the kitchen is neither large nor light enough.

'Shepherd,' continued he, 'with your good minister's leave and kind assistance, I propose to set up in this parish a Sunday-School, and to make you the master. It will not interfere with your weekly calling, and it is the only lawful way in which you can turn the Sabbath into a day of some little profit to your family, by doing, as I hope, a great deal of good to the souls of others. The rest of the week you will work as usual. The difference of rent between this house and the clerk's, I shall pay myself; for to put you in a better house at your own expense would be no great kindness. As for honest Mary, who is not fit for hard labour, or any out-of-door-work, I propose to endow a small weekly school, of which she shall be the mistress, and employ her notable turn to good account, by teaching ten or a dozen girls to knit, sew, spin, card, or any other useful way of getting their bread; for all this I shall only pay her the usual price, for I am not going to make you rich, but useful.'

'Not rich, Sir!' cried the Shepherd. 'How can I ever be thankful enough for such blessings? And will my poor Mary have a dry thatch over head? and shall I be able to send for the doctor, when I am like to lose her? Indeed my cup runs over with blessings. I hope God will give me humility.' Here he and Mary looked at each other and burst into tears. The gentleman saw their distress, and kindly walked out upon the green before the door, that these honest people might give vent to their feelings. As soon as they were alone they crept into one corner of the room, where they thought they could not be seen, and fell on their knees, devoutly blessing and praising God for his mercies. Never were heartier prayers presented, than this grateful couple offered up for their benefactors. The warmth of their gratitude could only be equalled by the earnestness with which they besought the blessing of God on the work in which they were going to engage.

The two gentlemen now left this happy family, and walked to the parsonage, where the evening was spent in a manner very edifying to Mr. Johnson, who the next day took all proper measures for putting the Shepherd in immediate possession of his now comfortable habitation. Mr. Jenkins' father-in-law, the worthy gentleman who gave the Shepherd's wife the blankets, in the first part of this history, arrived at the parsonage before Mr. Johnson left it, and assisted in fitting up the clerk's cottage.

Mr. Johnson took his leave, promising to call on the worthy minister and his new clerk, once a year, in his summer's journey over the Plain, as long as it would please God to spare his life. We hope he will never fail to give us an account of these visits, which we shall be glad to lay before our readers, if they should contain instruction or amusement.

THE SHEPHERD'S HYMN.

The Lord my pasture shall prepare,
And feed me with a shepherd's care;
His presence shall my wants supply,
And guard me with a watchful eye:
My noon-day walks he shall attend,
And all my midnight hours defend.

When on the sultry glebe I faint,
Or on the thirsty mountain pant,
To fertile vales and dewy meads
My weary, wand'ring steps he leads,
Where peaceful rivers, soft and slow,
Amid the verdant landscape flow.

Though in the paths of death I tread,
With gloomy horrors overspread,
My steadfast heart shall fear no ill;
For thou, O Lord, art with me still;
Thy friendly arm shall give me aid,
And guide me through the dreadful shade.

Though in a bare and rugged way,
Through devious, lonely wilds I stray,
Thy bounty shall my pains beguile;
The barren wilderness shall smile,
With sudden greens and herbage crown'd;
And streams shall murmur all around.

END.

No. 11.

'TIS ALL FOR THE BEST.

ASCRIBED TO MRS. HANNAH MORE.

"It is all for the best," said Mrs. Simpson, whenever any misfortune befell her. She had such a habit of vindicating Providence, that, instead of weeping and murmuring under the most trying dispensations, her chief care was to convince herself and others, that, however great might be her sufferings, and however little they could be accounted for at present, the Judge of all the earth could not but do right. Instead of trying to clear herself from any possible blame that might attach to her under those infirmities, which, to speak after the manner of men, she seemed not to deserve, she was always the first to justify Him who had inflicted them. It was not that she superstitiously converted every visitation into a punishment; she entertained more correct ideas of that God who overrules all events. She knew that some calamities were sent to exercise her faith, others to purify her heart; some to chastise her sins, and all, to remind her that this " is not her rest;" that this world is not the place for the full and final display of retributive justice. The honor of God was dearer to her than her own credit, and her chief desire was to turn all events to his glory.

Though Mrs. Simpson was the daughter of a clergyman, and the widow of a genteel tradesman, she had been reduced, by a succession of misfortunes, to accept of a room in an alms-house. Instead of repining at the change; instead of dwelling on her former gentility, and saying, " how handsomely she had lived once; and how hard it was to be reduced; and she little thought ever to end her days in an alms-house;" (which is the common language of those who were never so well off before;) she was thankful that such an asylum was provided for want and age; and blessed God that it was to the Christian dispensation alone that such pious institutions owed their birth.

One fine evening, as she was sitting, reading her Bible, on the little bench shaded with honey-suckles, just before her door, who should come and sit down by her but Mrs. Betty, who had formerly been lady's maid at the nobleman's house of the village of which Mrs. Simpson's father had been minister. Betty, after a life of vanity, was, by a train of misfortunes, brought to this very alms-house; and though she had taken no care, by frugality and prudence, to avoid it, she thought it a hardship and disgrace, instead of being thankful, as she ought to have been, for such a retreat. At first she did not know Mrs. Simpson; her large bonnet, cloak, and brown stuff gown, (for she always made her appearance conform to her circumstances,) being very different from the dress she had been used to wear when Mrs. Betty had seen her dining at the great house; and time and sorrow had much altered her countenance. But when Mrs. Simpson kindly addressed her as an old acquaintance, she screamed with surprise,

" What! you, madam! you in an alms-house, living on charity? you, who used to be so charitable yourself that you never suffered any distress in the parish which you could prevent ?"

" That may be one reason, Betty," replied Mrs. Simpson, " why Providence has provided this refuge for my old age. And my heart overflows with gratitude when I look back on his goodness."

"No such great goodness, methinks," said Betty; "why, you were born and bred a lady, and are now reduced to live in an alms-house."

"Betty, I was born and bred a sinner, undeserving of the mercies I have received."

"No such great mercies," said Betty; "why, I heard you had been turned out of doors, that your husband had broke, and that you had been in danger of starving, though I did not know what was become of you."

"It is all true, Betty, glory be to God! it is all true."

"Well," said Betty, "you are an odd sort of a gentlewoman. If from a prosperous condition I had been made a bankrupt, a widow, and a beggar, I should have thought it no such mighty matter to be thankful for; but there is no accounting for taste. The neighbors used to say, that all your troubles must needs be a judgment upon you; but I who knew how good you were, thought it very hard you should suffer so much; but now I see you reduced to an alms-house, I beg your pardon, madam, but I am afraid the neighbors were in the right, and that so many misfortunes could never have happened to you unless you had committed a great many sins to deserve them; for I always thought that God is so just that he *punishes us for all our bad actions, and rewards us for all our good ones.*"

"Ay, Betty; but he does it in his own way, and at his own time, and not according to our notions of good and evil; for his ways are not as our ways. God, indeed, punishes the bad and rewards the good; but he does not do it fully and finally in this world. Indeed he does not set such a value on outward things as to make riches, and rank, and beauty, and health, the rewards of piety; that would be acting like weak and erring men, and not like a just and holy God. Our belief in a future state of rewards and punishments is not always so strong as it ought to be; even now; but how totally would our faith fail if we regularly saw every thing made even in this world. We shall lose nothing by having pay-day put off. The longest voyages make the best returns. So far am I from thinking that God is less just, and future happiness less certain, because I see the wicked sometimes prosper, and the righteous suffer in this world, that I am rather led to believe that God is more just, and heaven more certain: for, in the first place, God will not put off his favorite children with so poor a lot as the good things of this world; and next, seeing that the best men here below do not often attain to the best things, why, it only serves to strengthen my belief that they are not the best things in His eye; and He has most assuredly reserved for those that love Him, such good things as 'eye hath not seen nor ear heard.' God, by keeping man in Paradise while he was innocent, and turning him into this world as soon as he had sinned, gave a plain proof that he never intended this world, even in its happiest state, as a place of reward. My father gave me good principles and useful knowledge; and while he taught me, by a habit of constant employment, to be, if I may so say, independent of the world, he, at the same time, led me to a constant sense of dependence on God."

" I do not see, however," interrupted Mrs. Betty, " that your religion has been of any use to you. It has been so far from preserving you from trouble, that I think you have had more than the usual share."

" No," said Mrs. Simpson; " nor did Christianity ever pretend to exempt its followers from trouble; this is no part of the promise. Nay, the contrary is rather stipulated; 'in the world ye shall have tribulation.' But if it has not taught me to escape sorrow, I humbly hope it has taught me how to bear it. If it has not taught me to feel, it has taught me not to murmur. I will tell you a little of my story. As my father could save little or nothing for me, he was very desirous of seeing me married to a young gentleman in the neighborhood who expressed a regard for me. But while he was anxiously engaged in bringing this about, my good father died."

" How very unlucky!" interrupted Betty

" No, Betty," replied Mrs. Simpson, " it was very providential; this man, though he maintained a decent character, had a good fortune, and lived soberly, yet he would not have made me happy."

" Why, what could you want more of a man?" said Betty.

" Religion," returned Mrs. Simpson. " As my father made a creditable appearance, and was very charitable and I was an only child, this gentleman concluded that he could give me a considerable fortune; for he did not know that all the poor in his parish are the children of every pious clergyman. Finding I had little or nothing left me, he withdrew his attentions."

' What a sad thing!" cried Betty.

" No, it was *all for the best:* Providence overruled his covetousness to my good. I could not have been happy with a man whose soul was set on the perishable things of this world; nor did I esteem him, though I labored to submit my own inclinations to those of my kind father. The very circumstance of being left pennyless produced directly the contrary effect on Mr. Simpson: he was a sensible young man, engaged in a prosperous business; we had long highly valued each other; but while my father lived, he thought me above his hopes. We were married; I found him an amiable, industrious, good-tempered man; he respected religion and religious people; but, with an excellent disposition, I had the grief to find him less pious than I had hoped. He was ambitious, and a little too much immersed in worldly schemes; and though I knew it was all done for my sake, yet that did not blind me so far as to make me think it right. He attached himself so eagerly to business that he thought every hour lost in which he was not doing something that would tend to raise me to what he called my proper rank. The more prosperous he grew, the less religious he became; and I began to find that one might be unhappy with a husband she tenderly loved. But one day, having been absent on business, he was brought in with his leg broken in two places."

" What a dreadful misfortune!" said Mrs. Betty.

" What a signal blessing!" said Mrs. Simpson. " Here, I am sure I had reason to say *all was for the best:* from that very hour in which my outward troubles began, I date the beginning of my happiness. Severe suffering, a near prospect of death, absence from the world, silence, reflection, and, above all, the divine blessing on the prayers and scriptures I read to him, were the means used by our merciful Father to turn my husband's heart. During this confinement he was awakened to a deep sense of his own sinfulness, of the vanity of all this world has to bestow, and of his great need of a Savior. It was many months before he could leave his bed. During this time his business was neglected. His principal clerk took advantage of his absence to receive large sums of money in his name, and absconded. On hearing of this great loss, our creditors came faster upon us than we could answer their demands; they grew more impatient as we were less able to satisfy them; one misfortune followed another, till at length Mr. Simpson became a bankrupt."

"What an evil!" exclaimed Mrs. Betty.

"Yet it led, in the end, to much good," resumed Mrs. Simpson. "We were forced to leave the town in which we had lived with so much credit and comfort, and to betake ourselves to a mean lodging in a neighboring village, till my husband's strength should be recruited, and till we could have time to look about us and see what was to be done. The first night we spent in this poor dwelling my husband felt very sorrowful, not for his own sake, but that he had brought so much poverty on me, whom he so dearly loved. I, on the contrary, was unusually cheerful; for the blessed change in his mind had more than reconciled me to the sad change in his circumstances. I was contented to live with him in a poor cottage for a few years on earth, if it might contribute to our spending a blessed eternity together in heaven. I said to him, instead of lamenting that we are now reduced to want all the comforts of life, I have sometimes been almost ashamed to live in the full enjoyment of them, when I have reflected that my Savior not only chose to deny himself all these enjoyments, but even to live a life of hardship for my sake; not one of his numerous miracles tended to his own comfort; and though we read, at different times, that he both hungered and thirsted, yet it was not for his own gratification that he once changed water into wine; and I have often been struck with the near position of that chapter in which this miracle is recorded, to that in which he thirsted for a draught of water at the well of Samaria. John, 1 : 2–4. It was for others, not himself, that even the humble sustenance of barley bread was multiplied. See here, we have a bed left us; (I had, indeed, nothing but straw to fill it with;) but the Savior of the world 'had not where to lay his head.' My husband smiled through his tears, and we sat down to supper. It consisted of a roll and a bit of cheese which I had brought with me, and we ate it thankfully. Seeing Mr. Simpson beginning to relapse into distrust, the following conversation, as nearly as I can remember, took place between us.

" He began by remarking, that it was a mysterious Providence that he had been less prosperous since he had been less attached to the world, and that his endeavors had not been followed by that success which usually attends industry.

" I took the liberty to reply: Your heavenly Father sees on which side your danger lies, and is mercifully bringing you, by these disappointments, to trust less in the world, and more in himself. My dear Mr. Simpson, added I, we trust every body but God. As children, we obey our parents implicitly, because we are taught to believe all is for our good which they command or forbid. If we undertake a voyage, we trust entirely to the skill and conduct of the pilot; we never torment ourselves with thinking that he will carry us east, when he has promised to carry us west. If a dear and tried friend makes us a promise, we depend on him for the performance, and do not wound his feelings by our suspicions. When you used to go your annual journey in the mail-coach, you confided yourself to the care of the coachman, that he would carry you where he had engaged to; you were not anxiously watching him, and distrusting, and inquiring at every turn. When the doctor sends home your medicine, don't you so fully trust in his ability and good will that you take it in full confidence? You never think of inquiring what are the ingredients, why they are mixed in that particular way, why there is more of one and less of another, and why they are bitter instead of sweet. If one dose does not cure you, he orders another; and changes the medicine when he sees the first does you no good, or that by long use the same medicine has lost its effect; if a weaker fail, he prescribes a stronger; you swallow all, you submit to all, never questioning the skill or the kindness of the physician. God is the only being whom we do not trust; though he is the only one who is fully competent, both in will and power, to fulfill all his promises; and who has solemnly and repeatedly pledged himself to fulfill them, in those Scriptures which we receive as his revealed will.

"Mr. Simpson thanked me for 'my little sermon,' as he called it; but said, at the same time, that what made my exhortations produce a powerful effect on his mind, was the patient cheerfulness with which he was pleased to say I bore my share in our misfortunes. A submissive behavior, he said, was the best practical illustration of a real faith.

"When we had thanked God for our supper we prayed together; after which we read the eleventh chapter of the Epistle to the Hebrews. When my husband had finished it, he said, "Surely, if God's chief favorites have been martyrs, is not that a sufficient proof that this world is not a place of happiness, nor earthly prosperity the reward of virtue? Shall we, after reading this chapter, complain of our petty trials? Shall we not rather be thankful that our affliction is so light?'

"Next day Mr. Simpson walked out in search of some employment, by which we might be supported. He got a recommendation to Mr. Thomas, an opulent farmer and factor, who had large concerns, and wanted a skillful person to assist him in keeping his accounts. This we thought a providential circumstance; for we found that the salary would serve to procure us at least all the necessaries of life. The farmer was so pleased with Mr. Simpson's quickness, regularity, and good sense, that he offered us, of his own accord, a little neat cottage of his own, which then happened to be vacant, and told us we should live rent-free, and promised to be a friend to us."

"All *does* seem for the best now, indeed," interrupted Mrs. Betty.

"We shall see," said Mrs. Simpson, and thus went on:

"I now became very easy and very happy; and was cheerfully employed in putting our few things in order, and making every thing look to the best advantage. My husband, who wrote all the day for his employer, in the evenings assisted me in doing up our little garden. This was a source of much pleasure to us; we both loved a garden, and we were not only contented, but cheerful. Our employer had been absent some weeks on his annual journey. He came home on Saturday night, and the next morning sent for Mr. Simpson to come and settle his accounts which were behindhand on account of his long absence. We were just going to church, and Mr. Simpson sent back word that he would call and speak to him on his way home. A second message followed, ordering him to come to the farmer's directly. We agreed to walk round that way, and that my husband should call and excuse his attendance.

"The farmer, more ignorant and worse educated than his ploughman, with all that pride and haughtiness which the possession of wealth, without knowledge or religion, is apt to give, rudely asked my husband what he meant by sending him word that he could not come to him till the next day, and insisted that he should stay and settle the accounts then.

"'Sir,' said my husband, in a very respectful manner, 'I am on my road to church, and am afraid I shall be too late.'

"'Are you so?' said the farmer. 'Do you know who sent for you? You may, however, go to church, if you will, so you make haste back; and, d'ye hear, you may leave your accounts with me, as I conclude you have brought them with you; I will look them over by the time you return, and then you and I can do all I want to have done to-day in about a couple of hours; and I will give you home some letters to copy for me in the evening.'

"'Sir,' answered my husband, 'I dare not obey you; it is the Sabbath.'

"'And so you refuse to settle my accounts only because it is Sunday?'

"'Sir,' replied Mr. Simpson, 'if you would give me a handful of silver and gold, I dare not break the commandment of my God.'

"'Well,' said the farmer, 'but this is not breaking the commandment; I don't order you to drive my cattle, or to work in my garden, or to do any thing which you might fancy would be a bad example.'

"'Sir,' replied my husband, 'the example, indeed, goes a great way, but it is not the first object. The deed is wrong in itself.'

"'Well, but I shall not keep you from church; and when you have been there, there is no harm in doing a little business or taking a little pleasure the rest of the day.'

"'Sir,' answered my husband, 'the commandment does

not say, thou shalt keep holy the Sabbath *morning*, but the Sabbath *day*.'

" 'Get out of my house, you puritanical rascal, and out of my cottage too,' said the farmer; ' for if you refuse to do my work, I am not bound to keep my engagement with you; as you will not obey me as a master, I shall not pay you as a servant.'

" ' Sir,' said Mr. Simpson, ' I would gladly obey you, but I have a Master in heaven whom I dare not disobey.'

" ' Then let him find employment for you,' said the enraged farmer; ' for I fancy you will get but poor employment on earth with these scrupulous notions; and so send home my papers directly, and pack out of the parish.'

" ' Out of your cottage,' said my husband, ' I certainly will; but as to the parish, I hope I may remain in that, if I can find employment.'

" ' I will make it too hot to hold you,' replied the farmer; ' so you had better troop off, bag and baggage; for I am overseer, and as you are sickly, it is my duty not to let any vagabonds stay in the parish who are likely to become chargeable.'

" By the time my husband returned home, for he found it too late to go to church, I had got our little dinner ready: it was a better one than we had for a long while been accustomed to see, and I was unusually cheerful at this improvement in our circumstances. I saw his eyes full of tears; and oh! with what pain did he bring himself to tell me that it was the last dinner we must ever eat in that house! I took his hand with a smile, and only said, ' The Lord gave, and the Lord taketh away, blessed be the name of the Lord.'

" ' Notwithstanding this sudden stroke of injustice, said my husband, 'this is still a happy country. Our employer, it is true, may turn us out at a moment's notice, because the cottage is his own; but he has no further power over us; he cannot confine or punish us. His riches, it is true, give him power to insult, but not to oppress us. The same laws to which the affluent resort, protect us also. And as to our being driven out from a cottage, how many persons of the highest rank have lately been driven out from their palaces and castles; persons, too, born in a station which we never enjoyed, and used to all the indulgences of that rank and wealth we never knew, and at this moment wandering over the face of the earth without a house and without bread, exiles and beggars; while we, blessed be God, are in our own native land; we have still our liberty, our limbs, the protection of just and equal laws, our churches, our Bibles, and our Sabbaths.'

"This happy state of my husband's mind hushed my sorrows, and I never once murmured; nay, I sat down to dinner with a degree of cheerfulness, endeavoring to cast all our care on 'Him that careth for us.' We had begged to stay till the next morning, as Sunday was not the day on which we liked to remove; but we were ordered not to sleep another night in that house; so, as we had little to carry, we marched off in the evening to the poor lodging we had before occupied. The thought that my husband had cheerfully renounced his little all for conscience' sake, gave an unspeakable serenity to my mind; and I felt thankful, that though cast down, we were not forsaken; nay, I felt a lively gratitude to God, that while I doubted not he would accept this little sacrifice, as it was heartily made for his sake, he had graciously forborne to call us to greater trials."

"And so you were turned adrift once more? Well, ma'am, saving your presence, I hope you won't be such a fool as to say *all was for the best* NOW."

"Yes, Betty, HE who does all things well, now made his kind Providence more manifest than ever. That very night, while we were sweetly sleeping in our poor lodging, the pretty cottage out of which we were so unkindly driven was burned to the ground by a flash of lightning, which caught the thatch and so completely consumed the whole little building, that had it not been for that merciful Providence who thus overruled the cruelty of the farmer for the preservation of our lives, we might have been burned to ashes with the house. 'It was the Lord's doing, and it was marvellous in our eyes.'—' O that men would therefore praise the Lord for his goodness, and for his wonderful works to the children of men!'

"I will not tell you all the trials and afflictions which befell us afterward. I would also spare my heart the sad story of my husband's death."

"Well, that was another blessing, too, I suppose," said Betty.

"O, it was the severest trial ever sent me," replied Mrs. Simpson, a few tears quietly stealing down her face. 'I almost sunk under it. Nothing but the abundant grace of God could have carried me through such a visitation; and yet I now feel it to be the greatest mercy I ever experienced. He was my idol; no trouble ever came near my heart while he was with me. I got more credit than I deserved for my patience under trials, which were easily borne while he who shared and lightened them was spared to me. I had, indeed, prayed and struggled to be weaned from the world; but still my affection for him tied me down to earth with a strong cord; and though I earnestly tried to keep my eyes fixed on the eternal world, yet I viewed it with too feeble a faith; I viewed it at too great a distance. I found it difficult to realize it. I had deceived myself. I had fancied that I bore my troubles so well from the pure love of God; but I have since found that my love for my husband had too great a share in reconciling me to every difficulty which I underwent for him. I lost him; the charm was broken; the cord which tied me down to earth was cut: this world had nothing left to engage me; Heaven had now no rival in my heart. Though my love of God was before sincere, yet I found there wanted this blow to make it more perfect. But though all that had made life pleasant to me was gone, I did not sink as those who have no hope. I prayed that I might still, in this trying conflict, be enabled to adorn the doctrine of God my Savior.

"After many more hardships, I was at length so happy as to get an asylum in this alms-house. Here my cares are at an end, but not my duties."

"Now you are wrong again," interrupted Mrs. Betty; "your duty is now to take care of yourself; for I am sure you have nothing to spare."

"There *you* aré mistaken again," said Mrs. Simpson. "People are so apt to fancy that money is all in all, that all the other gifts of Providence are overlooked as things of no value. I have here a great deal of leisure; a good part of this I devote to the wants of those who are more distressed than myself. I work a little for the old, and I instruct the young. My eyes are good; this enables me to read the Bible both to those whose sight is decayed and to those who were never taught to read. I have tolerable health, so that I am able occasionally to sit up with the sick; in the intervals of nursing I can pray with them. In my younger days I thought it not much to sit up late for my pleasure; shall I now think much of sitting up, now and then, to watch by a dying bed? My Savior waked and watched for me in the garden and on the mount; and shall I do nothing for his suffering members? It is only by keeping his sufferings in view that we can truly practise charity to others, or exercise self-denial to ourselves."

"Well," said Mrs. Betty, "I think if I had lived in such genteel life as you have done, I could never be reconciled to an alms-house; and I am afraid I should never forgive any of those who were the cause of sending me there, particularly that farmer Thomas, who turned you out of doors."

"Betty," said Mrs. Simpson, "I not only forgive him heartily, but I remember him in my prayers as one of those instruments with which it has pleased God to work for my good. O! never put off forgiveness to a dying bed! When people come to die, we often see how the conscience is troubled with sins, of which before they hardly felt the existence. How ready are they to make restitution of ill-gotten gain; and this perhaps for two reasons; from a feeling conviction that it can be of no use to them where they are going, as well as from a near view of their own responsibility. We also hear from the most hardened, of death-bed forgiveness of enemies. Even malefactors at Tyburn forgive. But why must we wait for a dying bed, to do what ought to be done now? Believe me, that scene will be so full of terror and amazement to the soul, that we need not load it with unnecessary business."

Just as Mrs. Simpson was saying these words, a letter was brought her from the minister of the parish where the farmer lived, by whom Mr. Simpson had been turned out of his cottage. The letter was as follows:

"Madam,

"I write to tell you that your old oppressor, Mr. Thomas, is dead. I attended him in his last moments. O may my latter end never be like his! I shall not soon forget his despair at the approach of death. His riches, which had been his sole joy, now doubled his sorrows; for he was going where they could be of no use to him; and he found, too late, that he had laid up no treasure in heaven. He felt great concern at his past life, but for nothing more than his unkindness to Mr. Simpson. He charged me to find you out, and let you know, that by his will he bequeathed you five hundred pounds, as some compensation. He died in great agonies, declaring with his last breath, that if he could live his life over again, he would serve God, and strictly observe the Sabbath. Yours, &c.

"J. JOHNSON."

Mrs. Betty, who had listened attentively to the letter, jumped up, clapped her hands, and cried out, " Now all *is for the best*, and I shall see you a lady once more."

" I am indeed thankful for this mercy," said Mrs. Simpson, " and am glad that riches were not sent me till I had learned, as I humbly hope, to make a right use of them. But come, let us go in, for I am very cold, and find I have sat too long in the night air."

Betty was now ready enough to acknowledge the hand of Providence in this prosperous event, though she was blind to it when the dispensation was more dark. Next morning she went early to visit Mrs. Simpson, but not seeing her below, she went up stairs, where, to her great sorrow, she found her confined to her bed by a fever, caught the night before by sitting so late on the bench, reading the letter and talking it over.

Betty was now more ready to cry out against Providence than ever. " What! to catch a fever while you were reading that very letter which told you about your good fortune, which would have enabled you to live like a lady, as you are! I never will believe this is for the best; to be deprived of life just as you were beginning to enjoy it!"

" Betty," said Mrs. Simpson, " we must learn not to rate health, nor life itself, too highly. There is little in life, for its own sake, to be fond of. As a good archbishop used to say, 'tis but the same thing over again, or probably worse; so many more nights and days, summers and winters; a repetition of the same pleasures, but with less relish for them; a return of the same, or greater pains, but with less strength, and perhaps less patience to bear them."

"Well," replied Betty, "I did think that Providence was at last giving you your reward."

"Reward!" cried Mrs. Simpson, "O no! my merciful Father will not put me off with so poor a portion as wealth; I feel I shall die."

"It is very hard, indeed," said Betty, "so good as you are, to be taken off just as prosperity was beginning."

"You think I am good just now," said Mrs. Simpson, "because I am prosperous. Success is no sure mark of God's favor; at this rate, you, who judge by outward things, would have thought Herod a better man than John the Baptist; and if I may be allowed to say so, you, on the principle that the sufferer is the sinner, would have believed Pontius Pilate higher in God's favor than the Savior, whom he condemned to die for your sins and mine."

In a few days Mrs. Betty found that her new friend was dying, and though she was struck at her resignation she could not forbear murmuring that so good a woman should be taken away at the very instant when she came into possession of so much money.

"Betty," said Mrs. Simpson, in a feeble voice, "I believe you love me dearly, you would do any thing to cure me; yet you do not love me so well as God loves me, though you would raise me up, and he is putting a period to my life. He has never sent me a single stroke which was not absolutely necessary for me. You, if you could restore me, might be laying me open to some temptation from which God, by removing, will deliver me. Your kindness in making this world so smooth for me, I might for ever have deplored in a world of misery. God's grace, in afflicting me, will hereafter be the subject of my praises in a world of blessedness." "Betty," added the dying woman, "do you really think that I am going to a place of rest and joy eternal?"

"To be sure I do," said Betty.

"Do you firmly believe that I am going to the 'assembly of the first born; to the spirits of just men made perfect; to God the Judge of all; and to Jesus the Mediator of the New Covenant?'"

"I am sure you are," said Betty.

"And yet," resumed she, " you would detain me from all this happiness; and you think my merciful Father is using me unkindly by removing me from a world of sin, and sorrow, and temptation, to such joys as have not entered into the heart of man to conceive; while it would have better suited your notions of reward to defer my entrance into the blessedness of heaven, that I might have enjoyed a legacy of a few hundred pounds!! Believe my dying words—ALL IS FOR THE BEST."

Mrs. Simpson expired soon after, in a frame of mind which convinced her new friend that "God's ways are not as our ways."

    God moves in a mysterious way,
      His wonders to perform:
    He plants his footsteps in the sea,
      And rides upon the storm.

    Deep in unfathomable mines
      Of never-failing skill,
    He treasures up his bright designs,
      And works his sovereign will.

    Ye fearful saints, fresh courage take;
      The clouds ye so much dread
    Are big with mercy, and shall break
      In blessings on your head.

    Judge not the Lord by feeble sense,
      But trust him for his grace;
    Behind a frowning Providence
      He hides a smiling face.

    His purposes will ripen fast,
      Unfolding every hour;
    The bud may have a bitter taste,
      But sweet will be the flower.

    Blind unbelief is sure to err,
      And scan his work in vain;
    God is his own interpreter,
      And he will make it plain.

Cowper

NO. 12.

PROFANE SWEARING.

It chills my blood to hear the blest Supreme
Rudely appealed to on each trifling theme!
Maintain your rank; vulgarity despise;
To swear is neither brave, polite, nor wise.
You would not swear upon the bed of death;
Reflect! your Maker now could stop your breath.
          COWPER.

THE excellent Mr. Howe, being at dinner with some persons of fashion, a gentleman expatiated largely in praise of King Charles I., introducing some harsh reflections upon others. Mr. Howe, observing that the gentleman mixed many oaths with his discourse, told him that, in his humble opinion, he had omitted a singular excellence in the character of that prince. The gentleman eagerly desired him to mention it, and seemed all impatience to know what it was. 'It was this, Sir,' said Mr. Howe: 'He was never heard to swear an oath in common conversation.' The hint was as politely received as given; and the gentleman promised to break off the practice.

The same Mr. Howe, once conversing with a nobleman in St. James's Park, who swore profanely in his conversation, expressed great satisfaction in the thought that there is a God who governs the world, who will finally make retribution to all according to their works; and 'who, my lord,' added he, 'will make a difference between him that sweareth, and him that feareth an oath.' His lordship immediately answered, 'I thank you, Sir, for your freedom; I take your meaning, and shall endeavor to make a good use of it.' Mr. H. replied, 'I have reason to thank your lordship for saving me the most difficult part of the discourse, which is the *application*.'

Another time, passing two persons of quality, who were talking with great eagerness, and *damned* each other repeatedly; Mr. Howe said to them, taking off his hat in a respectful manner—' I pray God, *save* you both:' for which handsome reproof they immediately returned him thanks.

The truly honorable Mr. Boyle, as eminent for philosophy as for morality, was so careful to avoid this profane custom, that he never mentioned the name of God in his conversation, without making an observable pause before it; that so he might both feel, and diffuse among the company, the veneration due to the sacred Majesty of the universe.

The brave Col. Gardiner took pains to prevent swearing in his regiment, at the head of which he would publicly declare his abhorrence of it, urging all his officers to avoid giving, by their example, any sanction to a crime which it was their duty to punish. A number of military gentlemen once dined with him at his house, when he addressed them with much respect, and begged leave to remind them that, as he was a justice of the peace in that district, he was bound by oath to put the laws against swearing into execution; and therefore entreated them to be upon their guard. Only one of the gentlemen offended on that day, who immediately paid the penalty, which was given to the poor, with the universal approbation of the company.

A moment's calm consideration will convince any rational person of the impropriety of this custom, which is inexcusable, irrational, vulgar, and profane.

It is *inexcusable.* There is less temptation to this vice than to any other. Some vices are excused by calling them constitutional; but, as Archbishop Tillotson observes, no man is born with a *swearing* constitution. It cannot procure credit to an assertion; because it is oftener used to confirm a rash or doubtful saying than a plain truth. The man who swears, seems to doubt his own veracity; and well may others suspect it; for how can we believe he will be true to man, who is false to God? Besides, the custom of swearing to truths may insensibly lead a man to swear to falsehoods. Persons addicted to this practice scarcely know when they swear; and some, when reproved for it, have sworn that they did not swear.

It is *irrational.* What greater proof of stupid ignorance can be given, than to use words without meaning? You call upon God (shocking to repeat) to *damn your eyes—your blood—your soul.* But have you considered what *damnation* is? It is a word of dreadful meaning! It is to be pronounced accursed of God in the day of judgment. It is to hear Jesus say, 'Depart from me, ye cursed, into everlasting fire, prepared for the devil and his angels.' But surely you do not mean this.

It is *vulgar*. That some *gentlemen* swear, is too true; but it can never be deemed the mark of a gentleman; for it is a vice common to the vilest characters in the lowest ranks of society. It produces the most disgraceful equality—it puts the honored, the learned, the polished, and the delicate upon a level with the most ignorant and depraved.

It is *profane*. Do you believe there is a God? Have you heard that he is the high and lofty One who inhabiteth eternity, before whom angels veil their faces—whose existence and terrible Majesty even the devils believe, trembling? Go, profane sinner, hide thyself in the dust, whence thou wast originally taken. Who art thou, impiously daring to set thy mouth against the heavens? You would not swear in the presence of the governor of the state; and will you treat the King of kings, the God of the whole earth, with less respect? You would perhaps refrain from swearing many hours together, if it were to exempt you from some temporal loss, or to procure some temporal gain; and do you treat the commands, the promises, and the threatenings of the Most High God, as if they were unworthy of your notice? The sovereign command of the Governor of the universe is, SWEAR NOT AT ALL. He, who said, 'Thou shalt do no murder,' hath also said, 'Thou shalt not take the name of the Lord thy God in vain'—and the awful sanction of this command is, 'for the Lord will not hold him guiltless that taketh his name in vain:' that is, he will punish him with signal vengeance—he will make him feel the thunder of his irresistible and destructive power.

Is the reader alarmed by the terrible sanction of the precept here cited? He has reason to be alarmed—yet let him not sink into despair. 'Let the wicked forsake his way, and the unrighteous man his thoughts, and let him return unto the Lord, and he will have mercy upon him, and to our God, for he will abundantly pardon.' Isaiah, 55 : 7. 'Christ died for the ungodly.' Rom. 5 : 6. Look, by faith, for pardoning mercy through his mediation, and thou shalt find that he who had compassion on Peter, will have compassion on thee : but it is proper that if thou hast polluted thy life in time past with oaths and curses, thou shouldst now, like him, weep bitterly, and repent sincerely.

Hitherto thy tongue has been thy shame, but from this time let it become thy glory. Let it be used to the honor of Him, whose word says, 'Bless, and curse not:'—and again, 'Let no corrupt communication proceed out of your mouth;' but 'that which is good to the use of edifying, that it may minister grace to the hearers.'

Besides these horrid oaths, which shock every decent ear, there is a vicious habit, indulged by many persons, otherwise moral, and among these even ladies themselves, of a thoughtless profanation of their Maker's name, on occasions the most trivial; as when they say, 'Good God! God forbid! God bless us! O Lord,' &c. &c. Such language proceeds from want of reverence for the best of Beings, and is as direct a violation of that command, 'Thou shalt not take the name of the Lord thy God in vain,' as the most vulgar and profane oaths.

THE SWEARER AND LITTLE CHILD

In a family at Shelton lived Mr. G——, a person much given to swearing. Mrs. F——, being a serious woman, had a daughter about four years old, that was remarkably attentive to every thing of a serious nature. This child would often remark, with great horror of mind, to her mother, how Mr. G. swore; and would wish to reprove him; but for some time durst not. One time she said to her mother, "Does Mr. G. say, 'Our Father?'" (a term by which she called her prayers.) Mrs. F—— could not tell. She then said, "I will watch, and if he does, I will tell him of swearing so." She watched him, and observed him saying his prayers privately in bed. Soon after this she heard him swear bitterly; upon which she said to him, "Did you not say, 'Our Father,' this morning? How dare you swear? Do you think he will be your Father if you swear?" He answered not a word, but seemed amazed, as well he might. He did not live long after this; but he was never heard to swear again. So true is that Scripture, "Out of the mouths of babes and sucklings hast thou ordained praise!"

PUBLISHED BY THE AMERICAN TRACT SOCIETY.

No. 13

CONDITION AND CHARACTER

OF

FEMALES

In Pagan and Mohammedan Countries.

The following pages contain a simple statement of facts. Their truth is attested by men of various characters and professions—by Protestants, Catholics, Infidels, and Pagans—by geographers, travelers, and missionaries; who all agree in representing the condition of the female sex in heathen countries as degraded and miserable in the extreme.]

It is difficult, perhaps impossible, to describe the wretchedness of heathen females, without wounding the feelings of the benevolent, or shocking the delicacy of the refined. But the truth must be told. The remedy can never be applied, unless the disease is known. The charity that kindles at the tale of wo, can never act with adequate efficiency till it is made to see the pollution and guilt of 600,000,000, now buried in the death-shades of heathenism. Shall we then, however painful the sight, shrink from the contemplation of their real state? We shall only *see* what they *endure*.

I. THEIR CONDITION.

1. *They are despised.* The heathen female is viewed with contempt from the morning of her existence. The birth of a daughter, in most unevangelized countries, is an occasion of sorrow. Frowned upon by her parents and relatives, her sex is often a sufficient reason for putting an immediate end to her existence; (1)* and if she

---

* The figures refer to a list of most of the writers and books on whose authority these statements are made, which the reader will find on the last page.

is permitted to live, it is only to witness the gathering cloud of darkness and misery, which hangs over the whole course of her life. Women in all Pagan and Mohammedan countries are regarded as inferior to men, created only to be subservient to their wants and pleasures. You cannot offer a greater insult to a Mohammedan in Persia than to inquire after the female part of his family, even were they dangerously ill.(2) Such contempt for the female character, and such opinions respecting the design of woman's creation, are sanctioned by the Koran, whose doctrines command the belief, and determine the practice, of 120,000,000 of the human race.

The "sacred books" of the Hindoos, whose precepts sway the minds of 100,000,000, speak thus: "In every stage of life, woman is created to obey. At first, she yields obedience to her father and mother. When married, she submits to her husband. In old age, she must be ruled by her children. During her life, she can never be under her own control." "Women have no business with the text of the Vedu. Having therefore no evidence of law, and no knowledge of expiatory texts, sinful woman must be as foul as falsehood itself."(3) Are such sentiments confined to the pages of their "sacred books?" No; they live in the heart, and govern the life of every Hindoo. Facts in proof and illustration of this will appear in the sequel.

But are females less despised, where no "sacred books" condemn them to perpetual disgrace and subjection? Contemplate their condition in the Society Islands before the introduction of Christianity. Men were considered "rah," sacred; while women were regarded as "noah," impure, or common. Men were allowed to eat several kinds of meat, cocoa-nuts, plantains, and other articles of food offered to the gods; which females were forbidden to touch, under pain of death. The fires, also, at which the food of the men was cooked, the baskets in which it was kept, and the houses in which they ate, were sacred; females being forbidden to use the former, or enter the latter, under the same fearful penalty.(4)

2. *Their education is neglected.* This is true of every rank, wherever the Bible has not rescued woman from degradation. Indeed, must not this naturally result from

the contempt in which she is held? Among rich and poor, in the families of princes and peasants, she is alike ignorant. Probably throughout the whole Pagan and Mohammedan world there does not exist a single school for the education of females, except those established by Christian benevolence. In Mohammedan countries they are sometimes instructed in embroidery, music, dancing, and such other external accomplishments as render them fitter instruments for their master's pleasure; but not a thought is bestowed upon the cultivation of the mind. Reading and writing are to them unknown. The immortal soul is utterly neglected.(5)

In Hindostan, not twenty in as many millions are blessed with the common rudiments of Hindoo learning.

In Ceylon, when the American missionaries arrived, not one in a district containing a population of 200,000 could read. The cultivation of the female mind is thought to be not only vain, but dangerous to the welfare of society; and the direst curses are denounced against the woman, who may aspire to the dangerous eminence of being able to read and write. It is supposed that the employments proper for woman do not require education: for she can sweep the house, cook the food, collect fuel, wait on her lord, and feed her children without it; and having discharged these duties with fidelity, the whole work of life is accomplished.(3)

A missionary, in conversation with some respectable natives, who were anxious to have schools established for boys, remarked that the Christian public were desirous of doing every thing in their power to establish schools for the instruction of girls. The oldest and most intelligent of them replied, "What have we to do with them? Let them remain as they are." The missionary reminded him that females were passing into eternity ignorant of the way of salvation, and in danger of perishing for ever. "They do not know how to go to heaven," replied the native; "but they know how to go to hell, and let them go."(6)

3. *They are not at their own disposal in marriage.* In some unevangelized countries they are betrothed by their parents in infancy, or childhood; in others, they are sold at a more advanced age, at prices varying ac-

cording to their beauty or rank. A Circassian female, fourteen years of age, who had been captured by the Cossacs, being told she was to be set at liberty, begged to remain their prisoner; because she feared her parents would sell her, and she might fall into the hands of masters less humane than the Cossacs.(7)

In some nations, custom, handed down from generation to generation, till it has become as strong as law, forbids a woman to reject proposals of marriage, from whatever man they come. Pleased or displeased, she must leave her parents, and the companions of her early years, to drag out the remainder of her earthly existence in subjection to the authority of a tyrant.(5) In Hindostan, the greatest disgrace is attached to the character of any female who remains unmarried after eleven years of age. So foul is the stain, that in order to avoid it, several who had passed that age were married to an aged Brahmin, when his friends were carrying him to the Ganges to die upon its banks.(3)

4. *The practice of polygamy prevents them from enjoying the affections of their husbands, and the happiness of domestic life.* This practice, so destructive of all conjugal felicity, prevails among the higher ranks in almost every Pagan and Mohammedan country. It is authorized by the Koran, which permits every man to marry four wives. But by the rich this limitation is commonly disregarded: with them, the number varies from the lawful four, to the three hundred, five hundred, fifteen hundred, or two thousand of the Grand Seignior.(8)

In Hindostan, the Kooleen Brahmins, considered the most holy of the whole Brahminical sect, claim, as a privilege of their order, the right to marry one hundred wives. Although they do not often exercise this right to its full extent, the number of their wives is frequently not less than forty or fifty.(9) As in Mohammedan, so in Pagan countries, the number of a man's wives is limited only by his income or inclination. The evils resulting from this unhallowed practice can be better conceived than described. Totally destructive of domestic peace, it renders every female within its influence, an object of constant and bitter persecution from the other wives of her husband, or a prey to the devouring envy, hatred, and malice, which continually rankle in her own bosom.

5. *They are liable to be divorced by their husbands at any moment, and left without means of support.* In Hindostan the husband may divorce his wife at pleasure. Says the "divine Munoo," "The woman who speaks unkindly to her husband, may be superseded by another without delay." Let him address her by the title "mother," and the marriage covenant is dissolved. This is the only bill of divorce requisite.(3) When thus cast out by her husband, the customs of society prevent her from obtaining an honorable livelihood.(10) In other countries, divorce is equally easy to the husband, and extremely common.

6. *Among the higher ranks in Mohammedan and partially civilized Pagan countries, they are secluded from the society of men.* In Hindostan and China, the wife of a man of rank and wealth is continually secluded, and closely guarded. She is not permitted to eat with her husband. See never mixes with company, even at her own house; and is never seen abroad with her husband, unless on a journey. A Hindoo female seeing an European lady walking arm-in-arm with her husband, exclaimed in the utmost astonishment, "O ma! what is this? Do you see? They take their wives by the hand, and lead them through the streets without the least shame!"(1)

In the houses of the higher class, the harem, or the women's apartment, is literally a prison. It is usually so situated and constructed, that the inmates can neither be seen from without, nor enjoy any prospect but that of an adjoining garden, surrounded with lofty walls. It is never entered by any male except the husband. The wife is seldom permitted to go abroad—never without being concealed in a close carriage, or having her face so enveloped that she could not be recognized even by the most intimate friend. If she does, it is at her peril. Says Col. Phipps, in an address before the Church Missionary Society, "At Alexandria, in Egypt, I have seen a Turk, at mid-day, in the open street, cut off a woman's head for no other reason than because he saw her without a veil, and her person was not concealed in her cloak"(6)

The strictness with which the inmates of the harem are guarded, may be learned from the following particulars respecting the women belonging to the seraglio of the Grand Seignior of Turkey. "Whenever they go abroad, which is very seldom, a troop of black eunuchs convey them to the boats, which are enclosed with lattices and linen curtains; or, if their excursion is on land, they are put into close chariots, and signals are made at certain distances, that no one approach the road through which they pass under pain of death. When the Sultan permits them to walk in the gardens of the seraglio they are cleared of every thing human, and a guard of black eunuchs, with drawn sabres, march on patrol. Any individual found in the gardens, even through ignorance or inadvertence, is instantly sabred, and his head laid at the feet of the Grand Seignior, who bestows a large reward upon the guard for his fidelity."(8)

This close confinement and seclusion places the wife entirely in the husband's power. Whatever abuse she may suffer, who shall redress her wrongs? Says a traveler, while residing at Constantinople, "The body of a young woman, of surprising beauty, was found one morning near my house. She had received two wounds, one in her side, the other in her breast, and was not quite cold. Many came to admire her beauty; but no one could tell who she was, no woman's face being known out of her own family. She was buried privately, and little inquiry was made for the wretch who had imbued his hands in her blood."(11) The Pacha of Acre, in Palestine, a few years since, put to death seven of his wives at one time with his own hands.(7)

7. *In the lower ranks, and in barbarous pagan countries, they are compelled to perform the most servile labors.* In Ceylon a recent traveler was surprised to see strong and healthy men engaged in washing, ironing, preparing muslin dresses, and other similar employments, while slender females were carrying heavy burdens through the streets, or laboring in the fields.

In China, where, on account of the vast number of rivers and canals, more business is done upon the water than in any other part of the world, women are obliged, in addition to what, in other countries, are considered their proper employments, to perform the duties of boatmen.(12.) On land they may be seen performing the various parts of agricultural labor, frequently with an infant on their backs; while their husbands are gaming, or otherwise idling away their time.(13) Barrows asserts that he has frequently seen the wife dragging the light plough, or harrow, while the husband was performing the easier task of sowing the seed. A Jesuit missionary assures us, that he has seen a woman and an ass yoked together to the same plough, while the inhuman husband was guiding it and driving his team.

What labors are exacted of the wife among uncivilized pagans, let the reader learn from one of their number, who, in describing her own, has described the condition of millions of her sex. A missionary in South America reproving an Indian mother for the destruction of her female infants, she replied with tears, " I would to God, father, I would to God that my mother had by my death prevented the distresses I endure, and have yet to endure, as long as I live. Consider, father, our deplorable condition. Our husbands go out to hunt, and trouble themselves no farther. We are dragged along with one infant at the breast and another in a basket. They return in the evening without any burden. We return with the burden of our children; and though tired with a long march, must labor all night in grinding corn to make chica for them. They get drunk, and in their drunkenness beat us, draw us by the hair of the head, and tread us under foot. And what have we to comfort us for slavery that has no end? A young wife is brought in upon us, who is permitted to abuse us and our children, because we are no longer regarded. Can human nature endure such tyranny? What kindness can we show to our female children equal to that of relieving them from such oppression, more bitter a thousand times than death? I say again, would to God my mother had put me under ground the moment I was born."(14)

8. *They are held in the most degrading subjection to their husbands.* From what has already been said, who can doubt that the Mussulman female, immured in the harem, must acquiesce in the will of her master? Especially when we recollect that the precepts of the Koran direct the husband to chastise his wife for any disobedience to his commands.

In Hindostan, women are required, not only by the enactment of legislators, but by the still more binding precepts of the pagan religion, to submit to the most degrading bondage. The Padma Purana, a book regarded with greater reverence and more strictly obeyed by many a deluded Hindoo than the word of the everlasting God by multitudes of nominal Christians, speaks thus: " When in the presence of her husband, a woman must keep her eyes upon her master, and be ready to receive his commands. When he speaks, she must be quiet, and listen to nothing beside. When he calls, she must leave every thing else and attend upon him alone. A woman has no other god on earth than her husband. The most excellent of all good works she can perform is to gratify him with the strictest obedience. This should be her only devotion. Though he be aged, infirm, dissipated, a drunkard, or a debauchee, she must still regard him as her god. She must serve him with all her might, obeying him in all things, spying no defects in his character, and giving him no cause for disquiet. If he laughs, she must also laugh. If he weeps, she must also weep. If he sings, she must be in an ecstacy. She must never eat till her husband is satisfied. If he abstains, she must surely fast; and she must abstain from whatever food her husband dislikes. When he goes abroad, if he bids her go with him, she must follow; if he bids her stay, she must go no where during his absence. Until he returns she must not bathe, clean her teeth, pare her nails, nor eat more than once a day."(10) By such impious and barbarous precepts the Hindoo husband is governed in the treatment of his wife. He never speaks her name, if he adheres strictly to his religion, but calls her " my servant," or " my dog." Nor may the wife speak the name of her husband, but must call him " my lord," or " the master of the house." Liable to chastisement from her husband, she deems that a happy day in which she escapes his cruel scourge.(1) A native convert to Christianity, speaking of the effect of the Gospel upon his conduct, stated, as the most decisive evidence of his conversion, that he had entirely ceased to beat his wife.

In Burmah, the wife and grown daughters are considered, by the husband and father, as much the subjects of discipline as the younger children. Hence it is not uncommon for females of every age and rank to suffer under the tyrannical rod of those who should be their kind **protectors** and affectionate companions.(15)

9. *Their lives are not valued.* In Greenland it is customary to bury aged helpless females alive. An Arab, in the north of Africa, asked his wife for his knife. She replied that she had lent it to a neighbor. "Do you not know," said he, "that you have no business to meddle with any thing belonging to me?" She acknowledged she had not, confessed her fault, expressed her sorrow, and offered to go immediately and bring it back. He replied, "I will see if I can't have a wife who will obey my commands better. I always told you not to meddle with any thing of mine." Then levelling her to the ground with one stroke of his club, he repeated his blows till she ceased to breathe. Neither man nor woman went near them, though her cries were heard through the whole tribe. In the evening the neighboring women dug a grave scarcely of the size of her body, into which they laid the naked corpse sideways, trode it down with their feet till it was level with the surface of the earth, and covered it with a heap of stones. The only notice taken of this inhuman deed was, that the council of the tribe fined the murderer four sheep, which he was required to cook for their supper. He paid the fine, and in two weeks married again.(16)

Col. Phipps, whose name has been already mentioned, says, "The rich and powerful in Hindostan not unfrequently punish the females of their families by causing them to be sewed up in a sack and thrown by night into a river or well. I have seen a rich Hindoo who was known to have destroyed several women in this manner. When the magistrate attempted to bring the wealthy culprit to punishment, he found that the very parents and kindred of the victims had been bribed to depose in a court of justice, that they had died a natural death. I have seen taken out of large wells several human skeletons, the remains of murdered heathen females; and I wish it to be distinctly understood that what I relate are facts which have come under my own personal observation."(6)

Such is the state of women in unenlightened countries. Degraded in her condition, exposed to continual persecution and insult, deprived of all that is delightful in domestic or social life, denied the blessings of education, excluded from the knowledge of God and the hopes of heaven; she is, in short, treated as a soulless being, whose highest aim should be to gratify the caprice and obey the commands of haughty and unfeeling man. But where in all the Pagan and Mohammedan world, where among the 600,000,000 of our race, to whom the Bible is unknown, is woman the companion of man? Where, the happy wife of the affectionate husband? Where, the honored mother of grateful children? Ask the islands of the sea, or the distant east. They cannot tell. Ask the native female of America. You have heard her mourn her unhappy fate. Ask the daughter of abused Africa. Her dying shrieks have told her tale of wo. She is every where *despised, neglected, afflicted, oppressed.*

II. Their Character.

1. *They are destitute of female delicacy.*—In many heathen countries, females, as if it were not enough to be destitute of those qualities of mind and heart which are the peculiar glory of their sex, disfigure their persons in such a manner as to destroy their native beauty and grace. They seem not only incapable of distinguishing between beauty and deformity, but also to have lost all sense of female propriety. Proofs of this are given in the writings of almost every traveler who has observed their customs. Among the multitude which might be adduced, let one or two suffice.

At the Society Islands it was formerly customary for every female to provide herself, immediately after marriage, with an instrument set with rows of shark's teeth, with which, upon the death of any of the family, they cut and mangled themselves in a most horrible manner; striking the head, temples, cheeks, and breast, till the blood flowed profusely, at the same time uttering the most deafening and agonizing cries. This was their mode of expressing intense joy, as well as grief. Nor were their amusements more becoming the female character. One was wrestling, in which females, even of the highest rank, engaged, in the presence of thousands of spectators of both sexes, not only with one another, but also with men.(4)

Who can, without disgust, describe the intolerable filthiness of their dwellings and food, and their want of personal cleanliness?(17, 20)

2. *They are superstitious.*—Is not this a natural consequence of ignorance? In Hindostan it is not uncommon to see females measuring the distance from temple to temple by falling prostrate every six feet, suspending themselves by hooks through the muscular parts of their backs, and in a thousand ways tormenting themselves to obtain the favor of their gods. "As I was walking out on a certain occasion," says an American missionary, "I saw two women in the middle of the road, rolling through the mud, which was then about a foot deep. Upon my approaching them and inquiring their object, they replied, 'We were sick, and vowed to our god that, if he would make us well, we would roll to his temple.' After expostulating with them some time, I was obliged to leave them, sick and weak as they were, to their infatuation, just at night, with three fourths of their journey still before them, and with a strong probability of their perishing before the night should be far advanced. Proceeding a few steps, I met a Brahmin, and pointing to the scene, expostulated with him for keeping the females in such ignorance and in the practice of such superstitions, appealing to his conscience that he knew better. He coldly replied, 'Ah, let them alone, let them alone; that's worship just suited to their capacities.' "(1)

Their superstition and ignorance render them the dupes of the most detestable and wicked impositions from the impious Brahmins. Among them, as among the ancient Israelites, barrenness is regarded as a calamity, and deliverance from it is often the subject of prayer to their gods; some of whom are believed to have power to remove it. Applicants are told to remain in the temple during the night, performing their devotions; and, if their worship is accepted, they will be visited by the god. They return home without the least suspicion of the horrid deception practised upon them by the Brahmins, supposing they have had intercourse with the deity of the temple. At other temples the same boon is promised on conditions *still more degrading and monstrous.* These present, during the festival months, one vast scene of impurity and wickedness.(10)

3. *They are* GENERALLY *guilty of transgressing the seventh commandment.* It is needless to dwell upon this topic. To assert the truth is scarcely tolerable to a mind of delicacy and refinement. Yet listen for a moment to what candid

men have said upon the subject. " It is a fact," says Rev. Mr. Ward, " which perplexes many of the well-informed Hindoos, that, notwithstanding the wives of Europeans are seen in so many mixed companies, they remain chaste while their wives, though continually secluded, watched, and veiled, are notoriously corrupt. I recollect the observation of a gentleman who had resided twenty years in Bengal, and whose opinion on such a subject is entitled to the highest regard, that 'the infidelity of Hindoo women was so great that he scarcely thought there was an individual among them who had always been faithful to her husband. A Brahmin, who would be far from disparaging his country, affirmed that 'he did not believe there was a single female in the large cities of Bengal who had not violated the laws of chastity.'"

But, in violating the laws of morality, do they not act in perfect obedience to the dictates of their religion? Many of the gods of India are gods of impurity. Their temples are brothels; their worship, unbounded licentiousness.

In consequence of their being married in childhood, thousands of Hindoo females are left in widowhood at an early age. Both law and public opinion take from them all means of supporting themselves in respectability. Driven to desperation by the miseries that overwhelmed them, hundreds have heretofore thrown themselves upon the funeral piles of their deceased husbands. The fate of the surviving widow is often worse than death. She can never marry, although her husband may have died when she was a mere child; but must remain in cruel bondage to her sons, or her husband's relations. Many, rather than endure the obloquy and servitude of widowhood among their friends, resort to the only means in their power of procuring support, and obtain a miserable subsistence by prostitution. Among these blinded, degraded beings, this mode of life is *honorable*, compared with widowhood; and widows generally give themselves up to it, in order to avoid disgrace!(1)

4. *They are " without natural affection."*—" The very periods," says a well known missionary, " when the infant of the Christian mother is to her an object of intense solicitude and of the deepest anxiety—times of sickness and distress—are those when the heathen mother feels that in her child she has a care and a trouble which she will not

endure: she stifles its cries for a moment with her hand, hurries it into a grave already prepared, and tramples to a level the earth under which *the offspring of her bosom is struggling in the agonies of death.*"(17)

At the Society Islands, two thirds of the children were murdered in infancy. Some mothers had thus consigned to the grave five, six, eight, or even more of their offspring. " I do not recollect," says Rev. Mr. Ellis, " meeting with a female in the islands, during the whole of my residence there, who had been a mother while idolatry prevailed, and had not imbrued her hands in the blood of her offspring." A similar statement is made by another missionary, who had spent thirty years on the islands.(4)

In India, frequent transgressions of the sixth commandment result from the disregard of the seventh. Mothers add to the sins already mentioned, that of destroying in the bud the fruit of their crimes. Not only the numerous widows in that country, but wives also procure abortion. Some are accustomed to do it annually. " The Pundit," [teacher,] says Mr. Ward, " who gave me this information, supposes that 10,000 infants are thus murdered in the province of Bengal every month; appealing in support of his opinion to the fact that many females are tried for these offences in the courts of justice in every zillah of Bengal, and that it was so common an event that every child knew it." Infants are also destroyed by offering them to the Ganges, burying them alive, suspending them in baskets on trees, to be devoured by ants and birds of prey; or exposing them to be torn in pieces by crocodiles, jackals, and tigers.

In China, this practice is scarcely less common. In the city of Pekin, so great is the number of infants exposed by their unnatural mothers, that a person is employed by government to go through the streets every morning with a part and gather up the children thus exposed, and cast them, the living and the dead without distinction, into a large pit appropriated to this purpose.

Such is a faint outline of the condition and character of the females in countries unenlightened by the Gospel.

Reader, pause for a moment! Behold 300,000,000 of your fellow-beings, formed by their Creator to constitute the fairest and loveliest portion of the human race, thus despised, oppressed, and sunk in ignorance and pollution! If there dwells in your breast the generous spirit of philanthropy, you cannot but inquire, "What can be done for their relief?" The sickly sentimentalist may turn away from this scene with disgust, the careless worldling may pass by with indifference, but no one whose heart glows with Christian benevolence can sit down without an effort to relieve their wretchedness. *What then must be done?* What, to rescue pagan woman from her bondage? What, to light up in her soul the consciousness that she possesses an immortal mind? What, to free her from the bondage of tyranny and superstition, to purify her soul, and to inspire in her bosom the hopes and the joys of heaven? All past experience, the history of the world, in every age and nation, gives but one answer. There is but one sun whose rays can penetrate the darkness that envelops these unhappy beings and pour the light of life into their benighted souls— it is the Sun of Righteousness. In vain do you look to literature, to science and the arts, as an adequate remedy. The females of ancient Greece and Rome were as degraded and as wretched as the females of Turkey and Hindostan; heathenism is essentially the same in every age and in every nation. But wherever the Gospel is made known and its sacred influence is diffused, it has rescued woman from her degradation and elevated her to her proper rank and standing in society. Mark upon the map of the world those countries where the Gospel is known and understood, and you mark at the same time the only nations where the rights of woman are understood and regarded.

That the Gospel still affords an effectual remedy for all the miseries of the suffering female, you have only to look at the various missionary stations of the present day. What was the condition and the character of the female in the Society and Sandwich Islands but a few years ago? Ignorance, impurity and infanticide were their characteristics. But what has the Gospel done?

Tahiti, one of the Society Islands, affords an answer.

"The commencement of the year 1815 was distinguished in the annals of this island," says Rev. Mr. Ellis, "by changes in society affecting the intellectual, religious, and domestic character of its inhabitants generally, but especially of the females. The withering influence of idolatry began to decline and give way to the humanizing, elevating power of Christianity. The food was no longer regarded as sacred, nor the fires as hallowed. In sickness and distress, the mother, the wife, the sister, the daughter, were no longer neglected. The social circle, the family board, the domestic altar, began to diffuse their life-giving joys. Instead of cruelty and contempt, the utmost tenderness is now manifested by the husband and father toward his wife and children. When the family carry their produce to trade with vessels, the first choice among articles purchased is given to the children, the next to the wife, and the husband takes for his portion whatever may remain. The female now enjoys the pleasure resulting from culture of mind, ability to read the sacred Scriptures and write her native language. Having become a proficient in needle-work, she has laid aside the native dress, consisting merely of a piece of cloth loosely thrown about the waist, and adopted the European style. Barbarous and masculine amusements are exchanged for visits of mercy to the sick and dying. The cruel mangling, dishevelled hair, and savage yell, are superseded by the solemn prayer and the funeral procession. The mild influence of Christianity has effected the entire abolition of infanticide, and revived the parental affection and tenderness originally implanted in the human bosom. The mother, formerly guilty of destroying her helpless offspring, may now be seen coming into the place of public worship with her little babe in her arms, gazing with evident tenderness upon its smiling countenance, or reading the word of God, and kneeling in prayer with those children who, but for the Gospel, would have been ushered into eternity ere their playful smiles had won the affections of the parent's heart.(4)

Christian female, compare your situation and prospects with those of your sex in pagan lands, and then say, what has the Gospel done for you! Every thing in life, in death, and in eternity, that can inspire you with the love of existence, you derive from the Gospel. To you then, in a special manner, is it "glad tidings of great joy." Your pagan sister appeals to you, she points to her ignorance, her superstition and wickedness; she entreats you to behold her degraded condition in this life, and her hopeless prospect in the life to come! She pleads with you, by these thrilling motives, for the light you enjoy; she appeals to your sympathy, your charity, your benevolence; she urges upon you the question, upon the decision of which her all depends—WILL YOU GIVE ME THE GOSPEL?

[AUTHORITIES.—1. Rev. Mr. Bardwell.—2. Sir R. K. Porter.—3. Rev. Mr. Ward.—4. Rev. Mr. Ellis.—5. Shobert.—6. Lond. Miss. Register.—7. Rev. Dr. Clarke.—8. Edin. Encycl.—9. Rev. Dr. Buchanan.—10. Abbé Dubois.—11. Lady Montague.—12. Mr. Wood.—13. Sir G. Staunton.—14. Cecil's Miss. Sermon.—15. Mrs. Judson.—16. Capt. Paddoch.—17. Rev. Mr. Stewart.—18. Rev. Dr. Ryan.—19. Barrows.—20. Lewis and Clark.]

END.

NO. 14.

PEACE TO THE TROUBLED.
AN AUTHENTIC NARRATIVE.

Ascribed to Rev. John Griffin, Portsea, England.

CALLING at a small cottage about five miles from ——, I found a poor woman, with four children, with whom the following conversation took place :—
"Good woman," said I, "your house, I observe, is sadly out of repair: I wonder how you do in the winter season; surely you must be very uncomfortable?" "It is but a poor place, indeed, Sir," she replied, "but it is a mercy that it is no worse. It is better than we deserve; and we are under the same kind Providence in the winter as in the summer." This unexpected reply led me to desire a farther conversation on the subject of religion. "I suppose you attend on public worship?" "I hope, Sir, we make conscience of worshipping God on the Sabbath and on other days." "I hope you do; but will you allow me to ask, What is it that inclines you to a practice which so many neglect?" "I will tell you, Sir.—About four years ago I was visited with a heavy and dangerous affliction; and being apprehensive that, if I died, I should perish for ever, I became very unhappy. I had such a sense of sin, and such apprehensions of the wrath of God, that I was a terror to myself and to those about me. As my affliction increased, and the danger became more apparent, I was increasingly wretched. Conceiving myself to be approaching the brink of hell, I cried to the Lord to have mercy on my poor soul, though I could scarcely entertain any hope of obtaining it. But it was my last and only resort. My husband and neighbors could not understand my case. I was to them an object of wonder and pity. My fever increased, and I was thought to be at the point of death. Several of my poor neighbors were about me, expecting every breath to be the last. 'She is just going,' said one of them. I could not speak, but was perfectly sensible, and heard those words; at which I thought, 'if I am going, I am going to hell.' It pleased God, however, to spare me; and I hope it was in mercy. From this time the fever abated, and I gradually recovered.

But my distress of mind did not abate. I considered that though God had spared me a little while, I was still the same vile, and guilty creature. I tried to pray, but could find no relief.

"I went to the minister of the parish, and told him the exercises of my mind from the beginning. He appeared to be much surprised, and said he supposed I must have been guilty of some great wickedness; and asked me what it was. I told him that I did not understand him. 'Why,' said he, 'you must have committed theft, or drunkenness, or fraud, or been unfaithful to your husband, or done some other great sin.'—'No, Sir,' said I, 'I desire to be thankful to God, I have been kept from all these outward evils; but do you not understand my meaning, Sir? I am a vile sinner *in the sight of God;* my heart is full of evil. Every thing I do is sinful: I am a ruined and undone creature: I fear that I am going to hell—and the thoughts of these things are terrible beyond what I can express.' 'O, poor woman,' replied he, 'you must not give way to such thoughts as these; you will go out of your mind: I would advise you to go into cheerful company; and, if you can read, get some diverting books; and, by degrees you will get the better of these gloomy apprehensions.'

"'O, Sir,' said I, 'I cannot think your advice is right. Surely this would be adding sin to sin: it would be acting contrary to my conscience, and therefore would increase the weight of my distress, instead of removing it.—He then advised me to come to the sacrament, live in peace and charity with my neighbors, and said I should be happy. Accordingly I took the sacrament repeatedly, but found no relief. The preaching too was unsuitable to my case; I wanted something to relieve my mind, but knew not what would do it.

"One Sabbath my husband and I, having been at public worship in the forenoon, (there being no service in the afternoon,) I persuaded him to go and hear a Mr. T. who preached about four miles distant. My eyes followed him as he entered the house and ascended the pulpit, but O, how I was affected during his prayer! He was so full in the confession of sin, particularly of heart sins; and so earnest in his petitions for mercy to poor sinners, pleading the merits and mediation of Christ as the only ground of hope. He prayed out my very soul! Never did I feel before as I did then. My expectations were raised to a high pitch. When he took his text I was al. attention. It was the former part of the parable of the sower. He began by describing those hearers that are compared to the way-side. The ground was hard, and did not receive the seed; and partly through ignorance, inattention, and the influence of Satan on the mind, no good was produced. Next he spoke of the stony-ground hearers. On these, he observed, some effect was produced; but it was of short duration, and at last came to nothing. Then he came to speak of worldly-minded hearers, who also brought no fruit to perfection. I followed him all through his sermon; but it was an awful one to me. I thought it all belonged to me. I went home with my mind more burdened than before. I saw that I was every thing that was vile and abominable; and could not help crying out, *Wo is me, for I am undone.*

"There was one thought which afforded me some relief. I had, till now, considered my case as singular; for I had never met with any person who had the same views and feelings with myself; but now I perceived there was a person who understood the state of my mind. I reflected on the prayer, and on the sermon; and my mind was filled with thought. Understanding that Mr. T. meant to preach upon the latter part of the parable the next Sabbath, I longed for its return all the week, that I might hear it through; hoping also that he might be directed to say something which would afford relief to my soul. Well, the Sabbath returned, and a delightful one it was to me! I was again greatly impressed and affected with the prayer; and when the minister described the good ground, he showed that it was originally all wild and barren; but that it was made good by the influence of divine grace. It was broken up by convictions of sin, which entering deeply into the soul of the sinner, caused him to see the exceeding sinfulness of sin, and to feel the plague of his own heart. Thus the spirit was made tender, and the mind teachable and prepared for the reception of the Gospel. Then he opened up the great truths of salvation through Jesus Christ, and directed the hearers to him as the only Savior from sin and the curse of the law to which they were exposed. He showed that pardon of sin, peace with God, justification and sanctification, all came freely to the chief of sinners, through the atonement and righteousness of Christ: and that these, being applied by the Spirit of God, were made effectual to their conversion—were productive of good fruit in the present life and in the life to come, of everlasting joy.

"I rejoiced that it was so. It was just such a salvation as I needed. My heart was filled with comfort—I was led to see the way of escape—a foundation was laid for my hope to rest upon—I returned home with joy; and could now attend to my family affairs with cheerfulness. From this time I attended constantly at the same place, and that with great delight; every Sabbath was a feast-day to me; and I have this additional comfort that my husband also attends constantly and cheerfully with me; and I trust that he is also converted to Christ. He now prays in his family, and we never lived so happily as we do now."

"I assure you," said I, "that your story is not a little interesting to me, and I hope you will serve the Lord faithfully." "I hope so," said she, "surely I can say from experience, that 'wisdom's ways are ways of pleasantness, and all her paths are peace.'"

"Well, good woman, can you read?" "Yes, Sir, I can now read better than I could before." "And what good books have you got?" "I have but one, Sir; and that is the Testament." "Let me look at it, if you please," "Dear Sir, I am ashamed to show it to you, it is such a tattered piece; for before I knew the worth of it, I let my children play with it; but now I take it to church with me, and when the minister mentions a text that is in it, I turn to it and read it. Handing me the book, she added, "*There is all St. John in it, Sir; and there is delightful reading in St. John!*" "Yes, good woman, there is; and I am glad that you have tasted the sweetness of it. Bless God that he has ever shown you the evil of your heart, and brought you to accept of Christ. Keep near the throne of grace. Train up your children in the fear of God, and may he be your eternal portion."

Putting into her hand the means of buying a new Bible and Testament, I then took my leave, trusting that, if I saw her not again on earth, I should meet her, through grace, in a better world.

PUBLISHED BY THE AMERICAN TRACT SOCIETY.

No. 15.
THE DOWNWARD COURSE OF SIN.

BY REV. ANDREW FULLER.

When our Savior spake of his making men *free*, the Jews were offended. It hurt their pride to be represented as slaves; yet slaves they were—and such is every sinner, however insensible of it, till Christ has made him free. And the longer he continues in this state, the more he is entangled, and the greater is the difficulty of making his escape. Sin is a master that will not suffer its slaves to rest, but is always hurrying them on from one thing to another, till, having finished its operations, it bringeth forth death. The way of sin is a way in which there is no standing still: it is a down hill-road, in which every step gives an accelerated force till you reach the bottom. Such is the import of those emphatic words of the apostle, "Ye were servants to iniquity, unto iniquity."

To be *a servant to iniquity* is descriptive of the state of every unconverted sinner. All may not be subject to the same kind of sins: one may be enslaved to drunkenness, another to uncleanness, another to covetousness, another to fashion, and another to self-righteous pride: but these are only different forms of servitude, suited to different tempers and constitutions: all are servants to iniquity; and all who continue such, are impelled, in a manner, to go on in their work, "servants to iniquity, unto iniquity." The proofs of this tendency to progression will appear in the following remarks.

1. He that yields himself a servant to sin, in any one of its forms, admits *a principle which opens the door to sin in every other form.* This principle is, that the authority of God is not to be regarded, when it stands in the way of our inclinations. If you admit this principle, there is nothing to hinder you from going into any evil which your soul lusteth after. You may not indeed be guilty of every bad practice; but, while such is the state of your mind, it is not the fear of God, but a regard to man, or a concern for your own interest, safety, or reputation, that restrains you. If you indulge in theft, for instance, you would, with the same un-

concern, commit adultery, robbery, or murder; provided you were tempted to such things, and could commit them with the hope of escaping punishment. It is thus that he, who transgresses the law "in one point, is guilty of all;" for He that forbids one sin, forbids all; and a deliberate offence against Him, in one particular, is as really a rejection of his authority as in many.

Moreover, if the mind be unrestrained by the fear of God, a regard for man will have but a feeble hold for it. Sin, in various shapes, will be frequently indulged in secret; and being so indulged, it will soon break out into open vices: for it is not in the power of a man, with all his contrivances, long to conceal the ruling dispositions of his soul. When king Saul had once disregarded the divine authority in his treatment of the Amalekites, there were no bounds to the evil workings of his mind; full of jealousy, envy, and malignity, he murders a whole city of innocent men, repairs to a witch for counsel, and at last puts an end to his miserable life.

2. Every sin we commit, goes to *destroy the principle of resistance*, and produce a kind of desperate carelessness. Purity of mind, like cleanliness of apparel, is accompanied with a desire of avoiding every thing that might defile; and even where this has no place, conscience, aided by education and example, is a great preservative against immoral and destructive courses; but if we once plunge into the vices of the world, emulation is extinguished. The child that is accustomed to rags and filth, loses all shame, and feels no ambition to appear neat and decent.

The first time a person yields to a particular temptation, it is not without some struggles of conscience; and when it is past, his soul is usually smitten with remorse; and, it may be, he thinks he shall never yield again; but, temptation returning, and the motive to resist being weakened, he becomes an easy prey to the tempter. And now the clamors of conscience subside, his heart grows hard, and his mind desperate. "There is no hope," saith he; "I have loved strangers, and after them I will go." Under the first workings of temptation he sets bounds to himself, "Hitherto I will go, and no farther;" but now, all such resolutions are of no account. The insect entangled in the spider's web can do nothing; every effort it makes only winds another thread round its wings; and after a few ineffectual struggles, it falls a prey to the destroyer.

3. Every sin we commit, not only goes to destroy the principle of resistance, but produces *an increased desire for the repetition of it;* and thus, like half an army going over to the enemy, operates both ways against us, weakening our scruples and strengthening our propensities. This is manifest in such sins as drunkenness, gambling, and fornication. It is one of the deceits of sin, to promise that, if we will but grant its wishes in this or that particular, it will ask no more; or to persuade its deluded votaries, that indulgence will assuage the torrent of desire; but, though this may be the case for a short time, sin will return with redoubled violence. It rises in its demands from every concession you make to it. He that has entered the paths of the destroyer can tell, from experience, that it is a thousand times more difficult to recede, than to refrain from entering. The thirst of the leech at the vein, and of the drunkard at his bottle, is but a faint emblem of the burnings of desire in the mind, in these stages of depravity.

4. If we yield to one sin, we shall find ourselves under a kind of necessity of *going into other sins, in order to hide or excuse it.* This is a truth so evident, that it needs only to be stated, in order to be admitted. Examples abound both in Scripture and common life. When sin is committed, the first thing that suggests itself to the sinner is, if possible, to conceal it; or if that cannot be, to excuse it. Adam first strove to hide himself among the trees of the garden, and when this refuge failed him, he alleged it was "the woman," and the woman, too, "that God gave to be with him," who tempted him to do as he did. Nearly the same course was pursued by David. Having committed a grievous crime, he first betakes himself to intrigue, in hopes to cover it; and when this failed him, he has recourse to murder; and this being accomplished, the horrible event is, with an air of affected resignation, ascribed to Providence: "The sword devoureth one as well as another." Nor is this the only instance wherein that which has begun in a wanton look, has ended in blood. What numbers of innocent babes, the offspring of illicit intercourse, are murdered, and one or both of their unhappy parents executed, for that which was resorted to merely as a cover for their wicked practices!

5. Every act of sin tends to form a *sinful habit;* or, if already formed, to strengthen it. Single acts of sin are as drops of water, which possess but little force; but, when multiplied, they become a mighty stream, which bears down all before it. The *drunkard* has no natural thirst for strong liquors. Some worldly trouble, or the love of loose company, first brought him to make free with them, but having once contracted the habit, though he knows he is every day wasting his substance, shortening his life, and ruining his soul, yet he cannot desist. Even under the power of stupefaction, he calls for more drink: his dreams betray his lusts: "They have smitten me," says he, "and I was not sick: they have beaten me, and I felt it not. When shall I awake? I will seek it yet again."—The *gamester*, at the first, thought but little of doing what he now does. He fell into company, it may be, with a card party, or had heard of a lucky adventure in the lottery, or knew a person who had made a fortune by a successful speculation in the stocks; so he resolves to try a little of it himself. He succeeds. He tries again; ventures deeper and deeper, with various success. His circumstances become embarrassed; yet having begun, he must go on. One more great adventure he hopes will recover all, and free him from his difficulties. He loses; his family is ruined; his creditors are wronged; and himself, it is not impossible, is driven to such means of support as shall bring him to an untimely end. The *debauchee* was once, it may be, a sober man. His illicit connexions might originate in what were thought, at the time, very innocent familiarities. But having once invaded the laws of chastity, he sets no bounds to desire: "His eyes are full of adultery, and he cannot cease from sin."

6. When the sinner becomes thus besotted in the ways of sin, there are commonly a *number of circumstances and considerations, beside his own attachment to it, which entangle his soul, and, if infinite mercy interpose not, prevent his escape.* He has formed connexions among men like himself. His interest, he thinks, will suffer. His companions will reproach him. The world will laugh at him. Many, in such circumstances, have been the subjects of strong convictions, have shed many tears, and professed great desire to return from their evil courses; yet, when it has come to the test, they have been too weak to recede:

having begun and gone on so far, they cannot relinquish it now, whatever be the consequence.

Reader, is this, or something like it, your case? Permit a well-wisher to your soul to be free with you. Be assured, you must return, or perish for ever, and that in a little time. Infidels may tell you there is no danger; but when they come to die, they have commonly discovered that they did not believe their own assertions. "Verily there is a God that judgeth in the earth;" and before him you must shortly give an account. Will you plunge yourself into the pit, whence there is no redemption? That tremendous punishment is represented as not prepared originally for you, but for the devil and his angels. If you go thither, you in a manner take the kingdom of darkness by force.

Let me add, it is not enough for you to return, unless, in so doing, you return to *God.* "Ye have returned, but not unto *me,*" saith the Lord. If I felt only for your credit and comfort in this world, I might content myself with warning you to break off your outward vices, and cautioning you against the inlets of future evils. Animals, though void of reason, yet, through mere instinct, fly from present danger. "In vain is the net spread in the sight of a bird." The fish of the sea avoid the whirlpool. And shall a man go, with his eyes open, into the net? Will he sail, unconcerned, into the vortex of destruction? But it is not from present danger only, or chiefly, that I would warn you to flee. My heart's desire and prayer to God for you is, that you may be saved from the wrath to come. Know then, that, though you should escape the grosser immoralities of the world, yet you may be still in your sins, and exposed to eternal ruin. Your danger does not lie merely, or mainly, in open vices. Satan may be cast out with respect to these, and yet retire into the strong holds of proud self-satisfaction.

It is not the outward spot that will kill you; but the inward disease, whence it proceeds. "From within, even from the heart, proceed evil thoughts, murders, adulteries, fornications, thefts, and blasphemies." Every outbreaking of sin in your life is a proof of the inward corruption of your nature. If this fountain be not healed, in vain will you go about to purify the streams. I mean not to dissuade you from "breaking off your sins," but to persuade you to "break them off by righteousness." But the only way in which this is to be done, is that to which our Savior directed in his preaching—" Repent, and believe the Gospel." All reformation, short of this, is only an exchange of vices. But if you can, guilty and unworthy as you are, renouncing all other hopes and dependencies, believe in Christ, you shall be saved. His blood was shed for sinners, even the chief of sinners. His obedience unto death was so well-pleasing to God, that any sinner, whatever has been his conduct or character, that comes to him in *his* name, pleading his righteousness, and his only, will be accepted for his sake. He has not only obeyed and died for such as you, but is now at the right hand of God, carrying into effect the great ends of his incarnation, life, and death. " Wherefore he is able to save to the uttermost, all them that come unto God by him, seeing he ever liveth to make intercession for them."

If, Reader, thou canst embrace this doctrine, it will heal thy malady. If, from thine heart, thou canst receive salvation as of mere grace, through the redemption of Jesus Christ, it is thine own. If thou canst confess thy sins upon the head of this sacrifice, " God is faithful and just to forgive thy sins, and to cleanse thee from all unrighteousness." God makes nothing of thy reformations, prayers, or tears, as a reason why he should accept and save thee; but every thing of what his Son has done and suffered. If thou canst be of his mind, making nothing of them in thy pleas and hopes for mercy, but every thing of Him in whom he is well-pleased, eternal life is before thee. And at what time this doctrine shall give peace to thy troubled soul, it shall purify thy heart in such a manner, that all thy former ways shall become hateful unto thee, and sobriety, righteousness, and godliness, shall be thy delight.

But if thy heart be still hardened in sin; if Jesus, and salvation by grace, through his name, contain nothing attractive, but rather what is offensive to thy mind; know this, "there is no other name given under heaven, among men, by which thou canst be saved;" and the remembrance of thy having once in thy life, at least, been told the truth, may not a little imbitter thy dying moments.

Happy are all they who, returning in the name of Jesus Christ to his Father and their Father, his God and their

God, are made free from sin, and have their fruit unto holiness! *They* too are *progressive,* but it is in a course the opposite of that which has been set before the reader. "The righteous shall hold on his way, and he that hath clean hands shall wax stronger and stronger." The service of God shall become more easy to him; truth shall appear more evident; the marks of his conversion shall multiply; his character shall strike its roots deeper; the hope of his perseverance shall continually renew its strength; and sorrow and joy, retirement and society, the dispensations of Providence and the ordinary means of grace, shall all contribute to make him more meet for the "inheritance of the saints in light."

Rev. Dr. Witherspoon has suggested these several steps in the downward course of sin.

1. Men enter and initiate themselves in a vicious practice *by smaller sins.* Heinous sins are too alarming for the conscience of a young sinner; and therefore he only ventures upon such as are smaller, at first. Every particular kind of vice creeps in in this gradual manner.

2. Having once begun in the ways of sin, he *ventures upon something greater and more daring.* His courage grows with his experience. Now, sins of a deeper die do not look so frightful as before. Custom makes every thing familiar. No person who once breaks over the limits of a clear conscience knows where he shall stop.

3. Open sins soon *throw a man into the hands of ungodly companions.* Open sins determine his character, and give him a place with the ungodly. He shuns the society of good men, because their presence is a restraint, and their example a reproof to him. There are none with whom he can associate, but the ungodly.

4. In the next stage, the sinner *begins to feel the force of habit and inveterate custom:* he becomes rooted and settled in an evil way. Those who have been long habituated to any sin, how hopeless is their reform! One single act of sin seems nothing; but one after another imperceptibly

strengthens the disposition, and enslaves the unhappy criminal beyond the hope of recovery.

5. The next stage in a sinner's course is *to lose the sense of shame, and sin boldly and openly.* So long as shame remains, it is a great drawback. But it is an evidence of an uncommon height of impiety, when natural shame is gone.

6. Another stage in the sinner's progress is to harden himself so far as to *sin without remorse of conscience.* The frequent repetition of sins stupifies the conscience. They, as it were, weary it out, and drive it to despair. It ceases all its reproofs, and, like a frequently discouraged friend, suffers the infatuated sinner to take his course. And hence,

7. Hardened sinners often come *to boast and glory in their wickedness.* It is something to be beyond shame; but it is still more to glory in wickedness, and esteem it honorable. Glorious ambition indeed!

8. Not content with being wicked themselves, they *use all their arts and influence to make others wicked also.* They are zealous in sinning, and industrious in the promotion of the infernal cause. They extinguish the fear of God in others, and laugh down their own conscientious scruples. And now,

9. To close the scene, those who have thus far hardened themselves, are *given up of God to judicial blindness of mind and hardness of heart.* They are marked out as vessels of wrath fitted to destruction. This is the consequence of their obstinacy. They are devoted to the judgment they deserve.

Reader! view it with terror.

PUBLISHED BY THE

AMERICAN TRACT SOCIETY,

No. 150 Nassau-street, New-York.

D. Fanshaw, Printer.

PIOUS RESOLUTIONS.

[The following Resolutions were written by one who, there is reason to believe, had made great progress in the christian life. They are recommended to the serious and repeated perusal of every reader.]

I WILL regard the favour and everlasting enjoyment of God, as the end of all my plans; and study to make the consideration of them influence, as much as possible, the minutest actions of my life.

I will regard the obedience, sacrifice, mediation, and intercession of Christ, as the only procuring cause of all those spiritual blessings which conduce to that end, as the pardon of sin, peace with God, and the sanctifying influence of his Spirit.

I will continually keep in mind my obligations to walk in Christ's steps, and to be holy as he is holy, without which I shall in vain hope to enter heaven; and I will ever pray for the Spirit of God, in the belief, that through his operation alone, can this holy frame be produced.

I will cultivate an habitual sense of God's presence, and of my accountableness to him; of the shortness of time, and of my obligations to improve it.

I will study for the future to appear well, not so much in the sight of man, as in that of God; and to that end, will be particularly watchful against the love of human praise or distinction, and the fear of shame; desisting from my purpose when I feel these to be my only motives, and endeavouring by prayer to overcome them when I perceive them to mix with such as are more pure.

I will consider love to God and zeal for his glory as my highest duties, and study to improve daily in these divine affections; and I will judge of my progress in them, not by transient fervours of the mind, but by my habitual temper, by my punctual performance of the self-denying duties of Christianity, by my cheerful acquiescence in all God's dispensations, and by the love, the humility, and the meekness, which I am enabled to exercise to those around me.

I will study to live a life of dependence on Christ, and

of faith in his word; making it the sole and exclusive measure of my belief and practice.

I will particularly study to restrain all wanderings of the mind in the public and private exercises of God's worship; to banish, as much as I can, vain and worldly conversation, and vain and worldly thoughts from my mind and lips, on the Lord's day; and to give all my household the time requisite for hallowing it.

I will guard against formality and vanity, especially in family worship; and strive to fit myself, by previous reflection and prayer, for its due performance.

I will be particularly guarded against the intrusion of impure thoughts. I will turn away my eyes from beholding what might lead to them, shut my ears against polluting conversation, and restrain my tongue from every licentious word; and I will carefully avoid every circumstance which I know to have formerly excited improper feelings, and forbid my thoughts to dwell for a moment on past scenes of sensual pleasure.

I will watch against every rising of covetous desire, and while I carefully repress all tendency to improper expense, or the careless profusion of any of God's gifts, I will seek out proper objects with whom to share those good things of which God has made me the steward, and of which he will require an account.

I will no longer put off, or leave the business of the present day or hour to some future time, but will apply myself to it, deny myself to sloth and the love of ease, and exercise a constant and self-denying attention to what is my proper work.

I will keep truth inviolate, in the smallest as well as in the greatest matters.

I will in no case affect knowledge which I have not

I will read no book but with attention; and I will read none which tends to inflame the mind, or to excite improper sentiments. I will be ready to communicate and also to receive knowledge; and I will be open to conviction, ever receiving correction and reproof meekly and thankfully, never questioning merely for the sake of dispute, nor ever retorting upon any reprover.

I will watch against all superciliousness in look or manner, all sourness of mind in dispute, all impatience of contradiction in my intercourse with all, whether common acquaintance, or the most intimate relative, as a wife, brother, &c. And I will listen with patience and kindness to the arguments and reasonings of others, however impertinent they may appear at the moment.

I will also watch against a selfish, exclusive attachment to my own comfort, and study to be equally solicitous for the comfort of others, and to repress every rising of impatience at the trouble which this may occasion me.

I will endeavour to cultivate a temper of more benignity towards all; and I will attend more to the outward expression of love and kindness, never allowing passion to dictate what I may say, but studying to act by others as I could reasonably wish to be dealt with.

I will watch particularly against all hastiness of spirit towards inferiors, and especially those who need my help; and will listen composedly to their representations, and render them all the justice and all the kindness in my power, consistently with my other duties.

I will not only not use railing words to any, but I will guard against every circumstance, in look and manner, which might tend unnecessarily to wound the feelings of others.

I will not allow the ill conduct of others towards me to lessen my kindness and good will to them.

I will not chide or correct my children in passion, nor use peevish language towards them; and previous to correcting them, I will use prayer to God; and I will not be turned aside by false pity, or by indolence, from duly correcting their faults, which I will ever remind them to be sins against God.

I will never use threatening language, but by way of prevention, and without any mixture of passion; and I will study not to allow my voice to be elevated above its ordinary tone, in talking with any.

I will guard against all excess in eating or drinking; never allowing complaisance for any to mar for a moment the clear exercise of my reason, or discompose my quiet, by leading me beyond the bounds of strict moderation.

I will, from this time forward, when not hindered by unavoidable circumstances, regularly devote at least one half hour in the morning, and one half hour in the evening, exclusively to those concerns which lie between God and my soul.

I will read every day in private a portion of Scripture, with meditation and prayer.

I will consider the study of my heart as one main business of my life; and I will enter every evening, if possible, into a serious review of the past day, and of the manner in which I have kept this engagement; and into a solemn consideration of the fitness of my soul for entering on the eternal world.

I will anxiously study to reform whatever I shall find amiss; and of whatever defect in the performance of my duty I may be sensible, whatever corrupt propensity I may discover, of whatever sinful thoughts, words, or actions, I may have been guilty, I will endeavour to improve them as an incitement more deeply to repent of sin, more highly to value the love of my crucified Redeemer, and more implicitly to rely on his atoning merits for pardon and acceptance, and on the sanctifying grace of the Holy Spirit, for victory over sin, and advancement in purity and holiness of heart and life.

May the Spirit of all grace fill my heart with heavenly wisdom, and form me anew in my Saviour's image. May the bright example of Jesus Christ be ever before my eyes; and may his lessons be ever graven on my heart. Through his blood may my defiled and guilty conscience be cleansed from all sin. May he reign in my heart, and ever continue the object of my ardent desires, of my undeviating reliance, of my cheerful homage, of my lively and active gratitude, and of my highest love. And may the God and Father of our Lord Jesus Christ, the Father of everlasting compassion, the God of grace and peace, sanctify me wholly; and through the blood of the everlasting covenant make me perfect in every good work to do his will, that I may be enabled ever to render to the Father, Son, and Spirit, one God, the praise and glory of all I have, am, or hope for. Amen.

PUBLISHED BY THE
AMERICAN TRACT SOCIETY

NO. 17.

PARLEY THE PORTER

AN ALLEGORY.

BY MRS. HANNAH MORE.

As he fell, he cried out, "O my master, I die a victim to my unbelief in thee, and to my own vanity and imprudence."—*See page* 12.

PUBLISHED BY THE

AMERICAN TRACT SOCIETY

AND SOLD AT THEIR DEPOSITORY, NO. 150 NASSAU-STREET, NEAR THE CITY-HALL, NEW-YORK; AND BY AGENTS OF THE SOCIETY, ITS BRANCHES, AND AUXILIARIES, IN THE PRINCIPAL CITIES AND TOWNS

VOL 1.   IN THE UNITED STATES.

PARLEY THE PORTER.

There was once a certain gentleman, who had a house or castle, situated in the midst of a great wilderness, but enclosed in a garden. Now, there was a band of robbers in the wilderness, who had a great mind to plunder and destroy the castle, but they had not succeeded in their endeavours, because the master had given strict orders to "*watch without ceasing.*" To quicken their vigilance, he used to tell them that their care would soon have an end; that though the nights they had to watch were dark and stormy, yet they were but few; the period of resistance was short—that of rest, eternal.

The robbers, however, attacked the castle in various ways. They tried at every avenue; watched to take advantage of every careless moment; looked for an open door, or a neglected window. But though they often made the bolts shake, and the windows rattle, they could never greatly hurt the house, much less get into it. Do you know the reason? It was because the servants were never off their guard. They heard the noises plain enough, and used to be not a little frightened, for they were aware both of the strength and perseverance of the enemy. But what seemed rather odd to some of these servants—the gentleman used to tell them, that while they continued to be afraid they would be safe; and it passed into a sort of proverb in that family, " Happy is he that feareth always." Some of the servants, however, thought this a contradiction.

One day when the master was going from home, he called his servants all together, and spoke to them as follows: 'I will not repeat to you the directions I have so often given you; they are all written down in THE BOOK OF LAWS, of which every one of you has a copy. Remember, it is a very short time that you are to remain in this castle; you will soon remove to my more settled habitation, to a more durable house, not made with hands. As that house is never exposed to any attack, so it never stands in need of any repair; for that country is never infested by any sons of violence. Here you are servants; there you will be princes. But mark my words, and you will find the same truth in THE BOOK OF MY LAWS: Whether you will ever attain to *that* house, will depend on the manner in which you defend yourselves in *this*. A stout vigilance for a short time will secure you certain happiness for ever. But every thing depends on your present exertions. Don't complain, and take advantage of my absence, and call me a hard master, and grumble that you are placed in the midst of a howling wilderness without peace or security. Say not, that you are exposed to temptations without power to resist them. You have some difficulties, it is true, but you have many helps, and many comforts to make this house tolerable, even before you get to the other. Yours is not a hard service; and if it were, " the time is short." You have arms, if you will use them; and doors, if you will bar them; and strength, if you will use it. I would defy all the attacks of the robbers without, if I could depend on the fidelity of the people within. If the thieves ever get in and destroy the house, it must be by the connivance of one of the family. *For mere outward attack can never destroy this castle, if there be no traitor within.* You will stand or fall, as you regard this fact. If you are finally happy, it will be by my grace and favour; if you are ruined, it will be your own fault.'

When the gentleman had done speaking, every servant repeated his assurance of attachment and firm allegiance to his master. But among them all, not one was so vehement and loud in his professions as old Parley, the Porter. Parley, indeed, it was well known, was always talking, which exposed him to no small danger; for, as he was the foremost to promise, so he was the slackest to perform. And, to speak the truth, though he was a civil spoken fellow, his master was more afraid of him, with all his professions, than he was of the rest who professed less. He knew that Parley was vain, credulous, and self-sufficient; and he always apprehended more danger from Parley's impertinence, curiosity, and love of novelty, than even from the stronger vices of some of his other servants. The rest, indeed, seldom got into any difficulty of which Parley was not the cause in some shape or other.

I am sorry to be obliged to confess, that though Parley was allowed every refreshment, and all the needful rest which the nature of his place permitted, yet he thought it very hard to be forced to be so constantly on duty. 'Nothing but watching,' said Parley; 'I have, to be sure, many pleasures, and meat sufficient, and plenty of chat in virtue of my office; and I pick up a good deal of news of the comers and goers by day; but it is hard that at night I must watch as narrowly as a house-dog, and yet let in no company without orders, only because there is said to be a few straggling *robbers* here in the wilderness, with whom my master does not care to let us be acquainted. He pretends to make us vigilant through fear of the robbers; but I suspect it is only to make us mope alone. A merry companion, and a mug of beer, would make the night pass cheerly.' Parley, however, kept all these thoughts to himself, or uttered them only when no one heard; for talk he must. He began to listen to the nightly whistling of the robbers under the windows, with rather less alarm than formerly; and was sometimes so tired of watching, that he thought it was even better to run the risk of being robbed once, than to live always in fear of robbers.

There were certain bounds in which the gentleman allowed his servants to walk and divert themselves at all proper seasons. A pleasant garden surrounded the castle, and a thick hedge separated this garden from the wilderness which was infested by the robbers, in which they were permitted to amuse themselves. The master advised them always to keep within these bounds. 'While you observe this rule,' said he, 'you will be safe, and well; and you will consult your own safety, as well as show your love to me, by not venturing even to the extremity of your bounds: he who goes as far as he dares, always shows a wish to go farther than he ought, and commonly does so.'

It was remarkable, that the nearer these servants kept to the castle, and the farther from the *hedge*, the more ugly the wilderness appeared. And the nearer they approached the forbidden bounds, their own home appeared more dull, and the wilderness more delightful. And this the master knew when he gave his orders; for he never either did or said any thing without a good reason. And when his servants sometimes desired an explanation of the reason, he used to tell them they would understand it when they came to *the other house:* for it was one of the pleasures of that house, that it would explain all the mysteries of this; and any little obscurities in the master's conduct, would then be made quite plain.

Parley was the first that promised to keep clear of the *hedge;* and yet was often seen looking as near it as he dared. One day he ventured close up to the hedge, put two or three stones one on another, and tried to peep over. He saw one of the robbers strolling as near as could be on the forbidden side. This man's name was Flatterwell, a smooth, civil man, " whose words were softer than butter, having war in his heart." He made several low bows to Parley.

Now Parley knew so little of the world, that he actually concluded all robbers must have an ugly look, which should frighten you at once ; and coarse, brutal manners, which would at first sight show they were enemies. He thought, like a poor ignorant fellow as he was, that this mild, specious person could not be one of the band. Flatterwell accosted Parley with the utmost civility, which put him quite off his guard; for Parley had no notion that he could be an enemy who was so soft and civil. For an open foe, he would have been prepared. Parley, however, after a little discourse, drew this conclusion, either that Mr. F. could not be one of the gang, or that if he was, the robbers themselves could not be such monsters as his master had described; and therefore it was folly to be afraid of them.

Flatterwell began, like a true adept in his art, by lulling all Parley's suspicions asleep; and instead of openly abusing his master, which would have opened Parley's eyes at once, he pretended rather to commend him in a general way, as a person who meant well himself; but was too apt to suspect others. To this Parley assented. The other then ventured to hint by degrees, that though the gentleman might be a good master in the main, yet he must say he was a little strict, and a little stingy, and not a little censorious. That he was blamed by the *gentlemen in the wilderness* for shutting his house against good company, and his servants were laughed at by people of spirit, for submitting to the gloomy life of the castle, and the insipid pleasures of the garden; instead of ranging in the wilderness at large.

'It is true enough,' said Parley, who was generally of the opinion of the person he was talking with, 'my master *is* rather harsh and close. But, to own the truth, all the barring, and locking, and bolting, is to keep out a set of gentlemen, who, he assures us, are *robbers*, and who are waiting for an opportunity to destroy us. I hope, no offence, Sir, but by your livery, I suspect you, Sir, are one of the gang, he is so much afraid of.'

Flatterwell. Afraid of me? Impossible, dear Mr. Parley. You see I do not look like an enemy. I am unarmed: what harm can a plain man like me do?

Parley. Why that is true enough. Yet my master says, that if we were once to let you into the house, we should be ruined, soul and body.

Flatterwell. I am sorry, Mr. Parley, that so sensible a man as you, are so deceived. This is mere prejudice. He knows we are cheerful, entertaining people; foes to gloom and superstition; and therefore, he is so morose, he will not let you get acquainted with us.

Parley. Well, he says you are a band of thieves, gamblers, murderers, drunkards, and atheists.

Flatterwell. Don't believe him; the worst we should do, perhaps, is, we might drink a friendly glass with you to your master's health; or play an innocent game of cards just to keep you awake, or sing a cheerful song with the maids: now is there any harm in all this?

Parley. Not the least in the world. And I begin to think there is not a word of truth in all my master says.

Flatterwell. The more you know us, the more you will like us. But I wish there was not this ugly hedge between us. I have a great deal to say, and am afraid of being overheard.

Parley was now just going to give a spring over the hedge, but checked himself, saying, 'I dare not come on your side, there are people about, and every thing is carried to my master.' Flatterwell saw by this, that his new friend was kept on his own side of the hedge by fear, rather than by principle, and from that moment he made sure of him. 'Dear Mr. Parley,' said he, 'if you will allow me the honour of a little conversation with you, I will call under the window of your lodge this evening. I have something to tell you greatly to your advantage. I admire you exceedingly. I long for your friendship; our whole brotherhood is ambitious of being known to so amiable a person.'—'O dear,' said Parley, 'I shall be afraid of talking to you at night, it is so against my master's orders.— But did you say you had something to tell me to my advantage?'

Flatterwell. Yes, I can point out to you how you may be a richer, a merrier, and a happier man. If you will admit me to-night under the window, I will convince you that 'tis prejudice and not wisdom which makes your master bar his door against us; I will convince you that the mischief of a *robber,* as your master scurrilously calls us, is only in the name; that we are your true friends, and only mean to promote your happiness.

'Don't say *we,*' said Parley, 'pray come alone, I would not see the rest of the gang for the world; but I think there can be no great harm in talking to *you* through the bars, if you come alone; but I am determined not to let you in. Yet I can't say but I wish to know what you can tell me so much to my advantage; indeed if it is for my good, I ought to know it.'

Flatterwell. (Going out, turns back.) Dear Mr. Parley, there is one thing I had forgot. I cannot get over the hedge at night without assistance. You know there is a secret in the nature of that hedge; you in the house may get over to us in the wilderness, of your own accord; but we cannot get to your side by our own strength. You must look about to see where the hedge is thinnest, and then set to work to clear away here and there a little bough for me; it wont be missed; and if there is but the smallest hole made on your side, those on ours can get through; otherwise we do but labour in vain. To this Parley made some objection, through the fear of being seen. Flatterwell replied, that the smallest hole from within would be sufficient, for he could then work his own way. 'Well,' said Parley, 'I will consider of it. To be sure I shall even then be equally safe in the castle, as I shall have all the bolts, bars, and locks between us, so it will make but little difference.'

'Certainly not,' said Flatterwell, who knew it would make all the difference in the world. So they parted with mutual protestations of regard. Parley went home, charmed with his new friend. His eyes were now clearly opened as to his master's prejudices against the *robbers;* and he was convinced there was more in the name, than in the thing. 'But,' said he, 'though Mr. Flatterwell is certainly an agreeable companion, he may not be so safe an inmate. There can, however, be no harm in talking at a distance, and I certainly wont let him in.'

Parley, in the course of the day, did not forget his promise to thin the hedge of separation a little. At first he only tore off a handful of leaves, then a little sprig, then he broke away a bough or two. It was observable, the larger the breach became, the worse he began to think of his master; and the better of himself. Every peep he took through the broken hedge, increased his desire to get out into the wilderness; and made the thoughts of the castle more irksome to him.

He was continually repeating to himself, 'I wonder what Mr. Flatterwell can have to say so much to my advantage. I see he does not wish to hurt my master, he only wishes to serve me.' As the hour of meeting, however, drew near, the master's orders now and then came across Parley's thoughts. So to divert them, he took THE BOOK. He happened to open it at these words, "My son, if sinners entice thee, consent thou not." For a moment his heart failed him. 'If this admonition should be sent on purpose,' said he,—'but no, 'tis a bugbear. My master told me that if I went to the bounds I should get over the hedge. Now, I went to the utmost limits, and did not get over.' Here conscience put in, 'Yes, but it was because you were watched.'—'I am sure,' continued Parley, 'one may always stop where one will; and this is only a trick of my master's to spoil sport; so I will even hear what Mr. Flatterwell has to say so much to my advantage. I am not obliged to follow his counsels, but there can be no harm in hearing them.'

Flatterwell prevailed on the rest of the robbers to make no public attack on the castle that night.

'My brethren,' said he, 'you now and then fail in your schemes, because you are for violent beginnings, while my soothing, insinuating measures, hardly ever miss. You come blustering, and roaring, and frighten people, and set them on their guard. You inspire them with terror of *you*, while my whole scheme is to make them think well of *themselves*, and ill of their master. If I once get them to entertain hard thoughts of him, and high thoughts of themselves, my business is done, and they fall plump into my snares. So let this delicate affair alone to me. Parley is a softly fellow, he must not be frightened, but cajoled. He is the very sort of man to succeed with, and worth a hundred of your sturdy, sensible fellows. With them we want strong arguments, and strong temptations; but with such fellows as Parley, in whom vanity and sensuality are the leading qualities, (as, let me tell you, is the case with far the greater part,) flattery, and the promise of ease and pleasure, will do more than your whole battle array. If you will let me manage, I will get you all into the castle before midnight.'

At night the castle was barricadoed as usual, and no one had observed the hole which Parley had made in the hedge. This oversight arose that night from the servants neglecting one of the master's standing orders,—to make a nightly *examination* of the state of the castle. The neglect did not proceed so much from wilful disobedience, as from having passed the evening in sloth and diversion; which often amounts to nearly the same.

As all was very cheerful within, so all was very quiet without. And before they went to bed, some of the servants observed to the rest, that, as they heard no robbers that night, they thought they might soon begin to remit something of their diligence in bolting, and barring; that all this fastening and locking was very troublesome; and they hoped the danger was now pretty well over. It was rather remarkable that they never made this sort of observations but after an evening of some excess, and when they had neglected their private business with their master. All, however, except Parley, went quietly to bed, and seemed to feel uncommon security.

Parley crept down to his lodge. He had half a mind to go to bed too; yet he was not willing to disappoint Mr.

Flatterwell, so civil a gentleman. To be sure, he *might* have bad designs, yet what right had he to suspect any body who made such professions, and who was so very civil. Besides, 'it is something for my advantage,' added Parley. 'I will not open the door, that is certain; but as he is to come alone, he can do me no harm through the bars of the windows; and he will think I am a coward, if I don't keep my word: no, I will let him see that I am not afraid of my own strength; I will show him I can go *what* length I please, and stop short *when* I please.' Had Flatterwell heard this boastful speech, he would have been quite sure of his man.

About eleven, Parley heard the signal agreed upon. It was so gentle as to cause little alarm. So much the worse. Flatterwell never frightened any one, and therefore seldom failed of any one. Parley stole softly down, planted himself at his little window, opened the casement, and spied his new friend. It was pale star-light. Parley was a little frightened, for he thought he perceived one or two persons behind Flatterwell; but the other assured him that it was only his own shadow, which his fears had magnified into a company. 'Though I assure you,' said he,' I have not a friend but what is as harmless as myself.'

They now entered into earnest discourse, in which Flatterwell showed himself a deep politician. He skilfully mixed up in his conversation, a proper proportion of praise on the pleasures of the wilderness; of compliments to Parley; of ridicule on his master; and of abusive sneers on the BOOK, in which the master's laws were written. Against this last he had always a particular spite, for he considered it as the grand instrument by which the master maintained his servants in allegiance; and when they could once be brought to sneer at the BOOK, there was an end of submission to the master. Parley had not penetration enough to see his drift. 'As to THE BOOK, Mr. Flatterwell,' said he, 'I do not know whether it be true or false; I rather neglect than disbelieve it. I am forced, indeed, to hear it read once a week, but I never look into it myself, if I can help it.'—' Excellent,' said Flatterwell to himself, ' that is just the same thing. This is safe ground for me ; for whether a man does not believe in THE BOOK, or does not attend to it, it comes pretty much to the same, and I generally get him at last.'

'Why cannot we be a little nearer, Mr. Parley?' said Flatterwell; 'I am afraid of being overheard by some of your master's spies; the window from which you speak is so high; I wish you would come down to the door.'—'Well,' said Parley, 'I see no great harm in that. There is a little wicket in the door, through which we can converse with more ease and equal safety. The same fastenings will still be between us.' So down he went, but not without a degree of fear and trembling.

The little wicket being now opened, and Flatterwell standing close on the outside of the door, they conversed with great ease. 'Mr. Parley,' said Flatterwell, 'I should not have pressed you so much to admit me into the castle, but out of pure disinterested regard to your own happiness. I shall get nothing by it, but I cannot bear to think that a person so wise and amiable, should be shut up in this gloomy dungeon, under a hard master, and a slave to the unreasonable tyranny of his BOOK OF LAWS. If you admit me, you need have no more waking, no more watching.' Here Parley involuntarily slipped back the bolt of the door. 'To convince you of my true love,' continued Flatterwell, 'I have brought a bottle of the most delicious wine that grows in the wilderness. You shall taste it, but you must put a glass through the wicket to receive it, for it is a singular property in this wine, that we of the wilderness cannot succeed in conveying it to you of the castle, without you hold out a vessel to receive it.'—'O, here is a glass,' said Parley, holding out a large goblet, which he always kept ready to be filled by any chance comer. The other immediately poured into the capacious goblet a large draught of that delicious, intoxicating liquor, with which the family of the Flatterwells have, for near six thousand years, gained the hearts and destroyed the souls of all the inhabitants of the castle, whenever they have been able to prevail on them to hold out a hand to receive it. This the wise master of the castle well knew would be the case, for he knew what was in men; he knew their propensity to receive the delicious poison of the Flatterwells, and it was for this reason that he gave them THE BOOK of his laws, and planted the hedge, and invented the bolts, and doubled the locks.

As soon as poor Parley had swallowed the fatal draught, it acted like enchantment. He at once lost all power of resistance. He had no sense of fear left. He despised his own safety, forgot his master, lost all sight of the house in the other country, and reached out for another draught, as eagerly as Flatterwell held out the bottle to administer it. 'What a fool I have been,' said Parley, 'to deny myself so long.'—'Will you now let me in?' said Flatterwell. 'Ay, that I will,' said the deluded Parley. Though the train was now increased to near a hundred robbers, yet so intoxicated was Parley, that he did not see one of them except his new friend. Parley eagerly pulled down the bars, drew back the bolts, and forced open the locks, thinking he could never let in his friend soon enough. He had however just presence of mind to say, 'My dear friend, I hope you are alone.' Flatterwell swore he was. Parley opened the door; in rushed, not Flatterwell only, but the whole banditti, who always lurk behind in his train. The moment they had got sure possession, Flatterwell changed his soft tone, and cried out in a voice of thunder, 'Down with the castle; kill, burn, and destroy.'

Rapine, murder, and conflagration, by turns, took place. Parley was the very first whom they attacked. He was overpowered with wounds. As he fell, he cried out, 'O, my master, I die a victim to my unbelief in thee, and to my own vanity and imprudence. O that the guardians of all other castles would hear me with my dying breath repeat my master's admonition, that *attacks from without will not destroy, unless there is some confederate within.* O that the keepers of all other castles would learn from my ruin, that he, who parleys with temptation, is already undone; that he, who allows himself to go to the very bounds, will soon jump over the hedge; that he, who talks out of the window with the enemy, will soon open the door to him; that he, who holds out his hand for the cup of sinful flattery, loses all power of resisting; that when he opens the door to one sin, all the rest fly in upon him, and the man perishes, as I now do.'

END.

No. 18.

FAMILY WORSHIP.

BY PHILIP DODDRIDGE, D. D.

This address may come into the hands of many who have long been exemplary for their diligence and zeal in the duties I am about to recommend. Such, I hope, will be confirmed, by what they read, in pursuing the good resolutions they have taken, and the good customs they have formed; and will also be excited more earnestly to endeavour to contribute towards introducing the like into other families, over which they have any influence, and especially into those which may branch out from their own, by the settlement of children and servants.

But I have those principally in view who have hitherto lived in the omission of family prayer.

While I write this, I have that awakening Scripture before me: "Pour out thy fury upon the heathen, that know thee not, and upon *the families that call not on thy name.*" Jer. x. 25. I appeal to you whether this does not strongly imply, that *every family*, which is not a *heathen family*, which is not quite ignorant of the living and true God, *will call upon his name.* Well may it then pain my heart to think that there should be a professedly *Christian family* whom this dreadful character suits; well may it pain my heart, to think of the *divine fury*, which may be poured out on the heads and on the members of it: and well may it make me desirous to do my utmost to secure you and yours from every appearance and possibility of such danger. Excuse the earnestness with which I may address you. I really fear, lest, *while you delay*, the *fire* of the divine displeasure should *fall upon you*. Gen. xix. 16, 17. And as I adore the patience of God in having thus long suspended the storm, I am anxious about every hour's delay, lest it should fall heavier.

What I desire and entreat of you is, that you would honour and acknowledge God in your families, by calling them together, every day, to hear some part of his word read to them, and to join, for a few minutes at least, in your confessions, prayers and praises to him. And is this a cause that should need to be pleaded at large by a great variety of united motives? Truly the petition seems so reasonable, and a compliance with it, from one who has not quite renounced religion, might seem so natural, that one would think the bare proposing of it would suffice. Yet experience tells, it is much otherwise. Some, who maintain a public profession of religion, have refused, and will continue to refuse, year after year.

Reflect, Sir, (for I address myself to every particular person,) seriously reflect on the *reasonableness of family religion*. Must not your conscience presently tell you, it is fit that persons who receive so many mercies together, should acknowledge them together? Can you in your mind be satisfied, that you and your nearest relatives should pay no joint homage to that God who hath set you in your family, and who hath given to you, and to the several members of it, so many domestic enjoyments? Can it be right, if you have any sense of these things, each of you in your own hearts, that the sense of them should be concealed and smothered there, and that you should never join in your grateful acknowledgments to him? Can you imagine it reasonable, that when you have a constant dependance upon him for so many mercies, without the recurrence of which your family would be a scene of misery, you should never present yourselves together in his presence to ask them at his hand? Upon what principle is *public* worship to be recommended and urged, if not by such as have their proportionable weight here?

Indeed the force of these considerations has not only been known and acknowledged by the *people of God* in all ages; we have not only *Noah* and *Abraham*, *Joshua* and *David*, *Job* and *Daniel*, each under a much darker dispensation than ours, as examples of it; but even the poor *heathen* had their household images, some of them in private chapels, and others about the common hearth, where the family used to worship them by frequent prayers and sacrifices. And the *brass*, and *wood*, and *stone*, of which they consisted, shall (as it were) *cry out against you*, shall rise up against you and condemn you, if, while you call yourselves the worshippers of the one living and eternal God, and boast in the revelation you have received by his prophets and by his Son, you presume to omit a homage which the stupid worshippers of such vanities as these failed not to present to them, while they called them their gods. Be persuaded then, I beseech you, to be consistent in your conduct. Either give up all pretences to religion, or maintain a steady and uniform regard to it, at home as well as abroad, in the family as well as in the closet or at church.

1. Consider the happy influence which the duty I am recommending might have upon the young members of your family, the *children* and *servants* committed to your care. For I now consider you as a parent and a master. *The father of a family* is a phrase that comprehends both these relations, and with great propriety, as humanity obliges us to endeavour to take a parental care of all under our roof. And indeed you ought to consider your *servants*, in this view, with a tender regard. They are probably in the flower of life, for that is the age which is commonly spent in service; and you should recollect how possible it is, that this may be, if rightly improved, the best opportunity their whole life may afford them, for learning religion, and being brought under the power of it. Let them not, if they should finally perish, have cause to testify before God in the day of their condemnation, that under your roof they learned the neglect and forgetfulness of God, and all that their pious parents, perhaps in a much inferior station of life to you, had in earlier days been attempting to teach them. Or, if they come to you quite ignorant of religion, as, if they come

from prayerless families it is very probable that they do, have compassion upon them, I entreat you, and endeavour to give them those advantages which they never yet had, and which it is too probable, as things are generally managed, they never will have, if you will not afford them.

But I would especially, if I might be allowed to borrow the pathetic words of Job, *entreat you by the children of your own body.* Job xix. 17. I would now, as it were present them all before you, and beseech you by the bowels of parental affection, that to all the other tokens of tenderness and love, you would not refuse to add this, without which many of the rest may be worse than in vain.

Give me leave to plead with you, as the instruments of introducing them into being. O remember, it is indeed a debased and corrupted nature that you have conveyed to them. Consider, that the world, into which you have been the means of bringing them, is a place in which they are surrounded by many temptations, and in which, as they advance in life, they must expect many more; so that it is much to be feared, that they will remain ignorant and forgetful of God, if they do not learn from you to love and serve him. For how can it be expected that they should learn this at all, if you give them no advantages for receiving and practising the lesson at home?

And let me further urge and entreat you to remember, that these dear children are committed to your special care by God their Creator, who has made them thus dependant upon you, that you might have an opportunity of forming their minds, and of influencing them to a right temper and conduct. And can this by any means be effectually done, if you do not at proper times call them together to attend to the instructions of the word of God, and to join in solemn prayers and supplications to him? At least, is it possible that it should be done any other way with equal advantage, if this be not added to the rest?

Family worship is a most proper way of teaching children religion, as you teach them language by insensible degrees—a little one day, and a little another; for to them *line must be upon line, and precept upon precept.* They may learn to conceive aright of the divine perfections, when they hear you daily acknowledging and adoring them; their hearts may be early touched with remorse for sin, when they hear your confessions poured out before God; they will know what mercies they are to ask for themselves, by observing what turn your petitions take; your intercessions may diffuse into their minds a spirit of love to mankind, a concern for the interest of the church and of their country; and your solemn thanksgivings for the bounties of Providence, and for the benefits of a spiritual nature, may affect their hearts with those impressions towards the gracious Author of all, which may excite in their little breasts love to him, the most noble and genuine principle of all true and acceptable religion. Thus they may embrace Christ in their earliest years, and grow in the knowledge and love of truth as they do in stature. Indeed, were this duty properly attended to, it might be expected that all christian families would, according to their respective sizes and circumstances, become nurseries of piety; and you would see, in the most convincing view, the wisdom of Providence, in making human infants so much more dependant on their parents, and so much more incapable to shift for themselves, than the offspring of inferior creatures are.

Let me then entreat you, my dear friends, to look on your children the very next time you see them, and ask your own heart, how can you answer it to God and to them, that you deprive them of such advantages as these—advantages without which it is to be feared your care of them in other respects will turn to but little account, should they be ever so prosperous in life. For what is prosperity in life, without the knowledge, and fear, and love of God? What but the poison of the soul, which swells and kills it? What but the means of making it more certainly, more deeply, more intolerably miserable? In short, not to mention the happy influence which family devotion may have on their temporal affairs, by drawing down the divine blessing, and by forming their minds to those virtues which pave the way to wealth and reputation, health and contentment, which make no enemies, and attract many friends; it is, with respect to the eternal world, the greatest cruelty to your children to neglect giving them those advantages which no other attentions in education, exclusive of these, can afford; and it is impossible that you should ever be able to give them any other equivalent. If you do your duty in this respect, they will have reason to bless you living and dying; and if you neglect it, take care that you and they come not, in consequence of that neglect, into a world where (horrid as the thought may seem) you will be for ever cursing each other!

2. Let me now press you to consider how much *your own interest* is concerned in the matter.

Your *spiritual* interest is concerned. Let me seriously ask you, do you not need those advantages for religion, which the performance of family duty will give you, added to those of a more secret and a more public nature, if peradventure *they* are regarded by you? These instructions, these adorations, these confessions, these supplications, these intercessions, these thanksgivings, which may be so useful to your children and servants—may they not be useful to yourself? May not your own heart have some peculiar advantage for being impressed, when you are the mouth of others in these domestic devotions, beyond what, in a private station of life, it is otherwise possible that you should have? Nay, the remoter influence they may have on your conduct, in other respects, and at other times, when considered merely, in the general, as religious exercises performed by you in your family, is to be recollected as an argument of vast importance.

A sense of common decency would engage you, if you pray with your family, to *avoid a great many evils*, which would appear *doubly evil* in a father or a master who kept up such religious exercises in his house. Do you imagine that, if reading the Scriptures, and family prayer, were introduced into the houses of some of your neighbours—drunkenness, and lewdness, and cursing, and swearing, and profaning the Lord's day, would not, like so many *evil demons*, be quickly driven out? The master of a family would not, for shame, indulge them, if he kept up nothing more than the *form* of duty; and his reformation, though only external, and at first on a kind of constraint, would carry with it the reformation of many more, who have such a dependance on his favour as they would not sacrifice, though, by a madness very prevalent among the children of men, they can venture to sacrifice their *souls* to every trifle.

And may it not perhaps be your more immediate concern, to recollect, that if you prayed with your family, you would *yourself* be more careful to *abstain from all appearance of evil?* 1 Thess. v. 22. You would find out a way to suppress that turbulency of passion which may now be ready to break out before you are aware, and other imprudences, in which your own heart would check you by saying, ' Does this become one that is by and by to kneel down with his domestics, his children, and servants, and adore God with them, and pray against every thing which displeases God, and makes us unfit for the heavenly world?' I will not say this will cure every thing that is wrong, but I believe you are already persuaded, it would often have a very good influence. And I fear it is the secret desire of indulging some irregularities without such a restraint, that, shameful as such a conduct is, hath driven out family prayer from several houses, and hath prevented its introduction into others. But if you have any secret disinclination of heart against it, in this view, it becomes you to be most seriously alarmed for your spiritual condition.

After this, it may seem a matter of small importance to urge the good influence which a proper discharge of family duty may have upon your own *temporal affairs*, both by restraining you from many evils, and engaging you to a proper conduct yourself, and also by impressing your children and servants with a sense of religion. And it is certain, the more careful they are of their duty to God, the more likely they will be to perform their duty to you. Nor can any thing strengthen your natural authority among them more, than your presiding in such solemnities, if supported by a suitable conduct. But I would hope, nobler motives will have a superior weight. And therefore, waving this topic, I entreat you, as the last argument, to consider,

3. The influence it may have on a *general reformation*, and on the *propagation of religion* to those who are yet unborn. You ought to consider every child and servant in your family, as one who may be a source, not only of life, but (in some degree) of character and happiness to those who are hereafter to rise into being; yea, whose conduct may in part affect those that are to descend from them in a remote generation. If they grow up, while under your eye, ignorant of religion, they will certainly be much less capable of teaching it to others: for these are the years of discipline, and, if they are neglected now, there is little probability of their receiving instruction afterwards. Nor

is this all the evil consequence; for it is highly probable, that they will think themselves sanctioned by your example in a like negligence, and so you may entail *heathenism*, under the name of christianity, on your descendants and theirs for ages to come. Whereas your diligence and zeal might be remembered and imitated by them, perhaps when you are in your grave; and the stock, which they first received from you, might with rich improvements be communicated to great numbers, so that *one generation after another* might learn to fear and serve the Lord. On the whole, God only knows what a church may arise from one godly family: what a harvest may spring up from a single seed; and on the other hand, it is impossible to say how many souls may at length perish by the treacherous neglect of a single person, and, to speak plainly, by your own.

These, Sir, are the arguments I have to plead with you, and which I have selected out of many more. And now give me leave seriously to ask you, as in the presence of God, whether there be not on the whole an unanswerable force in them? And if there is, what follows but that you immediately yield to that force, and set up Family Worship *this very day?* For, methinks, I would hardly thank you for a resolution to do it *to-morrow;* so little do I expect from that resolution. How can you excuse yourself in the continued omission? Bring the matter before God: He will be the final judge of it: and if you cannot debate the question as in his presence, it is the sign of a bad cause, and of a bad heart too, which is conscious of the badness of the cause; and yet will not give it up, nor comply with a duty, of your obligation to which you are secretly convinced, while in effect you say, "I will go on in this sin, and venture the consequence." O! It is a dreadful venture, and will be found *provoking the Lord to jealousy, as if you were stronger than he.* 1 Cor. x. 22.

God is represented as giving this reason to his angels for a particular favour to be bestowed on *Abraham*—*I know that he will command his children and household to keep the way of the Lord, that he may obtain the blessing promised.* Gen. xviii. 19. Did he not hereby intend to declare his approbation of the care which Abraham took to support religion in his family? And can it be supported in a total neglect of prayer?—Again, Do you not, in your conscience, think that the Spirit of God meant, that we should take Joshua for an example, when he tells us, that he resolved (and publicly declared the resolution) *that he and his house would serve the Lord;* (Josh. xxiv. 15.) which must express a religious care of his family too?—Do you not believe, that the blessed Spirit meant it as a commendation of *Job,* that he *offered sacrifices for all his children:* (Job, i. 5.) sacrifices undoubtedly attended with prayers; when he feared lest the gaiety of their hearts, in their successive feastings, might have betrayed them into some moral evil?—And was it not to do an honour to *David,* that the scripture informs us, that " he went home to bless his household," (2 Sam. vi. 20.) that is, to perform some solemn act of domestic worship, when he had been spending the whole day in public devotion?—And do you think, when our blessed Lord, whose life was employed in religious services, so frequently took his disciples apart to pray with them, that he did not intend this as an example to us, of praying with those under our special care, or in other words, with the members of our own family, who are most immediately so? Or can you, by any imaginable artifice, delude yourself so far as to think, that when we are solemnly charged and commanded to pray " with all prayer and supplication," (Eph. vi. 18.) this kind of prayer is not included in that apostolical injunction?

Were there not one praying family in the whole world, methinks it should instigate you to the practice, rather than tempt you to neglect it, and you should press on, as ambitious of the glory of leading the way. For what could be a nobler object of ambition, than to be pointed out by the blessed God himself, as Job was; of whom he said, with a kind of triumph, " Hast thou considered my servant Job, that there is none like him in the land, or even on the earth?" Job, i. 8. But blessed be God, the neglect we have supposed, is far from being universal. Let it however rejoice us, if God may say, " There are such and such families, distinguishable from those in their neighbourhood on this account; as prevalent as the neglect of family prayer is, *they* have the resolution to practise it, and, like my servant Daniel, fear not the reproach and contempt which profane and ungodly men may cast upon them, if they may but honour me and engage my favour; I know them; I hearken and hear, and a book of remembrance is written before me for them that fear me, and think on my name."

Say not you have no *time*. How many hours in a week do you spend for amusement, while you have none for devotion in your family? And do you indeed hold the blessing of God so very cheap, and think it a matter of so little importance, that you conclude your business must succeed the worse, if a few minutes were daily taken to implore it before your family? Let me rather admonish you, that the greater your business is, the more need you have to pray earnestly that your hearts may not be engrossed by it. And I would beg leave further to remind you, that if your hurry of business were indeed so great as the objection supposes, (which I believe is seldom the case,) prudence alone might suggest that you should endeavour to contract it. For there are certain boundaries beyond which a wise and faithful care cannot extend; and as an attempt to go beyond these boundaries has generally its foundation in avarice, so it often has its end in poverty and ruin. But if you were ever so secure in succeeding for this world, how dear might you and your children pay for that success, if all the blessed consequences of family religion, for time and for eternity, were to be given up as the price of that very small part of your gains, which is owing to the minutes you take from these exercises, that you may give them to the world? For you plainly perceive the question is only about them, and by no means about a strenuous application to the proper duties of your secular calling through the day. And if you will be rich upon such profane terms as are here supposed, (for truly I can call them no better than profane,) you will probably plunge yourself into final perdition, and may in the mean time "pierce yourself through with many sorrows;" while religious families will learn, by happy experience, that the blessing of the Lord, which they are so often imploring together, "maketh rich, and addeth no sorrow with it;" (Prov. x. 22.) or that "a little with the fear of the Lord is better than great treasures," with that intermingled trouble, (Prov. xv. 16.) which in the neglect of God must necessarily be expected.

As for *ability*, where the heart is rightly disposed, it does not require any *uncommon abilities* to discharge *family worship* in a decent and edifying manner. '*The heart of a wise*' and *good* '*man*,' in this respect, '*teacheth his mouth, and addeth knowledge to his lips;*' (Prov. xvi. 23.) and '*out of the fulness of it*,' when it is indeed full of pious affections, 'the mouth will naturally speak.' Luke, vi. 45. Plain, short sentences, uttered just as they rise in the mind, will be best understood by them that join with you; and they will be more pleasing to God than any thing which should proceed from ostentation and parade.

I must also desire you to consider, how many helps you may easily procure. The Scripture is a large and noble magazine of the most proper sentiments, and most expressive language, which, if you will attend to it with a becoming regard, will soon furnish you for this good work. We have too in our language a great variety of excellent *forms of prayer* for families as well as for private persons, which you may use, at least at first, with great profit. And if it is too laborious to you to learn them by heart, or if having learned them, you dare not trust your memory, what should forbid your *reading* them reverently and devoutly! I hope the main thing is, that God be reverently and sincerely adored; that suitable blessings, temporal and spiritual, be sought from him for ourselves and others; and cordial thanksgivings returned to him for the various gifts of his continual bounty.

If *opposition* be made in your family, you ought to let any in whom you discover it, know that your measures are fixed, and that you cannot and will not resign that just authority, which the laws of God and man give you in your own house, to their unhappy temper, or daring impiety.

May God give you resolution immediately to make the attempt! And may he assist and accept you, and scatter down every desirable blessing of Providence and of grace on you and yours! So that this day may become memorable in your lives, as a season from which you may date a prosperity and a joy hitherto unknown, how happy soever you may have been in former years: for very imperfect, I am sure, must that domestic happiness be, in which domestic religion has no part.

But if, after all, you will not be persuaded, you must answer it at last. If your children and servants grow up in the neglect of God, and pierce your hearts with those sorrows, which such servants, and especially such children, are likely to occasion; if they raise profane and profligate families; if they prove the curse of their country, as well as the torment and ruin of those most intimately related to them; the guilt is in part yours, and, I repeat it again, you must answer it to God at the great day, that you have omitted the proper and appointed method of preventing such fatal evils. In the mean time you must answer the omission to your own conscience, which probably has not been easy in former days, and in future days may yet be more unquiet. Yet, Sir, the memory of this address may continue to torment you, if it cannot reform you; and if you do not forsake the house of God, as well as exclude God and his worship from your own house, you will meet with new wounds; for new exhortations and admonitions will arm reflection with new reproaches. And in this uncomfortable manner, you will probably go on, till what has been the grief and shame of your life, become the affliction of your dying bed; nor dare I presume to assure you, that God will answer your last cries for pardon. The best you can expect, under the consciousness of this guilt, is to pass trembling to your final doom.—But whatever that doom be, you must acquit the friend who has given you faithful warning: and this address, transcribed as it were in the records of the divine omniscience, shall testify, that a matter of so great importance has not been kept out of your view, nor slightly urged on your conscience.

PUBLISHED BY THE

AMERICAN TRACT SOCIETY,

And sold at their Depository, No. 150 Nassau-street, near the City-Hall, New-York; and by Agents of the Society, its Branches, and Auxiliaries, in the principal cities and towns in the United States.

Fanshaw, Printer.

NO. 19.

THE MORAL MAN TRIED.

IN THREE DIALOGUES.

Minister. Good morning, neighbor. I find you have been early up and diligently employed : I see thriving in the world is a matter very near your heart.

Parishioner. Ay, Sir, all this is necessary. Meat and clothes must be provided, and this requires much diligence.

M. I would by no means discourage your industry. It is your duty to be " not slothful in business." But you know you have another calling—the soul must be fed and clothed too.

P. Doubtless the soul is the chief concern ; but I hope I do not neglect it ; I should be sorry you should think me so bad a man : I believe you have no reason—

M. No particular reason to be suspicious of you more than of many others. But when I look around, and observe the general unconcern about salvation in which men live, I am alarmed ; and with respect to the people of my charge, I think myself obliged to warn them of their danger.

VOL 1.

P. I hope you do not condemn us all: some of us indeed are wicked, swearing, drunken men; but we care not all so. You know that I attend church regularly; I never wronged any man in my life, and I pay every man his due.

M. And upon this you build your hope of heaven! If this is your foundation, I must tell you plainly it will leave you hopeless in the day of trial. Let us examine it by the word of God. "You never wronged any man." You mean perhaps you never robbed or cheated any person. I do not say you have, but still you have committed much sin, and done much hurt, not only to others, but especially to your own soul, by great and numberless offences against the holy law of God. Nay, you have broken every one of his commandments.

P. How can you have such an opinion of me? I never committed idolatry, murder, adultery—

M. Yes, all of them. Have you never loved any worldly thing more than God and his favor, nor feared any thing more than his displeasure, so as to neglect a known duty rather than draw upon yourself some temporal evil? This was a breach of the *first* commandment. The *second* commandment respects the manner of expressing the devotion of the heart; and therefore whatever in your service has been unbecoming, such as wandering thoughts, carelessness, and irreverence, is a breach of this commandment: so also is neglect of God's service. And here you will not pretend, I suppose, to be guiltless. Consequently, your coming to church in this careless unthinking manner deserves rather to be reckoned among your sins, than trusted to for justification before God. Every time you have used the Lord's name without any reverential sense of his majesty, you have broken the *third* commandment. Whenever you have neglected to attend on God's worship on the Sabbath without a necessary hindrance, suffered worldly thoughts to unfit you for God's service, done worldly business on that day that might have been done on another, and neglected to devote the whole to God, by reading, hearing, prayer, meditation, and useful conversation, you have profaned the Lord's day. The substance of these commands is, thou shalt love the Lord thy God with all thy heart; but you have come short of this, whenever you have not acted to the glory of God. Now what think you of your innocence with respect to the duties of the first table of the commandments?

P. I cannot pretend to justify myself with respect to God, but I am sure I have done no hurt to man.

M. You would not say so if you understood the spiritual nature and extent of God's law, as explained by our Lord in his sermon on the mount. Matt. 5. There you find that wantonness in the eye or heart is esteemed *adultery* in the sight of God; and causeless anger, and especially injurious language, is accounted a degree of *murder;* and who can acquit himself of these? If you take the same method to understand the other commandments, all parts of your behavior that are unsuitable to your station, all irreverence and rash censure of superiors, and all unkind and injurious treatment of those beneath you, will appear breaches of the *fifth* commandment. All evil speaking and repeating stories injurious to the character of others, contrary to the *ninth*, and all murmuring and discontent, envy and greediness, are sins forbidden by the *tenth*.

P. Then it seems there is but one commandment against which I have not sinned.

M. If you rightly know yourself and the law of God, you would not acquit yourself of that neither. Be not offended, I speak out of love to your soul. I do not think you a thief or a robber; yet have you never concealed the faults of what you sold, when you knew that ignorance of these was the very thing that induced the person to buy? Nay, have you not often recommended your goods in such general terms as were not consistent with strict truth? Have you not taken advantage of the necessity of a needy seller, and beat down his ware much below its real value? These will certainly witness against you.

P. Why, Sir, after this rate you condemn all the world. According to your account there is not a good man upon earth.

M. It is not my account, but the scripture account:— "There is none that doeth good, no, not one." Rom. 3 : 12.

P. I am glad then you do not think me worse than my neighbors. I hope I shall do as well as others, for all are sinners.

M. Therefore you think you need not be greatly troubled if you are so too, but hope to pass in the crowd. Does not some such thought lurk at the bottom? But what signify numbers with God, from whose all-searching eye no man can be concealed, and whose arm no man can resist or escape? Had you lived in Sodom, or the old world, this same thought might have lulled you to sleep in the prevailing sins, but would not have saved you from the tempest of fire.

P. After this rate you damn all the world.

M. Damn!—What word is that? It signifies to judge to eternal torment, to do which belongeth only to the righteous Judge. I would with all my soul rescue men from that misery. And with this view I now speak plainly and faithfully to you, and agreeably to the word of God.

P. Who then can be saved? Not you yourself. Pray, Sir, did you never sin?

M. Friend, be serious. The subject we are now upon is of the utmost importance. I have sinned as well as you; I have greatly sinned, and my sins have deserved eternal damnation. But as I hope, God has been pleased to awaken me to repentance; he has shown me my danger, and stirred me up to flee from the wrath to come. He has shown me also the way opened in the blessed Gospel of escaping the wages of sin. The offer of salvation there made I trust I have embraced, and obtained forgiveness, through faith in Jesus Christ.

P. I hope I have repented too; I am sure, if I offend God I am sorry for it afterward. And for faith—why I always believed.

M. If your *repentance* is sincere, and your *faith* lively and true, your state is safe and happy. But many persons deceive themselves by a dead faith and imperfect repentance. Are you willing to have yours tried?

P. I am, for the trial can do me no hurt. If I am safe, it is well; if not, I hope it is not too late to mend.

M. You say very right. First then, let us examine your *repentance.* Now, true repentance implies an affecting sense of sin, its odiousness and deformity, a hatred of it, a humiliation and self-loathing on account of it, an actual forsaking of it, and a turning to God by newness of life. Is your repentance such as this?

P. I hope it is.

M. Examine your feelings. The wages of sin is death, eternal death. Do you think you deserve this death?

P. As much as other men, for all are sinners; but God is merciful.

M. Do not now talk of other men. Do you think that *you* deserve eternal death?

P. If God should deal with me according to strict justice, I do; but as I think God is merciful, so I hope I shall do well enough.

M. I fear your notions of God's mercy are such as prevent true repentance. You seem to have hope of mercy without being sensible of your utter misery without it; to have applied the healing balsam before you were wounded. This is what the Almighty styles " healing the wounds of his people slightly." Now you seem in this matter to have deceived yourself. You never saw yourself in a state of sin and death; you never saw sin odious; you were never greatly afraid of perishing, nor saw that there was no help or strength in yourself; therefore you never fled to him who is a refuge " from the storm." And if you have never fled thus to Christ, as helpless and undone without him, it is plain that you are still without any saving interest in him. See how it was with these converts mentioned in the Acts of the Apostles; Peter's hearers were " pricked in their hearts, and said, Men and brethren, what shall we do?" The jailor came trembling, through a sense of his miserable condition, before he received forgiveness of sins. Paul was struck to the ground under a sense of guilt.

P. All these were infidels. I was born of pious parents, bred up to know good things, and always believed.

M. God does not deal with all exactly in the same way. But take heed you do not depend too much upon outward privilege. Search your heart and life. Have you not lived a long time as without God in the world? Instead of renouncing the world, the flesh, and the devil, have you not followed and been led by them? Have you not been led by the world in judging of things according to the opinions of men, in opposition to the word of God? Have you not in many things conformed to it, contrary to the commands of God? Have you not frequently obeyed your carnal lusts and inclinations, so as to violate the pure law of God, if not by actual offences, yet by indulging evil thoughts and living in lesser sins without concern? And has not the devil been for a considerable time your master, leading you to offend God by profaning his holy day; and that for the sake of such trifling pleasure as plainly argues that the love of God is not in you? And have you not continued in sin with little or no concern, hoping, notwithstanding, that all would be well? Nay, is not this still in some measure your case?—I see you acknowledge it is. It is plain then there is a necessity of turning unto God, and beginning all anew.

P. How must I begin anew?

M. By acknowledging that by your departure from God you have brought yourself into a state of sin and misery, estranged from God, inclined to evil, and therefore at enmity with God in your heart; and that for these things you deserve his wrath, and stand on the brink of ruin, covered with guilt, and fleeing to the Lord Jesus Christ for mercy.

P. I am willing to forsake all sin, turn to God, and do better.

M. These are good resolutions, but they do not seem to proceed from a right principle. You would forsake sin, and do better, I see, with some secret dependence upon your amendment and doings that these will fit you for acceptance and gain you an interest in Christ. But this is a legal spirit of self-dependence, a " going about to establish your own righteousness." When I see you acknowledge yourself sinful, vile, and base, and like Job abhorring yourself; when I see you sensible that you are unworthy of the least mercy, and that without the renewing of the Holy Spirit you can do nothing acceptable to God; when I see you renouncing your best deeds as defiled by sin, casting yourself before God as lost and helpless; having no hope in yourself, but supported only by the promise of salvation made in Jesus Christ; when this is not only the language of the tongue, but these convictions are deeply impressed on the heart—then I shall think a real work of grace is begun in your soul.

P. Why this is advising me to *despair!*

M. Indeed I would have you despair of all help from yourself, for till then you will not sufficiently value Jesus

Christ, nor fly to him as your only Savior "who came to preach deliverance to the captives," "to bind up the broken-hearted."

P. I believe all this may be necessary for a notorious sinner; but I have lived in some fear of God, attended church, and always believed.

M. I fear you never believed at all, properly speaking. At present it is plain your repentance has not been real. You never saw and felt your danger, and consequently never saw the necessity of escaping it. You always flattered yourself with some hopes that your state was safe, or certainly would be when you lived a little better; which was, at bottom, depending on yourself. With respect to the other branches of repentance, such as forsaking sin, it is evident to yourself you have lived without concern in some habitual sins; and as for turning *to* God, you were never sensible that you were turned *from* him.

Indeed (though you seem not to know it) the ruling principle in you, and every natural man, is a principle of selfishness and corruption. Instead of seeking to please God, you have all along been seeking to please yourself; to gratify corrupt nature by sensual delights, riches, worldly esteem, ease, or the like. This has been the moving principle of your whole conduct, instead of obeying that command, "*Do all to the glory of God.*" Nay, if you search narrowly, you will find in your heart *enmity against God.* For so says the apostle, "The carnal mind" (and such is every man's by nature) "is enmity against God." Rom. 8 : 7. And this enmity shows itself in opposing God's will, by doing what he has forbidden, and leaving undone what he has solemnly commanded. Have you not passed days and weeks without one serious thought of God, though you were all the time receiving mercies at his hand? Have you not banished and suppressed such thoughts when they have arisen in your mind? Have you not fled from serious thoughts of God and eternity as enemies to your peace, and drowned them in worldly cares, vain conversations, and idle amusements? Have you not thus fled from God? You know you have. Suffer me to be plain with you; hitherto you have gone wrong, been insensible of your danger, deceived yourself, and spoken peace to your soul when there was no peace. Continuing thus you must perish. Christ requires you to surrender your heart to him, confessing your sins and accepting of mercy through his blood and righteousness. "There is none other name under heaven among men whereby you can be saved."

DIALOGUE II.

M. I was in hopes of seeing you before now, neighbor, that we might have an opportunity of talking again on the same important subject.

P. Indeed, Sir, I must say I did not like what you said so well as then to wish to hear any more of it; but I am now convinced it was all true.

M. What has produced this change in your sentiments?

P. Your yesterday's sermon about the Day of Judgment. I have been very uneasy ever since I heard it; and I am greatly afraid that if the day of judgment was now come, it would find me unprepared.

M. It would be too late then to cry and hope for mercy. But what was it particularly that made you form such a judgment of yourself?

P. You showed us from the 25th chapter of Matthew, that judgment begins with a separation of the godly from the wicked; and that this must be according to a separation made between them in the present life. I am not sensible of any such change in me as you described, and am therefore afraid I am still in the state of sin in which you told us all men are by nature.

M. You have great reason to be afraid. I told you that those only would be esteemed *righteous* on that day who had fled to the Lord Jesus for righteousness to justify them, had been made holy by the Spirit of God creating in them a new heart, and had evidenced this change by a holy conversation through the remaining part of their life, how many or great soever their sins had been; and that the *wicked* were those that had lived and died without faith in Christ and the indwelling of God's Spirit, however orderly and decent their conduct was.

P. Ay, that it was terrified me. You told us that the most upright man had committed sins enough to condemn him if he died without an interest in Christ, and without being accepted as righteous through him.

M. Those who do not by faith fly for refuge to God's mercy in Christ, have no good works to be mentioned; for all they do is from a wrong principle, either for selfish and worldly ends, or in order to gain an interest in Christ, and pardon of their sins on account of their doings; which is seeking salvation by the law of works.

P. I see that all depends upon my obtaining, while on earth, mercy and forgiveness of all that is past; and that not on account of any thing done by me, but through faith in Jesus Christ. But what that faith is I know not: this I know, that I have been all along out of the way. I see that I have been daily offending God, by breaking his commandments, and pleasing myself, not him; and that now I stand under the guilt of thousands of sins, the least of which were enough to condemn me. Do, Sir, tell me " what must I do to be saved?"

M. What think you now of your good deeds?

P. I have none to think about. I see sin in every thing I do. My pride on account of not being so bad as others, my worldliness, my vanity and trifling spirit in prayer and hearing sermons, were enough to condemn me, if I had done nothing else.

M. And what do you intend to do?

P. I will do better, I will strive against sin, I will pray.

M. But all these duties, you say, have been heretofore mixed with sin; how then do you hope they will make you accepted now? Or, could you do these things ever so well, all is your necessary, bounden duty: the good deeds which you may do cannot make amends for past offences. On all these accounts, "by the deeds of the law shall no man living be justified."

P. I see no way—If ever there was a soul lost, I am he—What shall I do?

M. "Believe on the Lord Jesus Christ, and thou shalt be saved." Acts, 16 : 34. "This is the work of God, that ye believe in him whom he hath sent." John, 6 : 29. "And by him all that believe are justified from all things." Acts, 13 : 39. Come, naked, sinful, and helpless as you are, to God, through Christ, for mercy. "He is able to save to the uttermost all who come unto God by him, seeing he hath died for them, and ever liveth to make intercession for them." Heb. 7 : 25. He can wash you from the guilt of all your sins, destroy the power and dominion of sin in you, "sanctify you thoroughly in body, and soul, and spirit, and "present you to the Father without spot or blemish."

P. I have no manner of doubt of Christ's power to save, for he is the Son of God; but I fear I am not a fit person to be saved.

M. To determine that, look into your Bible. There it is said, "Christ Jesus came into the world to save sinners." 1 Tim. 1 : 15.

P. But he will not, he does not save *all* sinners.

M. That is because they will not come to him to be saved. Of this he complains, (John, 5 : 40,) "Ye will not come to me that ye may have life."

P. But I find certain conditions mentioned, which I fear I have not. It is said, "Repent, and believe the Gospel;" and "he that believeth, and is baptized, shall be saved."

M. If you are weary with the burden of sin, loathe it, and earnestly desire to be saved from the guilt and pollution of it, then go to Christ, who hath said, "Come unto me all ye that labor and are heavy laden, and I will give you rest."

P. But it is said, "Many will seek to enter in, and shall not be able;" and "not every one that saith unto me, Lord! Lord! shall enter into the kingdom of heaven." This makes me fear and keep at a distance.

M. To whom then do you intend to go?

P. I know not, for there is no other name under heaven whereby one may be saved.

M. Then apply to Christ; so escape the wages of sin, the curse of the law, and the wrath of God; fly to him for pardon and peace, grace and glory. Behold him on the cross, bleeding and dying for sinners—embrace and depend on God's promises in him.

P. I dare not thus embrace the promises, come to and depend on Christ, for I am utterly unworthy of the least **mercy.**

M. When do you think to make yourself worthy?

P. Never.

M. Then come to him just as you are, and accept unmerited mercy.

P. May I dare thus to come to Christ and depend upon him for salvation?

M. Do not depend upon my word, but hear the word of God. He *invites* you to come: " Ho! every one that thirsteth, come ye to the waters." Isa. 55 : 1. He *commands* you to come : " This is his commandment, that we should believe on the name of his Son Jesus Christ." 1 John, 3 : 23. He *promises* to receive those that come: " Him that cometh unto me I will in no wise cast out." John, 6 : 37. He *threatens* if you do not come : " He that believeth not shall be damned." Mark, 16 : 16.

P. But to whom are these words addressed?

M. To you, to me, and to every one that hears them : " Preach the Gospel to every creature." Mark, 16 : 15. They are addressed to those especially that see their want of salvation, because they alone will receive them: " Come unto me all ye that labor and are heavy laden, and I will give you rest." Matt. 11 : 28.

P. These arguments from Scripture stop my mouth. But still I cannot believe Christ will receive such a sinner as I am.

M. This stubborn unbelief is your deepest guilt. But consider again—God gave his only Son to death for this very purpose, *to save sinners;* for this he came into the world ; for this he labored, wept, and bled ; for this he reigns and intercedes in heaven. He is so far from being unwilling to save, that he is offended with those who will not come to him to be saved. When he was upon earth he wept over Jerusalem on this account.

P. I know not what to say.

M. What do you intend to do?

P. I am greatly afraid I shall never be saved. But I know there is no other way but God's free mercy in Christ. I feel that I must go to him, and if I perish it shall be at the foot of the cross, calling for mercy.

M. Continue this resolution, and all the precious promises of the Gospel are yours. Do not seek rest any where but in Christ. Beware lest worldly cares or pleasures, divert your attention from the things of God, and lest sin grieve the Holy Spirit. Remember it is said, "If a man draw back my soul shall have no pleasure in him."

DIALOUGE III.

P. Sir, I hope you will not be offended at the trouble I give you; but I want your advice very much.

M. You need no apology, my friend, I am glad to see any of the people of my charge when they need spiritual advice.

P. I have been for some time so as I never was in my life before; I have seen that my heart is a sink of sin, and that I deserve nothing but hell. You had no need to caution me against the danger of worldly cares and pleasures; for wherever I have been, or whatever I have been doing, my sins and hell have still been before my eyes.

M. What have you thought of your sins? In what light have they appeared to you?

P. Sins committed many years ago have now arisen in my mind and condemned me. The remembrance of the sins of my youth has followed me, as if committed but yesterday. And some awful Scriptures that I have heard and read seem to be the sentences of my condemnation. I believe I have thought a hundred times of these words, "The wages of sin is death."

M. Have you looked into your heart, and seen and lamented the corruption there?

P. I did not use to understand what you meant by *looking into the heart;* but I think I do now. I find in myself a strong inclination to many sins, and I am convinced that I deserve God's wrath for complying with these inclinations through my whole life. I have been led, by my own wicked heart, to delight in evil company; to talk of myself in an empty, vain manner; to be greedy after the world; to pass slightly over, or entirely neglect prayer or other duties, as a tedious burden; and to be guilty of other sins. I now desire to renounce sin, and live to the glory of God.

M. Trust not in your own strength: you may not yet

know your heart so well as you imagine. Be not deceived; such a cage of unclean birds as the heart of every man is by nature, is not easily cleansed from its various lusts and vile affections. Those that seem to be rooted out are perhaps only asleep for a season. Be watchful therefore; they may one day awake again. Some of them perhaps are only exchanged for others as bad and dangerous, such as pride, presumption, and the like.

P. Really, Sir, I fear I have been guilty of presumption. I was thinking what a sinful wretch I was, and what would become of me in the next world, when these words came strongly into my mind, "I will heal their backsliding, I will love them freely." I am sure they are somewhere in the Bible, but I cannot find them. They gave me much comfort and peace. Have I any right to regard this as the work of God?

M. I must desire some time to observe your temper and conduct, before I can solve this question. The words of Hosea which you mentioned, contain a sweet promise, and are free for every humble soul to embrace by faith. And as God has given you a sense of your sinful, helpless state, and a desire of turning to him; I hope the promise belongs to you, and that the comfort which you found in applying it to yourself proceeded from the Spirit of God. But remember the Savior's exhortation, *watch and pray*. The enemy of souls sometimes imitates these sensible experiences in order to deceive. And it is impossible to say how much our natural tempers and spirits may contribute thereto.

P. Pray, Sir, tell me plainly what you think of my state? As far as I know my own heart I would not willingly offend God for the whole world. I see and I rejoice that through Jesus Christ God can be just and justify him that believeth. I hope I believe and trust in him alone for salvation. I love those that seem to be his servants, and would go upon my hands and knees to do them good, or to make others like them. I love to hear his word, to pray, and to talk of heavenly things; and I think I could die with pleasure, if it were his will.

M. These are good signs. But rest not in any present attainments. The first love of the Israelites after passing the Red Sea, of the Galatians, and of the church of Ephesus, was great. But each of these grew colder afterward; and were reproved for it. You will have a continual warfare with sin to maintain. It is "he that endureth unto the end" that "shall be saved."

P. Sir, I believe you know my danger better than I do myself. Pray direct me to what I shall do.

M. Strive to "make your calling and election sure," and evident both to yourself and others, by "bringing forth the fruits of righteousness in a good conversation."

My first advice is, *Walk humbly with thy God.* Let the remembrance of your past life of sin and folly still cover you with shame. Recollect the many aggravating circumstances of a life hitherto spent in rebellion against God; during all which he daily heaped mercies upon you and yours; giving food and raiment, health and strength; and continued these mercies to you, while you forgot the hand that gave them, and returned evil for good.

He spared you in all your provocations, and at last opened your eyes to see your danger, stirred you up to avoid it, and now has given you hope, through grace, of obtaining eternal life. Thus compare what God has done with what you have deserved, and learn humility. Keep a watchful eye also upon the remains of indwelling sin. And let every sinful inclination, vain thought, backwardness to duty, and failure in it, teach you to be humble and fear. Thus, distrusting yourself, look up to God for continual support, like a helpless little child, to be assisted in every time of need.

My next advice is, *Keep a conscience void of offence.* If you have wronged any man, be not ashamed to acknowledge it, and according to your power make restitution, that the accursed thing may not cleave to you. Take heed that you grieve not the Spirit of God by unholy walking, lest you provoke him to forsake you. To this end watch over your heart, repress its first inclinations to sin, and be watchful of temptations from without; fixing your eye especially on the sin by which you have heretofore been most easily beset. If at any time sin prevail against you, do not endeavor to forget it, or hide it in your bosom; but go to God immediately; take shame to yourself; plead the Gospel promises to returning sinners, looking unto Jesus Christ as your all sufficient sacrifice and advocate with the Father; and never cease wrestling with God in prayer for pardon, until he again speak peace to your troubled soul, and fill you with a greater fear of offending him.

As I hope you are now planted in God's vineyard, be *fruitful*. Bear on your heart a sense of God's love to sinners in Jesus Christ. Consider in particular what God has done for you, in "calling you out of darkness into his marvellous light." Remember how you lay fast asleep in sin and fatal security, when God awakened you to see your danger and escape it. Think how many still go on in the same fatal path in which you trod. And let the sense of God's distinguishing love to you excite you to some return. "Love him because he first loved you." And let love to your heavenly Father influence your *thoughts*, and *words*, and *actions*.

Let your *meditations* of God be sweet and frequent. Lift up your heart to him that seeth in secret, and trieth the heart and reins. Seek a close communion with the Father of your spirit; and to this end endeavor to withdraw your thoughts from worldly things, and to raise your affections from earth to heaven, to those things which are not seen but by the eye of faith. Thus you may walk by faith, guided by it as the eye of the soul, and raised by it to heavenly mindedness; so as habitually to love and delight in God.

Instead of your former vain conversation, henceforth let your *tongue be employed to God's glory;* in praising his name, in making known to others his mercy in Christ; in warning sinners of their danger, and encouraging them that fear God to be bold and hearty in his service. Pray much for sinners around you; for the prosperity of Zion; and that the whole earth may be converted to God.

And let your *conduct* in life be such as becometh the Gospel. You are called to fight the good fight of faith; see that you faint not, neither be weary of well-doing. Show that you are *alive* unto God, by *living* unto God, by devoting yourself to his service, and by diligence therein. Do something for him that has done so much for you. Love all men, for they are the work of God's hands. Do good to all men, not excepting your enemies; let these have your prayers and forgiveness, and be ready to "overcome evil with good."

See also that you show the power of godliness in the conscientious discharge of *relative duties*. Be kindly affectionate and tender-hearted to all about you. To those of your family show yourself an example of gentleness, love, and forbearance. Show your regard for their souls as well as their bodies. Let your family and your acquaintance see that you have a new heart, by your leading a new life, and studying in all things to be conformed to the will and word of God.

Show a particular regard for " them that are of the household of faith," all the sincerely godly for Christ's sake. And to animate you to greater diligence in this work and labor of love, look forward with the eye of faith to that glorious day when Christ shall reward acts of mercy and love, done in his name, as if done to himself.

Quickened by this principle, and encouraged by this prospect, strive to grow in knowledge, in purity, faith, love, and godly fear, in meekness and every Christian grace. Study to promote God's glory, the welfare of all men, and such a disposition in your own soul as may render you meet to be a partaker of the inheritance of the saints in light. And in order to promote this work of sanctification in you, wait on God for his blessing in a conscientious use of all the means of grace.

P. Sir, I thank you. I see a great work before me; but, by God's help, I hope I shall be able to hold out to the end.

M. You must expect many difficulties and much opposition. The way to heaven is the way of the cross, and through much tribulation. The world, the flesh, and the devil are strong enemies, and they are closely leagued together. But be not discouraged; God is above all. Christ " ever liveth to make intercession for us," and to save in every difficulty those " that come unto God through him." Holy angels will be employed as your guardians; and all the truly godly will be your loving brethren and ready friends. " They that are for you are more than they that are against you." Be not your own enemy, and nothing can hurt you. Be not high-minded, but fear. " Happy is the man that feareth always."

PUBLISHED BY THE AMERICAN TRACT SOCIETY.
150 Nassau-street, New-York.

NO. 20.

REMEMBER THE SABBATH DAY, TO KEEP IT HOLY.

Such is the solemn order of Him, in whose hands our breath is, and whose are all our ways; and he is one who will not be mocked, and cannot be either escaped or resisted. His bounty permits us to spend six days in our worldly labor—not that a good man will forget his Maker for a single hour—but the seventh day is the Lord's by a peculiar claim: on it he rested from his work, when he had finished the earth, the heavens, and all their host. We are informed also, that he hallowed it—that is, made it holy—fixed it as the season when the tribute of gratitude and adoration should be paid him by the joyful multitude. Shall a man rob God? Or has God withdrawn his claim? No; he appears by an ordinance, lasting as the sun and moon, to have demanded the seventh part of our time for his immediate service and glory. Yet, is there no mercy in this appointment? Has he no respect to your advantage? Yes, much every way. Be assured, he needs neither your services nor you. You can neither shake nor establish his throne. It is for your sake that he appoints a Sabbath; it is then that he meets you with more abundant instruction. Thousands adore him in heaven for the appointment, which, while they sojourned on earth, became the means of preparing them for their high abode; and are there not tens of thousands, either here or in the world of darkness, whose neglect of such advantages has led them on to a character perfected in guilt, and to a state that ushers in the midnight of despair?

Acknowledge then the love of God. He hath *blessed* the Sabbath day. It is a day of special grace. The immortal King prepares inexpressible delights for those who keep it holy; he is well pleased when his creatures pay this mark of reverence and subjection; he will bless them eminently. And you know not how many more of these bright opportunities shall dawn. To *you*, it may be the last has already set, or is at this moment setting. Oh! look, before you sink into the gloom of death; look to the mercy of God in Jesus, and say, "Lord, it is enough; fain would I rebel no longer; subdue and pardon me at once." If such a prayer ascended from your heart, we should have every thing to hope. No more would you mispend a Sabbath, either by unnecessary absence from public worship, or by unsuitable employment on returning from it. You would anxiously inquire—"Where can I find the faithful minister, who cares for my soul, and will feed it with the bread of life?" Having found one, you would prove your gratitude by the constancy of your attendance, by aiming to fix in your memory the truths imparted, and by praying over the services of the day. You would not exclaim, "What a weariness it is to serve the Lord!" You would find no temptation to ask, "Where is the harm if I spend a part of the day in some diversions?" Your conscience would suggest, that, as far as you did so, you ceased to keep the day holy; reason might tell you that those diversions would effectually blot out the solemnities you had quitted, and a still higher principle would create such a preference for religious duties, that you would treat every thing which invited you away, not as a pleasing amusement, but as a deadly foe.

It is well for you, that you live in a country where the Sabbath is respected. We speak not of the manner in which it is to be feared the greater part express this respect, but of the opportunities that offer to those who are willing. Some are undoubtedly less favored than others; but there are few, especially in cities, towns, and their neighborhoods, who are entirely without opportunities; and even those who are farther removed from public ordinances, whose families confine them principally to the house, and whose stations there are the least favorable to religion; even such may manifest their good will. Let them so much the more abound in reading the Scriptures and in secret prayer. Perhaps the Lord of the Sabbath may remove the hinderances; or, if he please, the word of life shall be brought nearer to them, or their incumbrances shall lessen, or, what is better than all, their family connexions shall become like-minded with themselves. And who so likely to obtain this enlargement of privileges, as those who make the best use of privileges already in their possession?

Mournful as the neglect of the Sabbath is, and widely

as the crime prevails, let us be thankful that the Sabbath still exists, and that there are persons who know its value. It was well observed by Archbishop Sharp, that, "were it not for that happy institution, we should hardly see any face of religion among us; and, in a little time, should scarcely be distinguished from heathen." A Sabbath! it is the Christian's feast-day. It brings into view every thing that purifies, consoles, exalts, and makes happy. With angels he celebrates thereon the creation of the world, and the resurrection of his Savior. His affections toward his fellow-worshippers are drawn into lively exercise, he feels himself to be their kinsman, he shares with them the enjoyments of divine communion, and learns how to improve all the remaining days of the week. As the morning approaches, his happy soul meets it with a welcome, and were he to speak, it would be in language like what we borrow from a poet :

> Another six days' work is done,
> Another Sabbath is begun;
> Return, my soul, enjoy thy rest,
> Improve the day thy God has blest.
>
> Oh that our thoughts and thanks may rise,
> As grateful incense, to the skies;
> And draw from heaven that sweet repose,
> Which none but he that feels it knows.
>
> This heavenly calm within the breast,
> Is the dear pledge of glorious rest,
> Which for the church of God remains,
> The end of cares—the end of pains.
>
> In holy duties let the day,
> In holy pleasures, pass away;
> How sweet a Sabbath thus to spend,
> In hope of one that ne'er shall end!

Testimony of Sir Matthew Hale to the good effects resulting from a strict observance of the Sabbath; extracted from a letter to his grandchildren.

"I will acquaint you with a truth, that above forty years' experience and strict observation of myself have assuredly taught me. I have been near fifty years a man as much conversant in business, and that of moment and importance, as most men; and I will assure you I was never under any inclination to fanaticism, enthusiasm, or superstition.

"In all this time I have most industriously observed, in myself and my concerns, these three things:

1. "Whenever I have undertaken any secular business on the Lord's day, which was not absolutely and indispensably necessary, that business never prospered and succeeded well with me. Nay, if I had set myself that day but to forecast or design any temporal business, to be done or performed afterward, though such forecast were just and honest in itself, and had as fair a prospect as could be expected, yet I have always been disappointed in the effecting of it, or in the success of it. So that it grew almost proverbial with me, when any importuned me to any secular business that day, to answer them, that if they expected it to succeed amiss, then they might desire my undertaking of it upon that day. And this was so certain an observation of mine that I feared to think of any secular business that day, because the resolution then taken would be disappointed or unsuccessful.

2. "That always, the more closely I applied myself to the duties of the Lord's day, the more happy and successful were my business and employments of the week following. So that I could, from the loose or strict observance of that day, take a just prospect and true calculation of my temporal success in the ensuing week.

3. "Though my hands and mind have been as full of secular business, both before and since I was a judge, as it may be any man's in England, yet I never wanted time in my six days to ripen and fit myself for the business and employments I had to do, though I borrowed not one minute from the Lord's day to prepare for it, by study or otherwise. But on the other hand, if I had at any time borrowed from this day any time for my secular employments, I found it did further me less than if I had left it alone; and therefore, when some years' experience, upon a most attentive and vigilant observation, had given me this instruction, I grew peremptorily resolved never in this kind to make a breach upon the Lord's day, which I have now strictly observed for above thirty years. This relation is most certainly and experimentally true, and hath been declared by me to hundreds of persons, as I now declare it to you."

PUBLISHED BY THE AMERICAN TRACT SOCIETY

NO. 21.

THE
CLOSET COMPANION;
OR
A HELP TO SELF-EXAMINATION.

DIRECTIONS.

I. *Make conscience of performing this duty.* The necessity of it will appear, if you consider, 1. God has repeatedly commanded it. 2. The people of God have always practised it. 3. There is great danger of being deceived; for every grace in the Christian has its counterfeit in the hypocrite. 4. Many professors have been deceived, by neglecting it; and are ruined for ever. 5 Your comfort depends, in a great measure, upon knowing your real state.

II. *Be very serious in the performance of it.* Set your heart to the solemn work, as in the presence of the Searcher of hearts, who will judge the secrets of all men, in the great day. Heaven and hell are no trifles. The question before you is no less than this: Am I a child of wrath, or a child of God? If I should die when I have done reading this, where would this precious soul of mine be, for ever?

III. *Be impartial,* or you lose your labour; nay, you confirm your mistakes. On the other hand, resolve to know the *worst* of yourself, the very worst. Some are afraid to know the worst, lest they should fall into despair; and this fear makes them partial. Suppose the worst, and if, after serious examination, it should appear that you have neither faith nor repentance, yet, remember, your case is not desperate. The door of mercy is ever open to the returning sinner. It remains a blessed truth, that *whoever cometh to Christ, shall in no wise be cast out.*

On the other hand, be willing to know the *best* of yourself, as well as the *worst.* Do not suppose that humility requires you to overlook your graces, and notice only your corruptions.

IV. Judge of your graces by their *nature,* rather than their *degree.* You are to try inherent graces by the *touch-*

stone, not by the *measure*. The greatest degree is to be desired and aimed at, but the smallest degree is matter of praise and rejoicing. Do not conclude there is no grace, because there is some corruption; or, that the Spirit does not strive against the flesh, because the flesh strives against the Spirit.

V. Let not the issue of this trial depend at all upon your knowledge of the exact time of your conversion, or the particular minister or sermon first instrumental in it. Many are wrought upon by slow and insensible degrees. Grace increases like the day-light. No man doubts whether the sun shines at noon, because he did not see the day break.

VI. Take this caution, lest you stumble at the threshold. The question before you is not, Will God accept and save me, though a vile sinner, if I believe on Christ? But you are to inquire, *Am I now, at this time, in an accepted state?* The former question is already resolved by God himself, who cannot lie. His word positively declares, that every returning sinner shall be accepted and saved. This, being determined, is not to be questioned. But you are to try, whether you are *now* in a state of grace?

VII. Take care, that you do not *trust* on your self-examination, rather than on Christ. There is a proneness in our natures to put duties in the place of Christ.

VIII. Be not content merely to read over the following questions, but stop and dwell on each; nor suffer yourself to proceed to another, till you have put the first home to your conscience, and have got an honest answer to it.

IX. Examine yourself *frequently*. Seize every opportunity to do it. The Lord's day evening is a most suitable season. The oftener you perform this work, the easier it will become. If you do not obtain satisfaction at first, you may, by repeated endeavours; and a scriptural, solid hope, will amply repay your utmost labour.

QUESTIONS,

RESPECTING FAITH, AND ITS FRUITS.

I. Do I BELIEVE ON THE SON OF GOD? Surely this is an important question. My Bible assures me, that *he that believeth shall be saved.* Do I then believe? And here let me carefully distinguish between faith and its fruits. *What is faith?* The simple meaning of faith is, believing; and believing always refers to something spoken or written. Divine faith is the belief of a divine testimony, as John speaks, *He that hath received his testimony, hath set to his seal that* GOD IS TRUE. And on the contrary, the Apostle John says, *He that believeth not God, hath made him a liar, because he believeth not the record that God gave of his Son. And this is the record, that God hath given to us eternal life, and this life is in his Son.* I must first believe the *truth* of God, as revealed in his word; I must credit his report, and believe his testimony concerning Christ; and then *receive* and *trust upon Christ,* so revealed, for my own personal salvation. But to be more particular:

1. Do I really believe that I am a fallen creature—that I derived from Adam a nature wholly corrupt, depraved, and sinful—and that I am a child of wrath, by nature, even as others?—Have I ever considered the unspotted and infinite purity and holiness of God's nature, and that he abhors sin wherever he sees it?—Have I considered that his *law,* contained in the *Ten Commandments,* is a copy and transcript of that holy nature; and by comparing myself with that eternal rule of *right,* have I been led to see my horrible wickedness and vileness?—O what multitudes of sins have I committed in thought, word, and deed!—Am I really sick of sin, sorry for sin, and do I abhor myself as a vile sinner?

2. Have I duly considered what my sins have deserved? Do I sincerely think, that if God had sent me to hell because of my sins, he would have done justly?

3. Do I see my utter *helplessness,* as well as my sin and misery?—Am I perfectly assured, that I cannot by any works, duties, or sufferings of my own, save myself; but that if ever I am saved, it must be the effect of free mercy?

4. Are the eyes of my understanding enlightened, to know Christ?—What do I think of Christ? Who is he? Do I believe that he is *God manifest in the flesh,* uniting in his *one* person the human and divine natures: *man,* that he might suffer; and *God,* that he might redeem?—Do I know *why* he suffered; that it was to make satisfaction to divine justice for the injury done to God's law and gov-

erument, by man's sin?—Do I believe, that *the Father is well pleased for his righteousness' sake ; and that he has magnified the law, and made it honourable ?*—Do I therefore look upon Christ, as the only way to the Father ; as the only foundation to build on, the only fountain to wash in ?— Am I persuaded of his ability to save, to the utmost, all who come to God by him?

5. Am I satisfied from God's own Word and promise, that whoever, let him be ever so vile and wicked, cometh to Christ by faith, shall be saved?—the promise being without exception, *whosoever believeth on him shall not be ashamed.*

6. Am I led and assisted by the Spirit of God, to believe this general promise, in *my own particular case ?* As God has made no exceptions, why should I except myself? True, no tongue can tell how vile I have been ; only God knows the greatness of my sins, and the wickedness of my heart! But shall I then *reject Christ, and despair,* and so add to my other sins the worst and greatest sin of all, *Unbelief?* God forbid ! *It is a faithful saying, and worthy of all acceptation, that Christ came to save sinners.* Do I then, sensible of my sin, misery, and helplessness, look upon Christ as an all-sufficient Saviour, and commit my precious and immortal soul to him, relying upon him only, and endeavouring to rely upon him confidently, for eternal salvation?

Having thus examined my faith, let me proceed impartially to examine the *fruits and effects of my faith.*—Many pretend to faith, whose works give the *lie* to their pretensions ; let me, therefore, *show my Faith by my Works.*

QUESTION II. WHAT ARE THE FRUITS OF MY FAITH ? Does it produce those effects, which the word of God points out, as the proof and evidence of its sincerity, with respect to my *conscience,* my *heart,* and my *life ?*

1. *What are the effects of my Faith, as to my Conscience?* Do I rest from my former legal *attempts* to justify myself, going about to establish my own righteousness? Am I satisfied with Christ's righteousness, as a complete title to glory?—I read of *peace in believing.* Have I peace in my conscience ? Being justified by faith, have I peace with God ?—When my soul is alarmed by the remembrance of former sins, or those lately committed, how do I obtain

peace? Is it by forgetting them as soon as I can, and then fancying that God has forgotten them too?—Is it by resolving to do so no more, and so making future obedience atone for past offences?—Is it by performing religious duties, and so making amends?—Or is it by a fresh application to the pardoning, peace-speaking blood of Christ?—When my sins stare me in the face, and my duties themselves appear sins, whence, O my soul, proceeds thy comfort?—*Is it the blood of Christ, that purges my conscience from dead works?* —Does faith in the atonement free me from the dreadful apprehension of condemnation and wrath due to sin?— Do I, or do I not, look up to God, through the death of his Son, with freedom and delight?—If I have not this peace, why is it? What hinders? Either I do not clearly understand the nature of the Gospel, or I do not fully believe it; for it provides for every possible case. If I have this, blessed be God for it! Lord, help me to keep it, that it may keep me. Lord, I believe, help thou my unbelief.

2. *What are the effects of my Faith, as to my Heart and its affections?*

(1.) *Do I love God the Father?* Do I think of him, and go to him, as a loving Father in Christ? Have I the spirit of adoption, so that I cry, *Abba, Father?* Do I love him as the Father of mercies, the God of hope, the God of peace, the God of love?

(2.) *Do I love Christ?* To those who believe, he is precious; is he precious to me? Do I see infinite beauty in his person? Is he the chief among ten thousands to me, and altogether lovely? Do I admire the length, and breadth, and depth and height of his love? Is the language of my very soul, *None but Christ, none but Christ?* Is it my grief and shame, that I love him no more?

(3.) *Do I love the Holy Spirit?* Do I honour him as the great Author of light and life, grace and comfort? Do I maintain a deep sense of my dependance on his agency in all my religious performances? Do I desire my heart to be his temple? Am I cautious lest I quench his holy motions, or grieve him by my sins? Am I sensible, that without his influence I cannot pray, hear, read, communicate, nor examine myself, as I ought?

(4.) *Do I love God's law?* Do I delight in the law of the Lord, after the inward man, not wishing it less strict

VOL 1.

and holy, but loving it because it is holy? Am I as willing to take Christ for my *King* to rule over me, as for my *Priest* to atone for me? Do I hunger and thirst after righteousness? Do I pant, and long, and pray to be holy? Do I wish to be holy, as I wish to be happy? Do I hate all sin, especially that sin which most easily besets me, and labour daily to mortify it, and to deny myself?—Do I sigh for complete deliverance from remaining corruption, and rejoice in the hope of it through a holy Jesus? Do I long for heaven, that there I may be satisfied with his likeness?

(5.) *Do I love God's people?* Can I say to Christ, as Ruth to Naomi, *Thy people shall be my people?* Do I love them, because they love Christ, and bear his image? Do I feel a union of spirit with them, though they may not be of my party, or think exactly as I do? Can I say, *I know that I have passed from death to life, because I love the brethren?*

3. *What are the effects of my faith, as to my daily Walk and Conversation?* The word of God tells me, that he who is in Christ is a *new creature; old things are passed away; all things are become new.*—*If ye love me*, said Christ, *keep my commandments.* Let me review the commandments, and see how my love to Christ is manifested by my *obedience.*

(1.) Do I know and acknowledge God to be the only true God, and my God, and do I worship and glorify him accordingly? Is he the supreme object of my desire and delight? Do I trust him, hope in him, love to think of him? Do I pray to him, do I praise him, am I careful to please him?

(2.) Do I receive, observe, and keep pure and entire, all such religious worship and ordinances as God hath appointed in his word? How is it with me in secret prayer, in family prayer, in public prayer? With what views do I go to hear the preached Gospel, and what good do I get by it?

(3.) Do I make a holy and reverent use of God's names, titles, attributes, ordinances, word and works; avoiding the profanation or abuse of any thing whereby God makes himself known?

(4.) Do I keep holy to God the Sabbath-day, resting all that day from worldly employments, recreations, and conversation? And do I spend the *whole time* in public and private exercises of divine worship, except so much as is to be taken up in the works of necessity and mercy? Is the Sabbath my delight, and are the ordinances of God's house very precious to my soul?

(5.) Do I endeavour to preserve the honour, and perform all the duties, which I owe to my superiors, inferiors, or equals? remembering that true religion makes good *husbands, wives, children, masters,* and *servants.* If I am *really* holy, I am *relatively* holy.

(6.) Do I use all lawful means to preserve my own life and the life of others? Do I avoid all intemperance? Do I resist passionate tempers? Do I labour to promote the welfare of men's souls? Do I exercise love and compassion towards the poor and distressed, according to my ability? Do I freely forgive those who have injured me? Do I pray for them; and instead of hating, do I love my very enemies?

(7.) Do I earnestly strive to preserve my own and my neighbour's *Chastity,* in *heart, speech,* and *behaviour;* avoiding all incentives to *lust,* such as intemperance in food, lascivious songs, books, pictures, dancing, plays, and vile company; remembering that my body is the temple of the Holy Ghost?

(8.) Do I use the lawful means of procuring and furthering the wealth and outward estate of myself and others? Do I abhor every species of robbery and injustice? Am I strictly and conscientiously honest in all my dealings, not overreaching nor defrauding any person, in any degree?

(9.) Do I studiously maintain and promote truth between man and man; not only abhorring *perjury,* but hating all *falsehood?* And do I, as a professor of religion, avoid both ludicrous and pernicious lies, being as tender of my neighbour's character as of my own? Am I very cautious in making promises, and very careful to keep them?

(10.) Am I contented with the condition God has allotted me, believing that he orders all things for the best? And do I avoid envying my neighbour's happiness, or inordinately desiring any thing that is his?

Conclusion. And now, dear Reader, what is the result of your inquiry? Have you made a solemn pause at the close of every question, and obtained an honest answer? And are you, notwithstanding many imperfections, able to conclude, that your faith is of God's operation, and proved so to be, by its holy fruits? Then take the comfort, and give God the glory.

But if, on the other hand, the evidence of Scripture and your conscience is against you, and you are forced to conclude that your heart is not right with God—then, for God's sake, and for your soul's sake, cry instantly and mightily to him to have mercy upon you; remembering, that though your case is awful, it is not desperate; and that still you, even you, coming to Christ, shall in no wise be cast out.

SELF EXAMINATION.

'Tis a point I long to know,
   Oft it causes anxious thought;—
Do I love the Lord, or no?
   Am I his, or am I not?

Could my heart so hard remain,
   Pray'r a task and burden prove—
Ev'ry trifle give me pain—
   If I knew a Saviour's love?

Lord, decide the doubtful case!
   Thou who art thy people's Sun;
Shine upon thy work of grace,
   If it be indeed begun.

Let me love thee more and **more**,
   If I love at all, I pray;
If I have not loved before,
   Help me to begin to-day

THE EARL OF ROCHESTER.

This nobleman was distinguished as a great wit and a great sinner; and before he died, as a great penitent. Such he is described by the excellent Bishop Burnet, who personally knew him and attended him on his death-bed.

He had advanced to an uncommon degree of impiety, being a zealous advocate of Atheism. He had revelled likewise in the depths of debauchery, and had openly ridiculed all virtue and religion. But when, like the prodigal in the Gospel, he came to know himself, horror filled his mind, and drew from him the keenest self-reproaches. He was, in his own eyes, the vilest wretch on which the sun ever shone; and often wished that he had been a link-boy, a beggar, or a captive in a dungeon, rather than that he should so grossly have offended God.

Often when arguing with peculiar vehemence against God and religion, he felt the sting of an accusing conscience. At an atheistical meeting in the house of a person of quality, he undertook to be the champion of infidelity, and received the applause of the company; but his conscience so reproached him, that he exclaimed to himself, "Good God! that a man who walks upright, who sees the wonderful works of God, and has the use of his reason—should bid defiance to his Creator!"

These successive convictions, however, gradually wore off; and it was not till his last illness, which continued about nine weeks, that he appears to have been truly convinced and savingly converted. Then he saw "the exceeding sinfulness of sin," and learned the value of the atonement on which his hopes of pardon were founded. "Shall the joys of heaven," exclaimed he, "be conferred on me? O, mighty Savior, never, but through thy infinite love and satisfaction! O never, but by the purchase of thy blood!"

The Scriptures, which had been so often the subject of his merriment, now secured his esteem and inspired delight; for they had spoken to his heart: the seeming absurdities and contradictions, fancied by men of corrupt and reprobate judgments, vanished; and he was brought to receive the truth in the love of it. The fifty-third chapter of Isaiah, which was repeatedly read to him by Rev.

Mr. Parsons, was made particularly useful to him. Comparing it with the history of our Savior's passion, he saw the fulfillment of a prophecy written several ages before, and which the Jews who blasphemed Jesus still kept in their hands as an inspired book. He confessed to Bishop Burnet, that as he heard it read " he felt an inward force upon him, which so enlightened his mind and convinced him that he could resist it no longer; for the words had an authority which shot like rays or beams in his mind; so that he was not only convinced by the reasoning, which satisfied his understanding, but by a *power* which did so effectually *constrain him*, that he ever after as firmly believed in his Savior as if he had seen him in the clouds."

He had this chapter read so often to him that he " got it by heart, and went through a great part of it," says the Bishop, " in discourse with me, with a sort of heavenly pleasure, giving me his reflections on it; some of which I remember: '*Who hath believed our report?*' 'Here,' he said, 'was foretold the opposition the Gospel was to meet with from such wretches as he was.' '*He hath no form or comeliness; and when we shall see him, there is no beauty that we should desire him.*' On this he said, 'The meanness of his appearance and person has made vain and foolish people disparage him, because he came not in such a fool's coat as they delighted in.' Many other observations he made, which were not noted down; enlarging on many passages with a degree of heavenly pleasure, and applying various parts of it to his own humiliation and comfort. 'O, my God,' he would say, 'can such a creature as I, who have denied thy being and contemned thy power, be accepted by thee? Can there be mercy and pardon for me? Will God own such a wretch as I am?"

His faith now rested on Christ alone for salvation, and often would he entreat God to strengthen it; crying out, " Lord, I believe, help thou my unbelief." The grand enemy of souls failed not to assault him with many temptations; "But I thank God," said he, "that I abhor them all; and by the power of grace, which I am confident is sufficient for me, I have overcome them. It is the malice of the devil because I am rescued from him; and it is the goodness of God that frees me from all my spiritual enemies."

This noble convert gave many proofs of the soundness of his repentance; among which was his earnest desire to prevent the evil effects of his former writings and example. He gave a strict charge to the persons in whose custody he left his papers, that all his profane and lewd writings and pictures should be burned; and he desired all who attended him to publish abroad, that all men might know "how severely God had disciplined him for his sins by his afflicting hand; acknowledging that his sufferings would have been most just had they been ten times more heavy." His former visitations, he confessed, had produced some slight resolutions of reforming, arising from the present painful consequences of his sins; but now he declared that he had other sentiments of things, and acted upon other principles; that he possessed so great an abhorrence of all sin, that he would not commit a known sin to gain a kingdom.

To his former companions in sin he sent awful messages; and to some who visited him he gave the most solemn warnings. To one gentleman in particular he said, "O! remember that you contemn God no more. He is an avenging God, and will visit you for your sins; and will, I hope, in mercy touch your conscience sooner or later, as he has done mine. You and I have been friends and sinners together a great while, therefore I am the more free with you. We have been all mistaken in our conceits, and our persausions have been false and groundless; therefore God grant you repentance!" Seeing the same person again, he said, "Perhaps you were disobliged by my plainness yesterday; I spake the words of truth and soberness; I hope God will touch your heart."

Knowing the rock on which he himself had foundered, he expressed an earnest wish that his son might never prove one of those profane and licentious *wits* who pride themselves in denying God, and scoffing at religion; and that all his family might be educated in the fear of God. The following recantation he subscribed, and ordered it to be published to the world:

"For the benefit of all those whom I may have drawn into sin by my example and encouragement, I leave to the world this my last declaration, which I deliver in the presence of the great God, who knows the secrets of all hearts, and before whom I am to be judged; that from the bottom of my soul I detest and abhor the whole course of my former wicked life: and that I think I can never sufficiently admire the goodness of God, who has given me a true sense of my pernicious opinions and vile practices; by which I have hitherto lived without hope, and without God in the world; have been an open enemy to Jesus Christ, doing the utmost despite to the holy Spirit of grace; and that the greatest testimony of my charity to such is, to warn them, in the name of God, and as they regard the welfare of their immortal souls, no more to deny his being or his providence, or despise his goodness; no more to make a mock of sin, or contemn the pure and excellent religion of my ever-blessed Redeemer; through whose merits alone, I, one of the greatest of sinners, do yet hope for mercy and forgiveness. Amen. "J. ROCHESTER.

"*Delivered and signed June 19, 1680, in the presence of*
"ANN ROCHESTER. "R. PARSONS."

We now return to the death-bed experience of this converted nobleman, and mark the power of religion upon his mind in that important season. He seemed to have no desire to live, except to testify the truth of his repentance, and to bring glory to God. "If God," said he, "should spare me yet a little longer here, I hope to bring glory to his name proportionably to the dishonor I have done him in my whole life past; and particularly by endeavoring to convince others, and to assure them of the danger of their condition, if they continue impenitent; and to tell them how graciously God has dealt with me."

And when he came within the nearer views of death, about three or four days before his departure, he said, "I shall now die. But O what unspeakable glories do I see! what joys beyond thought or expression am I sensible of! I am assured of God's mercy to me, through Jesus Christ. O how I long to die, and to be with my Savior!"

Thus died this eminent subject of regenerating grace, July 26, 1680, being only in his 34th year; yet so was life worn away by his long illness and former licentious course, that nature gave up without a struggle.

The account published by Bishop Burnet gives the particulars of his conversion more at length, and the various conversations on divine things between them, under the title of "Some Passages in the Life and Death of John, Earl of Rochester;" of which the late Dr. Johnson entertained so high an opinion that he says, "the critic ought to read it for its excellence, the philosopher for its arguments, and the saint for its piety."

PUBLISHED BY THE AMERICAN TRACT SOCIETY

GOD A REFUGE.

There is not a son or daughter of Adam but has wants and woes. While the desire of happiness is predominant in every breast, there are multitudes who seek it by a life of continual labour and solicitude, and never find it. They form an erroneous judgment in respect both to the nature of real happiness, and the means of obtaining it. Man is possessed of two natures. He has an animal nature in common with other living creatures on the earth; and a spiritual, immortal nature, in common with angels. To make man happy, the wants of both natures must be supplied; and he must find some certain and sufficient refuge from the woes to which he is exposed. The union of soul and body is so close, and the sympathy between them so great, that wherever one is entirely neglected in the provisions for happiness which we make, the other will be a sufferer. Hence arises the dissatisfaction and wretchedness of those, who, while they pursue carnal enjoyments, make no preparation to satisfy the wants of their immortal souls.

When we look for a refuge in creatures, they always deceive us; but of this they give us warning. God has so formed every thing about us, that it speaks the language of admonition. Yonder ancient house, as we pass it, tells us that time impairs the structure reared by mortal hands; it whispers in the ear of reflection, that those who built it, and probably looked for peace and happiness within its walls, now moulder in the grave. Yonder ancient tree tells us, that he who planted it, and multitudes who have sat beneath its shade, are now in the shadow of death. When we pass the repository of the dead, innumerable voices issue from the tombs, and warn us that we have no refuge—no abiding place on earth. The very ground on which we tread every day admonishes us that it has been trodden by feet which are now undistinguishable from it. The constant changes and succession which we behold in all the world around us, warn us that there is no stability or security of any permanent happiness in terrestrial objects.

Vol. 1

The man who cannot say, 'My refuge is in God,' cannot say he has any refuge.—I ask you where you find a refuge in pain and distress? From these you cannot fly. It is not more certain that the sun will pursue his course to-day, than that these will overtake you. Will you fly to a physician? But how numberless are the cases in which no art can assist you; and how certain it is that a time will come, when such a refuge will only disappoint your hopes. Your past pleasures and your present possessions will then serve only to convince you of their vanity, because they cannot save you, be your cry ever so strong.—You have lost your property on the ocean, by accident or by fraud; you find yourself exposed to all the wants and mortifications of poverty, and your family involved with you in suffering. Where do you find a refuge? In the charity of your fellow men? This is a cold comfort. It is one which neither your pride will admit, nor their generosity extend, so as to constitute any adequate recompense for your losses. —You are persecuted by injustice, assailed by the tongue of slander, or have exposed yourself to the enmity of those who can do you much injury. Where is your refuge? Is it an appeal to the tribunals of your country? But these are so imperfect that they will neither blunt the dart nor extract the poison with which it has racked your breast.

Your country is divided by hostile parties, is threatened by foreign invasion, or is actually engaged in war; you tremble for the security of your family and friends, of your life, liberty, and property. Where is your refuge? Is it in the hope that your party, or your country, will prevail? But this is altogether uncertain; and if it were certain, the victory may cost you the loss of all for which you are alarmed.

The wife of your bosom, the dear child on which your affections are set, a beloved parent, or an affectionate relative, is taken away by death. Where is your refuge? In complaints? These will increase your misery. In weeping? This will administer no consolation. In plunging into worldly cares and pleasures? This will only be opening one source of misery to shut up another.

Your immortal soul, deluded so often in its hopes of happiness from carnal pursuits, will sometimes feel an aching void; the thoughts of guilt, of immortality, the fear of future judgments, will sometimes plant thorns in your pillow.

Where is your refuge? Will you drown all these anxieties in oblivion? Will you go to mirth, and wine, and thoughtless company, that you may cast them away? After all, they will return. There will be seasons in which they will overwhelm you; and on a death-bed, and in eternity, they will be a thousand fold worse than ever.

A few days more, and you will be gasping for breath; all human aid and skill will be useless; there is only another step, and you are on the ocean of eternity. Your pleasures, your riches, your gay friends, your honours, are now so many daggers to your soul, because they have drawn you away from God, and left you without any support in his place. Where is your refuge? Unhappy man! you have none. God will not receive you, when you have trifled with him so long; and the world is worse than nothing. You have only to draw another breath, and awake in the realms of despair.

You cannot say that I am describing fictions of the imagination to alarm you. The evils which I have enumerated are, in almost every instance, among those which no son or daughter of Adam can escape. Pain, distress, loss of friends, apprehensions of insecurity from national convulsions, despondencies at future prospects, agitations about death, which will tear you from every beloved earthly object; are woes from which no station nor circumstances will exempt you. I speak of real and certain evils, evils from which, if your peace is not made with God, you have not found, and cannot find, a refuge.

You confess yourself, that after all your efforts to find happiness from enjoyments of this world, you are disappointed. Thousands of times you have set your affections on objects which you have not been able to attain; and as many times more, you have found anticipation far exceed actual enjoyment. When you know that the most desirable objects on earth, if already in your possession, may not continue so for a single hour, it casts a gloom over your fairest hopes, which cannot be dissipated.

You have been driven about from object to object; one disappointment has followed another; and the only refuge you have found is in beginning the pursuit of some new object, which will end just as all the others have done. You are tossing from billow to billow on this tempestuous ocean, and the most you can expect is only a few days of fair weather before you are shipwrecked, for you are not directing your course to any haven which can afford you the least security.

You may wander through life in this hopeless manner after a resting place, but after all, there is no refuge but God. There is nothing short of him which can satisfy the desires of an immortal mind. The soul which emanated from God cannot be satisfied without returning to him. It may be stupified, benumbed, blinded, hardened, but cannot be satisfied. If you send me for a refuge to all the boasted wisdom of a philosopher whose fame has filled the earth, it will not meet my wants, nor support me under the sufferance of my woes. Two great systems have divided that class of men, and neither is at all adequate to the end in view. The one bids me harden myself against the wants and woes of life, and seek a refuge in *insensibility*. But when I ask for a refuge, I ask for support and comfort in all my trials as a man, and not to be turned into a block. The other bids me bury all my woes in *carnal pleasure*. But in sickness, in poverty, in misfortune, on a death-bed, when I most need a refuge, it is beyond my power to covet or indulge in such pleasures. Beyond all this, my nature will not support such a course. Sensual pleasures bring disease, disgust, and melancholy. They debase my soul, and make me like the brutes that perish. I ask for a refuge *in the time of my woes*, but I am directed to one which I cannot *then* enjoy. I ask for a refuge in my woes, that I may bear them as a man, and I am directed to become a *brute*.

The soul that has been brought to feel its need of support, can never find a refuge here. All the wisdom of men, and all the objects of time and sense, cannot discover or afford one. Every prop on which you lean will fall; and if you have no other security, your case is deplorable indeed.

When you contemplate the scene before you, and see the evils to which you are exposed, if you have the fears or feelings of a reasonable being, methinks you cannot but desire to find a sufficient refuge. Such a one the Psalmist points out: 'My refuge is in God.' He wrote this when his enemies were lying in wait to destroy him, and it was probable, according to human appearance, that he would fall into their hands. In the midst of these expected calamities, he found a refuge in God. He fled to it, was satisfied and supported,

God is the refuge which we all need. The soul that flies to God will find a *certain*, an *all-sufficient*, and an *eternal* refuge.

Let us consider these three characteristics. I find myself possessed of powers to enjoy happiness, or to suffer misery. I am placed in a world where suffering abounds, and where it is impossible to avoid it. My past experience has satisfied me that I cannot place my hopes of a refuge from trouble in any thing which this world can afford. It is all delusive, unstable, uncertain. I want some support under my trials which is not of such a nature; I want a refuge which is *certain*, whither I may fly without the possibility of being deceived. The Scriptures tell me, God is a refuge. In attentively considering this declaration, I find that he will afford that certainty of support which I need. My soul is sick with disappointment treading upon the heels of disappointment. I want somewhere to fix, so that I never shall be compelled to remove again. God will afford that certain refuge. God is unchangeable; 'the same yesterday, to-day, and for ever.' The support he gives to-day, he can give to-morrow and for ever. The Creator of the ends of the earth fainteth not, *neither is he weary*. Because he is subject to no *variableness nor shadow of turning*, creatures who fly to him, cannot be mocked and deluded by seeing the ground of their expectations perish. From everlasting he has not changed; and because he is above the operation of all causes which produce change, and *abideth for ever*, therefore he is a *certain* refuge.

Tired of perpetual change, the soul may *fix here*. The first great object of its inquiry is found.

When I am satisfied that I have found a refuge which is not mutable, and cannot mock my hopes, my next inquiry is, is this a *sufficient* refuge for all my wants and woes? In further contemplating the character of God, I find that he brought all creation into existence by a word of his power, that he constantly supports and directs all creatures and worlds; and that a single word from him can change, renew, or annihilate them. I find, therefore, that there is not a calamity which I fear, but he can avert it; or if this be not consistent with the course of his providence, he can soften it, and grant me a temper of mind which will bear me above it. When sickness invades, he can rebuke the disease, when friends or estate is lost, he can pour the balm of consolation into my wounded soul; when kingdoms are convulsed, he can speak them into peace, or direct his judgments to my benefit; when my sins come up against me and bow down my guilty soul, he can separate them from me. When death invades, he can make the eye beam with hope, which is about to close until the heavens are no more; he can enlighten my path through the valley of the shadow of death, and translate me from a vale of tears to the abodes of glory. Neither heaven, nor earth, nor hell, can alter his purposes, or defeat a single promise. If I trust in him, I have this security, "All things work together for good to them that love God." Here is not only support, a power of endurance in time of trouble, but an absolute promise that it shall be converted into a blessing. When an omnipotent and omnipresent God, who cannot deceive, engages this, it is all I can ask. My soul is satisfied with his sufficiency. There cannot be a want but it will be supplied, nor a wo but it shall be converted into a blessing. It is *enough*. The refuge is all-sufficient. Men or angels can ask for nothing more.

Once more; when I think of annihilation, or of ever being exposed to misery at any future season, however distant, I find within me something which shudders at the thought. My mind is therefore led to inquire particularly whether the refuge which God offers is not only *certain* and *all-sufficient* for the present, or for ages to come, but whether it will be *eternally the same*.

Here again light and comfort break in from on high. 'I the Lord change not.' From everlasting to everlasting he is God. 'The mountains shall depart, and the hills be removed; but my kindness shall not depart from thee, neither shall the covenant of my peace be removed, saith the Lord.' 'Wherefore God, willing more abundantly to show unto the heirs of promise the immutability of his counsel, confirmed it by an oath; that by two immutable things, in which it was impossible for God to lie, we might have strong consolation who have fled for *refuge* to lay hold on the hope set before us.' '*Jesus Christ the same yesterday, to-day, and for ever.*' He who is the same for ever will for ever be the same *refuge* he is now. On this awfully momentous subject, then, my fears may be hushed, when I have the security of a God of truth, that the refuge he affords will never fail. Without such an assurance the soul cannot be satisfied. Grant me a *certain* and *all-suffi-*

cient refuge for the present, and for millions of ages, and then tell me a time may come when it may fail, and you take away the anchor of my hope. Publish the tidings in heaven that their refuge is not eternal, and the songs of angels would instantly be converted into notes of wo. But blessed be God, such tidings will never reach the ear of a creature in the universe, who puts his trust in him.

All the important questions, then, about which my anxiety was exercised, are answered. Placed in a world of sin and wo, and deeply the subject of both, I find a refuge pointed out, where I may find security from them. My support is *certain*, it is *all-sufficient*, it is *eternal*.

Christians, you have fled to this refuge. Of all the inhabitants of this lower world, you have the most reason to rejoice. While afflictions are the ensigns of divine indignation to sinners, you hear, in the midst of your sufferings, a voice, saying, 'Whom the Lord loveth he chasteneth, and scourgeth every son whom he receiveth.' While you are called to trials, and wants, and sorrows, omnipotence and infinite mercy stand pledged that all things shall work together for good. What is it that brightens the countenance of that daughter of affliction? But yesterday she buried the husband of her youth: but a few weeks since she was reduced to poverty: and at this very moment her only surviving child lies at the point of death. Why, she has just been kneeling in her closet, where, if you could have listened, you might have heard her say, 'My cup of affliction is indeed full; yet, gracious God, not my will but thine be done. It is thine to command, but mine to obey. While thou art with me I am not forsaken. Thou gavest, and thou hast taken away, blessed be thy name. I ask for nothing more than submission to thy will, and for thy gracious presence. My Judge, my everlasting husband, I cast myself into the arms of thy mercy. Thou wilt not reject my cry in the hour of distress. Let me be thine, and I shall be comforted.'

Her cries have entered into the ears of the Lord of Sabaoth He has communed with her from off his mercy-seat. She has found a refuge.

What is it that calls forth a glow of hope from those cheeks growing pale in death, and those quivering lips? It is only a moment, and the soul will wing its flight to an unknown world, and enter on an unchangeable destiny.

Why, that soul, like the dying Stephen, has seen heaven opened, and Jesus standing on the right hand of God. If you could have heard its language, you might have discovered a cause for its triumph at this moment. 'When flesh and heart fail me, God is my strength and portion for ever. Into thy hands, merciful Saviour, I commit my soul, for thou hast redeemed it. *Though I walk through the valley of the shadow of death, I will fear no evil, for thou art with me. Come, Lord Jesus, come quickly.*' Do not be surprised to see the Christian triumph in the hour of death; he has found his *refuge*.

Sinners, whose peace is not made with God, you have found no refuge. You are like the troubled sea which casts up mire and dirt; and eternal truth has said, 'There is no peace to the wicked.' Your way is dark and leads to hell. If you mean to keep on in your present course, to set at defiance all the thunders of Sinai, and to mock at the invitations of redeeming mercy, then go your way. Eat, drink, and be merry. It is all the good you will have in this life; *more* than you will have in that which is to come. The inevitable hour of danger, distress, and death, approaches; and for this hour you have no *refuge*. O the miseries of your condition, when there is but a step between time and eternity, and when you are hastening away to the bar of an offended, almighty Judge, without a refuge from his wrath! If you will mock, mock now; now is your time. On a death-bed you will not mock. In hell you will not mock. There even the merciful Jehovah will pursue you with his thunders. You will then see your need of that refuge which has now been set before you, and which you now neglect.

PUBLISHED BY THE
AMERICAN TRACT SOCIETY,

And sold at their Depository, No. 150 Nassau-street, near the City-Hall, New York; and by Agents of the Society, its Branches, and Auxiliaries, in the principal cities and towns in the United States

ON

KEEPING THE HEART.

BY THE REV. JOHN FLAVEL.

THE *heart* of a man is the worst part, before it is regenerated, and the best, afterwards; it is the seat of principle, and fountain of actions; the eye of God is, and the eye of the christian ought to be, fixed principally upon the heart.

The greatest difficulty *in* conversion, is to turn the heart *to* God; and the greatest difficulty *after* conversion, is to keep the heart *with* God. Here lies the very stress of religion; this makes the way to life a narrow way, and the gate of heaven a strait gate. " Keep thy heart," it is written, " with all diligence; for out of it are the issues of life."

By the heart is meant the soul in general, or as an apostle calls it, the inner man; and by keeping the heart is meant the constantly watching over our thoughts, purposes and affections, in order to preserve us from sin, and maintain sweet and free communion with God.

The manner of performing it is, " with all diligence." The word is very emphatical, " Keep with all keeping;" and this vehemence of expression plainly implies how difficult it is to keep our hearts, and how dangerous it is to let them go.

The reason or motive is this, " out of it are the issues of life." As the spring in a watch sets all the wheels in motion, so the heart is the spring and the origin both of good and evil; " a good man out of the good treasury of his heart bringeth forth good things, and an evil man out of the evil treasury of his heart, bringeth forth evil things." Let me then draw your attention to this important truth :

That the keeping and right managing of the heart, in every condition, is the great business of the christian's life.

To keep the heart, necessarily supposes a previous work of sanctification, which has set the heart right by giving it a new spiritual bent and inclination. Man, by creation, had an understanding to know God, a heart to love him, and a will to obey him. Man, by his fall, is become a most disordered and rebellious creature, opposing his Maker as the first cause, by self-dependance; as the chief good, by self-love; as the highest Lord, by self-will; and as the last end, by self-seeking: thus man is the reverse of what he was, and the sad change is universal. His once illuminated understanding is clouded with ignorance; his once complying will, full of stubbornness; and all his once subordinate powers have cast off the dominion of his superior faculties. But by regeneration, this disordered soul is set right again. Sanctification is the renewing of the soul after the image of God; through which self-dependance is removed by faith; self-love, by the love of God; self-will, by subjection to the will of God; and self-seeking, by self-denial. The darkened understanding is again illuminated, the refractory will sweetly subdued, the rebellious appetite gradually conquered; and thus the soul which sin had universally depraved, is again restored and rectified. It should be the constant care of the regenerate man to preserve his soul in that holy frame into which grace has renewed it. This is an arduous work; for though grace has in a great measure rectified the soul, and given it an habitual and heavenly temper, yet sin often discomposes it again; so that even a renewed heart, like a musical instrument, though often tuned, is soon put out of tune again; the christian's heart, if lively in one duty, is often dull and disordered in another; to keep the heart then, is carefully to preserve it from sin which disorders it, and to maintain that spiritual and gracious frame which fits us for a life of communion with God. It includes in it the following duties:

1. Frequent observation of the frame of the heart. It is a hard thing to bring a man and himself together upon this important business. There are some who have lived forty or fifty years, and have had scarcely one hour's discourse with their own hearts all that while; but saints know that self-communion is of excellent use and advantage; the soul is made wise by sitting still in silence; it learns whether it is gaining or losing ground in the divine life.

2. It includes deep humiliation for heart evils and disorders, and earnest prayer for sanctifying grace: "Cleanse thou me from secret faults; create in me a new heart, and renew a right spirit within me." Saints offer many such petitions before the throne of grace; with these they fill their mouths, while they weep before the throne of mercy, "O for a better heart! a heart to love God more; to hate sin more; to walk more closely with God! Lord, deny me not such a heart, whatever else thou deniest me." It was observed of Mr. Bradford the martyr, that when he was confessing any sin, he would never give over confessing until he had felt some brokenness of heart for that sin; and when praying for any spiritual mercy, would never withdraw his petition till he had felt some relish for that mercy.

3. It includes a constant, holy jealousy over our own hearts. Quick-sighted self-jealousy is an excellent preservative from sin. He that would keep his heart, must have the eyes of his soul awake and open upon all the disorderly and tumultuous stirrings of his affections; if the affections break loose, and the passions are stirred, the soul must discover and surprise them before they come to a height. "O my soul, dost thou well in this? My tu-

multuous thoughts and passions, where is your commission?" Happy is the man that feareth always. By this fear of the Lord men depart from evil, shake off security, and preserve themselves from iniquity. He that will keep his heart, must act with fear, speak with fear, rejoice with fear, and pass the whole time of his sojourning here in fear; and all will be little enough to keep his heart from sin.

4. It includes the realizing of God's presence with us, and setting the Lord always before us. The people of God have found this of singular use to keep their hearts upright, and awe them from sin. When the eye of our faith is fixed upon the eye of God's omniscience, we dare not let out our thoughts and affections upon vanity. Holy Job durst not suffer his heart to yield to an impure, vain thought. " Doth he not see my ways, and count all my steps?"

Remember, christian, this heart work is the most *difficult* work thou hast to do. To shuffle through religious duties with a careless spirit, will cost no great pains; but to set thyself before the Lord, and tie up thy loose and vain thoughts to a constant and serious attendance upon him, will cost thee something. To attain a fluency of language in prayer, is easy; but to get thy heart broken for sin while thou art confessing it, and melted with free grace when thou art adoring God for it; to be really ashamed and humbled under a sense of God's infinite holiness, and to keep thy heart in this frame, not only *in* but *after* duty, will surely cost thee much pains. To repress the outward act of sin, and compose the outward part of thy life in a becoming manner, is no very difficult matter; the force of common principle can do this; but to kill the root of corruption, and to keep up a holy government, and to keep all well within, is no easy work.

Remember, it is a *constant* work: the keeping of the heart is a work that will never be finished till life is done; this labour and our life must end together; there is no time or condition in the christian life that will suffer an intermission of this work. It is in keeping watch over our hearts, as it was in keeping up the hands of Moses while Israel and Amalek were fighting below. Intermitting the watch over their own hearts a few minutes, cost David and Peter many a sad hour.

Remember, the keeping of the heart is a most *important* work.

Without this, we are but *formalists* in religion. God says, " My son, give me thy heart." When the heart is wanting, all our professions, gifts, and duties, go for nothing.

The *glory of God* is much concerned in it. From a neglected heart proceed those practices which cause the enemy to blaspheme; but when the heart is kept with all diligence, the life is fruitful in every good work; and it is written, " Herein is my Father glorified, that ye bear much fruit."

The *beauty of our conduct* arises from the heavenly frame and holy order of our minds. It is impossible that a disordered and neglected heart should ever produce a well ordered life; " out of the heart proceed evil thoughts, murders, adulteries." Mark the order—first, wanton or revengeful thoughts; then, unclean or adulterous practices. Is not this the reason why the discourses and duties of many christians are become so frothy and unprofitable? their communion both with God and one another runs so low. Where is that attracting beauty which used to shine from the conversation of the saints upon the men of the world? Time was, when their life and language were of a different strain from others; their tongues discovered them to be Galileans, wheresoever they were; but now, since vain speculations and fruitless controversies have prevailed, and heart-work and practical godliness are so much neglected, the case is sadly altered; their discourse is become like that of other men, who, if they come among such christians, may now " hear every one speak in his own language." And truly there is little reason to hope that we shall see this evil redressed, and the credit of religion again repaired, till christians take up this good old work again: when the salt of heavenly-mindedness is again cast into the spring, the streams will run clearer and sweeter.

Our *comfort* materially depends upon the keeping of our hearts. Be assured, my friend, if ever you hope for assistance in God's way, you must take pains with your own heart; you may expect your comforts upon easier terms; but I am mistaken if you ever enjoy them upon any other;

"Give all diligence," " Prove your own selves;" this is the Scripture way.

There was once a pious man, who, in the infancy of his religion so vehemently panted after the infallible assurance of God's love, that for a long time together he earnestly desired some voice from heaven: this, after many desires and longings, was denied him; but, in time, a better was afforded, in the ordinary way of searching the word and his own heart. Another good man was once driven by temptation upon the very borders of despair: at last, being sweetly settled and assured, one asked him how he attained it? he answered, " not by any extraordinary revelation, but by subjecting his understanding to the Scriptures, and comparing his own heart with them." It is indeed the office of the blessed Spirit to witness with your spirits. But be assured, my friends, God will not indulge lazy and negligent souls with the comforts of assurance; he will not so much as seem to patronise sloth and carelessness; his command has united our care and comfort together; the comfort of our souls rises and falls with our diligence in this work. " Keep thy heart then with all diligence."

The *improvement of our graces* depends upon the keeping of our hearts. Grace never thrives in a negligent and careless soul. The habits of grace are planted in the heart, and the more deeply they are fixed, the more thriving and flourishing grace will be. We read of being rooted and grounded. Grace in the heart is the root of every gracious word in the mouth, and of every holy work in the hand. Now, in a heart not kept with care and diligence, these fructifying influences are stopped and cut off; a multitude of vanities break in, and devour its strength. The heart is as it were the pasture, where a multitude of thoughts are fed every day; a heart diligently kept, feeds many thoughts of God in a day. " How precious are thy thoughts to me, O God! How great is the sum of them! If I should count them, they are more in number than the sand; when I awake I am still with thee." And as the gracious heart feeds and nourishes *them*, so they nourish and feast the *heart*. " My soul is filled with marrow and fatness, when I remember thee upon my bed, and meditate on thee in the night-watches.

My soul followeth hard after thee; thy right hand upholdeth me." The careless heart makes nothing of duties or ordinances, and yet these are the conduits of heaven, whence grace is watered and made fruitful. A man may go with a heedless spirit from ordinance to ordinance, abide all his days under the choicest teachings, and yet never be improved by them; heart-neglect is a leak in the vessel; no heavenly influence can abide where it is found. The heart that lies open and common is like the highway, free for all passengers, on which the birds of the air alight to devour the seed which is scattered there. It is not enough to hear, unless we take heed how we hear: we may pray, and not be better, unless we watch unto prayer.

The *stability of our souls in the hour of temptation* will depend much upon the care we take in keeping our hearts. The careless heart is an easy prey to Satan in the hour of temptation: if he wins the heart, he wins all; for it commands the whole man; and, alas! how easy a conquest is a neglected heart! It is the watchful heart that discovers and suppresses the temptation before it comes to its strength.

You have now heard that the keeping of the heart is the great work of a christian, in which the very life and soul of religion consist, and without which all other duties are of no value with God. Hence then I shall infer,

1. That the pains which many persons have taken in religion are but lost labour, and will never turn to account. Many glorious works are wrought by men, which will be utterly rejected, because the heart was not right with God. This is the fatal rock upon which thousands of vain professors split for eternity. O how many hours have some spent in hearing, praying, reading; and yet, as to the main end of religion, they might as well have done nothing. Thou that hast put off God with heartless duties, that hast acted in religion as if thou hadst been blessing an idol that could not search or discover the heart, how wilt thou abide the coming of the Lord? With what face canst thou so often tell him that thou lovest him, when thou knowest in thine own conscience that thine heart is not with him?

2. Hence I also infer, for the humiliation even of upright hearts, that unless the people of God spend more

time and pains about their hearts than they generally do, they are never likely to do God much service, or to enjoy much comfort. I may say to the christian that is remiss and careless in keeping his heart, "Thou shalt not excel." It grieves me to see how many christians there are, who go up and down dejected and complaining that they live at a poor low rate both of service and comfort: and can they expect it should be otherwise, as long as they live at such a careless rate? O how little of their time is spent in their closet in searching, humbling, and quickening their hearts! You say your hearts are dead; and do you wonder they are so, as long as you keep them not with the fountain of life? If your bodies had been dieted as your souls have been, they would have been dead too. Never expect better hearts, till you take more pains with them. He that will not have the sweat, must not expect the sweet, of religion. O christians, I fear your zeal and strength have run in a wrong channel; and we must take up this complaint of you. "They have made me keeper of the vineyards, but my own vineyard have I not kept."

Fruitless controversies have taken us off from practical godliness, and made us puzzle our heads when we should have been searching our hearts. O how little have we minded those words of the apostle, "It is a good thing that the heart be established with grace, and not with meats!" Would it not be better, christians, if the questions agitated among the people of God were such as these: "How may a soul discern its first declinings from God?" "How may a backsliding christian recover his first love?" "How may the heart be preserved from unseasonable thoughts in duty?" "How may a bosom sin be discovered and mortified?" O christian, it is time to be ashamed of this carelessness.

Another cause of neglecting our hearts is found in earthly encumbrances. O how has this wilderness entangled us! Our discourses, nay, our very prayers and duties, are infected by the world. We have had so much work without doors, that we have been able to do but little within. Alas! that christians who stand at the door of eternity, and have more work upon their hands than this poor moment of intervening time is sufficient for, should yet be filling both their heads and hearts with trifles!

3. If the keeping of the heart is so important a business—if so many dear and precious interests are included in it, then let me call upon the people of God every where to apply themselves to this important work. O christians, study your hearts, watch your hearts, keep your hearts; get into your closets; you have been strangers in this work too long; you have trifled about the borders of religion too long; this world has detained you from your great work too long; will you not now resolve to look better to your hearts? What I beg of you is, that you would commune, frequently and in earnest with your own hearts; that you would not suffer trifles to divert you, that you would keep a more true and faithful account of your thoughts and affections; that you would seriously demand of your own hearts, at least every evening, what have been their employments through the day.

The studying, observing, and diligent keeping of your hearts, will greatly *help your understanding* in the high concerns of religion. A man may discourse clearly and profoundly of the nature and effects of faith, the troubles and comforts of conscience, and the sweetness of communion with God, who never felt the efficacy and sweet impression of these things upon his own mind; but O! how dark and dry are these notions, compared with his upon whose heart they have been acted! When such a man reads David's Psalms, or Paul's Epistles, he is ready to exclaim, "O! these holy men speak my very heart! Their doubts are mine, their troubles mine, and their experience mine."

Your care and diligence in keeping your hearts will prove one of the best *evidences of your sincerity.* If self-jealousy, care and watchfulness, are thy daily employment, it strongly argues thy sincerity: for what but the sense of the divine eye, what but the real hatred of sin, could put thee upon these secret duties, which lie out of the observation of all creatures?

How fruitful, sweet, and comfortable, would *ordinances and duties* be to us, if our hearts were better kept! O what delightful communion we should have with God, if our meditations of him were more constant! A christian whose heart is in a good frame, gets the start of all others that come with him in that duty: they are tugging to get

VOL 1.

up their hearts to God; now trying one argument, and then another, to quicken and affect them; and sometimes go away as bad as they came; sometimes the duty is almost ended before their hearts are warmed and enlivened; out all this while the prepared heart is in its work. Prayers and sermons would appear to you very different from what they now do, were your hearts more prepared: you would not go away dejected and drooping; you would then have a fulness of matter for prayer, a rich supply for all your addresses to God.

By this, the decayed *power of religion will be recovered again* among professors. O that we might see the day, when professors should be no more content with a name to live, being spiritually dead! When the majestic beams of holiness shall awe the world, and command reverence from all that are about them! When they shall warm the hearts of all that come near them, so that men shall say, " God is with these men of a truth!"

Professors of religion, would you recover your credit? Would you again obtain an honourable testimony in the conscience of your very enemies? Then keep your hearts; watch your hearts. It is the earthliness of your hearts that has made your lives so unprofitable; you first lost sight of God, and communion with him; then your serious and heavenly deportment among men; and, by that means, your interest in their consciences. For the credit then of religion, for the honour of your profession, keep your hearts.

By diligence in keeping our hearts, we should prevent and *remove the fatal scandals and stumbling-blocks* out of the way of the world. " Wo to the world, because of offences!" Does not shame cover your faces, do not your hearts bleed within you, to hear of the scandalous fall of many loose professors? How is that worthy name blasphemed! And how are the hearts of the righteous made sad! By this the world is prejudiced against Christ and religion, and those who had a general love and liking to the ways of God are startled and quite driven back. How are the consciences of careless professors often overwhelmed in trouble, God inwardly excommunicating their souls from all comfortable fellowship with himself and the joys of his salvation! What words can express the high importance and the interesting consequences of this work? Every thing puts a necessity, a solemnity, a beauty, upon it.

If the people of God would more diligently keep their hearts, how exceedingly would the *communion of saints be sweetened!* "How goodly then would be your tents, O Jacob, and thy tabernacles, O Israel!" Were professors duly humbled under the evil of their own hearts, how charitable, how tender, would they be to others! They would strive no more, no more would they rashly censure; but they would forbear and forgive, keeping the unity of the Spirit in the bond of peace.

By this the *comforts of the Spirit*, and precious influences of all ordinances, would be fixed, and much longer preserved in our souls than they are. How is it, christians, that these comforts remain no longer with us? Doubtless, it is because we suffer our hearts to grow cold again; we have our hot and cold fits by turns; and this is owing to our unskilfulness and carelessness in keeping the heart.

I would now direct you to some spiritual *means for keeping the heart.*

1. Furnish your hearts richly with the word of God, which is the best preservative against sin; let it dwell with you richly in all its commands, promises, and threatenings; in your understanding, memory, consciences and affections; and then it will preserve your hearts. "Thy word have I hid in my heart, that I should not sin against thee." Conscience cannot be urged or awed by forgotten truth; but keep it in the heart, and it will keep both heart and life upright. "The law of his God is in his heart, none of his steps shall slide;" or if they do, the word will recover the straying heart again. We never lose our hearts till we have first lost the powerful impression of the word.

2. If ever you mean to keep your hearts with God, call them frequently to account; the oftener the heart meets with rebukes and checks for wandering, the less it will wander; if every vain thought were retracted with a sigh, every excursion of the heart from God with a severe check, it would not dare so boldly and frequently to digress and step aside; those actions which are committed with reluctance, are not committed with frequency.

3. He that means to keep his heart, must carefully ob-

serve its first declinings from God, and stop it there. Little sins, neglected, will quickly become great, and will increase to more and more ungodliness. Men little think to what a proud, vain, wanton, or worldly thought, may grow; "behold how great a matter a little fire kindleth!"

And now, my dear fellow christians, let me solemnly charge you to lay these things to heart; count over the benefits that will arise from a well-ordered heart. Is it a small matter to have your weak understanding assisted by divine wisdom? To have your sincerity cleared? Your communion with God sweetened? Your endangered souls guarded from sin? Your lips filled with prayer? Is it a small thing to have the decayed power of godliness again recovered, all fatal scandals removed, the communion of saints restored to its primitive glory, and the influences of ordinances abiding on the souls of saints? If these are blessings worth seeking, then surely it is an important duty to keep your hearts with all diligence! Be not discouraged, christian, with the difficulty of the work: the time is coming, when thou shalt be discharged from thy labour, from thy tears and sorrows; when all darkness shall be removed from thine understanding, when all vanity shall be removed from thy thoughts, and they shall be everlastingly and delightfully exercised upon the supreme goodness and excellence of thy God and Saviour, from whom they shall never start any more, like a broken bow; and these corruptions, which thou seest to-day, thou shalt see them no more for ever; and when thou shalt lay down the weapons of prayers, tears, and groans, and put on the armour of light, not to engage in battle, but to triumph for ever, through him who has loved you, and left you this gracious encouragement, "To him that overcometh will I grant to sit with me in my throne, even as I also overcame, and am set down with my father in his throne."

No. 25.

THE EFFECTS OF ARDENT SPIRITS

UPON

THE HUMAN BODY AND MIND.

BY BENJAMIN RUSH, M. D.

By ardent spirits, I mean those liquors only which are obtained by distillation from fermented substances of any kind. To their effects upon the bodies and minds of men, the following inquiry shall be exclusively confined.

The effects of ardent spirits divide themselves into such as are of a prompt, and such as are of a chronic nature. The former discover themselves in drunkenness; and the latter in a numerous train of diseases and vices of the body and mind.

I. I shall begin by briefly describing their prompt or immediate effects in a fit of drunkenness.

This odious disease (for by that name it should be called) appears with more or less of the following symptoms, and most commonly in the order in which I shall enumerate them.

1. Unusual garrulity.
2. Unusual silence.
3. Captiousness, and a disposition to quarrel.

4. Uncommon good humor, and an insipid simpering, or laugh.

5. Profane swearing and cursing.

6. A disclosure of their own or other people's secrets

7. A rude disposition to tell those persons in company, whom they know, their faults.

8. Certain immodest actions. I am sorry to say this sign of the first stage of drunkenness sometimes appears in women, who, when sober are uniformly remarkable for chaste and decent manners.

9. A clipping of words.

10. Fighting; a black eye, or a swelled nose, often mark this grade of drunkenness.

11. Certain extravagant acts which indicate a temporary fit of madness. These are singing, hallooing, roaring, imitating the noises of brute animals, jumping, tearing off clothes, dancing naked, breaking glasses and china, and dashing other articles of household furniture upon the ground or floor. After a while the paroxysm of drunkenness is completely formed. The face now becomes flushed, the eyes project, and are somewhat watery, winking is less frequent than is natural; the under lip is protruded—the head inclines a little to one shoulder—the jaw falls—belchings and hickup take place—the limbs totter—the whole body staggers. The unfortunate subject of this history next falls on his seat—he looks around him with a vacant countenance, and mutters inarticulate sounds to himself—he attempts to rise and walk: in this attempt he falls upon his side, from which he gradually turns upon his back: he now closes his eyes and falls into a profound sleep, frequently attended with snoring, and profuse sweats, and sometimes with such a relaxation of the muscles which confine the bladder and the lower bowels, as to produce a symptom which delicacy forbids me to mention. In this condition he often lies from ten, twelve, and twenty-four hours, to two, three, four, and five days, an object of pity and disgust to his family and friends. His recovery from this fit of intoxication is marked with several peculiar appearances. He opens his eyes and closes them again—he gapes and stretches his limbs—he then coughs and pukes—his voice is hoarse—he rises with difficulty, and staggers to a chair—his eyes resemble balls of fire—his hands tremble—he loathes the sight of food—he calls for a glass

of spirits to compose his stomach—now and then he emits a deep-fetched sigh, or groan, from a transient twinge of conscience; but he more frequently scolds, and curses every thing around him. In this state of languor and stupidity he remains for two or three days before he is able to resume his former habits of business and conversation.

Pythagoras, we are told, maintained that the souls of men after death expiated the crimes committed by them in this world by animating certain brute animals; and that the souls of those animals, in their turns, entered into men, and carried with them all their peculiar qualities and vices. This doctrine of one of the wisest and best of the Greek philosophers, was probably intended only to convey a lively idea of the changes which are induced in the body and mind of man by a fit of drunkenness. In folly, it causes him to resemble a calf—in stupidity, an ass—in roaring, a mad bull—in quarrelling and fighting, a dog—in cruelty, a tiger—in fetor, a skunk—in filthiness, a hog—and in obscenity, a he-goat.

It belongs to the history of drunkenness to remark, that its paroxysms occur, like the paroxysms of many diseases, at certain periods, and after longer or shorter intervals. They often begin with annual, and gradually increase in their frequency, until they appear in quarterly, monthly, weekly, and quotidian, or daily periods. Finally they afford scarcely any marks of remission either during the day or the night. There was a citizen of Philadelphia, many years ago, in whom drunkenness appeared in this protracted form. In speaking of him to one of his neighbors, I said, " Does he not *sometimes* get drunk?" " You mean," said his neighbor, " is he not *sometimes* sober?"

It is further remarkable, that drunkenness resembles certain hereditary, family, and contagious diseases. I have once known it to descend from a father to four out of five of his children. I have seen three, and once four brothers, who were born of sober ancestors, affected by it; and I have heard of its spreading through a whole family composed of members not originally related to each other. These facts are important, and should not be overlooked by parents, in deciding upon the matrimonial connexions of their children.

II. Let us next attend to the chronic effects of ardent spirits upon the body and mind. In the body they dispose to every form of acute disease; they moreover *excite* fevers in persons predisposed to them from other causes. This has been remarked in all the yellow fevers which have visited the cities of the United States. Hard drinkers seldom escape, and rarely recover from them. The following diseases are the usual consequences of the habitual use of ardent spirits, viz.

1. A decay of appetite, sickness at stomach, and a puking of bile, or a discharge of a frothy and viscid phlegm, by hawking, in the morning.

2. Obstructions of the liver. The fable of Prometheus, on whose liver a vulture was said to prey constantly as a punishment for his stealing fire from heaven, was intended to illustrate the painful effects of ardent spirits upon that organ of the body.

3. Jaundice, and dropsy of the belly and limbs, and finally of every cavity in the body. A swelling in the feet and legs is so characteristic a mark of habits of intemperance, that the merchants in Charleston, I have been told, cease to trust the planters of South Carolina as soon as they perceive it. They very naturally conclude industry and virtue to be extinct in that man, in whom that symptom of disease has been produced by the intemperate use of distilled spirits.

4. Hoarseness, and a husky cough, which often terminate in consumption, and sometimes in an acute and fatal disease of the lungs.

5. Diabetes, that is, a frequent and weakening discharge of pale or sweetish urine.

6. Redness, and eruptions on different parts of the body. They generally begin on the nose, and after gradually extending all over the face, sometimes descend to the limbs in the form of leprosy. They have been called " Rum buds," when they appear in the face. In persons who have occasionally survived these effects of ardent spirits on the skin, the face after a while becomes bloated, and its redness is succeeded by a death-like paleness. Thus, the same fire which produces a red colour in iron, when urged to a more intense degree, produces what has been called a white heat.

7. A fetid breath, composed of every thing that is offensive in putrid animal matter.

8. Frequent and disgusting belchings. Dr. Haller relates the case of a notorious drunkard having been suddenly destroyed in consequence of the vapour discharged from his stomach by belching, accidentally taking fire by coming in contact with the flame of a candle.

9. Epilepsy.

10. Gout, in all its various forms of swelled limbs, colic, palsy, and apoplexy.

11. Lastly, madness. The late Dr. Waters, while he acted as house pupil and apothecary of the Pennsylvania Hospital, assured me, that in one-third of the patients confined by this terrible disease, it had been induced by ardent spirits.

Most of the diseases which have been enumerated are of a mortal nature. They are more certainly induced, and terminate more speedily in death, when spirits are taken in such quantities, and at such times, as to produce frequent intoxication; but it may serve to remove an error with which some intemperate people console themselves, to remark, that ardent spirits often bring on fatal diseases without producing drunkenness. I have known many persons destroyed by them who were never completely intoxicated during the whole course of their lives. The solitary instances of longevity which are now and then met with in hard drinkers, no more disprove the deadly effects of ardent spirits than the solitary instances of recoveries from apparent death by drowning, prove that there is no danger to life from a human body lying an hour or two under water.

The body, after its death, from the use of distilled spirits, exhibits, by dissection, certain appearances which are of a peculiar nature. The fibres of the stomach and bowels are contracted—abscesses, gangrene, and schirri are found in the viscera. The bronchial vessels are contracted—the blood-vessels and tendons in many parts of the body are more or less ossified, and even the hair of the head possesses a crispness which renders it less valuable to wig-makers than the hair of sober people.

Not less destructive are the effects of ardent spirits upon the human mind. They impair the memory, debilitate the understanding, and pervert the moral faculties. It was probably from observing these effects of intemperance in drinking upon the mind, that a law was formerly passed in Spain

Vol 1.

which excluded drunkards from being witnesses in a court of justice. But the demoralizing effects of distilled spirits do not stop here. They produce not only falsehood, but fraud, theft, uncleanliness, and murder. Like the demoniac mentioned in the New Testament, their name is " Legion," for they convey into the soul a host of vices and crimes.

A more affecting spectacle cannot be exhibited than a person into whom this infernal spirit, generated by habits of intemperance, has entered: it is more or less affecting, according to the station the person fills in a family, or in society, who is possessed by it. Is he a husband? How deep the anguish which rends the bosom of his wife! Is she a wife? Who can measure the shame and aversion which she excites in her husband? Is he the father, or is she the mother of a family of children? See their averted looks from their parent, and their blushing looks at each other! Is he a magistrate? or has he been chosen to fill a high and respectable station in the councils of his country? What humiliating fears of corruption in the administration of the laws, and of the subversion of public order and happiness, appear in the countenances of all who see him! Is he a minister of the Gospel? Here language fails me. If angels weep—it is at such a sight.

In pointing out the evils produced by ardent spirits, let us not pass by their effects upon the estates of the persons who are addicted to them. Are they inhabitants of cities? Behold! their houses stripped gradually of their furniture, and pawned, or sold by a constable, to pay tavern debts. See! their names upon record in the dockets of every court, and whole pages of newspapers filled with advertisements of their estates for public sale. Are they inhabitants of country places? Behold! their houses with shattered windows—their barns with leaky roofs—their gardens overrun with weeds—their fields with broken fences—their hogs without yokes—their sheep without wool—their cattle and horses without fat—and their children, filthy and half clad, without manners, principles and morals. This picture of agricultural wretchedness is seldom of long duration. The farms and property thus neglected and depreciated are seized and sold for the benefit of a group of creditors. The children that were born with the prospect of inheriting them are bound out to service in the neighborhood; while their parents, the unworthy authors of their misfortunes, ramble into new and distant settlements, alternately fed on their way by the hand of charity, or a little casual labor.

Thus we see poverty and misery, crimes and infamy, diseases and death, are all the natural and usual consequences of the intemperate use of ardent spirits.

I have classed death among the consequences of hard drinking. But it is not death from the immediate hand of the Deity, nor from any of the instruments of it which were created by him: it is death from *suicide*. Yes—thou poor degraded creature who art daily lifting the poisoned bowl to thy lips—cease to avoid the unhallowed ground in which the self-murderer is interred, and wonder no longer that the sun should shine, and the rain fall, and the grass look green upon his grave. Thou art perpetrating, gradually, by the use of ardent spirits, what he has effected suddenly by opium or a halter. Considering how many circumstances from surprise, or derangement, may palliate his guilt, or that (unlike yours) it was not preceded and accompanied by any other crime, it is probable his condemnation will be less than yours at the day of judgment.

I shall now take notice of the occasions and circumstances which are supposed to render the use of ardent spirits necessary, and endeavor to show that the arguments in favor of their use in such cases, are founded in error, and that in each of them ardent spirits, instead of affording strength to the body, increase the evils they are intended to relieve.

1. They are said to be necessary in very cold weather. This is far from being true, for the temporary warmth they produce is always succeeded by a greater disposition in the body to be affected by cold. Warm dresses, a plentiful meal just before exposure to the cold, and eating occasionally a little gingerbread, or any other cordial food, is a much more durable method of preserving the heat of the body in cold weather.

2. They are said to be necessary in very warm weather. Experience proves that they increase instead of lessening the effects of heat upon the body, and thereby dispose to diseases of all kinds. Even in the warm climate of the West Indies, Dr. Bell asserts this to be true. " Rum," says this author, " whether used habitually, moderately, or in excessive quantities in the West Indies, always diminishes the

strength of the body, and renders men more susceptible of disease, and unfit for any service in which vigor or activity is required."* As well might we throw oil into a house, the roof of which was on fire, in order to prevent the flames from extending to its inside, as pour ardent spirits into the stomach to lessen the effects of a hot sun upon the skin.

3. Nor do ardent spirits lessen the effects of hard labor upon the body. Look at the horse, with every muscle of his body swelled from morning till night in the plough, or a team; does he make signs for a draught of toddy, or a glass of spirits, to enable him to cleave the ground, or to climb a hill? No—he requires nothing but cool water and substantial food. There is no nourishment in ardent spirits. The strength they produce in labor is of a transient nature, and is always followed by a sense of weakness and fatigue.

* See his "Inquiry into the causes which produce, and the means of preventing diseases, among British officers, soldiers, and others, in the West Indies."

DANGER FROM ARDENT SPIRITS.

Every man is in danger of becoming a drunkard who is in the habit of drinking ardent spirits—1. When he is warm. 2. When he is cold. 3. When he is wet. 4. When he is dry. 5. When he is dull. 6. When he is lively. 7. When he travels. 8. When he is at home. 9. When he is in company. 10. When he is alone. 11. When he is at work. 12. When he is idle. 13. Before meals. 14. After meals. 15. When he gets up. 16. When he goes to bed. 17. On holidays. 18. On public occasions. 19. On any day; or, 20. On any occasion.

END.

No. 26

SIN, NO TRIFLE.

WHAT a strange world is this in which we live! The Prince of light and the prince of darkness—good men and bad men—holiness and sin—are all made objects of sport and ridicule. However, it is dangerous folly to jest with serious things; and Solomon teaches that they are "fools" who "make a mock at sin." Prov. 14 : 9. *Here* we see children doing mischief and then laughing at it, in which, alas! they are often encouraged by ungodly parents; *there* the drunkard boasts of his excesses, the debauchee of the number of his victims, and the gamester of the fruits of his art and deceit. Thus many, at every period of life, glory in their shame!

Wicked men triumph when they see blemishes in the character of the righteous. What manner of persons ought Christians then to be in all holy conversation and godliness, that they may cut off the pleas of gainsayers, and put to silence the ignorance of foolish men.

Friendly reader, art thou tempted to countenance, by a laugh, or a smile, or in any other way, what thou canst not inwardly approve? We entreat thee to weigh well the following considerations:

1. He who laughs at sin, laughs *while God frowns.*

"God is angry with the wicked every day." Psal. 7 : 11. What is it that excites his anger? What is that by which his Spirit is vexed and grieved? What is that which occasions the sword of vengeance to hang over the heads of sinners? "The wrath of God is revealed from heaven against all ungodliness and unrighteousness of men." Rom. 1 : 18. And if the wrath of a king be as the roaring of a lion, how dreadful must be the wrath of the Almighty God!

2. He who makes light of sin makes light of *the miseries of mankind*, all of which are occasioned by sin. We live in a vale of tears, in which prisons, and hospitals, and innumerable other receptacles of wo, impress the solemn truth, that the misery of man is great upon him Eccl. 8 : 6.

> Ah! little think the gay, licentious proud,
> Whom pleasure, power, and affluence surround,
> They, who their thoughtless hours in giddy mirth,
> And wanton, often cruel riot, waste;
> Ah, little think they while they dance along,
> How many feel, this very moment, death,
> And all the sad variety of pain. THOMSON.

3. To sport with sin, is to sport with *death*. For sin entered the world, and death followed sin. Rom. 5 : 12. And death has made this world like Golgotha, a place of skulls—not a fit place then for profane merriment. If all the carcasses of all the dead were collected into one vast pile, and it should be asked, "Who slew all these?" (2 Kings, 10 : 9.) the answer must be, "Sin slew them all."

> Death stands between eternity and time,
> With open jaws—on such a narrow bridge
> That none can pass but must become his prey.

4. For a man to laugh at sin, is to laugh at what renders him *odious* in the sight of all holy beings, and unrepented of will prove his *ruin*. Will any one make sport with his own disease? Sin is a disease. It is poisonous —it is fatal too, unless the Balm of Gilead (the blood of Christ) be applied in time. Sin produces degradation and shame. When a man laughs at his sin he laughs at the fraud by which he has cheated himself. His conduct is not less absurd than wicked. It is the folly of an odious wretch laughing at his own pollution.

5 To make light of sin, is to make light of the *pains*

of hell. For sin opened the bottomless pit. Sin is the parent of the worm that dieth not. Sin kindles the flame which shall never be quenched. Sin leads to the place of weeping, and wailing, and gnashing of teeth.

O careless, thoughtless sinner! Is it a light thing to fall into the hands of the living God—to feel the weight of his curse—to dwell with everlasting burnings? Canst thou expect to enjoy sinful mirth and jovial companions in hell, from whence the smoke of their torment ascendeth up for ever and ever? Consider this, ye that forget God, lest he tear you in pieces, and there be none to deliver. Consider this before the great day of his wrath is come. Think on your ways, and turn your feet to his testimonies. In those testimonies you will find a Savior revealed. His name is Jesus. Behold, now is the accepted time, behold, now is the day of salvation. Believe on the Lord Jesus Christ and thou shalt be saved.

6. To sport with sin is to sport with *the sorrows of Jesus.* And this, considering the dignity of the person of Christ, is the most solemn and awful consideration that can be suggested. It were less guilty to sport with fellow-creatures than with the Son of God. Never did any person suffer so much from contempt as Jesus did. He was blindfolded and buffetted, and in the grossest manner insulted by the rabble in the high priest's hall. "Then did they spit in his face." Matt. 26 : 67. Herod and his men of war set Jesus at naught. In mockery he was invested with a purple robe. A reed was put into his hand for a sceptre, to ridicule his pretensions to a kingdom. And when he was expiring in agony (O horrid to relate,) they mocked the pangs in which he died. Passing strangers wagged their heads, and said, "If thou be the Son of God, come down from the cross." The chief priests, scribes, and elders, said, with bitter sarcasm, "He saved others—himself he cannot save." And even the thieves, who were crucified with him, cast the same in his teeth.

You perhaps say, that had you been there you could not have joined in such cruel mockery and murder! But recollect that in trifling with sin you "crucify the Son of God afresh, and put him to open shame." And can you, O wanton sinner, join your voice to theirs, to insult him; can you trifle with Jesus, and make light of his prayers,

his tears, and groans, and bloody sweat, and dying agonies!
O be persuaded to trace his footsteps to Calvary. There
stand and gaze, pause and ponder. If at such a place,
with such a scene, you can still trifle with sin, and thus
sport with the sorrows of Jesus, your heart must be hard
indeed—harder than the rocks which rent, more insensible
than the dead which came up from their graves! At the
sight of such obduracy, how must angels feel? "More
struck with grief or wonder, who can tell?"

> Around the bloody tree they pressed with strong desire,
> That wond'rous sight to see, the Lord of life expire!
> And could their eyes have known a tear,
> In sad surprise had dropt it here. DODDRIDGE.

"Consider this, ye that forget God," and make a mock
of sin," lest your hearts become *still harder*, and lest he
"tear you in pieces and there be none to deliver." For
remember "if we sin wilfully after that we have received
the knowledge of the truth, there remaineth no more sacrifice for sin."

> Who laughs at sin, laughs at his Maker's frowns,
> Laughs at the sword of vengeance o'er his head;
> Laughs at the great Redeemer's tears and wounds,
> Who, but for sin, had never wept or bled.
>
> Who laughs at sin, laughs at the numerous woes
> Which have this wicked world so oft befell;
> Laughs at the whole creation's groans and throes,
> At all the spoils of death, and pains of hell.
>
> Who laughs at sin, laughs at his own disease;
> Welcomes approaching torture with his smiles,
> Dares at his soul's expense his fancy please,
> Affronts his God—himself of bliss beguiles.
>
> Who laughs at sin sports with his guilt and shame,
> Laughs at the errors of his senseless mind;
> For so absurd a fool there wants a name
> Expressive of a folly so refin'd. JOS. STENNET.

PUBLISHED BY THE

AMERICAN TRACT SOCIETY,

And sold at their Depository, No. 150 Nassau-street, near the City-Hall, New-York; and by Agents of the Society, its Branches, and Auxiliaries, in the principal cities and towns in the United States.

No. 27.

PARENTAL DUTIES.

It is the perpetual and universal law of nature, for the parent of every species to care for its offspring. The wild beast that roams through the forest, and the bird of prey that builds her nest in the cliffs of the rock, provide, each, for their young, and teach them the most suitable means for preserving their existence, and providing for all their wants. It is indeed a rare thing for a woman to "forget her sucking child," or even for a man to be altogether void of "natural affection;" but we too often see that their concern extends only to inferior objects. To provide food and raiment for the body, to preserve it from the dangers to which it is exposed, and so to cherish the dawn of reason and cultivate the human mind as to fit the individual to be an ornamental member of society, are indispensable duties; but they are not all. "These ought ye to have done, and not to leave the other undone." Luke, xi. 42.

We are going to urge upon you, parents, especially upon you, professedly christian parents, duties far more excellent in their nature, and far more weighty in their consequences, than any to which we have alluded. We are going to urge upon you a becoming solicitude for the *souls* of your children. Here is indeed a treasure committed to you in trust, which carries with it a high degree of responsibility: this is a stewardship of which you must one day give account; and an awful day will it indeed be to you, if you have in any measure contributed to the eternal ruin of your children, or if you have not assiduously used all the means which might any way have proved conducive to their salvation.

He who knoweth the end from the beginning, and who searcheth the heart, foresaw that the Father of the faithful would show proper regard to this important duty, and thus commends his fidelity: "For I know him, that he will command his children, and his household after him; that they shall keep the way of the Lord, to do justice and judgment." Gen. xviii. 19. David also, when his latter end was approaching, gave this solemn and appropriate charge to his successor. "And thou, Solomon, my son, know thou the God of thy father, and serve him with a perfect heart, and with a willing mind; for the Lord searcheth all hearts, and understandeth all the imaginations of the thoughts; if thou seek him, he will be found of thee; but if thou forsake him, he will cast thee off for ever." 1 Chr. xxviii. 9. We have another interesting example to place before parents in the following passage: "And it was so, when the days of their feasting were gone about, that Job sent and sanctified them, and rose up early in the morning and offered burnt offerings, according to the number of them all; for Job said, it may be that my sons have sinned and cursed God in their hearts. Thus did Job continually." Job, i. 5. These good men all exemplified the character of wise and affectionate parents, looking to the *souls* of their children as the first and most essential point, knowing that this was infinitely more important than any thing which related to their interest in the present world. All such parents as regard the earthly advantage of their children, and neglect their souls, act a part as unwise as it is unjust and cruel.

PARENTAL DUTIES.

The following was among the first and most solemn injunctions given to the Israelites: "Therefore shall ye lay up these my words in your heart, and in your soul, and bind them for a sign upon your head, that they may be as frontlets between your eyes. And ye shall teach them to your children, speaking of them when thou sittest in thy house, and when thou walkest by the way, when thou liest down, and when thou risest up." Deut. xi. 18, 19.

Those parents who occupy themselves in the discharge of those parental duties which this Tract earnestly recommends, are employed in the most honourable manner; they are employed in a way which is likely to yield more solid and permanent pleasure than it is possible to derive from the most fascinating scenes of worldly gayety and splendour. But we have to deplore this melancholy truth, that parents forego the honour and pleasure attendant upon this line of duty; the religious instruction of their children being neglected. Nor does this complaint attach only to one class of society; this criminal conduct is pursued alike by the learned and the illiterate, by the rich and the poor.

The ignorance and irreligion of the younger branches of many families may be easily accounted for. Observe the evil habits, and that profligacy of manners, in which the parents indulge. Those who are in good circumstances are frequently from home, at the theatre, the ball, or the card party: while their children (at least in many instances) are left under the care of ignorant and vicious servants; or hurried to those haunts of folly at hours so unseasonable as to injure their health, and to endanger their lives. On the other hand, many parents who are poor, and devoted to idleness and drinking, leave their ragged and dirty offspring to rove through the streets from morning till night, and to pick up all those vulgar and profane expressions, and all those vicious habits, which it is well known are learned there.

The first step which will most effectually contribute to a diminution of ignorance and vice in the young, is to awaken in the minds of parents a just, a strong sense of the nature and extent of the duty which they owe their children. This is correcting the evil at the fountain head; and this evil being corrected, streams of blessings will flow abroad, and produce the most effectual and lasting benefits. Then the state of the rising generation, which has long been a barren wilderness, shall become a fruitful field. Then the prevailing anxiety among parents shall be thus expressed: " That our sons may be as plants grown up in their youth, that our daughters may be as corner stones, polished after the similitude of a palace." Ps. cxliv. 12.

Christian ministers may render great assistance in this good work. Let them constantly and earnestly aim to impress upon the minds of parents the vast importance not only of family prayer, but of family instruction, especially catechising. Indeed, it would be well if there were in all our congregations, schools of instruction for the full-grown and aged, too many of whom are unhappily themselves too defective in knowledge to be able to teach their children either the doctrines or the duties of true christianity. To those, however, who have ability and leisure to instruct their families, but either want courage to commence, or patience to continue the practice, *ministers* should in public show the importance of this needful, but much neglected duty.

Let us indulge the hope that we are addressing many parents who already feel the propriety and importance of the advice we are now giving. They are saying with considerable solicitude, " What is to be done to accomplish this great end, and what are the means most likely to make an effectual impression upon the minds of our children ?" We would cherish your zeal in this good work, we would aid you, if possible, in the discharge of this duty. Often read, and labour to carry into effect the advice of the inspired volume :—" Train up a child in the way he should go, and when he is old he will not depart from it." Prov. xxii. 6. You will see the wisdom, and feel the importance, of this work, only in the proportion in which you feel the worth of your own souls, and are yourselves giving all diligence to obtain salvation and eternal life; and when you feel it your privilege and duty, you will not only assiduously direct all your zeal and talents to carry it into effect, but you will constantly and earnestly pray to God to crown your labour with his blessing.

In a small Tract designed for general distribution among

various classes, it is impossible to be so minute and explicit as we might be if it was designed for one circle only; much therefore must be left to the judgment of readers, who, if properly awakened to feel the magnitude of the subject, will not long remain in doubt as to the line of duty to be pursued. It is not indeed necessary to give a precise plan for the discharge of this duty. Persons differently circumstanced may adopt very different methods; but the good effect may be nearly the same. All that we can do is to offer some hints that will apply to the subject generally.

If parents would become instructers, and render their habitation the school of genuine wisdom, they must render home agreeable, they must treat their children as friends, and, by an open and kind behaviour, conciliate their friendship and esteem; otherwise the most wise and profitable advice will be lost. If it is conveyed in an authoritative, domineering, austere manner, it will excite disgust and revolt, while mildness and affection soften the mind, and allure it to the love of that which is good. The one thing is injurious as the boisterous hail storm, the other beneficial as the copious dew, or the warm and gentle shower.

One of the first objects of parental attention should be, to weaken the energy, check the growth, and prevent, as much as possible, the breaking forth of the corrupt and sensual propensities of the human heart, which being deceitful above all things and desperately wicked, sends forth nothing but corrupt and polluted streams. You must especially watch over and aim to subdue and destroy the master passion, (or to use Scripture language,) the sin which easily besets them. Evil propensities in the minds of youth, like weeds in the garden, by indulgence take deeper root and grow more vigorous; you will find it most easy to destroy them soon after their first appearance.

Carefully watch the dawn of reason, and as their infant minds begin to expand, labour to throw light upon them. The vacant and playful hour may be improved for instruction. They are never tired of asking questions; never do you be weary of answering them, and aim to give all their inquiries a useful, that is, a moral and religious turn. You may make their instruction a matter of amusement; and even teach them the most weighty truths in regard to God, their own souls, and another world, in a way most congenial to their natural disposition. The lessons you give them in this way, will be received with more willingness, and in some instances, will make a more lasting impression than those which are given in a formal manner, attention to which costs them more time and labour. Indeed, parents should begin early to converse with their children in the most free and unrestrained manner; some parents have used themselves to spend half an hour in conversation and prayer with each of their children individually, and it has produced the best effect. There is not an object, or an occurrence, which passes under their notice, but, while it furnishes the child with matter of inquiry, will also furnish the parent with a subject or lesson of instruction; especially be careful to improve seasons of mercy and affliction.

Parents cannot begin too soon to allure their children to read and love the word of God; for although some branches of it are sublime and elevated above the full grasp of the most enlarged and soaring mind, yet there are other parts suited, both in subject and language, as well to the capacity as to the age and circumstances of children. It was, no doubt, at a very early period, that the mother and grandmother of Timothy began to teach him the Holy Scriptures; their example is worthy the imitation of every parent, and their success affords a strong encouragement to diligence and perseverance. Joseph, Samuel, and Josiah, are all delightful patterns of early piety; and modern times furnish many instances in which parents have, under the divine blessing, in the use of the Scriptures, sown the seeds of eternal life in the hearts of their children, even in their tenderest years.

Let it be your daily and persevering effort to impress their minds with profound reverence for the name of God. Guard them against even the most trifling instance which would either express or imply a want of respect for the Lord's day. Cherish in their minds an habitual regard to truth; assure them that lies told in jest, and those which are told for gain, or to avoid suffering, are all contrary to the Scriptures, and offensive to God. As soon as prudence and circumstances will allow, carry them to the house of

God, that they may not only see and hear God's people join in acts of devotion, but themselves also try to lisp his praise; for out of the mouths of babes and sucklings he can perfect his own glory. Children receive religious impressions much earlier in the house of God than we are aware of, and therefore it is criminal in parents not to give them all the advantages of God's instituted worship. If you send them to boarding schools, it should be a matter of conscience with you to select religious ones.

It is very important indeed that parents should endeavour to give the minds of their children a right direction as to the choice of books and company. It is a maxim delivered to us upon high authority, that " evil communications corrupt good manners;" and indeed the experience of every age has justified and illustrated this solemn truth. Circulating libraries, and the companions with which many young persons resort to these repositories of every thing delusive to the imagination, and destructive to the morals of the young, should be assiduously guarded against, as generally leading to the most destructive consequences. The real tendency of the greater part of the reading furnished by novels and romances, is to mislead the understanding, corrupt the heart, and prepare the way for a dissolute and vicious course of practice. Indeed, not a few of the books alluded to, deserve to be burned by the hands of the public executioner. The writer speaks from his own knowledge, when he says, that some of the worst of this kind, jest books, &c. are printed upon a very coarse paper, and hawked among servants from door to door, at the expense of only a few cents each. Let parents be on their guard also against the general course of public amusements; for the sparks of evil which irreligious books and companions first kindle in the mind, are too frequently blown into a flame, and break forth in the most tremendous manner through their influence. It is evident that the generality of public entertainments, adapted both to the rich and the poor, can answer no other purpose in the young people of both sexes, than to feed " the lust of the eye, the lust of the flesh, and the pride of life." And yet so deluded are the multitude, that these things pass current for *innocent amusements!*

Be it remembered by parents, that in vain they furnish

their children with good advice, and bring them under the influence of wholesome restraints, if they themselves do not practically exemplify the excellency and importance of pure and undefiled religion. Let the temper, the conversation, and the conduct of the parent then, be a pattern of every thing wise and good. He is sure to be an unsuccessful preacher to his children, who is not a practical one. Is it possible that your children will be influenced to choose and follow that which is good, upon your recommendation, if your whole practice is so diametrically opposite as to justify them in addressing to you that old and mortifying proverb, " Physician, heal thyself."

But peradventure, Reader, you see the importance of this subject; you are alive to your duty; you are applying yourself to it with becoming zeal; you are anxiously watching for the fruit of your labour; and your mind is often divided between hope and fear as to its issue. I congratulate you on the honourable nature of your employment, you work for eternity; I congratulate your children that they are privileged to have such parents; I congratulate the country that there is reason to hope you will bequeath to it, in the persons of your children, industrious, peaceable, and useful members of society; I congratulate the church of God, that perhaps, ere long, these children shall come and tell what God hath done for them, saying, " God hath heard the prayers of our dear parents, he hath blessed their instructions and example to the salvation of our souls, and now we love the house and ordinances of God. We abhor the assemblies of the wicked, and desire to be united to the congregation of the righteous: we now see that the wages of sin is death; that the broad, the crowded way leadeth to destruction; and, blessed be God, we have now learned to say of religion by happy experience, ' Her ways are ways of pleasantness, and all her paths are peace'." Prov. iii. 17.

But alas! there are too many parents insensible to their duty, who totally neglect the souls of their children; to them we would address some of those considerations which tend to show their folly and sin, and which may, under the blessing of God, awaken their attention to this service, the neglect of which when attached to persons bearing the christian name, and themselves professing to know and believe christianity, is not only inexcusable, but doubly criminal. It is the duty of every christian to endeavour to his utmost to spread the knowledge and salvation of Christ among his fellow creatures, but especially among his own children. If he who provides not temporally for his own household, has denied the faith, and is worse than an infidel, what shall we say of those parents who use no endeavour to save their children's *souls*? Their offence is greater, and their punishment will be awful indeed.

The soul is infinitely more precious than the body. It is immortal, it is depraved, it is in danger of being eternally lost. Oh! pity, pray for, and seek its eternal salvation. The immense value of the souls of your children is expressed in the most striking language by our Lord: " What is a man profited if he shall gain the whole world and lose his own soul?" How little have those parents thought of and felt this truth, who confine all their care for their children merely to clothing and feeding, and preserving them from external evil, or promoting their well-being in society. All these things bear relation only to time; the advantages arising from them will soon have an end. But if, by instructing them in the things of God, you save their souls, you confer upon them a substantial and eternal good. All that you do for them short of aiming at their eternal happiness, is trivial and insignificant. Although you should procure for them riches, honours, and large possessions; what will these avail when their souls are required? What will these avail, if they lift up their eyes in hell at last?

You are bound to instruct your children in the ways of God, as you regard your own interest. What fruit have you a right to expect from your children, if you leave them to walk in the way of their own hearts, and in the ways of sin? They will be so far from adding to your comfort, that they will be as thorns in your sides; they will despise both your authority and your affection; they will waste your property in riot and dissipation; they will daily wound your peace, pierce your heart through with many sorrows, and finally, it may be, bring down your gray hairs with sorrow to the grave. Read the history of Eli, who when his sons made themselves vile, restrained them not; read the character, conduct, and end of David's two

VOL 1.

sons, Absalom and Adonijah; of the latter, it is said, "His father had not displeased him at any time, in saying, Why hast thou done so?" 1 Kings, i. 6.

Look around you, and on every side you will see parents reaping the bitter fruits of their impious indifference to the instruction and salvation of their children.

In urging upon parents their obligation religiously to instruct their children, we may appeal to their patriotism. They are bound to regard this duty by all the love they bear to their country. Religion and morals are the glory and strength of a country. "Righteousness exalteth a nation, but sin is a reproach to any people." What an irreparable injury do ignorant and ungodly parents entail upon their country, by leaving to it uninstructed and ungodly children! They become the scourge of the neighbourhood in which they live; they often become depredators upon the property of others, help at a very early period of life to crowd our jails, and end their wretched course in infamy and disease, if not by the hands of a public executioner. It is true, you do not accompany them to the haunts of vice and dissipation; you did not teach them to cheat and plunder their neighbours; but you neglected to teach them the fear of God; you neglected to warn and admonish them; you did not pray with them and for them; you did not teach them to observe the Sabbath; nor take them with you to the house of God; instead of restraining their passions, you indulged them; instead of bringing them up in the ways of truth and holiness, you led them into the paths of sinful pleasure; and thus you initiated them into that course, in which their own passions and the temptations of the devil still keep them, progressively advancing in wickedness, until they finish their life, (it may be,) blaspheming their God, and cursing the negligence and irreligion of their parents.

But consider also the awful destiny of human beings; they are to enter, according to their character, a state of endless blessedness or endless misery.

As for you, yet a little while and you must give an account of yourselves unto God. When God gave you children, he in fact said to you, "Take these children, and bring them up for me." You should also remember, that the children of this age are to be the men and women of the next. The advantages arising out of the religious instruction you give your children, will not be confined to your own or to their life, but may be perpetuated to the third and fourth generation. This encouragement is beautifully expressed, and strongly urged in the following passage: " For he established a testimony in Jacob, and appointed a law in Israel, which he commanded our fathers, that they should arise and make them known to their children; that the generation to come might know them, even the children which should be born; who should arise and declare them to their children; that they might set their hope in God, and not forget the works of God, but keep his commandments." Ps. lxxviii. 5, 6, 7.

Think of the pleasure of being useful to the souls of your children, of being *spiritual* parents to them, and having them as your crown of rejoicing in the great day, so that you may then say, " Here am I and the children whom thou hast given me." This will be a source of inexpressible delight; this will make heaven a heaven indeed. But on the other hand, to be any way assisting to the eternal misery of your children—awful thought! horrid affliction! it is more than human nature can sustain. Wretched indeed will ye parents be in that awful day, if your children are lost through your neglect.

Take then this friendly remonstrance in good part, and in a dependance upon God aim to instruct and save the souls of your children.

PARENTAL EXAMPLE.

All endeavours to make right impressions on the mind of a child will very generally be found ineffectual, if the character of the parent does not correspond with his instructions, and inspire his child with esteem and affection. It is surprising how God honours his own image among men. Faint as it is, even in the best, still its proximity gives it effect, and it exercises a portion of his own sovereign power over the hearts of his creatures. This has been found to be the case in a remarkable manner among savage and idolatrous nations, when holy men have lived for a length of time among them as Missionaries. Every one must be struck with the effect produced by living examples of the christian graces, on reading accounts of the Moravian Missions; and still more, perhaps, when, in the history of India, he finds what a wonderful ascendancy the holy Swartz obtained over the Hindoos of all ranks, from the highest to the lowest. But it is unnecessary to look so far from home, to be convinced of this truth. We every day see it exemplified among ourselves in the respect and affection which good men generally acquire, when their light has long shone before the same neighbourhood. If the beauties of the christian character thus recommend themselves to persons of mature age, whose evil habits are often so confirmed, and whose tastes are so vitiated, it will not be matter of wonder that they should have peculiar charms for the minds of children. Let a parent exhibit this character with consistency and prudence, and he will seldom fail to be loved and revered by his children. And when this is the case, what authority will belong to his example! what weight to all his admonitions! what ready attention will be paid to his very wishes! The difficulties of education will be wonderfully smoothed. Ill humour, distaste to particular studies, impatience under restraints, eye-service and deceit, a disposition to look on a parent as a hard master, not to mention other evils, will be in a very great degree avoided. But in proportion as a parent fails to resemble in character that Divine Being who appoints him, as it were, his vicegerent in his family, this picture will fail to be realized; and in the worst cases it will be reversed. Let, then, every parent look well to his own example.

No. 28.

THE SPOILED CHILD.

A GENUINE NARRATIVE OF FACTS.

BY W. C. BROWNLEE, D. D.

See page 5.

The valley that is bounded by L—— and S——y hills, in the county of M——, and State of N—— ——, is remarkable for its beauty and fertility. The sluggish stream of the P—— winds slowly in its serpentine course through the midst of it, and waters a succession of well-cultivated farms. The inhabitants used to be among the most church-going, and happy people in that district of the country; until by the influence of General —— and a club of his friends, the spirit of infidelity, and with it, dissipation and corrupt morals crept in among them.

John C——l was one of the wealthiest and most influential men in the valley. Every thing was neat and well arranged in his mansion, and the outbuildings, and every nook and corner of the fences, and the whole farm, displayed the

Vol. 1.

hand of the tasteful and diligent cultivator. He was one of those men who retained the rural simplicity of the first settlers of our country. He had received the usual substantial English education of his day; his mind was one of a high order; his judgment was discriminating; his memory retained, with unusual tenacity, what he had read. In his whole deportment there was just such a dignity and air of pleasantness as one might expect to find in a Christian who had long walked with God; who had daily studied his Bible; who had a warm and benevolent heart; who had, next to the pastor, been the leading man in the parish; who had been in the magistracy, was honored in his county, and had always been accustomed to be consulted in matters of delicacy and public interest. The exterior was worthy of such a mind: he was a tall, venerable man, the patriarch of the valley.

His house was five miles from the village church: and yet no man was more punctual in his attendance. It was never recollected, even by an enemy, that he was in any instance late. The secret of it was this: he rose as early on a Sabbath morning as on days of business; and it was a part of his religion not to give any offence, or disturb others, during the worship of God, by coming in late. Beside, he loved God's sanctuary: his heart was early there: and it was natural that he should wish to join in the first ascriptions of praise to God. No ordinary storm would prevent him from being, summer and winter, in his place. If it rained, he put on a great-coat; for he always rode on horseback: and if it stormed severely, he would put on *two*. And when he reached the church, usually among the foremost, he would gravely observe that it seemed greatly to be desired that the rain should cease, that those who dwelt close by might venture into the house of God; adding, that if, like himself, they had five long miles to come, they would probably prize in a higher degree the privilege of the sanctuary.

The domestic arrangements of his family seemed also, in all respects, befitting his Christian character and profession. And his wife, endowed with singular prudence and the other Christian graces, seemed a true helpmeet. Every morning and evening the whole family was assembled around the domestic altar, and the worship of the Most

High performed with great reverence. In the busiest seasons he would frequently say to his laborers, "My friends, we always find time to take our daily food; let us also take time to worship the Lord our God; and remember, *prayers and provender never hinder a journey.*"

Here were all the elements of happiness, usefulness, and honor, apparently combined. Surely, his neighbors would say, Mr. C———l must be a happy man; rich in this world's goods, and rich in the grace of God; honored in the church; esteemed and respected by all in the social and political circles; possessed of a fine constitution, and enjoying uninterrupted health: what is there to disturb his mind or mar his peace?

But it had been long observed by the pastor that there was some secret worm at the root of his joys; and it became, at length, manifest to all his intimate friends. The grace of God will, indeed, carry a Christian through any afflictions: it will give buoyancy to his mind and spirits in the darkest and most distressing hours. Our heavenly Father's face shining upon us, will disperse the heaviest clouds: an humble and believing view of the Redeemer pleading for us at the very moment when we are like to be overwhelmed by the waves of sorrow, will send a foretaste of heaven's joy into our wounded souls; and when the Holy Comforter seals upon our hearts the consolations of his grace, we can praise him, even in the valley of the shadow of death.

But of all the sorrows which befall a Christian, that which comes nearest to his heart, paralizing his mind and drinking up his joys, is the outbreaking of wickedness in his children.

Mr. C———l had a son, he was his eldest child and his only son. On this child he had doated: he had made an idol of him. This is the besetting sin of Christian parents, especially those who are, by natural temperament, unusually kind-hearted and affectionate. It is indeed a strong and overpowering temptation. We doat on our offspring: they become *spoiled* children: and such is the ordering of divine Providence, we, who had sinfully indulged them, and "spared the rod" when we ought to have employed it to drive away folly from the young heart, according to the command *f*

God, learn, to our sorrow, that they are employed, in our old age, as the rod in God's hand to chastise our criminal indulgence!

It has been unfeelingly asserted, particularly by some who are unfriendly to religion, that "pious parents have generally very wicked children." But facts do not warrant the assertion. On the contrary, the fact of an eminent Christian, whether minister or layman, having a profane child, always calls forth *very* marked attention as something which the public did not expect in such a family: whereas it is never a wonder with any one, that wicked and profane children should proceed out of wicked and profane families. The Christian parent, however, in the hour of sorrow for the waywardness of his children, will make great searchings of heart into the causes of it. The promise of God is full before him, he seeks not to pervert or modify its import, "Train up a child in the way he should go, *and when he is old he will not depart from it*." He bemoans his delinquencies in many, yea, in innumerable instances, which the eyes of the world have never perceived, but which his own delicate conscience promptly discovers. Such was the fact with the father, whose character we have been describing. No enlightened Christian, perhaps, was ever more ready to admit his delinquencies before God; or more earnest, by prayer and supplication, to regain the ground he had lost, and subdue what had hitherto baffled his skill.

It was on one of those beautiful days in our autumn, when every thing in the country is smiling under the profusions of the divine beneficence, that Doctor F. the Pastor of the village of B———, made a visit to Mr. C———l, who was a ruling elder in his church.

He found him sowing his fields with the winter grain. He would not permit him to desist from his labor, and thereby interrupt the arrangements of the day: but he walked side by side with him, discoursing on general topics; and finally, on the state of the church, and the happy prospect of an answer to their prayers, in a revival of religion. For often had that village been blessed with seasons of refreshings from the presence of the Lord; accompanied by a rich ingathering of souls: and there were now some cheering evidences of another outpouring of the Spirit.

While they were thus engaged, the son of Mr. C———l, a lad about seventeen years of age, approached to mock: he groaned, and made singular grimaces, or laughed aloud, as he walked immediately behind his father: and at the end of the ridge next to the house, having caught up a young animal, he contrived, by tormenting it, to make it utter one continued yell: this he did in defiance of the solemn rebukes of the Pastor, and the entreaties and threats of his too indulgent parent. An end had been thus put to all regular conversation; and at this last outrage the aged father wept in silence, and sought to conceal his tears as he hurriedly sowed his field.

This ebullition of youthful fury had been caused, it was afterward discovered, by the father's peremptory refusal of the usual supply of money. Like too many parents, foolishly indulgent, he had yielded to the dominion which his only son possessed on his heart, and had given liberally and often: this only created an appetite for more: he soon found himself compelled to give liberally, simply to get rid of his importunate duns. And having made the discovery which, as a wise man, he ought to have anticipated as naturally as any common effect from a common cause, that this free indulgence with money had led him into habits of dissipation, and that the present solicitation was made to enable him to take the lead at a "frolic" in the tavern of the adjacent village, he had positively refused him. The young man now left his father's presence with a threat that " he would have money, and just that sum which he needed; if not one way, at least by another, which he (his father) might *conjecture*."

This was too much for a tender parent's heart to endure. He took hold of the Pastor's arm and led him to the shade of an aged apple-tree; and placing him beside his wife, who had joined him by this time, he sat down and wept.

"My poor ruined boy!" was all he could now utter in his grief. His wife and the Pastor also burst into tears.

" I now see my error," said the afflicted parent, after a short pause, as if awakened from the sleep of long delusion: "my eyes are opened to the calamity that has befallen us. But, oh! Sir," he added, as he grasped the Pastor's hand, "how can I retrace my steps? O my God have mercy, have mercy on my poor spoiled child! God of my fathers, who didst in thy tender compassion bring me into thy fold, look in mercy on my poor son! Thou, O Lord, didst convert a Manasseh, and didst arrest a persecuting Saul in his wicked course on the way to Damascus to murder thy saints, and didst reclaim the sottish prodigal: O have mercy on my son! Let the riches of thy grace, Father in heaven, triumph one day in his return to thee and to his parents' heart! You may well ask me, dear Pastor, why I do not correct him. Could I succeed in detaching him from his companions, then, perhaps, I might do it with some hope; but until that be done, correction may only drive him to a more desperate resistance; or, more probably, to a final abandonment of my roof; and ultimately to the commission of some fearful crime; and thence— my soul is tortured at the bare possibility of it—to a public and ignominious suffering! But I have not yet revealed the secret cause of all this mischief. There is a demon in him, which sets at defiance Christian discipline and the rod of correction: yes, in him, young as he is—I mean THE LUST OF STRONG DRINK! This, with the influence of vicious companions, has, I am grieved to say, seared, as with a hot iron, the sensibilities of his conscience and of natural affection. O! I look back on the past, and I see my fatal errors staring me in the face!"

"Did you not commit a great error," said the Pastor with tenderness, "in not sustaining the discipline under which his *teacher* sought judiciously and faithfully to bring the daring and turbulent spirit of this youth? This I once recollect to have witnessed, and ventured to predict the result."

"We did, dear Pastor, we did," was the answer, as he cast his eyes on his afflicted wife with more of sorrow than reproof, "we did: and here is an exceedingly great evil under the sun, and an error committed by almost every parent. The teacher is one of the most useful officers in the republic; one of the most necessary and influential office-bearers among us; one who walks forth over the land, bearing the future destinies of our country and the church, as it were, in his hand: he has the training of the rising generation, the hope of our country and of the church of God! What an important, what a responsible office! Yet, how often, and how much is it despised! and it is miserably ill paid moreover, and still worse treated! When the schoolmaster would bring the wayward spirits of our spoiled children under a wholesome discipline, both parents are, in too many instances, in arms against him. And their ill-timed and foolish pity fails not to sustain the boy in open and daring rebellion against his teacher, and in the repetition of fresh crimes. This parental interference, by paralyzing the arm of salutary discipline, has helped to consummate the ruin of many a hapless youth!"

" This has been a fatal error," said the almost heart-broken wife; " but this is not all: frivolous excuses, I remember to my sorrow, would be sustained by us, for neglecting his evening tasks; the slightest indisposition, and (I am mortified to think how easily we were deceived) that, too, very often pretended, and our excessive anxiety about the " *dear child's*" *health*, would be reason enough for allowing him to absent himself whole days from school. And then, from our foolish fondness, he would gain permission from us to rove about from house to house, and, what was worse, to absent himself whole nights from his parental roof. It is thus that a young mind acquires, at too early an age, a taste for company: its inexperience lays it open to cruel temptations, while it is too young to derive, without a parent or a teacher's guidance, any real benefit from it. This early taste, or I should rather say, this passion for company, together with a plentiful supply of money from indulgent parents, has laid the foundation of utter ruin to many thousands and tens of thousands of youth. And I know it to my sorrow, dear Pastor, that in the young and inexperienced mind, where we are not busy in sowing the good seed of God's word, the evil one is very busy and successful in sowing tares."

" How easy it is to see errors," said the father, " when the bandage of our delusions is thus torn from our eyes. Ah! Sir, experience is the mother of wisdom. One of our principal errors was that of allowing our child to *associate with vicious boys*, until they had so entwined themselves around his heart, that no influence or authority of ours could detach him from the snare. And often, I remember it with the bitterness of remorse, when I should have wooed him over with kindness, I have, in my wrath, reproached the character of his associates to his face. The consequence was just such as every wise student of human nature must have observed. His galled spirit clung closer and closer to them, as they were persecuted by me for his sake. There is a witchery in a young profligate's companions, which parents have never duly conceived. It is the result of that depravity which pervades the human heart, and which makes us averse to all that is good, and swift to learn and to practice what is evil. One hour's influence of profligate company on a young mind may not be effaced by days and months, and even years of parental labor and prayer."

"And, my friends," said the Pastor, "there was a defect in your efforts to win over his *love for the house of God.* I have always lent my countenance to the practice of our good old fathers, which is still kept up in our church, of bringing the children into the house of God on the holy day of rest. God, by the mouth of his servant Joel, commanded the children, and even the babes at the breast, as well as the elders and the people, to be assembled before him in the solemn convocation. And our Redeemer, in the days of his humiliation, charged parents and the disciples 'not to forbid little children when coming unto him,' 'for of such,' said he, 'is the kingdom of heaven.' We must train them up, in infancy, by our prayers, privately, and in the house of God; and in riper years, by parental and pastoral instruction. And thus, by the grace of God, we can beget a respect, and a love for the courts and the ordinances of God in the young and tender mind."

"Yes, dear Pastor," cried the father, "here, in the weakness of our hearts, did we commit another great error. The slightest excuses were often sustained; and 'the dear child' must be spared the journey, and the pain of going to church, and of sitting so long, and being confined so long in church! And there was another error, as serious on our part, by which the mischief was consummated. When we were urgent to overcome his aversion to the church, which we invariably found to be strengthened by every fresh indulgence and permission to stay at home, he would then, to get rid of our importunity and command, beg permission to go to the church in the next village, which happened to be nearer. And in order to induce him to go *somewhere* to the house of God, we thus left him, or rather abandoned him to himself. That which we ought to have anticipated and feared, did take place. His vicious companions took the charge of him; and they led him, not into the house of God, but into the village taverns! Whole Sabbaths had he thus spent before we made the appalling discovery!"

"And then," said the Pastor, "did not your too fond and compliant hearts place *funds too profusely* at his disposal, even from the first?"

"Ah! Sir," cried the father, "that was my next error, which, perhaps, gave pungency and fatality to the rest. I gave him money, first, because '*I loved the dear child:*' then I gave him money, because I saw other parents giving liberally to their children: and then, I gave him money, because my pride said, *my only son shall not be behind his comrades in any thing:* and, finally, I confess that latterly I gave many sums purely out of self-defence, or an indolent aversion to resistance, simply to get rid of his importunate duns! And now I can say, from experience, that these ill-timed donations to children fail not to beget *new wants*, and *new appetites*, and *new desires*. This evil is like the dropsy in the natural body, it increases by its own means of indulgence: the more water the dropsical man drinks the more thirsty he becomes, and the more inveterate is his disease rendered by every fresh draught. That parent who lavishes 'pocket money' on his child, before he has acquired sound principles and prudence to control his passions, and a spirit of enlightened charity and good taste to make a wise use of it, exerts his influence directly to initiate him into habits of gambling, intemperance, gluttony, and their attendant revolting vices. He furnishes the means of gratification; he lays the train, and puts into the hands of his child the lighted torch and the match ready to be applied! All this, alas! to my sorrow, have I done. And when, at length, I did awaken to the frightful consequences, now too evident in the confirmed habits of vice in my poor ruined boy, I found myself adding another error to the former, and thereby helping on the mischief. When I was dunned with incessant clamors to supply the appetite which my folly helped to create, I have replied fiercely, adding reproach and insult to refusal, instead of making the effort with paternal kindness and love to reclaim him. What was the result? Just what you have witnessed, and what might have been anticipated in one whose conscience is seared, and who is prepared for the most debased and debasing conduct; just that which is practised by unprincipled and ruined sons and apprentices every day. He actually abstracted property, article after article, weekly; he even drove off, in my absence, the sheep and young cattle, to pay his *debts of honor;* namely, his tavern and gambling debts! And, O! Sir, I am well aware, that within an hour he has been repeating this robbery on his father!"

"It is a desperate case!" said the Pastor, after a long pause of sorrowful silence. "But, all that you have been alluding to, my dear friend, are only the branches of the evil you deplore. If you go farther back than to his boyhood at school, perhaps you may discover the *root*. And, my dear Madam," continued he, in the most tender and respectful manner, "I allude to *a mother's earliest influence* over the young heart, to show how much depends on a mother's care; not by any means to insinuate that you, like Eve, were first in the transgression. But did you not miss, in his early infancy, or at least in the earliest part of his boyhood, the grand opportunity of establishing your parental authority in the heart of your dear boy?"

"I fear I did," said she, with great emotion; "and often have I bewailed it. Ah! Sir, I am assured that a child is capable of receiving instruction, ay, and of being spoiled, as it regards religious matters, sooner than most mothers have any just conception of. I did, indeed, long for the grace of God to sanctify his soul—and earnestly, if I know my own heart, did I pray for this. But, on review, it is a question involving serious doubt with me, whether I did labor aright, or use the means of God's grace in a skilful and judicious manner, to convey the truth into his young heart, and establish there a sense of God's authority, and thence, of my own as a parent. I did not make, I fear, a scriptural effort to melt down his heart, by causing the knowledge, and thence the fear of the great God, Creator, Preserver, Redeemer, and Judge, to distil, as it were, drop by drop, on his mind and heart; and by teaching him to pray to God as soon as reason dawned, and as soon as he could lisp a word. The first word I should have taught him, the first sentence I should have made him breathe out, should have been 'THOU GOD SEEST ME!' And then, again, I fear I did not take sufficient care to sooth his spirit when ruffled, and subdue by reason and kindness his little fits of violence and brawlings, and woo him over by love, and firmness. I have known a mother do this by singing softly a melting hymn on the ear of her little child; and by teaching it also to sing a sweet and plaintive hymn, as well as to pray with infant lisp, *to him the great God who always sees us!* Awe and submission to God, I am fully persuaded, is the only true basis of genuine and unaffected submission and reverence to parents. It must be so, if it be a moral virtue, and not mere instinct. And there are no genuine morals without a principle of religion. Hence the pagan is described as 'without natural affection:' the parent sacrifices his child, and the child his parent; and we have painful evidence, that a profligate child is likewise without natural affection! O! it was here I failed: I see my error: I should never have given up: I should have daily renewed my efforts: I should have labored and wrestled in prayer; until, by the grace of God, I saw the fruits of my exertions showing themselves in filial reverence and submission, based on the fear and the love of God."

She paused, and wiped her flowing tears. "These are not tears of sorrow and despair, dear Pastor," she added, after she had composed herself, "neither are these the conjectures of a theorist. I saw my error with my boy; God, I trust, was my guide in training that dear child, my daughter, who is advancing to us: she is not only a sweet child to comfort us in our sorrows—I have reason to believe that God has changed her heart; and I know not that she has ever needed a reproof from her dear father these three years past. But I am interrupting you; you were about to say something"——

At this moment the daughter came up; a beautiful girl of fourteen or fifteen years; who cast a look of tender anxiety on her parents; and, saluting the kind pastor, with the frank and blushing simplicity of innocence, as she presented her hand to receive his cordial welcome, she sat down by her mother's side. The pastor went on.

"I have learned, from painful experience," said he, "that many parents, and even some of them the most pious, are apt to prove defective in *two* grand points; in their domestic discipline; and the early training of their children.

"They are defective in the *matter* employed to train them, and in the *manner* of applying the proper matter. Some parents I have found defective in both of these: some in the former: others in the latter."

"Have the goodness to explain yourself more fully," said the father. The Pastor went on.

"To understand how a parent may be defective in the *matter* which he is to employ in the training of his children, you need only to recollect that vital godliness, as Mrs. C———l has just now hinted, is the only true basis of all genuine morality; and therefore of all pure moral order, such as is pleasing in the eyes of God, in families, as well as in the community. I do not deny that there may be morals, even lovely morals, and virtuous deportment in a person destitute of true religion. And I also admit that these are good and valuable in their place, and so far as they go. Our blessed Savior looked on the young man spoken of in the Gospel, who had, in the exterior, kept the commandments, '*and loved him,*' though his heart was as yet a stranger to vital piety. We instinctively love such a character, while we are disgusted with vice and profligacy. But all those lovely and beautiful traits are, nevertheless, radically defective: they can no more be compared with the virtues and morality of the Gospel, I mean '*the beauties of holiness,*' than the apples said to grow on the margin of the Dead Sea, to these golden apples of a skilful hand's engrafting, which you see richly clustering on that magnificent tree before us. The former were fair, very fair, to human view; but they were light and deceptive; the interior was filled up with black dust, emblematical of the depraved and unconverted heart of the mere moralist. But the latter, these rich apples on that grafted tree, are solid, sound to the core, and delicious. 'Neither circumcision, nor uncircumcision,' that is to say, no exterior virtues, or accomplishments, or mere profession, 'availeth any thing' 'before God at his bar, for our personal justification and acceptance—no, nothing but our Redeemer's righteousness:' and for morals, '*nothing but a new creature.*'

"And this, my dear friends, opens up the true secret why the philosopher and moralist, who trust in human virtue alone, with all its defects, have *never* succeeded in this matter. There is nothing in philosophy, there is nothing in the most eloquent declamation on virtue, nothing in the most persuasive words of man's wisdom, that can ever convey the life, or spirit, or principle of vital religion into the human heart, after having conquered all the opposition from the devil, the world, and the flesh. Hence these never did, and they never can convert a man; they never have made, they never can make a true Christian. They may appear to be limpid streams; but they are the streams of Damascus; not the divinely appointed and health-giving waters of the River of the God of Israel. The life of the Spirit of God is not in them. 'If any man be in Christ Jesus, he is a new creature.' 'I through the law, am dead to the law, that I might LIVE unto God. I am crucified with Christ: nevertheless I live; yet not I, but Christ liveth in me: and the life which I now live in the flesh, I live by the faith of the Son of God, who loved me, and gave himself for me.' Hence, it is only when we are risen with Christ, that we seek those things which are above,' and do 'mortify our members,' and bring forth the fruits of holiness in 'good works which God hath ordained that we should walk in them.'

"It is easy to see, then, that where 'the life of Christ' is wanting, no fruits of holiness *can* be produced: this 'life of Christ' wanting, the very basis of *pure* morality is wanting.

"But the Spirit of God is the only author of this life. For this is the testimony of God, 'We are his workmanship, created anew in Christ Jesus,' 'by the washing of regeneration, and the renewing of the Holy Ghost.' Eph. 2 : 10; Titus, 3 : 5.

"**And in the production of the 'new creation,'** the Holy

Ghost employs, not the moral declamation, and the enticing words of the philosophy of this world; not the persuasions of 'science falsely so called;' these may be useful and ornamental in their place: they may be as choice pearls: but what are pearls to a hungering and thirsting soul? what are pearls to the famished Arab in the dry and barren wilderness? It is the voice of God only that raises the dead: it is the precious truth of the Gospel alone which the Holy Ghost employs to convince and convert sinners: it is the bread and the water of life alone, that can bring back the fainting spirit of man, and can sustain the life of God in the soul. The words of our Lord are explicit on this point. 'We are born again, not of corruptible seed, but of incorruptible, by the word of God, which liveth and abideth for ever And this is the word which, by the Gospel, is preached unto you.' And, under a deep sense of our responsibility, and in the faithful and diligent use of all the means and ordinances appointed of God, 'we purify our souls in obeying the truth, through the Spirit, unto unfeigned love of the brethren,' 'and building up ourselves on our most holy faith, praying in the Holy Ghost, we keep ourselves in the love of God,' and 'grow in grace,' till we come unto the perfect man; to the measure of the stature of the fulness of Christ.'

" And, I need not tell you, my friend, how fruitless would be your labor in planting, in this beautiful orchard of yours, a tree, 'twice dead,' which had been, long ago, 'plucked up by the roots:' or, how fruitless would be your utmost diligence and painstaking in plowing and sowing these fine fields of yours, if you throw in the *wrong seed*. He who resorts to human means, and human wisdom only, in the training of his family, and adopts the world's cold and lifeless morality, instead of 'the living and powerful word' of God's Gospel, is actually sowing *tares* instead of *wheat* He may toil late and early; but he will, at the last, be mortified to find that the crop will be *tares*, and nothing but *tares!* This, my dear friend, is the dangerous result of erring in the *matter* of training."

" Ah! dear Pastor," exclaimed Mr..C———l, " it may be that I have erred in the skillful use of all this; but not, as I trust, in the *matter* itself. What you have kindly recited are the truths which my soul loves. We have erred, I think, less in the *matter*, than in the *manner* of applying them. Will you, dear Pastor, have the goodness briefly to notice the usual failures here."

"Touching this matter," said the Pastor, "it is not only our duty, but a pleasure to copy the manner of our divine Master in all points practicable. Now, it must have struck you that our Lord exhibited the most perfect kindness, tenderness, and benevolence, in the whole manner of his instruction. Let us, then, put kindness, tenderness, and benevolence foremost, in the list of the graces of parental government. Let our whole souls flow forth in kindliest emotions. O! let us ever think of the unutterable value of the souls of children entrusted to our care; let us lose no opportunity, let us spare no pains to pluck them as brands from the burning. Let us never cease to woo over their souls to Christ, by our entreaties, by our tears, by our prayers, by our love, by our example. Knowing the terrors of the Lord, let us use the most touching persuasions which the yearning of parental love can suggest.

"But, alas! how often do parents err in this point! The error sometimes arises from an irritable temper; passion overwhelms reason and reflection; we do not stop to recollect how much our own dear parents bore with our waywardness and follies: we forget how much, and how long our heavenly Father has borne with us; we forget how inconsistent is this hasty spirit with the character of Christian parents, who must be 'apt to teach;' and therefore, patient and long suffering. The error sometimes proceeds from a failing leaning to virtue's side. A Christian has warm and strong feelings of piety; these hurry him on; and he does not exercise calm reflection, so as to make the proper and necessary allowances for youth's thoughtlessness and follies. But did our Father in heaven bear with us? Did our Master forgive us ten thousand *talents*, and shall we not bear with our children, and forgive them a hundred *pence*? Shall we, who profess to be the children of the light, not remember that we must subdue the young heart by the discipline of truth, applied with labor and prayer, not by force or the spirit of persecution!

"And permit me also to add here, that we who are parents are often a good deal defective in another valuable quality, or virtue, if you will allow me to call it so—I mean, *cheerfulness*. To the absence of this, and the influence of moroseness, may we not, in a great measure, ascribe the aversion so manifest in many young people, of the higher and middling ranks, to the topic of religious conversation? In all our allusions and conversations on the matter of religion, we should carefully study to make it what it is in sober reality, the most lovely and the most charming thing in the world!

"Much wisdom and spiritual skill are required in making a cheerful and exhilarating improvement of the *Sabbath evening*. In recalling to memory and reviewing the duties and exercises of the day, we should studiously endeavor to make our fireside and Sabbath evening conversations the most delightful and most captivating possible to the young mind. There are some parents and masters of families so stern, so awful, so morose in their manner, that their exhibitions of the lovely Gospel of Christ are really revolting to young persons. They seem to mistake sternness for solemnity, moroseness for zeal, and a spirit to find fault with and chide every one, for a spirit of piety and purity. They seem as if they took a pleasure in picturing out religion, not as an angel in robes of glory, but as a dark and lowering demon, come to rob us of our joys! This cannot fail to excite disgust. To this cause, and also, in an equal, if not superior degree, to another cause—I mean the total absence of all religious conversation at a parent's fireside, do I ascribe that prevailing dislike for religious conversation among young people.

"But, my dear friends, while I recommend *cheerfulness*, I would implore every Christian parent to be on his guard against the want of a proper and becoming gravity. An ill-timed *levity* has, in many instances, produced lasting and most injurious consequences. Gravity and cheerfulness are perfectly consistent, and even congenial: it is the former which prevents the latter from degenerating into utter levity. Never, on a Sabbath evening, and never on a religious subject, should becoming gravity permit the introduction of *wit and levity;* far less, 'foolish talking or jesting, which are not convenient.' It was one of that learned and truly godly man, President Edward's recorded rules of life, 'never to say a thing on the Lord's day which would excite *mirth* or *a laugh.*' This should be strictly observed by every Christian parent and master of a family. We may be perfectly cheerful without mirth and laughter. Let every thing be in its proper place, and always seasonable.

"There is another defect in the *manner*, which I cannot omit; the want of a due equanimity of temper. This is usually betrayed by impatience and irritation. It is of essential importance not only to be on our guard against these; but to have the mind cured of them, as an exceeding great evil. A parent should never use the rod until he is convinced, on cool recollection, that it is his imperative duty to have recourse to it: he should never correct a child until he has convinced him of his error and crime: he should never correct a child in a passion; to do so is to indulge a spirit of revenge; not to exercise salutary parental discipline. His whole manner should indicate to the child that he administers the correction with the utmost reluctance, and from a painful sense of duty. An estimable friend of mine had an untoward son: he had committed a crime against the laws of the household: he took him into the family circle, spent some time in explaining to him the nature and the evil of that crime, and laying the rod down, he said, 'It is my duty, my child, to correct you; but I will do it in the fear of God. Let us first pray.' The whole family circle threw themselves on their knees, while he poured out, with deep emotions, and many tears, a prayer for his stubborn and rebellious child: the culprit alone remained standing: but the prayer and tears of his father melted his refractory heart, and he kneeled down also. The correction was administered with evident distress; but it was light, for the child bowed instantly in submission and penitential confessions. And to my knowledge it was the last he ever needed. He is still alive; and a more dutiful and excellent son you will not readily find.

"There is another defect which is originated by a parent's constitutional indolence and aversion to the trouble and pain of discipline. This dangerous failing has made many a parent criminally yield to his own ease or natural feelings.

"And finally, my friends, a painful defect shows itself in the *want of a proper unity between the parents*. One parent *scolds* when he ought to administer solemn but affectionate rebukes; while the other parent takes the child's part, and makes an apology for it: one of the parents corrects in wrath; the other interferes, and pities the 'poor child' and insists that it shall not be corrected. The child thus creates an insurrection in the family, and contrives to escape in the unseemly brawl. The result is, that he laughs at the weakness of both parents, and soon begins to set parental authority at defiance."

While the Pastor was uttering the last *three specimens of parental delinquency* in the *manner* of conducting family discipline, the elder and his wife, having turned their eyes mutually on each other with more of sorrow than reproach, began to testify their unaffected grief: they were both bathed in tears. It had occurred to them that this was the main origin and source of the evil which they were now bitterly deploring.

Toward evening the Pastor, previous to his departure, took some pains to find out the youth; and bringing him in, placed him by his father's side, and addressed another of his pastoral admonitions to him. There was a dignity in the Pastor's manner which seldom failed to command the awe and attention of this young man, when in his common moods. It is true, he had insulted him in the field, but it was in a gust of passion, which was now, for a season at least, soothed into a calm. But the Pastor knew not the depth of that youth's depravity: he was silent, but unsubdued.

The Pastor commenced his address to him in a tone of unaffected tenderness, while he sought to conceal the tears which coursed down his cheeks: but it had no effect on him. He rose by degrees into the most touching pathos, as he addressed himself to the youth's conscience: then he spread out before his mind the terrors of the law and the majesty of the Almighty; and told him of the coming hour of death, of judgment, and an eternal retribution.

"My poor boy!" cried the Pastor, with the utmost tenderness, "I will not fail to tell thee thy duties, whether thou wilt hear, or whether thou wilt forbear. It is the command of God to cherish in thy soul the principle of *filial affection.* 'Hearken to thy father that begat thee, and despise not thy mother when she is old.' And remember, my child, that the basis of this affection and veneration which you owe your parents, is a holy veneration of God. And O were there a principle of piety toward God in your heart, you would not thus break the hearts of your parents. In proportion as a child has the fear of God before his eyes, he is dutiful and affectionate. And in proportion as the fear of God is banished from the mind, the child is unnatural, stubborn, and rebellious. The drunkard and the gambler exhibit a mournful evidence of this: they would shuffle the implements of their folly and crime at a father's death-bed: they would make their last stake on a mother's coffin!

"In addition to filial affection, I charge you to render a corresponding reverence and honor: carry it in all your looks; be courteous, gentle, and kind; shun petulance and the distressing spirit of contradiction, even when you may be confident that you are in the right. Never utter a disrespectful word of them to others: he who can do this, *even when they are in error*, lessens the dignity of his family, and detracts from his own honor: like the pious sons of Noah, always throw a veil over their frailties and failings; and always be ready to defend them from the tongue of slander. And in a particular manner show the substantial evidence of your filial reverence and honor, by a dignified deportment before *all men*, in your intercourse with the world. I would not ask a higher compliment from a child of mine than this, I mean as it regards temporal honors.

"In addition to this, my child, God enjoins it on you to render to your parents a prompt filial *obedience* in all things. Always lend a willing ear to them in all their instructions. Yield up your heart to their injunctions promptly: humble yourself under their admonitions and reproofs: bow down with filial submission under their corrections, whether expressed in words, or in a temporary exile from their presence, or by the rod of correction. Consult with them frankly, and make them your counsellors and guides; especially in matters of such importance as your establishment in life, the choice of your employment and business, the choice of your company and companions, and in a sp:cial manner your early attachments and choice of a companion, and in all your spiritual concerns.

"And, finally, fail not to give them endearing evidences of your filial *gratitude*. This includes in it, love for the benefits received, and a high value put on them, on account of their proceeding from persons beloved and dear: it includes *affection* to the persons of the donors, joy at the reception of favors, and a prompt disposition to render back what it can, in return for them.

"And now, young man, these duties are enjoined by the awful authority of God speaking to you in his holy word, and by the mouth of your honored parents; and enforced by the captivating example of our Lord Jesus Christ toward his mother in early life, and as, in a most touching manner, while expiring on the cross, he recommended her, in his last moments, to the beloved disciple, with whom she should find reverence, affection, and a home! John, 19 : 25, 26. Moreover, God has enforced this duty by a promise of long life and prosperity; and when this duty is rendered by faith and love to God's authority, it receives its eternal reward in the heavens. On the contrary, hear the denunciations of Heaven against the rebellious and wicked child : 'Cursed be he that setteth light by his father and his mother: and all the people shall say Amen. Deut. 27 : 16. 'The eye that mocketh at his father, and despiseth to obey his mother, the ravens of the valley shall pick it out, and the young eagles shall eat it.' Ah! young man, look on these weeping parents, and say, can you dare pursue the course which will bring down their gray hairs with sorrow to the grave?"

Having finished his admonitions he kneeled down with the afflicted parents, and uttered a fervent prayer for them, while he did not forget in his holy wrestlings their poor prodigal son; for he felt that he had received his ministry of the Lord, and watched for souls as one who knew he was soon to be called to give his last account—even for those who might be *lost*, as well as for those who should be *saved!*

* * * * * * * * *

The writer of this Tract succeeded that venerable minister in the pastoral charge of the church of B———; and when he came into the charge, the Pastor, and Mr. C., and his wife also, had all departed this life. They all died in great peace and joy in the Holy Ghost. Mr. C. died first, and shortly after him his wife, after closing their often-renewed and solemn entreaties and admonitions to their only son, to return to the Lord God of his fathers, and eschew the miseries of the second death; and enforcing these admonitions with many tears, and by all the solemnities of their trial and experience of a dying bed! The Pastor had accepted the invitation to take on him the presidency of a college, and died in a few months after entering on his official duties.

John C———, the son, was the husband of an amiable lady, and the father of several beautiful children, when I first visited his mansion. He had been, for a season, reformed, to appearance at least; and had sustained a tolerably decent character for about a year after he had been married to his excellent wife. But now he had added the crime of a boasted and obstinate infidelity to the most disgusting habits of intemperance. And having once returned to them, his latter end was worse than the beginning. He was now a miserable and degraded man, lost to all self-respect, and reckless of character and public opinion; his wife, once the most beautiful and happy woman in the valley, was now a broken-hearted and haggard being; and his own children, to complete his misery and degradation, fled at his approach, and hid themselves from his presence. His fine estate was now involved in debt, and every thing around him indicated the condition of one fast sinking into ruin. His person, formerly athletic and handsome, exhibited a revolting spectacle. He had been visited with several attacks of the *delirium tremens*, or the drunkard's brain fever, and yet he would daily drink incredible quantities of the poisonous liquid which was drowning him in perdition!

I remember as distinctly as if it had been only yesterday, the last visit which I paid him. I was accompanied by an elder of the church, who had for some years filled the place of his venerable father. He received us kindly; he was sober, for it was rather early; he sat down on my left side, the elder on the other; his meek and humble wife, with her three pretty little children, casting anxious and sorrowful looks at their father, placed themselves over against us. A deep and painful silence prevailed for some minutes. Every thing about the chamber, and about the house, on which the eye could rest, exhibited tokens of desolation and wretchedness. This was the inheritance of a SPOILED CHILD—the house of a drunkard and infidel!

"Will you, Sir, bring me your father's Bible?" A smile, not of pleasure, but that of the scorner, played over his face; nevertheless, he rose and brought it out, covered with dust and cobwebs.

This led me to notice the very different use which the good old man, his father, made of that book, and the use which all good men would make of it. He smiled contemptuously, but said nothing, for his wife cast a beseeching look on him, tempered with her winning sweetness, rendered more touching by her unaffected sorrow.

It was a long visit we paid him; and we endeavored, by the help of divine grace, to improve our time. We set before him, after reading the nineteenth psalm, a brief outline of the authenticity and divinity of the Holy Scriptures; and begged respectfully his attention to it. "Ah! Sir, this points out to you the good old way in which your fathers walked, and found rest and happiness: I appeal to your own experience if you have ever tasted one drop of happiness or peace in your wanderings from these ways." He turned away from the discussion with a sally of ridicule; yet in that sarcastic laugh a child might have seen that he felt miserable in his soul. His wit had pierced his own conscience.

We turned to another subject—the nature and the worth of the immortal soul. "O let the son of your father remember the words of Him whose lips never spoke falsehood, even Him whose lips, as the Lord God of Hosts liveth, will ere long judge you at his tribunal! O hear his words, "What is a man profited, though he should gain the whole world, and lose his own soul? or what shall a man give in exchange for his soul?" O what will you feel—what will you say—what will you do, when you are in the last awful conflict—in the act of leaving this world!—and soon

—soon will you be summoned to leave it! As the Lord liveth, and as your soul liveth, there is only a step between you and death! O what will you feel—what will you say—what will you do, when the eternal world in all its fearful realities, in all its overpowering glories and terrors, shall burst on your astonished and disembodied soul! O hear me—return to the Lord God of your father! I beseech you, by Him who loved us, and gave himself for us—by him who died on the cross for us—by the Lord Jesus Christ, I beseech you, return to your God! By the memory of that dear old man your father—by the memory of his tears, and prayers, and vows—by the memory of that dear saint of God, now in heaven, your mother, who bare you, and nursed you in her bosom, and wept and prayed over you—whose last prayer and sigh were breathed from her dying lips for you—O return to your God; and break off your sins by repentance and faith in the Lord Jesus Christ!"

He burst into tears, and placing his hands on his face, bowed himself down, his face on his knees, and wept aloud.

We all kneeled down and prayed: the miserable man kneeled close by me: my heart was utterly overcome: I poured out my soul in almost incoherent words: I implored the outpouring of the Holy Ghost on him, his wife, and his dear little children. Every one of us wept: the very children sobbed: and I shall never forget the scene: the floor where the prodigal son bowed his head was wet with his streaming tears.

The sun was now setting: we took our leave of him with a cordial embrace: he led us to our horses, and on parting besought us to visit him soon again.

But, alas! it was our last interview with him. I never saw him more. I was called into a neighboring State on business of the churches, and I was absent two weeks. The first news I learned, as I alighted at my own door, on my return, was the appalling intelligence that POOR JOHN C—— WAS DEAD, AND BURIED!

I learned in brief his last moments from the Elder who had accompanied me on my last visit, and who had seen him when dying. Poor C—— was attacked with fits: he raved in his deliriums: at intervals he recovered his senses, and for a season was somewhat composed in his mind, but expressed deep compunctions and sorrow for his evil ways and doings. When he felt himself dying, he became awfully alarmed: he seemed actually frantic: the very bed shook under him; as if with supernatural strength, he tried to raise himself up; and shrieked out for some moments, " O Lord Jesus, have mercy on me! God of my father, have mercy on me! O Christ, have mercy on me!—O curses, curses on the head of General ——— who seduced me from the ways of my father's God into his infidel ways!—Curses on my vicious companions, who taught me to break the Sabbath, and to dishonor and disobey my father and mother! And led me into taverns, instead of the church of my fathers! O mercy, mercy, Lord, on me, a poor miserable outcast!"—Thus he continued wailing, sometimes crying for mercy, and frequently uttering fearful imprecations. In a few hours, during which there was nothing but horror and distraction in the family, his strength, though the strength of a giant, became utterly exhausted; and his spirit, with an agonizing struggle, took its everlasting flight!

This, as reported to me, was the end of the SPOILED CHILD.—In these solemn facts we set up a beacon, to give an awful warning to Parents, of the fatal rock on which they also may strike. " Avoid it; pass not by it; turn from it, and pass away!" " O let us hear and fear, and do no presumptuous sin!" Let us labor for the conversion of our dear children, like those who feel that they are laboring to "pluck brands from the devouring fire!" We pronounce not on the final destiny of poor John C———; but who of us, I beseech you, would wish our children to follow his course of life, or to die his appalling death?

END

No. 29.

THE CHILD'S
GUIDE TO PRAYER.

BY REV. DR. WATTS.

My dear Young Friends,

Give me leave to propose to you a few serious considerations, to awaken your desires to *seek after God, and to pray to him in your early years.*

1. *Consider who and what God is.*

Have you not been told that he is an Almighty Being, who made the heavens, and the earth, and the sea, and all things that are in them? that he is a Spirit, and that he is every where present, though you cannot see him? that he knows all things that you do, and that he can do all that you desire of him? that he is holy, and hates sin, and yet that he is very good and full of mercy, even to his sinful creatures? that he is the greatest, the wisest, and the best of beings? And does he not expect you should love and honor him, who is so great and so good? Is he not your heavenly Father? Did he not make you to love, and serve, and worship him? And how can you pretend to serve and love him, if you never *pray* to him! Could you but see him, you would think him the most lovely and most excellent of all beings, and should you not then be exceedingly desirous to be more acquainted with him, and seek to obtain his love?

2. *Consider who and what you are.*

Are you not young creatures, that a few years ago had no being at all, and cannot preserve your own lives? And is it not of high concern to you to be acquainted with that God, and to pray to him upon whom your very being depends? He that made you can destroy you. Besides, are you not sinful creatures? Do not your own hearts and consciences tell you that you have done many things amiss, and that you have provoked that God who made you, to be angry with you, and to take away all your comforts? And are you willing to continue under his anger for ever? Do you know how terrible is the anger of God, who can make you miserable in this world and in that which is to come? And is he not very gracious, to call upon such sinners as you are to pray to him? Is it not necessary, therefore, that you should come humbly before him, and fall down on your knees and confess your sins, and entreat him to lay his anger aside, and to love you, notwithstanding all your offences? This leads me to the third consideration.

3. *Consider what are your wants.*

Do you not stand in daily need of food and raiment, that you may not suffer sharp hunger and cold? Do you not want the continuance of your health, that you may not pine away with sickness and pain? Can you keep yourselves alive, or can any of your friends keep you from dying? Do you not know, that God is the author of all your comforts, and it is on him you depend for daily food and clothing, for health and strength, for recovery from sickness, and preservation from death? It is from God that you must seek all these things, by prayer.

Are you not exposed to dangers every day, and every night? Do you not want the care of God to keep you? to preserve you from mischief, from fires, and from all evils of every kind? And since you deserve nothing at the hand of God, can you suppose he will watch over you, and cover you from all evil, if you never call upon him, nor ask his favour?

Do you not know that you have a soul as well as a body, and that you want spiritual blessings for your souls, as well as temporal blessings for your bodies?

Since you are guilty creatures, do you not greatly want the forgiveness of your sins? Have you not been taught, that your sins have deserved great punishments, both here and hereafter? And are you not desirous to be delivered from this punishment? But can you expect God will pardon and deliver you, if you never pray?

And since you cannot do any thing to make recompense to the great and holy God for your offences, how speedily should you apply to Jesus Christ, the Son of God, who now dwells in heaven, and who did once make recompense by his death for the sins of men? He is the great Mediator between God and man. How earnestly should you pray, that you may enjoy the benefit of his mediation, and that he may bring you into a state of peace with God? How should you cry to God, that he would forgive you, for the sake of his well beloved Son? Since you are sensible that you are guilty sinners, you should not be easy one day, without seeking to God for mercy.

Remember, also, that though your sins were pardoned, yet you have a sinful nature in you, ready to offend God continually. Do you not find yourselves ready to commit new sins? Are you not soon ready to be angry, to strike, or call ill names? Are you never ready to grow uneasy and fret, if other children have better things than you? Are you not ready to disobey your parents, or to spend your time in play, when you should be at work, or learning your book? Are you not sometimes inclined to hide your faults by telling a lie? Do not you find yourselves ready to learn evil words, or to wish evil to others, or take something privately that is not allowed you, or to do something that is forbidden? Do you not see, then, how much you need to pray for the grace of God, to keep you from sin daily?

And are not your minds too ignorant of God, and heavenly things? Is it not a pleasure to think, that God has promised his own Holy Spirit, to instruct you in the understanding of holy things, as well as to help you in doing your duty? This is a blessed promise, indeed, to poor ignorant and sinful creatures, such as we are. But can you think God will give his grace, or his Holy Spirit, to them who never pray to him? Do you not read in your Bible, "If fathers give good gifts to their children, how much more shall your heavenly Father give the Holy Spirit to them that ask him?" Do not you know, that you cannot live here always? Have you not been taught that your body must die, and turn to dust, and that your soul, which cannot die, must then go into another world? Have you not been told that Jesus Christ is now gone to heaven, to take care of his people when they leave this world? And do you think Jesus Christ will take care of your soul, when it comes like a stranger into that other world, if you have not committed and entrusted it into his hands by prayer?

You must stand before God, the judge of all, when you die; and are you prepared to stand before God, if you have not obtained a good hope that God loves you? There are but two places in the other world, heaven and hell. Heaven for the righteous, who love God and pray to him; and hell for the wicked, who neither pray to him nor love him. And can you ever hope that God will save you from hell, and receive you to dwell with himself, and with his Son Jesus Christ, if you never pray to him for these blessings?

4. *Consider what your mercies are.*

How kindly has God dealt with you? Has he not given you parents and friends, who by his order provide food and raiment, and every thing convenient for you? How many poor children want these comforts, and are exposed to hunger and cold! Have not your parents and friends taken care that you should be taught to read, and learn many things for your good? Do you not know, that it was God who put it into their hearts, and also made them able to do it? How many thousand poor creatures are there in the land, who know nothing of God, and cannot read a word! Is it not God who has made this happy difference between you and them? And should you not praise him for his goodness? Have you not seen other children blind, or lame, or foolish? Is it not God who has given you your limbs and your senses? Is it not the same good God, that gives you health and peace, night and day; and are you not bound to thank him for these mercies? What! would you live like the brute beasts, who eat and drink and sleep, and take no notice of the great God, from whose hand all blessings come?

5. *Consider what relation you stand in to others.*

Have you not a father and mother that you are bound to honour and love? and would you never pray, that God would bestow his best blessings on them, and make them live long to bring you up in his fear? Have you not brothers or sisters, or other friends and relations? And have you no mercies to ask of God for them? Do not your teachers desire that you should pray to God to bless them, that they may the better instruct you? They pray for you, and you should pray for them.

Since, then, dear children, there are such a multitude of reasons that urge you to pray to God; since you see it is your constant duty, and your highest interest; if you would be safe and happy in this world, or the world to come, delay no longer, but begin this religious work immediately; and I humbly pray, that God would abundantly assist and bless you therein, that you may learn, from your own experience, how sweet and profitably a thing it is to call upon the name of the Lord.

ADVICE RELATING TO PRAYER.

BY THE SAME AUTHOR.

1. SEEK out a proper time to retire alone by yourself, morning and evening, at those seasons wherein you have no other necessary business or duty.

And here I would persuade myself, that parents or masters, who take due care of the souls of children, would not only admonish and encourage them to seek God in secret, morning and evening, but would point out a proper place for their retirements. This is easily done in private families; and they should make some observations, whether children observe these seasons or not. In some schools, I have heard there are certain seasons in the day, which are called "the half hour," that are ordained on purpose for children to retire; and if they cannot be entirely alone, yet, at distant parts of their chambers, they may lift their hearts, and their low voices, to God in worship.

In the morning, I would generally say, the earlier the

better. For if you lose the first opportunity, you will often find that you will be utterly hindered from praying, by other things that may happen. Besides, it is best to call upon God early, and begin the day with religion, that you may beg a blessing on yourself, and on all your business that day. Do not begin with the world in the morning, before you have been with God. In the evening, I cannot say the later the better; but rather embrace the first convenient evening hour that offers, lest you be drowsy. However, it is much better to pray late, than not to pray at all. If, at any time, you are hindered in the morning, be sure, if possible, that you be not hindered in the evening too. But the best way is, to keep pretty nearly the same seasons, every day, for your morning and evening retirements, if your circumstances will allow it.

2. Seek a proper and convenient place for your secret retirements. It is no matter what the place, if it be free from all disturbance. A bedchamber is generally a proper place for those who have not the conveniency of closets. Be not afraid to go alone, though it may be sometimes in the dark; you are going to meet with God, and he is ever near to them that call upon him. The presence of God is an almighty security against all manner of evils. Nothing can hurt you while God is with you.

3. If you have time, in your secret worship, read a chapter or two, and a psalm, before you pray. For my part, I could wish there were select portions of Scripture chosen out, and printed by themselves, for children to read in private. However, for want of this, I would recommend the book of Genesis, and of Exodus as far as the twentieth chapter, and the book of Proverbs, and the four Gospels, with some practical chapters out of the epistles, and especially the book of Psalms, to be the chief subjects of their reading in secret, in their younger years. The book of Proverbs abounds in useful lessons of prudence, and instructions of piety. The book of Psalms is full of prayers and praises. And let the word not be read in a careless and hasty manner, but with diligent attention, and with an endeavour to remember something of it every day.

4. Leave your business and sports, and all thoughts of them, behind, when you retire for worship. Let your spirit be composed to great seriousness when you begin to

pray. The reading of a chapter will help to compose your thoughts, and fix them more on divine things. Fall down upon your knees before God in a humble posture, and remember, that you are come into the presence of the Great God, that you are going to speak to the Majesty of heaven, before whom angels worship, and at whose name devils tremble. Take heed, therefore, that you do not trifle with him, nor take his holy name in vain. He sees your heart, he knows all your thoughts, and he observes all your wanderings. And for your encouragement also remember, that he takes kind notice of every sincere desire that rises from your heart.

5. Take heed that you speak not any thing to God in prayer, which is not the sincere thought and desire of your own soul. See to it, that your heart agree to the words of your prayer, or else do not utter them before God. "God is a Spirit; and they that worship him must worship him in spirit and in truth." He hates a hypocrite, who speaks what he does not mean. Speak nothing, therefore, which is not suitable to your present case, and is not the sense of your own heart.

6. Take notice, every day, what good or evil falls out relating to you, and by this means, perhaps, you will often have some particular thing in your mind to mention before God; it may be, some sin to confess, some sorrow to complain of, some blessing to desire, or some mercy to give thanks for. Then be sure to speak it with freedom, in your own language. The great God, who hears the young ravens when they cry, will much more take notice of the voice and language of young children, when they pray to him; and he understands the meaning of your heart, though your expressions may not be so proper as you could wish.

7. If any person whatsoever takes notice of your retiring daily to pray to God in secret, never be ashamed of it, nor leave off prayer for fear of being seen or known to be religious. If you are ashamed of worshipping God your heavenly Father, in this world, God will be ashamed to own you for one of his children, in the world to come.

8. When several children join together in prayer, take care that nothing be done with rudeness or confusion, but let all decency and gravity be practised. Let not him that speaks begin, till all are come in, and have fallen down

on their knees; and let every one attend to the words spoken, and lift up his heart to God, in all the several sentences; that the prayer of every one may be accepted of God, and that God may delight to answer the united prayers of children, and pour down his blessing on so religious a family.

9. To sum up all, I should add in the last place: Let all your behaviour in the world, both toward God and toward superiors and toward your fellows, be such as becomes those who profess religion, and pray to God morning and evening. Let a pious care to please God, and a fear of offending him, run through all your speeches and actions. Honour and obey your parents and teachers; love your brothers and sisters; be courteous and kind to all; abstain from all evil words and sinful works; for your prayers will be useless if you continue in wilful sins. The prayers of the wicked, who will not repent, are " an abomination to the Lord."

Make it appear, that your hearts are sincere and honest in your prayers to God, by endeavouring always to avoid those sins which you have confessed, as well as to practise those duties in which you have prayed God to assist you; and let it be your daily care to obtain all those blessings, as far as in you lies, which you have asked God to bestow upon you. Thus, while prayer and practice go together, you will become christians indeed, you will be the comfort and joy of your friends in this world, you will always find acceptance with God through the mediation of Jesus Christ, and in the world to come, be made happy to all eternity. Amen.

PUBLISHED BY THE

AMERICAN TRACT SOCIETY,

And sold at their Depository, No. 150 Nassau-street, near the City-Hall, New-York; and by Agents of the Society, its Branches, and Auxiliaries, in the principal cities and towns in the United States.

No. 30.

THE BENEVOLENCE OF GOD.

Go to Calvary! What a wonderful scene strikes our senses! The heavens grow black—the rocks burst asunder—the thunder of the Lord waxeth louder and louder—the vail of the magnificent temple is rent asunder by an invisible hand—the dead arise, and appear in the holy city! What event do these prodigies attest?—*Page* 5.

PUBLISHED BY THE

AMERICAN TRACT SOCIETY,

150 NASSAU-STREET, NEW-YORK.

D. Fanshaw, Printer.

THE BENEVOLENCE OF GOD.

```
———— Survey the wond'rous cure!
And at each step let higher wonder rise!
Pardon for infinite offence! and pardon
Through means that speak its value infinite!
A pardon bought with blood!—with blood divine!
With blood of Him I made my foe!
Persisted to provoke! though woo'd and aw'd,
Blest and chastis'd, a flagrant rebel still!
A rebel, 'midst the thunders of his throne!
Nor I alone! a rebel universe!
My species up in arms! not one exempt!
Yet, for the foulest of the foul he dies,
Most joy'd for the redeem'd from deepest guilt!
As if our race were held of highest rank,
And Godhead dearer as more kind to man!           Young.
```

GOD IS LOVE.—1 John, iv. 8.

PROOFS of the divine benevolence may be gathered from the widely-extended scene of the visible creation, and also from the harmonious operations of providence; but it is proposed at present to restrict ourselves to those which arise from the great scheme of redemption. Allow us then,

1. To advert to the *character* and *condition* of those for whom it has been devised, as a proof that *God is love*.

It is generally acknowledged, that we are affected by the tale of misery in a degree which bears some proportion to the original state of the sufferer, or the superior endowments which he possesses. Suppose, for example, two individuals were labouring under the same sentence of condemnation: the one, a man of a strong mind, a fascinating genius, a brilliant imagination, whose figure and whose manners bore the marks of the most exquisite polish, and who had moved in a high orbit of existence; the other a comparatively mean, ignorant, and uncultivated being;

over which would your sympathy spread with the most delicate sensibilities? and if mercy could be obtained *only* for *one,* to which would you rush to administer it? We know! But, *My thoughts are not your thoughts, neither are your ways my ways, saith the Lord.* From the lofty heights of eternity, Mercy looked down, and beheld the angelic and the human nature involved in guilt, and in misery; but the passed by the nature which presented the strongest physical and intellectual attractions, to rescue man, 'doomed to die'—man, in whose warm bosom no love to God was cherished, but the most deep-rooted enmity—on whose moral character no lineaments of the divine image could be traced, but rather the evil passions which degrade and defile—and who occupied such an insignificant station in the vast universe, that if he had been annihilated he would scarcely have been missed. *For verily he took not on him the nature of angels; but he took on him the seed of Abraham.*

And what part of the human race calls forth this spontaneous expression of benevolence? We know that the moral character of man varies, from the most delicate amiability, to the most brutal and savage ferocity; and if *we* had been permitted to have speculated on the exercise of mercy, we should have predicted that it would have been monopolized by the most virtuous;—we should have concluded, that the amiable, the intelligent, and the honourable, would have been admitted to a participation of its blessings, while the more debased and ignorant would have been left to perish in their sins. But, saith the Lord, *My thoughts are not your thoughts, neither are your ways my ways.* It is true, the more virtuous are not denied mercy, but it is not confined to them;—they are not forbidden to indulge the hope of final happiness, but they are not permitted exclusively to enjoy it. The Gospel of Jesus Christ makes provision for the salvation of the chief of sinners; and frequently those whom men abhor become the objects of its compassion, while the self-complacent, and the self-righteous, are left under the delusions of their own fancy. Hence said our Lord to the elders and chief priests of Israel, who trusted in themselves that they were righteous, and despised others, *Verily I say unto you, that the publicans and the harlots go into the kingdom of God before you.* How pure and ardent must be that love, which could pass by the angels who kept not their first estate, to rescue fallen man from the awful peril of his condition—and which often passes by those who appear, in many respects, very attractive members of the human family, to save the most guilty, the most depraved, and the most unhappy!

2. The superior state of bliss to which man is ultimately to be raised, is another proof that *God is love.*

Man, when created, was placed in the garden of Eden; and if ever a local residence was favourable to human felicity, Eden could boast of unrivalled charms. Intersected with flowing streams—decorated with the most majestic trees, and with the choicest shrubs and flowers creation could supply—rendered melodious by the varied, yet harmonious notes of the feathered tribe—and visited by the occasional presence of the King Eternal—who threw over his uncreated glories a visible form, which, softening their radiance, added, if not to their grandeur, yet to their beauty. Here man dwelt. His eye gazed on a cloudless sky—his ear listened to the song of the earliest bird—his nostrils inhaled the breath of uncorrupted morn—his heart felt the sublimity of bliss. He sinned—Discord rushed from her retreat—Misery started up from every bower in Paradise—the thunder of the divine displeasure rolled in the loud and lengthened peals over the once tranquil place —and when concealed, as he thought, amidst the thick-set trees, the voice of insulted Majesty was heard, saying, *Adam, Where art thou? And he said, I heard thy voice in the garden, and I was afraid, because I was naked; and I hid myself. And he said, Who told thee that thou wast naked? Hast thou eaten of the tree whereof I commanded thee that thou shouldest not eat?* The ground is immediately accursed—the agent of seduction is at once doomed to punishment—and man is driven from his beloved abode into the wide world, in which he has wandered from that fatal hour to the present, the slave of passion, and the victim of grief. Multifarious rites have been practised, and the most costly sacrifices have been offered up, to appease the vengeance of Heaven: but it still goes forth against the children of disobedience. But must *we* despair? No. *For God so loved the world, that he gave his only-begotten Son, that whosoever believeth in him should not perish, but have everlasting life.*

And you who believe in Christ will attain a higher state

of honour and of bliss, than you would have acquired if the catastrophe of the fall had never happened.

A higher state of *honour*.

Had man never sinned, he would have stood in the relation of a servant, or a subject of the great King; but now, being mystically united to Jesus Christ, and adopted by an act of grace, he bears the endearing epithet of a son. *But when the fulness of the time was come, God sent forth his Son, made of a woman, made under the law, to redeem them that were under the law, that we might receive the adoption of sons.*

A higher state of *felicity*.

Had man never sinned, his felicity would have run on in a smooth and even current, liable to no fluctuations—no impediments—no swellings. His removal from earth to heaven, if that event had ever taken place, would have increased his happiness, but we have no means of ascertaining the exact proportion. But now, trace a redeemed sinner through this scene of mortality and of wo, till you behold him before the throne of God, and of the Lamb; and while conscious that he enjoys all the sources of bliss which he would have enjoyed had he entered glory from a Paradisiacal state of innocence, you will perceive that his most exalted felicity arises from his redemption. *Unto him that loved us, and washed us from our sins in his own blood, and hath made us kings and priests unto God and his Father; to him be glory and dominion for ever and ever.* Amen.

3. The means by which this state of future felicity is obtained, is another decisive proof that *God is love.*

What are the means? Go to Calvary! What a wonderful scene strikes our senses! The heavens grow black—the rocks burst asunder—the thunder of the Lord waxeth louder and louder—the vail of the magnificent temple is rent asunder by an invisible hand—the dead arise, and appear in the holy city! What event do these prodigies attest? Tell us, ye ministering spirits, who dwell near the throne of the Eternal! That *God is love!* What! love selecting for its heralds the eclipse—the earthquake—and the tempest! Yes! Amidst these awful movements of Nature, in her disturbed condition, we behold God giving his only-begotten Son for the salvation of man; and his death, which consummates the scheme of mercy, is the event which these strange prodigies announce! He dies, *the just for the unjust, that he might bring us to God.*

But could not the salvation of man have been effected by some other expedient? The question is improper. It is not our province to dictate to the Redeemer the terms of our redemption, nor the means by which it is to be accomplished. Such are the means which infinite wisdom has devised for our salvation; and if we reject them, *there remaineth no more sacrifice for sins, but a certain fearful looking for of judgment, and fiery indignation which shall devour the adversaries.*

4. The method by which we enjoy the blessings of this scheme of redemption—the extent to which they are to be conveyed—and the provision which is made to guard against their universal rejection, are other proofs that *God is love.*

The leading blessings which flow to us through the redemption that is in Christ Jesus are, remission of sin—the sanctification of our nature—consolation suited to the varied afflictions of life—and the prospect of eternal glory.

How is the remission of sin to be obtained? Are you required, like the modern pagan, to undertake a distant and dangerous pilgrimage, leaving your family exposed to the insults of the proud, and liable to the pressure of want? No! *For through Christ we have access by one Spirit unto the Father. In whom we have redemption through his blood, the forgiveness of sins, according to the riches of his grace.*

How is your nature to be purified? Are you, like the deluded Hindoo, to expose yourself to the scorching heat of a tropical sun? are you to submit to the deep laceration of self-inflicted torture, before you can be redeemed from the bondage of corruption, and regain that high elevation of moral excellence from which you are fallen? No! *God purifieth your hearts by faith.* Faith brings before the mind those facts, and those doctrines—those promises, and those threatenings, which strongly tend to destroy the *love* of sin, and to subdue its *power.*

How are the consolations of mercy obtained? Not by the incantations of superstition, nor the mere force of philosophical reasoning; but by the belief of those exceeding great and precious promises with which the Scriptures abound. And is not faith the evidence of things unseen, as well as the substance of things hoped for? *Therefore being justified by faith, we have peace with God, through our Lord Jesus Christ: by whom also we have access by faith into this grace wherein we stand, and rejoice in hope of the glory of God.*

Under the Levitical dispensation, Mercy seemed confined to one place, and her blessings were almost exclusively confined to one people. Her residence was within the vail, and from between the cherubim she uttered her responses to the tribes of Israel. But now she has taken the wings of the morning, and following the course of the sun, her going forth is to be from the end of the heaven, and her circuit to the ends of it, and no human being to be hid from the light thereof. Did not our Lord declare that *this Gospel of the kingdom shall be preached in all the world for a witness unto all nations?* See him before his ascension, even while the scars of Golgotha were still fresh on his sacred person, gathering around him his faithful apostles, and hear the last injunction which fell from his lips. *Go ye into all the world, and preach the Gospel to every creature. He that believeth and is baptized shall be saved; but he that believeth not shall be damned.*

Wherever man resides, thither the scheme of redemption may be conveyed: and though it abounds, in its historical details, in references and allusions to the phenomena of the country in which it was revealed, and in which it was perfected, and to the civil and religious customs of the people to whose care it was first intrusted, yet neither its doctrines, nor its precepts—neither its rites, nor its institutions, discover any local peculiarities which would restrict its progress, or limit its duration.

And though these blessings are to be conveyed through the instrumentality of men who possess no ability to secure their reception, yet these men stand in alliance with an invisible agency, which can make the barbarian and the Scythian, the bond and the free, willing in the day of Jehovah's power. Hence our preachers are not dependant for success on the force of moral suasion; neither do they expect to triumph over the passions and prejudices of the human heart by the splendour of evidence, or the charms of eloquence—regarding themselves as the mere instruments through whom the Holy Ghost exerts his almighty energy. And who can withstand, when he arises to promote the growing empire of the Redeemer? What mind can remain impervious to the rays of truth, when he exhibits it? What prejudices can retain their strong hold, when he sends forth the subduing efficacy of his grace? *My word,* saith the Lord, *shall not return unto me void; but it shall accomplish that which I please, and prosper in the thing whereto I send it.*

And now consider what PRACTICAL INFLUENCE this love of God should have on our minds.

1. The benevolence of God, as displayed in the scheme of redemption, should become a subject of *intense meditation.*

Nature throws out attractions, in some of her departments, which invite the traveller to leave his home, and his country, only to gaze on them. And when he reaches the enchanted spot, from whence he can see the lofty pyramid, losing its top amidst the clouds of heaven—or the long extended valley, where vegetation, in her varied forms, puts forth all her magnificence and beauty—where the burning mountain is casting up its liquid flames—or the cataract is thundering amidst the solemn stillness of deserted declivities, into what transports is he thrown!—nor is it till the scenes become familiar to his senses, that he has power to take a sketch, or describe an object. He passes on till he sees the splendid monuments of ancient times mouldering in ruins; but does he not feel rich in mental excitement, amidst the desolations which Athens, which Corinth, which Jerusalem still exhibit? And shall the unconscious scenes of nature which, after the lapse of a few more centuries, will form part of the general conflagration—shall the mutations of Providence, which are only serviceable as they make us wiser and better, awaken the most impassioned interest in the breast of the sentimental traveller? and shall the great scheme of redemption by the death of Jesus Christ, pass rapidly over the mind, as though it were too unimportant to fix our attention? God forbid! But we must not conceal from you the astonishing fact, that it is treated with cold neglect by the great majority to whom it is revealed. They deem it low and worthless; and they attempt to vindicate their conduct by saying, with the unbelieving Jews, "Which of the scribes or rulers—which of the learned or dignified of our church, make it the theme of their beautiful addresses, or eloquent harangues? Which of our celebrated men of science, discrimination, and taste, make it the object of their study, or the subject of their discourse? Does not the preaching of it provoke contempt, and expose the minister to the degrading imputation of fanaticism?" And yet angels, fascinated by its charms, suspending their studies of nature, and their lofty pursuits in heaven, descend from the celestial world to look into it; and whilst they look, they discover new beauties and new wonders incessantly arising, which induce them again to look, and continue the research. They bend, and again they bend their lofty minds, and cannot quit the object; and by their conduct they seem to unite with the Apostle, in his admiration of the incomparable *excellency of the knowledge of Christ Jesus their Lord.* And shall angels, who have no direct interest in this subject, be captivated by its beauties, and shall we remain insensible to them? Shall they turn away from the overpowering grandeur of the heavenly world, to pry into the hidden mysteries of the cross, and shall we treat them with indifference? God forbid! But it cannot be that you who have felt the burden of sin, will ever be guilty of such a crime. It cannot be that you, who have derived from it your purest joy and your most sublime anticipations, will ever be accused of such a species of criminal folly and base ingratitude. You can adopt the language of the Apostle, as descriptive of the deep interest which you take in this supremely important subject;—*God forbid that I should glory, save in the cross of our Lord Jesus Christ.*

2. It ought to become a subject of *devout imitation. Herein is love, not that we loved God, but that he loved us, and sent his Son to be the propitiation for our sins. Beloved, if God so loved us, we ought also to love one another. If we love one another, God dwelleth in us, and his love is perfected in us.*

If you wish to cherish and display that spirit of benevolence towards others, which God has manifested in the scheme of human redemption, it will be absolutely necessary that you should take that specific view of their character and condition which the Sacred Writers have given us. There are many christians in modern times, who will weep over the ruins of Carthage, and pour forth their bitter lamentations near the site where Athens once displayed her unrivalled grandeur—who will mingle their sympathies with the sufferers of Ionia and Marathon, who were doomed to witness the extinction of science, and the destruction of empire;—who contemplate the fall of man from his original state of purity and honour with cool indifference, or impiously declare that he is as pure and as perfect as when first formed by the power of Jehovah. They speak in raptures of the dignity and happiness of the human species, even while the groans of misery are issuing from almost every receptacle of humanity—and unblushingly assert, that no derangement has taken place in the social system, though the history of man is little more than the public record of his ambition, cruelty, fraud, and injustice. To reason with such men is an act of folly, as they seem, on this subject, incapable of feeling the force of the most palpable evidence; and the only course which remains to us, is to pity their incorrigible insensibility, and to guard ourselves against the neutralizing and paralyzing influence of their opinions. To expect that such men will ever become the philanthropists of the age in which they live, would be no less visionary, than to expect that the author of all evil would, if permitted, come and repair the moral injury which he has done amongst us. And though they may, from birth, and accidental associations, stand connected with christianity in some of the external forms of her establishment, yet they are no less devoid of her spirit than the avowed infidels, who reject her revelations as fabulous, and her pretensions as absurd.

You must view man as a fallen and a guilty creature, before you will feel the tenderness of pity for him. You must view him as in a state of rebellion against the authority of God, and as exposed to the terrors of his righteous displeasure, or you will never feel that deep and paramount anxiety on his behalf which will impel you to aim at his salvation. You must not allow the few *social* virtues, which *sometimes* bud and blossom on his character, to induce you to suppose that his moral condition, in relation to God, is less awful and perilous than the Scriptures represent—or that he stands in less need of the cleansing efficacy of the blood of atonement, and the purifying influence of the Holy Spirit, than when he appears in the more repelling form of the bold and profligate transgressor!

Be ye, then, imitators of God; and as he has given his only-begotten Son, to die, *the just for the unjust*, do all in your power to convey a knowledge of this fact to every human being. Suffer no false principles of reasoning—no selfish calculations—no considerations of personal ease, to induce you to suppress your tender pity—to smother your strong anxieties—or to withhold your zealous exertions, till all the members of the human family know the only true God, and Jesus Christ whom he hath sent, whom to know is life eternal.

Often meditate on the conduct of the Lord Jesus Christ; *who, being in the form of God, thought it not robbery to be equal with God; but made himself of no reputation, and took upon him the form of a servant, and was made in the likeness of men; and being found in fashion as a man, he humbled himself, and became obedient unto death, even the death of the cross.* And why should you meditate on the original dignity, and on the abasement of the Redeemer, but to possess the same spirit of condescension and benevolence which he so gloriously displayed? Meditate on the greatness of his humiliation—on the intensity of his sufferings—on the ardour of his love—and go forth into the world with the same mind—and let every place you visit, and every individual with whom you come in contact, feel the moral influence of your christian benevolence. The world may reproach you for your fanaticism, if they see you devoted to the cause of Christ; and may impeach your good sense, if you speak in raptures of the love of God to man, as displayed in the plan of redemption; but be regardless of its revilings, and offer the same apology for your conduct which the Apostle once offered for his own, and his fellow-labourers:—*For the love of Christ constraineth us.*

But if you reject this scheme of redemption, or treat it with cool indifference, how shall you escape from the overflowings of the divine displeasure? Do you not know, on the authority of the Scriptures, that *the Lord Jesus shall be revealed from heaven with his mighty angels, in flaming fire, taking vengeance on them that know not God, and that obey not the Gospel of our Lord Jesus Christ: who shall be punished with everlasting destruction from the presence of the Lord, and from the glory of his power; when he shall come to be glorified in his saints, and to be admired in all them that believe.*

IT IS FINISHED.

Hark! the voice of love and mercy
   Sounds aloud from Calvary;
See, it rends the rocks asunder—
   Shakes the earth, and veils the sky!
     "It is finish'd!"—
Hear the Saviour—dying—cry.

It is finish'd!—O what pleasure
   Do these precious words afford!
Heav'nly blessings, without measure,
   Flow to us from Christ the Lord.
     It is finish'd!—
Saints, the dying words record.

Finish'd—all the types and shadows
   Of the ceremonial law;
Finish'd—all that God had promis'd;
   Death and hell no more shall awe:
     It is finish'd!
Saints, from hence your comforts draw.

Ransom'd ones, approach the table—
   Taste the soul-reviving food:
Nothing's half so sweet and pleasant
   As the Saviour's flesh and blood.
     It is finish'd—
Christ has borne the heavy load.

Tune your harps anew, ye seraphs—
   Join to sing the pleasing theme;
All on earth, and all in heaven,
   Join to praise Emmanuel's name,
     Hallelujah!
Glory to the bleeding Lamb!   *Burder's Col.*

No. 31.

KNOCKING AT THE DOOR.

AN APPEAL TO YOUTH.

BY REV. J. SCUDDER,
MISSIONARY IN CEYLON.

Behold a Stranger at the door!
He gently knocks, has knock'd before;
He's waited long, is waiting still:
You treat no other friend so ill.

O lovely attitude! He stands
With melting heart and loaded hands!
O matchless kindness! and He shows
This matchless kindness to His foes.

But will He prove a friend indeed?
He will, the very friend you need:

The friend of sinners—yes, 'tis He
With garments dy'd on Calvary.

Rise, touch'd with gratitude divine,
Turn out His enemy, and thine,
That soul-destroying monster sin,
And let the heavenly stranger in.

Admit Him, ere his anger burn;
His feet departed, ne'er return.
Admit Him, or the hour's at hand
You'll at His door rejected stand.

MY DEAR YOUNG FRIEND—As you have been instructed in Christianity from your early years, you are so well acquainted with it as to be prepared to admit that you are a sinner, and as such, exposed to the wrath and curse of God. You are equally prepared to admit that you must repent of sin, believe in Christ, and make an unreserved and unconditional surrender of your all to Him, as the only conditions upon which God will save you. But though you have a speculative knowledge of these things, I fear they do not affect your heart. I fear that, if the angel of death should be commissioned to cut you down at this moment, you would be lost for ever.

That affecting passage on which the above hymn is founded is peculiarly adapted to your condition: "Behold, I stand at the door and knock; if any man hear my voice and open the door, I will come in to him, and sup with him, and he with me." The person spoken of as knocking at the door is *the ever-blessed Jesus,* the friend of sinners. He it is who left the joys of heaven, came into this world, and died in ignominy and shame upon the cross, that poor sinners might escape eternal burnings and be raised to the joys of heaven.

VOL 1.

The same love which constrained Him to shed his precious blood for you, constrains him to follow you in all your wanderings from him, with entreaties that you will not ruin your soul. And though you have hitherto turned a deaf ear to them, his patience is not yet wearied out.

The figure of *knocking at the door* is very beautiful, and points out in the strongest manner the wonderful compassion of the Savior toward sinners. He may very properly be compared to a stranger, who comes to the door of sinners hearts, and knocks for admission, with the most important tidings which ever greeted the ears of men. One would suppose that, the moment they were communicated, they would be received with the utmost rejoicing, and the bearer welcomed with ten thousand thanks. The reverse of this, however, is generally the case. He is treated with indifference, and often with supreme contempt. That man who would treat a stranger who had knocked at his door, in the manner that sinners treat the Savior while knocking at the door of their hearts, would be looked upon as very uncivil, and worthy of being discarded from our society. Should I tell you, my young friend, that you are the very person who has treated your Savior with an incivility which you would blush to use to a passing stranger? You may start back with horror, and perhaps weep at the very mention of it. You may probably tell me, that you pray and read your Bible, and are strict in your attendance at the house of prayer, and are therefore wrongfully accused. But you must remember, that as long as you do not turn your back upon the vain world, and give yourself entirely to your Savior, you treat him not only with incivility, but with contempt. "Give me thy heart," is his language to you—"Lord, I cannot give up the pleasure of the world, therefore I cannot give it to thee" is yours to him. I need hardly add, that as long as this is the case, even your prayers and reading the Bible are an abomination in his sight, and will only enhance your condemnation if you at last perish. "If any man come to me, and hate not his father and mother, and wife and children, and brethren and sisters, yea, and his own life also, he cannot be my disciple."

The various ways in which the Savior knocks at the door of your heart, show his tender concern for you. Some of these I will mention.

1. He knocks *by his Holy Word*. This has been in your hands for years, and often reminded you that you are a perishing sinner. It abounds with all manner of warnings and incentives to make you flee to Jesus Christ, the ark of safety, ere the deluge of divine wrath overtake you, and you are swept away by it into the ocean of eternal fire. The torments of hell are pointed out by it in such glowing colors, that you can, as it were, see the lake of fire and brimstone; and its miserable victims weeping, and wailing, and gnashing their teeth, and gnawing their tongues for pain, and blaspheming the God of heaven, because of their pains and sores. The joys of heaven it also points out in the most attractive manner; and assures you that if you will embrace Christ as your Savior, you shall soon be put in possession of them, and reign as a king and priest in his Father's kingdom, where all tears shall be wiped from your eyes, where there shall be no more death, neither sorrow nor crying, neither shall there be any more pain.

2. Christ knocks at the door of your heart *by his ministers*. One would suppose that it would be unnecessary for him to do any thing more than to have his word put into your hands. The reverse, however, of this is in a most melancholy manner manifested to be the case. He has therefore stirred up men by the Holy Ghost, and set them apart for the express business of explaining this word to you, and using every other endeavor to pluck you as a brand from the burnings. The knocks which the Lord Jesus has given by them are loud and awfully alarming. Methinks the alarm in which a person would be thrown, who should be awaked by a rap at his door, and find himself in the midst of flames, would bear but a little proportion to that which you ought to feel when they show you the lake of fire and brimstone, with the smoke of the torments of the damned ascending for ever and ever, into which you are in danger of being momently plunged. Think of the favors the Savior has conferred upon you by enabling you to sit under the stated ministry of his word. You have had the opportunity, from Sabbath to Sabbath, to hear of the concerns of your soul, while hundreds of millions do not know there is such a day. He who has been set your overseer by the Holy Ghost, often retires from holding intercourse with his fellow-men, in order to study what he shall

say to awaken you to a consideration of your soul's concerns, and after having, on his knees, with tears, supplicated the divine blessing, he affectionately delivers the message to you. Has he not often told you, that by nature and by practice you are a sinner, and that you must be born again by the Holy Spirit; that you must repent of every sin, accept of Christ as your Savior and love him above the things of the world, or be lost for ever? Has he not described to you, with all his powers of eloquence, the love of the Redeemer? Has he not taken you with him to the garden of Gethsemane, and shown him to you, sweating, as it were. great drops of blood? Has he not often shown him to you, scourged and crowned with thorns? Has he not often told you of his painful march up the hill of Calvary, bearing the cross to which he was to be nailed? Has he not often shown you the wounds made by the nails which pierced his hands and his feet? Has he not often repeated, in your hearing, the doleful exclamation which escaped his lips just before he expired, "My God, my God, why hast thou forsaken me?" Does not the Savior, also, now knock at the door of your heart by *me*, as you read these pages?

3. Christ knocks at the door of your heart when he sends *sickness and other afflictions* upon you, and when, by fierce diseases, he is sweeping away hundreds around you into eternity. Though young, you probably know what sickness is. Tell me, when your body has been racked with pain, and wearisome days and nights have been appointed to you, has not the thought of death come into your mind; and have you not, as it were, been constrained for a moment to give your reflections to this, to you, I fear, most melancholy subject? Has not the thought of eternity taken hold of you, and made you tremble? Has not the awful gulf over which you were hanging, suspended, as it were, by a thread, made you almost scream with wild amazement; and have you not involuntarily exclaimed, Save me, Lord, or I perish? When you have followed the remains of your friends to the house appointed for all the living, has not the thought come into your mind that you must soon follow, and at that moment have you not been ready to say, "Vanity of vanities, all is vanity," except religion? When multitudes have been cut down by pestilence, have you not been filled with most anxious fears lest death should surprise you?

And when you have heard your Savior saying unto you, "Be thou also ready, for in an hour thou thinkest not, the Son of man cometh," have you not told him, Lord, I will prepare: let what will come, I am resolved hereafter to be thine. And have you not, after all this, not merely gone as far as Ananias and Sapphira in keeping back a part, but have you not kept back *the whole of the price?*

4. Christ knocks at the door of your heart by *his Holy Spirit.* The Holy Spirit, the third person in the ever-blessed Trinity, is sent for the express purpose of convincing men of sin, of righteousness, and of a judgment to come; and though often resisted, he frequently follows them wherever they go. By the way, in the house, on the bed, in the night-watches, he acts the part of a kind friend, and reveals to them that all is not right between God and their souls; that the course they are pursuing is ruinous, and that it is high time for them to attend to their spiritual concerns. Tell me, my dear young friend, does not the Holy Spirit come to you at times, and inspire you with feelings of the nature here described? Do you not, when experiencing his influences, feel that it is a solemn thing to die, and that if you should die immediately you must be lost for ever? Sometimes, when you lie down on your bed at night, are you not almost distracted when you reflect upon your conduct during the day, and does not a sigh proclaim the distress within; or are you not so pressed at times, that you even proclaim with an audible voice the words once used by one in your situation, "If I should die this night, my soul would be in hell?" Especially when, in the house of prayer, you hear of the joys of heaven and the torments of the damned, and learn from the word of God that you have none of the qualifications for heaven, do you not at times come to the resolution that you will, without delay, give up this vain world and dedicate yourself to Christ? And do you not endeavor to put this resolution in force, and continue to endeavor, until some card party, or ball, or other vain amusement, or some light book, or even some small domestic concern, has lulled your conscience to sleep— yes, to sleep, perhaps until awakened by the gnawing of that worm which is to prey upon the ungodly for ever.

Having pointed out some of the methods by which Christ

knocks at the door of your heart, I will for a moment speak of THE GREAT MOTIVE which he holds out to induce you to admit him: "*I will sup with him, and he with me.*" The blessings of the Gospel are fitly compared to a feast. The spiritual supping here alluded to, relates to that delightful communion which takes place between Christ and the believer. The Savior fills his mind with that peace and comfort which the world can neither give nor take away, which enables him to rejoice under the afflictions of life, and even to look upon death with composure. Death is called the king of terrors, and he is indeed so to the ungodly. But to him who sups constantly on the love of his Savior, whose treasure is in heaven, he is a conquered enemy. The apostle Paul could even challenge death to tell him where was his sting, and the grave, where was its victory. I am fully aware that the worldling will tell you that Christians are gloomy, unhappy beings, and would fain persuade you that happiness is to be found alone in his ranks. But you must remember that he is very unfit to sit in judgment upon things of which he knows nothing. Were a Hottentot to see a Herschel so engaged in his contemplations of the heavenly bodies as to be lost to every object around him, he would be ready enough to pronounce him a madman. Let him, however, enjoy his intellectual feast for an hour, and he would long to be a participater in his joys. The worldling must taste the pleasures of religion before you are to pay the least regard to his suppositions. He who addresses you was once a worldling. Religion then possessed no charms. But the scene has been altered. He has tasted its pleasures, and is happy to assure you that he would not give one hour of the enjoyment he has found in it for all the pleasures you have ever enjoyed. Nothing, my dear young friend, can be more preposterous, than for one who has no other portion than this world, to talk of enjoying happiness. I should as soon expect to hear of a man who was going to the gallows, talking of enjoying happiness. What, a man be happy, when the God who made him is his enemy, and against whom, it may be, the gates of heaven are barred for ever! a man be happy, who, ere to-morrow's sun arise may be writhing and weltering in the flames below! Go to the death-bed of such an one, and you learn what the pleasures are of which he boasts.

It is related of the Hon. Sir Francis Newport, that when near death, he looked toward the fire and said: "O that I might lie upon that fire for a hundred thousand years to purchase the favor of God! but it is a fruitless wish. Millions of millions of years will bring me no nearer the end of my tortures than one poor hour. O eternity, eternity, who can discover the abyss of eternity! O that I were in hell, that I might feel the worst; and yet I dread to die, because that worst will never have an end. When will be the last breath, the last pulse, that shall beat my spirit out of this decayed mansion into the desired region of death and hell! O, it is at hand; but I am afraid again, to die. Ah, the forlorn state of one that has no God to fly to for peace and comfort!" The last expression he made use of was, "O the insufferable pangs of hell and of damnation!"

"O time, time," cried out young Altamont, "it is fit that thou shouldst thus strike thy murderer to the heart! How art thou fled for ever! A month! O for a single week! I ask not for years, though an age were too little for the much I have to do. Remorse for the past throws my thoughts on the future. Worse dread of the future strikes it back on the past. I turn and turn, and find no ray; and is there another hell? O thou blasphemed, yet indulgent Lord God! Hell itself will be a refuge if it hides me from thy frown."

When you have left these scenes, go and see the follower of the Lord Jesus, with the view of the king of terrors before him, and learn the pleasures of religion. "I am going to Mount Zion," said the Rev. Dr. Payson, "to the city of the living God, to the heavenly Jerusalem, to an innumerable company of angels, to the general assembly and church of the first born, and to God the judge of all. The celestial city is full in my view. Its glories beam upon me. Its breezes fan me. Its odors are wafted to me. Its sounds strike upon my ears, and its spirit is breathed into my heart. Nothing separates me from it but the river of death, which now appears as an insignificant rill, that may be crossed at a single step, whenever God shall give permission. The Sun of righteousness has been gradually drawing nearer and nearer, appearing larger and brighter as he approached; and now he fills the whole hemisphere, pouring forth a flood of glory, in which I seem to float like an insect in the beams of the sun, exulting, yet almost trembling, while I gaze on this excessive brightness, and wondering with unutterable wonder why God should deign thus to shine upon a sinful worm. A single heart and a single tongue seem altogether inadequate to my wants. I want a whole heart for every separate emotion, and a whole tongue to express that emotion." Again, "I can find no words to express my happiness. I seem to be swimming in a river of pleasure, which is carrying me on to the great fountain." "Last night I had a full clear view of death as the king of terrors; how he comes and crowds the poor sinner to the very verge of the precipice of destruction, and then pushes him down headlong. But I felt that I had nothing to do with this, and I loved to sit like an infant at the feet of Christ who saved *me* from this fate. I felt that death was disarmed of all his terrors: all that he could do, would be to touch me and let my soul loose to go to my Savior." "My soul, instead of growing weaker and more languishing as my body does, seems to be endowed with an angel's energies, and to be ready to break from the body and join those around the throne." "I have suffered twenty times, yes, to speak within bounds, twenty times as much as I could in being burnt at the stake, while my joy in God so abounded as to render my sufferings not only tolerable but welcome." "God is literally now my all in all; while he is present with me, no event can in the least diminish my happiness, and were the whole world at my feet, trying to minister to my comfort, they could not add one drop to the cup." "It seems as if the promise, 'God will wipe away all tears from their eyes,' was already fulfilled in me, as respects tears of sorrow. I have no tears to shed now but those of love and joy and thankfulness."

The death-bed scenes of those who have now been mentioned of course I did not witness; but I have witnessed others both of the righteous and the wicked. I have seen the joy of the one and the distress of the other. Never shall I forget the awful death of a young person who was a patient of mine. After I told her she must die, she inquired with deep anxiety, "Cannot I live a month, cannot I live two weeks?" She died three or four days afterward. I visited her about half an hour before this mournful event. She was then deranged. Would that I could present her before you as she appeared while reason retained its powers, that you might hear the solemn warnings she gave to the young not to put off repentance as she had done. Methinks you would weep, if you never wept before. Horror past imagination sat lowering upon her brow, while she stood shuddering and aghast upon the tremendous precipice. I heard her doleful cries. She fell—I saw her no more.

> " In that dread moment, how the frantic soul
> " Raves round the walls of her clay tenement;
> " Runs to each avenue, and shrieks for help,
> " But shrieks in vain ! How wishfully she looks
> " On all she's leaving, now no longer hers.
> " A little longer, yet a little longer—
> " O might she stay to wash away her crimes,
> " And fit her for her passage ! Mournful sight;
> " Her very eyes weep blood, and ev'ry groan
> " She heaves is big with horror; but the foe,
> " Like a staunch murd'rer, steady to his purpose,
> " Pursues her close, through every lane of life,
> " Nor misses once the track, but presses on,
> " Till forced at last to the tremendous verge,
> " At once she sinks."

What is to be the end of the young friend to whom I am writing, remains to be seen. That your state is beyond all conception dreadful at the present, I very much fear. Day after day is hastening you on to eternity, and your work for it is not yet begun. O how dreary and dark and disconsolate is your path ! No sun of righteousness ever sheds one ray of light upon it. No dews from the heavenly world ever distil upon it. The God who made you looks with no approbation upon you. No Savior looks down from heaven to greet you with his smiles. No Holy Ghost descends to take possession of your body and make it his temple. The awful curses of a broken law are denounced against you. The angel of death stands with his sword drawn, waiting only to receive the command to cut you down and cast you into outer darkness. Nothing, nothing but the mere mercy of that God who is angry with you, keeps you from hell one moment. How bitter the thought, that though the sun may oft arise rejoicing in his course, you are groping the dark road to death; that all the lights of heaven are extinguished upon your path, and the shades of premature night may have spread their blackness over your undying spirit!"

My appeal has already swelled to a great length, but I cannot yet persuade myself to leave off writing. I am reminded that this may be the last effort I shall ever make for the salvation of your soul. It is therefore of the utmost importance that I use every argument in my power to constrain you to open the door of your heart and admit your Savior. God is my witness, that I long to meet you in heaven; but this is altogether impossible, unless I can persuade you to give up the pleasures of this world in which you are deeply immersed, and dedicate yourself unreservedly to his service. My dear young friend, you believe the Gospel; you believe you must embrace it, or be lost. How then is it that you do not let it engross your most solemn and immediate attention? You well know that it is the only thing really worthy of your consideration, and why will you suffer yourself to neglect it a moment longer? Tell me, are you willing to lose your soul for the sake of enjoying a few worldly pleasures for a season? Would such a choice be wise? Let me entreat you to step into that grave-yard which you so often pass, and view the mouldering corpses of those who a short time ago led in the ball-room or at the card party, and ask them, what they think of such pleasures now. O! methinks, if they could speak, they, even they, would address you in such language as you never yet have heard. They would tell you in such vivid strains of eloquence of that lake of fire and brimstone of which they heard while in the house of God, but which they disregarded, and in which all their pleasures have terminated, that the very "caul of your heart," would be rent in pieces, and you would, ere you left the spot, cry out, "If this be the end of those who seek their happiness from the world, 'my soul, come not thou into their secret, unto their assembly, mine honor, be not thou united.'" Sin, though seemingly sweet in the commission, yet at last "biteth like a serpent, and stingeth like an adder."

"Happy is the man that findeth wisdom. Her ways are ways of pleasantness, and all her paths are peace." Would that I could persuade you to make trial of them. One single draught from her cup would divest you of all relish for those imaginary pleasures which now dazzle your sight. Peradventure this may, with the divine blessing, be the case. I will turn supplicant and beseech you to make such a trial.

"I entreat you by the majesty of that God in whose

name I come, whose voice fills all heaven with reverence and obedience—I entreat you by the terrors of his wrath, who could speak to you in thunder, who could, by one single act of his will, cut off this precarious life, and send you down to hell—I beseech you by his mercies, his tender mercies, by the bowels of his compassion, which still yearn over you as those of a parent over a dear son, a tender child, whom, notwithstanding his former ungrateful rebellion, he earnestly remembers still—I beseech you further, by the name and love of our dying Savior—I beseech you by all the condescension of his incarnation, by the poverty to which he voluntarily submitted, that you might be enriched with eternal treasures, by all the gracious invitations which he gave, which still sound in his word, and still coming, as it were, warm from his heart, are sweeter than honey and the honey comb—I beseech you by the memory of what he suffered, as well as of what he said and did; by the agony which he endured in the garden, when his body was covered with a dew of blood—I beseech you by all that tender distress which he felt, when his dearest friends forsook him and fled, and his blood-thirsty enemies dragged him away like the meanest of slaves, and like the vilest of criminals—I beseech you by the blows and bruises, by the stripes and lashes which this injured sovereign endured while in their rebellious hands, by the shame of spitting, from which he hid not that kind and venerable countenance—I beseech you by the purple robe, the sceptre of reed, and the crown of thorns which this King of glory wore, that he might set us among the princes of heaven—I beseech you by the heavy burden of the cross under which he panted, and toiled, and fainted, in the painful way to Golgotha, that he might free us from the burden of our sins—I beseech you by the remembrance of those rude nails which tore the veins and arteries, the nerves and tendons of his sacred hands and feet, and by that invincible, that triumphant goodness, which, while the iron pierced his flesh, engaged him to cry out, ' Father, forgive them, for they know not what they do'—I beseech you by the unutterable anguish which he bore when lifted up on the cross, and extended there as on a rack for six painful hours, that you open your heart to those attractive influences which have drawn to him thousands and tens of thousands—I beseech you by all that insult and derision which the Lord of glory bore there, by that parching thirst which could hardly obtain the relief of vinegar; by that doleful cry, so astonishing in the mouth of the only-begotten of the Father—My God, my God, why hast thou forsaken me—I beseech you by that grace which subdued and pardoned a dying malefactor; by that compassion for sinners, by that compassion for you, which wrought in his heart, long as its vital motion continued, and which ended not when he bowed his head, saying, 'It is finished,' and gave up the Ghost—I beseech you by all the triumphs of that resurrection, by which he was declared to be the Son of God with power; by the Spirit of holiness—I beseech you by the memory of all that Christ has already done; by the expectation of all he will further do for his people—I beseech you at once by the sceptre of his grace, and by the sword of his justice, with which all his incorrigible enemies shall be slain before him, that you do not trifle away these precious moments while his Spirit is thus breathing upon you; that you do not lose an opportunity which may never return, and on the improvement of which your eternity depends—I beseech you by all the bowels of compassion which you owe to the faithful ministers of Christ, who are studying and laboring, preaching and praying, wearing out their time, exhausting their strength, and very probably shortening their lives for the salvation of your soul, and of souls like yours—I beseech you by the ruin of those who have trifled away their days, and perished in their sins; and by the happiness of those who have embraced the Gospel, and are saved by it—I beseech you by the great expectation of that important day, when the Lord Jesus shall be revealed from heaven; by the terrors of a dissolving world, by the sound of the archangel's trumpet, and of that infinitely more awful sentence, 'Come, ye blessed,' and 'Depart, ye cursed,' with which that grand solemnity shall close— I beseech you, finally, by your own precious and immortal soul, by the sure prospect of a dying bed, or a sudden surprise into the invisible state, and as you would feel one sparkle of comfort in your departing spirit when your flesh and your heart are failing—I beseech you by your own personal appearance before the tribunal of Christ, by all the transports of the blessed, and by all the agonies of the damned, the one or the other of which must be your everlasting portion—I affectionately entreat and beseech you, in the strength of all these united considerations, as you will answer it to me, who may in that day be summoned to testify against you; and what is unspeakably more, as you will answer it to the eternal Judge, *that you now make choice of Christ, and his appointed way of salvation, and solemnly devote yourself to God in the bonds of an everlasting covenant.*"

And now, my dear young friend, what will you do? Considering yourself in the immediate presence of the heart-searching and rein-trying God, before whom all you do will be reviewed at the final day, I ask you, will you, or will you not *now* open the door of your heart and admit your Savior? I must have an answer. I charge you in the most solemn manner, and in his name, not to stir from the spot where you are without giving it to me. Upon the determination of THIS MOMENT, perhaps, hangs your everlasting salvation, or everlasting damnation. "Quench not the Spirit," "Grieve not the Spirit," is the command of heaven. Will you then, in defiance of this command, continue to grieve Him any longer? I pause for an answer. What is it? Is it, that you do from *this moment* give up the world, repent of every sin, and dedicate yourself to your Savior in an everlasting covenant not to be broken? If so, throw yourself at his feet, tell him you are a wretch undone, deserving nothing but his vengeance. Tell him, that though you have trampled upon his blood, you will in his strength do so no more, but be his for ever. Plead with him, with tears of blood, to give you the influences of his Holy Spirit, to create in you a clean heart, and renew within you a right spirit, without which you are eternally undone, and continue to plead, until you hear him saying, Go in peace, thy sins are forgiven thee. If this should be the result of my exertions in your behalf, how happy should I be. How happy would all the angels in heaven be. They would chant an anthem to your conversion. How happy, too, would God the Father be to welcome you, a lost child, to his bosom. How happy would the blessed Redeemer be to see of the travail of his soul; and how happy would the ever-blessed Spirit be to make your body the temple of his residence.

But it may be that a result of an entirely different nature

will take place. It may be that you will not comply with the injunction God gives you by me, to dedicate yourself to Christ NOW. In view of the pleasures of the world, and the opposition and ridicule you may have to meet with from your gay companions and others, you may think it best to put off the consideration of this momentous subject to a more convenient time. If such a thought is passing through your mind, cast it out at once. O cast it out, I entreat you. No more harbor it for a moment, than you would harbor the deadly adder in your bosom. Remember that a more convenient season may never arrive. Death may close your eyes in as unexpected a manner as he did those of a young man of whom I have been lately reading, and your body be entombed in yonder church-yard before to-morrow's setting sun. But even should you live for many years to come, you have no reason to believe that you will have as convenient a season as the present. Your heart will grow daily harder and harder, and of course you will find it more and more difficult to embrace the Savior. Look at the aged. Are they more ready to seek him, after having spent fifty or sixty years in sin, than they were when young? The reverse in general is the case. Beside, you do not know that God will continue to hold out any encouragement for you to come to him after *this very moment.* "My Spirit," he has declared, "shall not always strive with man." Many are the sad monuments of his desertion. An instance I will transcribe for your warning.

"I was once called, says a venerable clergyman, to visit a young lady who was said to *be in despair.* She had at some time previous been serious, and had, it was hoped, resolutely set her face Zionward. In an evil hour some of her associates, gay, pleasure-loving young ladies, called on her to accompany them to a ball. She refused to go. The occasion, the company, the parade and gayety, were all utterly dissonant with her present feelings. With characteristic levity and thoughtlessness, they urged her, ridiculed her Methodism, railed at the cant and hypocrisy of her spiritual guides, and finally so far prevailed, that with a desperate effort to shake off her convictions, and regain her former carnal security, she exclaimed, '*Well, I will go, if I am damned for it.*' God took her at her word. The blessed

Spirit immediately withdrew his influences, and instead of the anxious sigh and loving desire to be freed from the body of sin and of death, succeeded by turns the calmness and horrors of despair. The wretched victim knew that the Spirit had taken his final leave: no compunctions for sin, no tears of penitence, no inquiries after God, no eager seeking of the 'place where Christians love to meet,' now occupied the tedious hours. Instead of the bloom and freshness of health, there came the paleness and haggardness of decay. The wan and sunken cheek, the ghastly glaring eye, the emaciated limb, the sure precursors of approaching dissolution, were there. The caresses of friends, the suggestions of affection, all were unheeded. The consolations of piety, the last resource of the miserable, were to her but the bitterness of death. In this state of mind I was called to visit her. When I entered the room where she was, and beheld her pale and emaciated, and reflected that the ravages of her form *without* but faintly shadowed forth the wreck and desolation within, I was almost overpowered. Never had I conceived so vivid an idea of the wo and misery of those who had 'quenched the Spirit.' I proposed prayer. The word threw her into an agony. She utterly refused. No entreaties of friends, no arguments drawn from the love of God, from the fullness and freeness of atoning blood could prevail to shake her resolution. I left her without having been able to find a single avenue to her heart, or to dart one ray of comfort into the dark bosom, which, to all human view, was soon to be enveloped in the blackness of darkness for ever. Never shall I forget the dreadful expression of that ghastly countenance, the tones of that despairing voice. The impression is as vivid as though it had been but yesterday. O that all the young, gay, thoughtless ones, who stifle the convictions of conscience and repress the rising sigh, who dance along on the brink of utter reprobation and despair, would read and lay to heart the warning which the last hours and death of this young lady are calculated so forcibly to give."

That God should withdraw his Spirit from those who resist him, is a matter of no wonder. You very well know, that if one comes to your door day after day, and is received with unkindness, he will leave you, no more to return. You, my dear young friend, have resisted the knocks which the

Savior has been giving the door of your heart by his Spirit, day after day, and month after month, and, O dreadful to relate, year after year. To-day! he is knocking, perhaps *for the last time*. If you reject him, I shall not at all wonder if he abandons you to your own ways, to be filled with your own devices. I shall not at all wonder if *this day* a seal is put in heaven to your everlasting damnation.

And now, my young friend, I bid you an affectionate farewell. It will be but a little while before you and I are summoned before the tribunal of the Judge of all the earth. When we meet there, if this Tract should rise up in judgment against you, as it certainly will, if you are found on his left hand, I think you will allow that I have acted the part of a kind friend, and done what I could for your spiritual welfare. Very probably what I have written will be hastily read by you, and afterward unheeded, uncared for, and but little thought of. This indifference, however, cannot always last. Your seasons of reflection will certainly come. If not in a dying hour, they will in the judgment-day; and they will make your heart sink and die within you, when in common with all whose sins are not washed away in the blood of the Lamb, you hear the awful sentence pronounced against you, " Depart, ye cursed, into everlasting fire prepared for the devil and his angels." And when millions and millions of years shall have rolled away, and you are constrained by the gnawings of the worm which never dies, and by the torments of that fire which never is quenched, to lift up your voice and say, " How long, O Lord, yet how long"—and when the voice of infinite justice proclaims " FOR EVER"—with what wailings and bitter lamentations will you look back and remember the transactions of *this day*—when you deliberately and voluntarily *chose the world, instead of the Savior, as your portion!*

THE END.

DAY OF JUDGMENT.

That a just God will render to every man according to his character and works, is a dictate of reason. Conscience also intimates to every man when he sins, that he deserves to be punished; and when we see or hear of great crimes committed by others, such as murders, perjuries, robbery, or treachery, we feel something within us demanding that such should receive condign punishment. But we see that the wicked are not always punished, in this world, according to their evil deeds; it seems reasonable therefore to expect that there will be a judgment after death.

We are not left, however, to the mere dictates of reason on this subject; God, in his word, has revealed, in the clearest manner, that there will be a day of reckoning, at the end of the world. This day is appointed, and will certainly come. It is not so certain that we shall ever see the sun rise again, as it is that we shall see the day of judgment. The Lord Jesus Christ is also appointed to act as Judge on that day: "because he hath appointed a day in which he will judge the world in righteousness by that Man whom he hath ordained." Acts, 17:31. "For we must all appear before the judgment-seat of Christ; that every one may receive the things done in his body, according to that he hath done, whether it be good or bad." 2 Cor. 5:10.

When this awful day will arrive, is a profound secret, not revealed to any creature in the universe. But we know that it will come suddenly and unexpectedly on those who shall then be on the earth. As it was in the days of Noah and of Lot, so will it be in the Day of Judgment Men will be pursuing their common worldly business and amusements, without apprehension of danger, when the sound of the last trump shall be heard, (for the trumpet shall sound,) and the Son of Man shall be seen coming in the clouds of heaven.

The race of man shall not cease from the earth until that day comes. There will then be a generation of living inhabitants (probably very numerous) in the world. These will never die as other men, but they will undergo a change equivalent to death and a resurrection; in a moment, in the twinkling of an eye, they shall be changed. But all they that are in their graves shall hear the voice of God, and shall come forth, great and small. No sooner shall the trumpet sound, than the scattered dust of unnumbered millions shall resume its proper place in every man. No matter where it lies, or how widely it may have been scattered, one word of the Almighty God is sufficient to bring it to its place, and animate it with new life. The multitude which will then start up into life cannot be conceived, it will be so great. There will stand Adam and all his posterity—there will stand those who lived before the flood, and those who have lived since— there will be seen the ancient patriarchs, Noah, Abraham, Isaac, and Jacob; and the inspired prophets and apostles —there will appear kings, emperors, nobles, and their subjects—the learned philosopher and the ignorant multitude—ministers and their congregations, parents and their children, masters and their servants—all, all coming forward to the grand tribunal. Not one of our whole race will be absent from this great assembly. There, Reader! shall you and I stand, trembling or rejoicing.

It is useless to inquire where room can be found for so great a multitude to stand, for this will be a day of miracles. All the wonders ever exhibited before will be nothing to the wonders of this day. Indeed, all that is natural will end on this day; and every thing will be miraculous. The sun will no longer rise and set; the moon no longer give her light, and the stars shall no longer appear in the firmament. Heaven will appear to have come down to earth, for the King of kings and Lord of heaven will be visible to all, with all his own glory and that of his Father. And all the holy angels will appear in attendance, standing round his throne, ready to execute his orders, whether of justice or of mercy.

When all things are prepared—when the Judge has taken his seat on the tribunal, and all men are brought before him, the judicial process will begin; "*and the books will be opened.*" What books these are, except one, which is "the book of life," we are not informed; but we may be sure that one is the book of God's law; and another the record of human actions which is in the "book of" God's "remembrance." It is not necessary to think of more. These contain all that is necessary for conducting the trial of every man. The one contains the law, and the other the testimony. But every thing will be conducted with the most perfect equity. Every man will be judged for his own deeds, and according to that knowledge of the law which he had opportunity of acquiring. The omniscience of the Judge will enable him to estimate with perfect exactness all the circumstances of every action; every thing which aggravates guilt, and every thing which palliates it, will have due consideration. They who lived under the Patriarchal dispensation will be judged according to the light and advantages then enjoyed; they who lived under the Mosaical economy will be judged by the law of Moses; and they who enjoyed the clear light of the Gospel, will be dealt with in a manner accordant to their advantages; while they who enjoyed no external revelation, will be judged by that law written on the hearts of all men.

The things which shall be brought under the eye of the Judge, and exhibited to the view of the universe, are, all deeds done in the body—whatsoever a man hath done, whether good or bad. Every secret thing. "For God shall bring every work into judgment, with every secret thing, whether it be good, or whether it be evil." Eccl. 12 : 14. Every idle word. "I say unto you, that every idle word that men shall speak, they shall give account thereof in the day of judgment." Matt. 12 : 36. The thoughts of the heart shall also be made manifest. Every unholy desire; every proud, envious, or malicious thought; every secret purpose of iniquity; every unhallowed temper; every rebellious, and discontented, and ungrateful feeling toward God and his government, will be brought into judgment.

And the inquiry will extend not only to positive acts, but also to omissions of duty. Great as is the number of the acts of wickedness, the catalogue of omissions will be greater, and not less criminal. The first sin of this sort which will claim the attention of the Judge, will be the omission to entertain and cherish right sentiments toward God. No more heavy charge will be brought against any individual on that day, than that he neglected to love the Lord his God with all his heart, and soul, and mind, and strength. This is the total violation of the first and greatest command, and the fountain of all other iniquities. The neglect to believe on the Lord Jesus Christ when he was offered to us a complete Savior in the Gospel, will, to the unfruitful hearers of the word, be an accusation of the highest kind. The heinousness and enormity of unbelief, which now affects the consciences of men so little, will on that day appear in a glaring light. It will not be strange if it should call forth reproaches upon the unhappy culprit, from devils, who never had a Savior provided, and from heathen, who never had a Savior offered to them. In that account which our Lord has given of the process of the judgment, in the twenty-fifth chapter of Matthew, the neglect of kindness to the saints, by visiting, comforting, and aiding them, is the only thing mentioned. Whatever else, then, may be noticed, we are sure this will not be forgotten. The whole passage is so solemn and interesting, that it deserves our deepest attention: "When the Son of man shall come in his glory, and all the holy angels with him, then shall he sit upon the throne of his glory. And before him shall be gathered all nations; and he shall separate them one from another, as a shepherd divideth his sheep from the goats: and he shall set the sheep on his right hand, but the goats on the left. Then shall the King say unto them on his right hand, Come, ye blessed of my Father, inherit the kingdom prepared for you from the foundation of the world: for I was an hungered, and ye gave me meat: I was thirsty, and ye gave me drink: I was a stranger, and ye took me in: naked, and ye clothed me: I was sick, and ye visited me: I was in prison, and ye came unto me. Then shall the righteous answer him, saying, Lord, when saw we thee an hungered, and fed thee? or thirsty, and gave thee drink? When saw we thee a stranger, and took thee in? or naked, and clothed thee? or when saw we thee sick, or in prison, and came unto thee? And the King shall answer and say unto them, Verily I say unto you, inasmuch as ye have done it unto one of the least of these my brethren, ye have done it unto me. Then shall he say also unto them on the left hand, Depart from me, ye cursed, into everlasting fire, prepared for the devil and his angels: for I was an hungered, and ye gave me no meat: I was thirsty, and ye gave me no drink: I was a stranger, and ye took me not in: naked, and ye clothed me not: sick, and in prison, and ye visited me not. Then shall they also answer him, saying, Lord, when saw we thee an hungered, or athirst, or a stranger, or naked, or sick, or in prison, and did not minister unto thee? Then shall he answer them, saying, Verily I say unto you, inasmuch as ye did it not to one of the least of these, ye did it not to me. And these shall go away into everlasting punishment: but the righteous into life eternal." Matt. 25 : 31–46.

And let it be well considered, that most of the sins which are mentioned in the discourses of Christ, as the ground of condemnation, are *sins of omission.* The slothful servant, who prepares not himself, is the wicked servant, who will be cast into outer darkness. The man who wrapped his talent in a napkin and buried it, is condemned out of his own mouth. "For to him that knoweth to do good (of any kind) and doeth it not, to him it is sin." James, 4 : 17.

Many who prided themselves in their inoffensive lives and harmless behavior, will find, when the books are opened, a catalogue of omissions which will startle them with horror, and overwhelm them with confusion. And as actions externally good will then be examined by One who has a full view of the motives from which they proceeded, and the end which the agent had in view, is it not certain that many religious actions will then appear to have been mere hypocrisy? that many actions, apparently just and benevolent, were mere efforts of pride and selfishness? and that a life civil and blameless in the eyes of men, was a mere cloak which covered a heart full of unclean lusts? Our most intimate friends here, will be astonished when they see our secret iniquities and wicked motives exposed to view. Crimes the most detestable will be found in the skirts of those who passed through life without suspicion. O how many secret murders, perjuries, thefts, blasphemies, and adulteries, will then be brought to light! How much injustice, fraud, cruelty, oppression, pride, malice, revenge! The cries of the injured, the widow and the orphan, always enter into the ears of the Lord, and he now comes to avenge them. Cruel persecutors of God's church and people, though clothed in purple, and almost adored, when living in the world, will now be brought to a severe account. The blood of the martyred saints, from beneath the altar, has been long crying out, " How long, O Lord, holy and true, dost thou not judge and avenge our blood on them that dwell on the earth?" Rev. 6 : 10. And now the day of retribution has arrived.

What will be the length of time occupied with the judgment we know not. It is called *a day*, but it will differ exceedingly from all other days; and in its duration, probably, as well as in other respects. Our wisdom is to attend to what is revealed, and to repress a vain curiosity in regard to other matters. We may rest assured that the whole process will be wisely conducted, and that complete justice will be done. *The Judge of all the earth will do right.* He will not condemn the innocent, nor clear the guilty. And his judgment will be most impartial. There will be no respecting of persons. The king and the beggar will stand upon equal ground, and will be judged by the same rule. Those who in this world were reviled and slandered, and had no opportunity of clearing up their character, will then be vindicated, and lies and reproaches will have effect no more.

But here a serious difficulty occurs. It may be said: "If the law of God is the rule of judgment, and if all sins are brought into judgment, then certainly every human being must be condemned; 'for all have sinned and come short of the glory of God.' According to this view, none can be saved." To remove this difficulty, let it be remembered, that besides the book of the law, there is another book which will be produced there, written from the foundation of the world. This is called THE BOOK OF LIFE. This contains the names (and they shall never be blotted out) of all those who have washed their robes and made them white in the blood of the Lamb. These he has undertaken to present to God without spot or wrinkle or any such thing. They will appear on that day clothed with the righteousness of the Redeemer. The Judge on the throne is their covenanted Surety. He answers to every accusation made against them. But notwithstanding "there is no condemnation to them that are in Christ Jesus;" notwithstanding none can "lay any thing to the charge of God's elect;" yet they also shall be brought into judgment. When all things are prepared, and the whole assembly is collected before the august tribunal, a separation will be made of the great congregation into two parts; the righteous, and the wicked. The former will be placed on the right hand of the Judge, and with them he will commence. But no sooner shall their numerous sins be brought to view, than it will be made to appear that they are pardoned through the blood of Christ. When the books are opened, a long account will appear against them; but on the other hand it will be seen that the whole is freely forgiven, through the riches of grace in Christ Jesus. But a most exact account will be taken of all their good works; and they will be mentioned to their honor, and rewarded as though no imperfection had cleaved to them. The least act of kindness done to any of Christ's followers will be magnified and rewarded as if done to Christ himself: even the giving a cup of cold water to a disciple, in the name of a disciple, shall not lose its reward. Persons in the lowest state, servants and slaves, who performed their duty faithfully, shall not be forgotten in that day, for "whatsoever good thing any man doeth, the same shall he receive of the Lord, whether he be bond or free." Eph. 6:8. But they who suffered persecution and death for righteousness' sake, will be most highly distinguished, and most signally rewarded. "Blessed are ye when men shall revile you, and persecute you, and shall say all manner of evil against you falsely, for my sake. Rejoice and be exceeding glad; for great is your reward in heaven." Matt. 5:10, 11. They also who have labored much in promoting the Redeemer's kingdom, will receive a reward proportioned to their works of faith and labors of love. But none who have done good shall fail of their reward. Every one shall receive according to what he hath done; and every one will be satisfied; for the lowest place in glory is a situation too dazzling for our present conceptions, and the whole is a matter of pure grace. These works, considered in themselves, deserve no reward. But it is the will of God that every holy desire, every good word and work, in the members of Christ's body, should receive a mark of his favor, to the honor and glory of him who is their Head, and who died for their salvation.

When the gracious sentence, "*Come, ye blessed, inherit the kingdom prepared for you from the foundation of the world*," is pronounced, the righteous shall be caught up to the Lord, and shall be seated by his side, and be united with him in the remaining transactions of that great day; for it is written, "The saints shall judge the world;" and, "Know ye not that ye shall judge angels?"

The case of the righteous being disposed of, then will come the awful transaction of pronouncing sentence on the wicked. They will, indeed, have anticipated the sentence. By this time they will be certain of their doom; but the scene itself will far exceed all apprehensions before entertained. To behold the face of inflexible justice turned toward them—to hear the irreversible sentence of condemnation, and that too from the mouth of the benevolent Son of God—to feel in the inmost soul the justice of the sentence—to be as certain of everlasting damnation as they are of existence—are things concerning which we can speak now, but of which we can form but very feeble conceptions, compared with the dreadful reality. In all his existence there will probably be no moment in which the sinner's anguish will be so poignant as in this, when the Judge shall say, "DEPART, YE CURSED, INTO EVERLASTING FIRE, PREPARED FOR THE DEVIL AND HIS ANGELS." Matt. 25:41. Every word in this tremendous denunciation will pierce through the soul with more insufferable pain than ten thousand daggers. It is reasonable to think, that every person against whom it is pronounced, will endure as much misery at that moment, as in the nature of things is possible. And if this were all, the prospect would be appalling; but to be doomed to endless misery in fire, with the devil and his angels!—who can bear the thought without horror and dismay? Yet, as sure as God is true, will this sentence be executed on every impenitent sinner. Men may reason and cavil now, but then every mouth shall be stopped. That the cry of despair and horror will be heard through the great multitude is certain—such a great and bitter cry as was never heard before. But it is all in vain; repentance comes too late. The day of grace is for ever past. The Gospel dispensation is ended. This is the consummation of all things. No change in condition can ever be expected. They that are saved have their salvation secured by the oath and promise of God; and they who are lost, have their damnation sealed for ever and ever, by a judicial sentence which can never be revoked. And from this sentence there is no appeal. There is no higher tribunal to which the cause may be transferred. Neither can any resistance be made to the execution of the sentence. They who are now bold and daring in their blasphemies and rebellion, will then find that they are in the hands of a sin-avenging God. It will belong to the holy angels, who are mighty in power, to execute the sentence of the Judge. "So shall it be," said our blessed Savior, "at the end of the world: the angels shall come forth, and sever the wicked from among the just, and shall cast them into the furnace of fire: there shall be wailing and gnashing of teeth." Matt. 13 : 49, 50. And it will be as impossible to escape as to resist. The rocks and mountains will not cover them. They cannot cease to exist. Go where they will, God is there to execute deserved wrath upon them. They will therefore be obliged to "go away into everlasting punishment." Matt. 25 : 46.

The devil and his angels will also be judged on that day, but of the particular nature of the trial we are not informed. All that we know is, that "the angels which kept not their first estate, but left their own habitation, he hath reserved in everlasting chains, under darkness, unto the judgment of the great day." Jude, ver. 6. They are now miserable, but their cup is not full; therefore they cried out when they saw Jesus, "Art thou come to torment us before the time?" Matt. 8 : 29. At the breaking up of this great assembly, the present system of the world will be destroyed. "For, the heavens and the earth which are now, by the same word are kept in store reserved unto fire, against the day of judgment and perdition of ungodly men." 2 Pet. 3 : 7.

Reader! deeply fix in your mind the certainty and importance of the transactions of this last, great day. Meditate upon it as a reality in which you have a momentous interest. Let every other day, as it passes, put you in mind of this in which all others will end. Consider also that it draws near. Every moment bears us on toward the great tribunal. Mockers may say, Where is the promise of his coming? "but the day of the Lord will come as a thief in the night, in which the heavens shall pass away with a great noise, and the elements shall melt with fervent heat; the earth also, and the works therein shall be burnt up." 2 Pet. 3 : 10.

O Reader, whoever thou art, let me entreat you to inquire without delay, whether you are prepared for the scrutiny and judgment of this coming day? Have you made your peace with God? Have you repented of all your sins? Are you in union with Christ by faith? Have you any clear scriptural evidence that your sins are pardoned? What says conscience to these inquiries? Be assured, if your own heart condemns you, God, who is greater than your heart, and knoweth all things, will much more condemn you. But your situation is not like that of them whose day of grace is ended. You are yet in the place of reconciliation. You have yet a little time before you—God only knows how much. *Now* then, hear the voice of warning—hear the voice of mercy. *Now* "*strive to enter in at the strait gate.*" *Now* forsake your sins and live. Accept the offered grace—"*lay hold on eternal life.*"

Let no consideration induce you to delay your conversion. The importance of salvation—the uncertainty of life—the danger of provoking the Holy Spirit to abandon you—the example of thousands who have perished by procrastination—should urge you to lose no time, but to fall in with the gracious invitation of the Gospel. But if you will refuse, then prepare to meet an angry God! Harden yourself against the terrors of the Almighty; summon all your fortitude to hear your dreadful doom from the Judge of quick and dead. But I forbear—there is no fortitude or patience in hell.

Reader! art thou advanced in years? Let thy gray hairs, and pains, and wrinkles admonish thee that thou art near to judgment; for what if death intervene, yet after death all preparation is impossible. Just as death finds us, so will judgment. "In the place where the tree falleth, there it shall be." Eccl. 11:3. Consider also that the number of your sins is in proportion to the number of your days. Long life will prove a dreadful curse to those who die in their sins.

But if thou art in youth, or in the vigor of manhood, remember that thy life is a vapor; that most men do not live out half their days; and that of those who shall appear before the judgment-seat, comparatively few will have finished their course of three score years and ten. "Remember now thy Creator in the days of thy youth." Eccl. 12:1. "Behold, the Judge standeth before the door." James, 5:9. Others have been suddenly taken away from your side. They also intended to make preparation hereafter; but while they were pleasing themselves with the prospect of many years, and were saying, "Soul, take thine ease, thou hast much goods laid up for many years," God said, "Thou fool, this night is thy soul required of thee. Be ye therefore ready also, for at such an hour as ye think not, the Son of man cometh." "*Behold, the ax is laid at the root of the tree,*" and now perhaps thou art spared, on account of the prayer of some kind intercessor, for one year. This, for aught thou knowest, may be thy last year. If so, it behoves you to make good use of your time and privileges. Let the idea of the judgment be ever before your mind. There you must appear—there you must stand and render up your account—there you must be filled with overwhelming shame and terror—there you must hear the awful final sentence, which will fix your doom irreversibly, unless by a speedy repentance, and by faith in Jesus Christ, you flee from the wrath to come.

May God, of his infinite mercy, cause the truths which you have read in this Tract to sink deeply into your mind; and by the light of his Holy Spirit lead you to just views of your own condition, and to saving views of the Lord Jesus Christ, the only Redeemer of lost sinners! Amen.

CHRIST COMING TO JUDGMENT. *

Lo, he comes—the King of glory!
  With his chosen tribes to reign;
Countless hosts of saints and angels
    Swell the mighty conqueror's train;
      Now in triumph,
Sin and death are captive led.

See the rocks and mountains rending—
  All the nations fill'd with dread!
Hark! the trump of God—proclaiming
    Through the mansions of the dead—
      " Come to judgment—
" Stand before the Son of Man!"

Now behold the dead awaking;
  Great and small before him stand;
Not one soul forgot, or missing;
    None his orders countermand;
      All stand waiting—
For their last decisive doom!

Hear the Chief among ten thousand
  Thus address his faithful few:
" Come, ye blessed of my Father,
    " Heaven is prepar'd for you:
      " I was hungry—I was thirsty—I was naked—
" And ye minister'd to me."

But how awful is the sentence—
  " Go from me, ye cursed race,
" To that place of endless torment—
    " Never more to see my face:
      " I was hungry—I was thirsty—I was naked—
" Ye to me no mercy show'd."

Now awake, ye slumbering virgins,
  Trim your lamps—the bridegroom's near;
Let your loins with truth be girded;
    Signs proclaim, he'll soon appear:
      Mark! the fig-tree,
Budding, shows the summer's near

Jesus, save a trembling sinner,
  While thy wrath o'er sinners roll;
In this gen'ral wreck of nature,
  Be the refuge of my soul:
Jesus, save me! Jesus, save me! when the lightnings
  Blaze around from pole to pole.

NO. 33.

REDEMPTION.

BY JOSEPH JOHN GURNEY,

A MEMBER OF

THE SOCIETY OF FRIENDS.

PUBLISHED BY THE AMERICAN TRACT SOCIETY.

"This is a faithful saying, and worthy of all acceptation, that Jesus Christ came into the world to save sinners."—1 Tim. i. 15.

THE mercy of God in Christ Jesus is a subject which I have long been accustomed to regard as superior to all others, in point of interest and importance. Conscious, in some degree, of the perfect purity of an omnipresent Deity, as well as of the corruption of my own heart, I rejoice in the assurance that means are provided through which the stain of my sins may be washed out, and through which I may be accepted with favour by the Author of all true happiness. Nor is it wonderful that I should entertain for others whom I love, an earnest, and even painful solicitude, that they also may be brought to the discovery of this *way of escape*, and may come to acknowledge Jesus Christ, the Lord of glory, to be "the propitiation for their sins"—their "resurrection," and their "life."

Animated by these feelings, I cannot but be willing, according to the best of my ability, to communicate scriptural information on the great doctrine of *Redemption;* and most happy shall I be to assist any anxious inquirer, on this all-important article of the christian faith. Since, however, I am well aware how useless it is to attempt the formation of a superstructure without laying a foundation, I shall take the liberty, in the first place, of stating two or three propositions, which will be found necessary to the validity of my future observations, but upon which it is far from my design to enter into any detailed argument.

Let it be observed, in the first place, that *christianity is to be received, not as a moral science of human invention, but as a religion revealed to mankind by the Creator himself, and promulgated upon his authority.* In reference to this primary position, there are a few particulars of evidence to which it may be desirable for us shortly to advert.

1. That the writings of which the New Testament consists are genuine—that they were written in the apostolic age, and by the individuals with whose names they are inscribed—is a point evinced to be true by a greater variety and quantity of evidence than has probably ever been brought to bear on a similar subject. We may adduce, *in the first place*, a multitude of christian writers, from the first century downwards, who have made innumerable quotations from the various parts of that sacred volume: *secondly*, many canons or lists of the books of the New Testament, and commentaries on its several parts, composed at various times during the second, third, and fourth centuries of the christian era: *thirdly*, versions of the New Testament into a variety of foreign dialects; some of which versions (for example, the Syriac, the old Latin, and the Sahidic) were probably written in the course of the second century: *fourthly*, the heathen enemies of christianity, (especially Celsus, Porphyry, and Julian,) who, in their attacks on the divine authority of our religion, were so far from denying the genuineness of the New Testament, that they frequently referred to it, as written by the apostles and evangelists. And *lastly*, these external evidences are abundantly confirmed by numerous internal indications of a genuine origin: for example, the Hebraistic Greek, in which the whole volume is composed—a dialect which distinguishes it from all the works of the fathers, and plainly indicates both its real date and the country of its authors; the absence of anachronisms; the uniformity of style subsisting in those several parts of

it which are attributed to the same authors; and, above all, the exactness with which (on a comparison with other allowed sources of information) it is found to unfold, in an incidental manner, the customs and circumstances of the Jews, Romans, and Greeks, during the age of Christ and his apostles.

Nor can we with any reason question the correctness of the *text* of the New Testament; for although the early multiplication of copies naturally gave rise to some unimportant various readings, it obviously afforded an ample check upon any wilful alteration of the common record. In the numerous manuscripts of the Greek Testament now existing, some of which are of very considerable antiquity, in the early versions, and in the quotations made by the ancient fathers, modern critics have found sufficient criteria for the settlement of the sacred text; and the result of their indefatigable inquiries is this—that the New Testament, as christians for several centuries past have been accustomed to read it, continues unimpaired—that it has not been deprived of a single article of faith, a single historical narration, or a single moral precept.

2. It being a well established point, that the writings of which the New Testament consists, are the genuine work of the evangelists and apostles, we may, in the next place, observe that the history, related in those writings, is credible and true. In support of this proposition, it might be sufficient to remark, that the gospels were composed by four honest, simple, and independent writers; two of whom were apostles, and eye-witnesses of the facts which they relate, and the other two companions of apostles, and in full possession of the exact sources of information. With regard to the book of Acts, the truth of the history contained in it is evinced in a highly satisfactory manner, (as Paley has ingeniously shown in his 'Horæ Paulinæ,') by a variety of incidental accordances between that book and the epistles of Paul.

It is true that the history of Jesus is a miraculous history, and therefore requires for its confirmation a greater quantity and higher degree of evidence than could reasonably be demanded to secure the belief of history in general. But the evidences, of which we are in possession, are amply sufficient to meet the peculiarities of the case. That these miraculous events really occurred, rests on the especial testimony of all the original promulgators of the Gospel. Not only have Matthew, Mark, Luke, and John, recorded them in their writings, but it is plain that the apostles in general grounded their preaching of the Gospel on the authority of these facts. Acts, ii. 22. x. 38. That principal miracle, more particularly, the resurrection of Jesus Christ from the dead, was an event to which, in an especial manner, they uniformly bore witness. Acts, i. 22. iv. 33. Now that the testimony of the first preachers of the Gospel, on the subject of these miracles, was *true*, must be allowed, for the following plain reasons :—1. Because it was the *accordant* testimony of *numerous* witnesses: 2. Because the written records of these supernatural events abound in the internal marks of simplicity, candour, and entire fidelity: 3. Because, on the one hand, the miracles to which the apostles bore witness, were of such a nature, that they could not possibly have been themselves deceived respecting them; and, on the other hand, the real integrity and goodness which these persons displayed, absolutely preclude the supposition that they intended to deceive others: 4. Because they confirmed the truth of their testimony by lives of unexampled self-denial, and by a willing submission to innumerable sufferings, and even to the *infliction* of death itself: 5. Because, in further proof of the truth of their declarations respecting Jesus Christ, they were enabled to work miracles themselves. This fact is repeatedly recorded in the book of Acts: it is proved, *first*, by the appeals which the apostle Paul, in his authentic letters, has made to the miracles wrought by him, in the presence of *those very persons* whom he thus addresses; as well as to the supernatural powers with which some of those persons were themselves endowed; (Rom. xv. 19. 1 Cor. xiv. 2 Cor. xii. 12.) And, *secondly*, by a known result, for the production of which such extraordinary interpositions of divine power appear to have been essential—I mean the wonderfully extensive promulgation of early christianity, not only without the assistance of human authority, but in direct opposition to the systems, habits, and prejudices, of the whole heathen world.

The miracles of Jesus Christ and his apostles, therefore,

really took place; they were *true miracles*. Now we acknowledge that God created all things, and instituted those general laws by which the order of nature is regulated and maintained; and miracles are supernatural infractions of those general laws, and changes, in that order. Every reasonable theologian will allow that no *creature* can possess any inherent, independent power of controverting the designs, or of interrupting the harmonious arrangements, of an omnipotent God; and hence it follows, according to my apprehension, that all true miracles, like the original creation, are to be regarded as the especial work of God himself. If, however, it is granted, that a certain limited and controlled power over the order of nature has sometimes been permitted, for especial purposes, to be exercised by evil spirits, such an allowance by no means affects the christian miracles; which not only proclaimed their own divine origin, by their astonishing variety and greatness, but were wrought in direct attestation of a professed revelation from God, and for the furtherance of ends perfectly consistent with his justice, holiness, and mercy. Christianity, then, was attested by supernatural events, of which the Deity was the sole and immediate author; a fact to which nothing similar can be predicated either of Mahometanism, or of any of the religious systems of the heathen: christianity, therefore, and christianity *only*, is the religion of God.

3. It appears, in the third place, to be a clear and undeniable position, that the actual knowledge of the future is an attribute peculiar to the Divine Being. No one, who admits the existence of the one God, will refuse to allow that in point of both knowledge and power, he is placed at an infinite distance above all his creatures—that while he regulates the course of events according to his own will, none of those creatures are his counsellors, and none of them are capable of penetrating his secret designs and intentions. From these premises, it follows that all prophecies, which, by their exact fulfilment, are proved to have proceeded, not from intellectual sagacity and human conjecture, but from actual fore-knowledge, must have been inspired, or dictated by the Almighty himself; and further, that the religion which is attested by such prophecies, is a divinely authorized religion.

That christianity is attested by true prophecies, is a fact capable of easy proof. Jesus Christ was a prophet, and during his conversation among men, accurately predicted a variety of events, which were then future; especially his own death and resurrection, and the circumstances by which they were to be attended; the out-pouring of the Holy Ghost; and the approaching sufferings of the Jews, with the destruction of their city and temple. But perhaps the most striking prophecies which attest the truth of christianity, are those contained in the Old Testament, and relating to our Saviour himself. The writings of the Hebrew prophets are replete with the promises of a great spiritual deliverer, denominated the Messiah, who was appointed to appear in the world at a certain period declared by the prophet Daniel. In various parts of these writings, (composed as they were by a number of unconnected persons, living at different periods,) it is predicted that this long-expected deliverer should arise, according to the flesh, out of the seed of Abraham; (Gen. xxii. 18.) and from the family of David; (Isa. xi. 1. Jer. xxiii. 5.) that he should be born, miraculously, of a virgin; (Isa. vii. 14.) that his birth-place should be Bethlehem; (Micah, v. 2.) that his outward situation should be of a very humble description; (Isa. liii. 2.) that he should be engaged in proclaiming glad tidings, and in relieving the sufferings of mortality; (Isa. lxi. 1.) that his character should be distinguished for gentleness, kindness, faithfulness, and all righteousness; (Isa. xi. 4, 5, 6. xliii. 1—3;) that nevertheless the Jews would refuse to believe in him; (Isa. liii. 1.) that he should be despised, rejected, and persecuted of men; (Isa. liii. 3, 4. Ps. xxii.) that he should be betrayed by one of his familiar friends, and that his followers should be scattered from him; (Ps. xli. 9. Zech. xiii. 7.) that he should be led as a lamb to the slaughter, and be as a sheep dumb before his shearers; (Isa. liii. 7.) that he should be cut off, yet not for himself; (Dan. ix. 26.) that his body should not see corruption, nor his life be left in the grave; (Ps. xvi. 10.) finally, that he should ascend into heaven; (Ps. lxviii. 18.) and that he should exercise an universal and never-ending government over mankind. Ps. lxxii. 8. Isa. ix. 7. Dan. vii. 14. In addition to these leading facts, there are predicted in the Old Testament, a number of minor particulars respecting the life and death of the Messiah; and, to complete their wonderful statement, the prophets, whilst they depict the circumstances of his human nature, and especially his many humiliating sufferings, describe him nevertheless *as one possessing the name and character of Jehovah himself.* Ps. xlv. 6. Isa. vii. 14. ix. 6. xxxv. 4. xl. 3. 10, 11. Jer. xxiii. 5. Zech. ii. 10—13. Mal. iii. 1.

At the time appointed for the appearance of the Messiah, Jesus was born, of the seed of Abraham, of the family of David, at Bethlehem, of a virgin. We find him living in a humble outward condition—engaged in preaching the Gospel, in healing the sick, and in relieving every species of bodily and mental distress—meek, gentle, kind, faithful, and fulfilling all righteousness—not believed by the Jews—despised, rejected, and persecuted of men—betrayed by his familiar friend—forsaken in the hour of trial by all his followers—led as a lamb to the slaughter—dumb in the presence of his persecutors—cut off, but not for himself—rising from the dead—ascending into heaven, and assuming a spiritual government over men—fulfilling in his own character and circumstances a variety of minor particulars—*and all these things in precise accordance with the predictions of the Old Testament.* More particularly, in the midst of his humiliations and distresses, and notwithstanding the lowliness and piety of his human character, we find him, in agreement with those predictions, receiving the homage, asserting the character, displaying the powers, and described by the titles, which appertain to Jehovah himself. Matt. xiv. 33. John, xx. 28, 29. Matt. ix. 2—6. xii. 6. 8. xviii. 20. John, v. 21—23. x. 28—30. xiv. 9. 23. xvi. 7. Rev. ii. 23. Matt. viii. 3. 8—13. *compare* Acts, ix. 34. Luke, viii. 24. Matt. xii. 25. John, xvi. 19. 30. *compare* Rev. ii. 23. John, xx. 22. John, i. 1. Rom. ix. 5. Rev. xix. 16.

When a lock and key precisely correspond, though they be of a simple character, a presumption arises that they were intended for one another. When, instead of being formed in a simple manner, they are respectively complex and curiously wrought in different directions, and nevertheless correspond; such a presumption is exceedingly strengthened. But when the lock is not only complex and curiously wrought, but contains such an extraordinary and wonderful combination of parts as to be absolutely sui generis, and without parallel; when, among all the keys in the world, none present even a slight approach to a correspondent conformation, except one; and by that the lock is easily and exactly fitted—then, surely, is all doubt on the subject discarded; and it becomes a moral certainty that the lock and key proceeded from the same master hand, and truly appertain to each other. Now this is a familiar but precise representation of the evidence afforded, by a comparison between the Old and New Testaments, that the prophecies concerning Jesus Christ were true prophecies; that they were inspired by an omniscient God; and, therefore, that the religion which they attest is a religion of divine origin.

4. It is generally allowed by all persons who confess the existence and unity of God, (whether they are believers in the christian revelation or otherwise,) that he is a Being not only of infinite power and knowledge, but of the highest moral perfections. A comprehensive view even of natural religion leads to an easy admission of the declarations of the sacred writers that God is just, holy, true, bounteous, and merciful. Such being the moral attributes of our heavenly Father, we cannot refuse to allow, that it is our *reasonable service* to walk in his fear, to worship him with devotion of spirit, to obey his law, to promote his glory, and more especially to *set our love* upon him with the whole heart. And yet it is a fact, to which the history of past ages and present observation bear alike the most decisive testimony, that, by mankind in their unregenerate condition, this reasonable service is set aside and neglected. Now christianity, considered as a religious system, consisting of both doctrines and precepts, and applied by faith to the heart—that is to say, comprehensive and vital christianity—is unquestionably the means of so transforming men, that in the dispositions of the soul, and in the regulation of the conduct, they come to " render unto God the things that are God's."

But further—when the true christian is thus introduced to a peaceful communion with the Father of spirits, he is gradually weaned from his evil passions, and becomes conformed, in his own person, to the *moral attributes* of the

Deity. As the face of a man is seen reflected in the mirror, so are those attributes seen *reflected* in his life and conversation. Pretenders to religion—the mere professors of the christian name—form no exception to this observation, because they have no real connexion with our argument; but of those persons who place a full reliance upon Christ as their Saviour, and who have yielded themselves *without reserve* to his guidance and government, it may with truth be asserted, that they are created anew in the *image of their Maker*. Undoubtedly they have still to contend with innumerable infirmities, and with many corrupt inclinations; and they can readily acknowledge, that, in the sight of the Most High, they are less than nothing, and vanity. Nevertheless, in the integrity of their words and actions, in the purity of their intentions and conduct, in their kindness, charity, and long-suffering towards all around them, they *show forth* the truth, the holiness, and the love, of that Being from whom alone all their virtue is derived.

Lastly, christianity procures for mankind a pure and substantial happiness. The true christian is happy far above all other persons, for various reasons: because, though his sins have been many, he is reconciled to the Father, through the mediation of the Son; because, notwithstanding his natural weakness, he is enabled to walk in the way of righteousness, by the power of the Holy Spirit; because a sense of the divine love and approbation dwells in his heart; because he is taught to regard every tribulation as a moral discipline directed to greater good; and, lastly, because he is animated by the expectation of a future joy, perfectly unsullied in its nature, and eternal in its duration.

Now the several excellent results which have formed the subject of these observations, have never been adequately produced in men by any principles, except those of christianity; but by the principles of christianity, when cordially embraced and fully submitted to, they are produced *without fail*. Experience may convince us that the contrivance of so comprehensive, so extraordinary, and so operative a moral system, was placed far beyond the reach of human invention: like the works of nature, it can be traced to nothing less efficacious than the wisdom, the power, and the love, of God.

Christianity, therefore, is the religion of God; and since it is impossible that in bringing his reasonable creatures into true piety, virtue, and happiness, the God of all truth should employ a mere illusion, it plainly follows that christianity is *true*—that its doctrines are real, its hopes substantial, its promises and threatenings certain.

5. Christianity, then, being the religion of God—the true, and only true religion—where are we to find an *authorized* record of the doctrines of which it consists? I answer, not in the scholastic productions of polemical divines; not in the treatises of modern and uninspired theologians; not in the declarations of any particular church: but in the genuine compositions of inspired men; *in the Holy Scriptures of the Old and New Testament.*

The genuineness of the New Testament is a point to which I have already adverted. That of the various books of history, law, psalmody, and prophecy, which compose the Old Testament, is satisfactorily evinced by the quotations made from these writings in every part of the New Testament; by a Greek version of the Hebrew Scriptures, written at a date long prior to the christian era; by the plain testimony of Josephus, Philo, and other Jewish writers; by the care which the ancient Jews are known to have exercised, in order to the incorrupt preservation of their sacred books; by the fact that, before the captivity, the law of Moses was often read in public, and that after the captivity, the reading of both the law and the prophets formed a regular part of the synagogue service; and, lastly, by a variety of internal evidences, derived from language and style, from the circumstantiality of description and narrative, and from the mutual yet incidental accordance of part with part.

It being admitted that the Scriptures of the Old and New Testament are genuine, that the Gospel history is true, and that Christ was a divinely commissioned teacher; we are placed at once in possession of satisfactory evidence that these writings were given by inspiration of God. That such was the fact, as it regards the Old Testament, is expressly declared by the apostle Paul; (2. Tim. iii. 16.) and the testimony of this apostle on the subject, is confirmed by that of Jesus Christ himself, who, in his conversations with the Jews, and with his disciples, frequently referred to the Jewish Scriptures in such a manner as plainly to attribute to them an absolute and unquestionable authority. With respect to the New Testament, we learn from the authentic history which it contains, that the persons by whom it was written, (especially the apostles who composed the greater part of it,) were directly inspired; and inspired for the purpose of promulgating christian truth. Whether it was by preaching or by writing that they performed the service thus committed to them, it is indisputable, (since the Gospel history is true,) that their doctrine rested not on their own authority, but on that of the Divine Being whom they served, and flowed from no other source than his Holy Spirit. See Matt. x. 18—20. Luke, xxiv. 46—49. John, xiv. 26. Acts, ii. 4. 1 Cor. ii. 3—5, &c.

Inspiration, it may be remarked, operates under various circumstances, and is bestowed in various measures. Now that the inspiration of the apostles and of some of their companions was of a very high and plenary description, may be inferred from a most important fact already noticed—viz. that they were endued with the power of working miracles. The *work* of God confirmed the *word* of God. The signs and wonders which the Lord displayed through the agency of those gifted men, afforded a specific and irresistible evidence, that he was also the author of their doctrine, in whatsoever form that doctrine was delivered.

To the external proofs of which we are thus in possession, that the Holy Scriptures were given by inspiration, and that their contents are therefore to be received as of *divine authority*, are to be added many powerful internal evidences. He who takes a sound and comprehensive view of the wonderful variety and richness of the sacred records—of the admirable moral harmony which pervades the whole volume—of the perfect adaptation of the preparatory system, as described by Moses and the prophets, with the fulness of Gospel light as revealed to us in the New Testament—of the practical excellence of those doctrines, precepts, and sentiments, which distinguish the Bible from all other books, or which, in other books, are simply borrowed from the Bible—will presently confess, not only that the religion unfolded in the Scriptures is divine, but that the *record itself* must be traced not to the unassisted efforts of fallible men, but to the spirit of perfect wisdom—*to the mind which cannot err.*

The Scriptures, then, are a *divinely inspired* record of religious truth. If I am told that there is much in the Bible which even the learned cannot understand, and some things, perhaps, which the wicked have perverted to evil purposes, I would observe in reply, that in this respect there is an obvious analogy between the *written word* and the *works of God;* for there is much also in the science of nature itself, which the wise cannot comprehend, and which the vicious have misapplied to evil. And I would further remark, that the Scriptures are not intended to gratify the curiosity, or to illuminate the speculations of worldly wisdom; but to instruct the humble and devotional reader, and to teach the simple and the meek the way to heaven. To such as these, whatsoever be their condition in life, or their measure of mental cultivation, the Bible, as to every main doctrine, and every practical principle, is explicit and intelligible. While the divine law is so accordant with the conclusions of profound reasoning, that the most enlightened philosophers have yielded to it their willing homage, it is also so plain, that when it is received with simplicity and godly sincerity, " the wayfaring man, though a fool, shall not err therein."

6. Having thus briefly surveyed some of the principal evidences, from which the conclusion is safely deduced that christianity is true, and that the Bible contains a genuine and divinely inspired record of all its truths,—we may now proceed to inquire what things that sacred volume declares respecting God, ourselves, and Jesus Christ.

There is nothing by which the Scriptures are more eminently distinguished,—nothing by which their importance and divine origin are more clearly evinced,—than by the information which they impart respecting the nature and character of *God.* Much light indeed, on this great subject, may be derived from the works of the Deity which surround us on every side, and which proclaim, in intelligible language, his wisdom, power, and goodness; and also from that moral sense of his own existence and authority, which, (however it may in numberless instances be depraved and perverted,) he appears to have impressed universally on the mind of man. But the knowledge which we derive from natural religion respecting God, is, in a wonderful manner, augmented and *completed* in the records of his revealed will. We learn from the Scriptures that there is no other God but JEHOVAH—that he exists from eternity to eternity—that he is the creator, governor, and preserver, of the universe—that he is omnipresent, omnipotent, omniscient, and perfectly wise—that in him we live, and move, and have our being—that he is the author of the moral law—that he is the source of every good and perfect gift, and more especially of everlasting life—that he is holy, just, true, faithful, righteous, long-suffering and merciful—that he is *love;* a tender and compassionate Father to those who walk in his fear and obey his law—that, eternal and infinite as he is, he graciously extends his immediate care to the most minute interests of his creatures—that not a sparrow falleth to the ground without him, and that he numbers the very hairs of our heads. It is more particularly to our present purpose to observe, that the Deity is ever described in the Bible as a Being of absolute purity; so that in his sight every species of iniquity, whether in thought, word, or deed, is abominable. Hence it follows, " that he" will by no means clear the guilty, and that " without holiness no man shall see the Lord."

Here I would remark, that while the inspired writers bear the most ample and decisive testimony to the unity of the Supreme Being—while the great principle that God is *one*, lies at the very foundation of their scheme of religion, and pervades it in every part—we nevertheless learn, from many of their declarations, that in that great scheme of mercy which he has ordained for our salvation, the ONE GOD has manifested himself to mankind, as the FATHER, the SON, and the HOLY SPIRIT.

The mode of that distinction and of that union which we believe to subsist in the Divine nature, is placed far beyond the reach of our limited comprehension, and can never be a fit subject either for speculation or for definition; but the doctrine that there *is* such a distinction, and that there *is* such a union, will never cease to be highly prized by those persons who are aware of its practical influence and operation. I may confess that it has long appeared to me to be a sound and necessary deduction, not only from the passages of Scripture in which the Creator, the Redeemer, and the Comforter, are upheld to view as the common sources of our spiritual good, and the common objects of our faith and allegiance, but from all those also in which there is a distinct reference to the divinity either of the Son or of the Spirit. See Matt. xxviii. 19. John, xiv. 26. xv. 26. xvi. 13—15. 2 Cor. xiii. 14, *comp.* John, i. 1—3, &c. Acts, xiii. 2. 1 Cor. xii. 11. 2 Cor. iii. 17.

Respecting ourselves, the Scriptures reveal many truths of the highest importance to us. From various declarations contained in them, we plainly learn, that man is endued not only with a frail body, but with a soul; and that when the body perishes, the soul continues to exist; (Matt. x. 28. xvi. 26. 1 Thes. v. 23. Heb. x. 39. Luke, xvi. 19—31. xx. 38. xxiii. 42, 43. 2 Cor. v. 1—8.) that moreover, in a day to come, the dead will be raised in a body incorruptible and spiritual; (John, v. 28, 29. 1 Cor. xv.) that this short life is the only time appointed for our probation; and that, in another world, we shall all stand before the judgment-seat of Christ, and shall then, according to our works, be rewarded with everlasting happiness, or punished with everlasting misery. Matt. xxv. 31—46. Rom. ii. 6—11. xiv. 10. Rev. xx. 12—15. The Scriptures, moreover, declare that man was created in the moral similitude of God—that, yielding to the temptations of the devil, he fell from that image—that now, being a fallen and depraved creature, he is, *in his unregenerate nature*, prone to wickedness—that his heart is " deceitful above all things, and desperately wicked," that " all have sinned and come short of the glory of God"— that " they are together become unprofitable; that there is none that doeth good, no not one;" and that thus "*all the world*" is " become guilty before God;" (Jer. xvii. 9. Rom. iii. 1—19. 23. *compare* Isa. liii. 6. Matt. xv. 19.) And " except a man be born again he cannot see the kingdom of God." John, iii. 3.

Such are the awful statements contained in the sacred volume respecting *ourselves*. Where, then, is there any hope for us, who are fallen, corrupt, inclined to sin, and, in so great a multitude of particulars, sinners; and who are therefore separated in our natural state from a just and holy God, and are plainly liable to eternal separation from him in the world to come? Truly our hope is only in the *mercy* of God, through the Saviour of men. *A Saviour, or I die—a Redeemer, or I perish for ever!*

Lastly, therefore, we may inquire, what is the doctrine of the Bible respecting our Lord and Saviour Jesus Christ? We read in Scripture, that he is the Word—the Son of God the Father almighty—that in the beginning, before the world was created, and from everlasting, he was *with God*, (John, i. 1. xvii. 5. *comp.* Mic. v. 2.)—that by him all things were created that are in heaven, and that are in earth, (Col. i. 16. Heb. i. 2. 10.)—that without him was not any thing made that was made, (John, i. 3.)—that he was the light and life of men, (John, i. 4. 9.)—that he and the Father are *one*, (John, x. 30.)—that he is *God*, (John, i. 1.) Jehovah our righteousness, (Jer. xxiii. 5.) the mighty God, (Isaiah, ix. 6.) the true God, (1 John, v. 20.) the great God, (Tit. ii. 13.) God over all, (Rom. ix. 5.)— that he is the searcher of the reins and the hearts, knows what is in man, and bestows upon his servants all their spiritual gifts and graces, (Rev. ii. 23. Acts, ii. 33. 2 Cor. xii. 9. Eph. iv. 11.)—the object of faith, prayer, glorification, and all worship, (John, iii. 16. Acts, vii. 59, 60. 2 Cor. xii. 8. Heb. i. 6. xiii. 21. Rev. v. 13.)— that he "filleth all in all." (Eph. i. 23.)—that he is "the same yesterday, and to-day, and for ever;" "the Alpha and Omega, the beginning and the ending, the first and the last." Heb. xiii. 8. Rev. xxii. 13. The Bible further declares, that when the fulness of time was come, "God sent forth his Son, made of a woman, made under the law," (Gal. iv. 4.)—that the Word became flesh, (John, i. 14.)—that he was born a child into the world, and really took our frail nature upon him, being made in all points like unto his brethren, yet without sin, (Heb. ii. 14.)— that he went about doing good, healing the sick, giving sight to the blind and hearing to the deaf, raising the dead to life, and preaching the Gospel to the poor—that he was betrayed into the hands of wicked men, and died on the cross—that on the third day he rose from the dead, and that he ascended to the right hand of the Majesty on high, being restored to that state of infinite and unsearchable glory which he possessed in the Father's presence before the world began, (John, xvii. 5. Heb. i. 3.)—that now he is exalted of the Father, far above all principality, and power, and might, and dominion, and every name that is named, not only in this world, but also in that which is to come, (Eph. i. 21.)—finally, that he will bring to a termination the whole economy or dispensation of which he is the Mediator, by coming again with all his holy angels, for the final and universal judgment of quick and dead, when the wicked " shall go away into everlasting punishment, but the righteous into life eternal." Matt. xiii. 40—42. xxiv. 30, 31. xxv. 46. 1 Cor. xv. 25—28.

7. Having thus adduced some of the principal declarations of Scripture respecting the nature and history of our Lord Jesus Christ, I may proceed, without further delay, to the consideration of that *doctrine of Redemption*, for the elucidation of which this Tract is principally intended; and I may commence by putting a very simple question. What could be the mighty and equivalent purpose for which this infinitely glorious Person, the Son of God, who is one with the Father, and is himself the everlasting Jehovah—should so marvellously condescend and humble himself as to take our nature upon him, in that nature to undergo every species of contumely and contradiction of sinners, and finally to die on the cross a cruel and shameful death?

When we reflect on the perfect adaptation which always subsists, and which is generally apparent in the operations both of nature and of providence, between the cause and the effect, the means and the end—when we thus take analogy as the ground of our reasoning—we can scarcely avoid perceiving how strong an improbability attaches to the supposition, that SUCH AN ONE should not only come into the world, but should live, suffer, and die, as a man, for the *single* purpose of *revealing* the truth. Experience teaches us that any inspired person, whose divine mission was attested by miracles, might have been an adequate instrument for that purpose; for it is evidently on this simple ground that christians are unanimous in giving their credence to the doctrines delivered to the Jews by Moses, and to the followers of Christ by the apostles. No doubt, to reveal the truth was one of the offices of our blessed Saviour—that chief of prophets: nor are we to forget, that it was another of his offices, by his holy and merciful life and conversation on earth, to institute that perfect *pattern* after which the conduct of his disciples, in all future ages, was to be formed and regulated. But important and salutary as these offices were, the peculiar circumstances of the case are such, as inevitably lead us to believe, that in humbling himself from the height of his divine glory—in assuming our frail and suffering nature—and in subjecting himself even to the death of the cross—the Son of God had yet higher, nobler, and *more comprehensive* purposes in his view. When we consider the infinite dignity and absolute omnipotence of our heavenly Visiter, and the marvellous love which he has displayed in visiting us, we cannot fail to conclude that such a dispensation of divine mercy towards us was intended to supply *all* our spiritual need. Now were we, through the means of that dispensation, to receive nothing but information, precept, and example, our need would be far indeed from being supplied. Powerless and corrupt as we are, we should still be left to perish in our sins, and the light, thus communicated to us, would only aggravate our wo, and render our destruction more terrible. Where is the individual who understands the plague of his own heart, who is not aware that he stands in need, not only of information, but of reconciliation with God; not only of light, but of life; not only of precept and example, but of a disposition to obey the one and to follow the other? Yes, my dear Reader, the Gospel of our Lord and Saviour is no message of glad tidings to us, unless it proclaims to us *indemnity and cure.* In this way, and in this only, will it supply *all* our spiritual need.

This plain course of reasoning leads us at once to the conclusion, that Christ did indeed come in order to bestow upon us, not only information and precept, but pardon. But happily this is a subject on which we are not left to any conclusions of our own formation. It is one on which the declarations of Holy Writ are equally abundant and explicit.

The very first passage of Scripture in which the Messiah is alluded to, proclaims the great purpose of his mission. "I will put enmity," said Jehovah to the serpent, "between thee and the woman, and between thy seed and her seed; *it shall bruise thy head*, and thou shalt bruise his heel." Gen. iii. 15. Christian commentators generally allow, that by the seed of the woman is here intended the Messiah, and that by the serpent is represented the devil, the author of all moral evil. We therefore learn from the prophecy, that Christ was to bruise the serpent's head; or, in other words, to destroy the devil and his works. Compare Heb. ii. 14. "For as much, then, as the children are partakers of flesh and blood, he also himself took part of the same; *that through death he might destroy him that had the power of death, that is the devil*"—and 1 John, iii. 8, "He that committeth sin is of the devil, for the devil sinneth from the beginning. For this purpose the Son of God was manifested, *that he might destroy the works of the devil.*" It was by means of *his death*, that the Messiah was to obtain a complete victory over our spiritual adversary; a doctrine which perfectly accords with Isaiah's celebrated prophecy respecting his vicarious and propitiatory sufferings: "Surely he hath borne our griefs, and carried our sorrows; yet we did esteem him stricken, smitten of God, and afflicted. But he was wounded for our transgressions; he was bruised for our iniquities; the chastisement of our peace (or whereby our peace is procured) was upon him; and with his stripes we are healed. All we, like sheep, have gone astray: we have turned every one to his own way: and the Lord hath laid on him the iniquity of us all. *He was oppressed, and he was afflicted:* he is brought as a lamb to the slaughter, and as a sheep before her shearers is dumb, so he opened not his mouth. Therefore will I divide him a portion with the great, and he shall divide the spoil with the strong; because he hath poured out his soul unto death; and he was numbered with the transgressors, and he bare the sin of many, and made intercession for the transgressors." Isa. liii. 4—12.

That this consolatory passage of Scripture relates to our Lord Jesus Christ, is proved, partly by strong internal evidence, and partly by the repeated testimony of the authors of the New Testament. Who does not perceive that it proclaims pardon for the sinner, through the sufferings and death of a Saviour? The same doctrine is powerfully expressed in the words addressed by Jehovah to the Messiah, as recorded in the prophecies of Zechariah :— " As for thee also, by *the blood of thy covenant* I have sent forth thy prisoners *out of the pit wherein is no water :* turn ye to the strong hold, ye prisoners of hope." Zech. ix. 11, 12.

Such are the declarations of prophecy respecting that mighty propitiation for sin, which was to distinguish the introduction of the Gospel dispensation; nor ought it to be forgotten that the whole sacrificial institution of the Jews was " a shadow of good things to come," and had a direct relation to the same doctrine. This observation applies in a very especial manner to the slaying of the Lamb in the passover, and to the offering up of the bullock and goat on the great day of atonement. For Jesus Christ, " the Lamb slain from the foundation of the world," is described by the apostle Paul as " our passover," who " is sacrificed for us ;" (1 Cor. v. 7.) and we are plainly taught, in the epistle to the Hebrews, that the High Priest who offered up the victims, first " for his own sins, and then for the people's," and who, on that solemn occasion, entered into the holiest place and sprinkled the blood over the mercy seat, was but the type of that Saviour who is entered into the heavens for us, who sprinkles his blood on our hearts, and who " by *one offering* hath perfected for ever them that are sanctified". Compare Lev. xvi. with Heb. ix. x.

But in order to that destruction of the works of the devil which was to be effected by the Messiah, there was need not only of a propitiatory sacrifice, but of a powerful redeeming influence. Accordingly, in those prophecies of the Old Testament which are acknowledged by both Jews and christians to relate to the times of the Messiah, we find many clear promises of the more abundant effusion of such an influence on the Lord's people, and of its practical and internal operation. " Thus saith the Lord that made thee and formed thee from the womb, which will help thee; fear not, O Jacob my servant, and thou Jesurun whom I have chosen. For I will pour water upon him that is thirsty, and floods upon the dry ground. I will pour MY SPIRIT upon thy seed, and my blessing upon thine offspring." Isa. xliv. 2, 3. " Then will I sprinkle clean water upon you, and ye shall be clean:

from all your filthiness, and from all your idols, will I cleanse you. A new heart also will I give you, and a new spirit will I put within you; and I will take away the stony heart out of your flesh, and I will give you an heart of flesh. And I will put MY SPIRIT within you, and cause you to walk in my statutes; and ye shall keep my judgments and do them." Ezek. xxxvi. 25—27. Precisely consonant with these passages is the description given by Jeremiah of the principal characteristics of the New Covenant: " But this shall be the covenant that I will make with the house of Israel. After those days, saith the Lord, I will put my law in their inward parts, and write it in their hearts; and will be their God, and they shall be my people. And they shall teach no more every man his neighbour, and every man his brother, saying, Know the Lord: for they shall all know me, from the least of them unto the greatest of them, saith the Lord; for I will forgive their iniquity, and I will remember their sin no more." Jer. xxxi. 33, 34.

The blessings which were thus to distinguish the New Covenant are represented by Isaiah as the " sure mercies of *David*," that is, of the Messiah, the descendant of David, who was appointed in the counsels of the Most High to be " a witness to the people, a leader and commander to the people ;"— (Isa. lv. 1—4.) and from the various descriptions given to us, in the prophetical writings, of the universal authority and never-ending government of this Prince of Peace, we can scarcely avoid deducing the inference, that he was himself to dispense those spiritual gifts, and to conduct those powerful internal operations, by which his dominion over the hearts of men was to be obtained and secured. Accordingly, we learn from Psalm lxviii. 18. that on his ascension into glory, the Messiah was to " *lead captivity captive*," and receive " *gifts for men ;*" and Malachi has announced the sudden appearance and spiritual work of our Redeemer, in the following sublime language : " Behold I will send my messenger, and he shall prepare the way before me: and the LORD whom ye seek shall suddenly come to his temple, even the Messenger of the covenant whom ye delight in; behold he shall come, saith the Lord of hosts : but who may abide the day of his coming, and who shall stand when he appeareth? *for he is like a refiner's fire, and like fuller's soap. And he shall sit as a refiner and purifier of silver; and he shall purify the sons of Levi, and purge them as gold and silver, that they may offer unto the Lord an offering in righteousness.*" Mal. iii. 1—3.

Thus then it appears from the concurrent declarations of those ancient prophets who spake of Christ beforehand " as they were moved of the Holy Ghost," that the dispensation of the Gospel was " to finish the transgression, and to make an end of sins, and to make reconciliation for iniquity, and to bring in everlasting righteousness, and to seal up the vision and prophecy, and to anoint the MOST HOLY." Dan. ix. 24.

Let us now direct our attention to the New Testament. When the angel Gabriel predicted to the virgin Mary the approaching birth of her Son, he added, " Thou shalt call his name *Jesus*, (or the Saviour,) for he shall *save* his people *from their sins.*" Matt. i. 21. By John the Baptist, also, the approaching Saviour of men was announced in the same character: " Behold the Lamb of God," said he, " which *taketh away the sin of the world.*" John, i. 29.

By our blessed Lord himself the great object of his coming was frequently and explicitly declared: " The Son of man is come to seek and to *save* that which was *lost.*" Luke, xix. 10. " The Son of man came not to be ministered unto, but to minister, and to *give his life a ransom for many.*" Matt. xx. 28. " This is my blood of the New Testament which is shed for many, for the remission of sins." Matt. xxvi. 28. " As Moses lifted up the serpent in the wilderness, even so must the Son of man be lifted up; that *whosoever believeth in him should not perish, but have eternal life.* God sent not his Son into the world to condemn the world, but that the world through him *might be saved.*" John, iii. 14. 17. " I am the living bread which came down from heaven: if any man eat of this bread, he shall live for ever: and the bread that I will give is my flesh, which *I will give for the life of the world.*" John, vi. 51. After his ascension also, when he delivered to the converted Paul an apostolic commission, he said, " I have appeared unto thee for this purpose, to make thee a minister and a witness—delivering thee from the people and from the Gentiles, to whom now I send thee, to open their

VOL 1.

eyes, and to turn them from darkness to light, and from the power of Satan unto God, that they may receive forgiveness of sins, and inheritance among them which are sanctified, *by faith that is in me.*" Acts, xxvi. 16—18.

A multitude of declarations to the same effect were made by our Lord's apostles. From these a few passages may be selected, by way of specimens, from the writings of John, Peter, and Paul.

JOHN.—" Whosoever committeth sin transgresseth also the law; for sin is the transgression of the law. And ye know that he was manifested *to take away our sins:* and in him is no sin. Whosoever abideth in him, sinneth not." 1 John, iii. 4—6. " In this was manifested the love of God towards us, because that God sent his only-begotten Son into the world, that we might live through him. Herein is love, not that we loved God, but that he loved us, and sent his Son to be the *propitiation* for our sins. And we have seen and do testify, that the Father sent the Son to be the Saviour of the world." 1 John, iv. 9, 10. 14. " What are these which are arrayed in white robes? and whence came they? These are they which came out of great tribulation, and have washed their robes and made them white in the blood of the Lamb. *Therefore are they before the throne of God,*" &c. Rev. vii. 13—15.

PETER.—" For as much as ye know that ye were not redeemed with corruptible things, as silver and gold, from your vain conversation received by tradition from your fathers; but with the *precious blood* of Christ, as of a lamb without blemish and without spot." 1 Pet. i. 18, 19. " Because Christ also suffered for us—who his own self bare our sins in his own body on the tree, that we, being dead to sin, should live unto righteousness: by whose stripes ye were healed; for ye were as sheep going astray, but are now returned unto the Shepherd and Bishop of your souls." 1 Pet. ii. 21. 24, 25.

PAUL.—" Therefore by the deeds of the law there shall no flesh be justified in his sight; for by the law is the knowledge of sin. But now the righteousness of God without the law is manifested, being witnessed by the law and the prophets; even the righteousness of God which is by faith of Jesus Christ unto all, and upon all them that believe; for there is no difference: for all have sinned and come short of the glory of God; being justified freely by his grace through the redemption that is in Christ Jesus; whom God hath set forth *to be a propitiation through faith in his blood*, to declare his righteousness for the remission of sins that are past, through the forbearance of God: to declare, I say, at this time, his righteousness: that he might be just, and the justifier of him which believeth in Jesus." Rom. iii. 20—25. "For as by one man's disobedience many were made sinners, so by the obedience of one shall many be made righteous. Moreover the law entered that the offence might abound. But where sin abounded, grace did much more abound: that as sin hath reigned unto death, even so might grace reign, through righteousness, unto eternal life, by Jesus Christ our Lord." Rom. v. 19—21. "For the wages of sin is death, but the gift of God is eternal life, through Jesus Christ our Lord." Romans, vi. 23. "Christ also loved the church, and *gave himself* for it: that he might sanctify and cleanse it with the washing of water by the word: that he might present it to himself a glorious church, not having spot or wrinkle or any such thing; but that it should be holy and without blemish." Eph. v. 25—27. "Who hath delivered us from the power of darkness, and hath translated us into the kingdom of his dear Son, in whom we have redemption through his blood, even the forgiveness of sins. And you that were sometime alienated, and enemies in your mind by wicked works, yet now hath he reconciled; in the body of his flesh through death, to present you holy and unblamable, and unreprovable in his sight." Col. i. 13, 14. 21, 22. "For the grace of God, that bringeth salvation, hath appeared to all men; teaching us, that, denying ungodliness and worldly lusts, we should live soberly, righteously, and godly, in this present world; looking for that blessed hope and the glorious appearing of our great God and Saviour Jesus Christ: who gave himself for us, that he might redeem us from all iniquity, and purify unto himself a peculiar people, zealous of good works." Tit. ii. 11—14.

Justification through the blood of Christ, and sanctification by his Spirit, are very usually treated as distinct doctrines; but different as they are in one point of view, it is nevertheless evident, from the tenor of these extracts, that they are inseparably connected. Both are essential to the work of salvation; both originate in the same divine mercy, and both are described, by the sacred writers, as arising out of the sacrifice of the Son of God. Was Christ " set forth" of the Father, to be " a propitiation through faith in his blood?" Did he bear " our sins in his own body on the tree?" Did he thus *give himself* for us? It was not only for the " remission of sins that are past," and for the justification of penitent believers, but also that " he might sanctify and cleanse" his church—" that he might redeem us from all iniquity"—that our consciences might be " purified from dead works, to *serve the living God*"— " that we, being dead to sin, should *live unto righteousness.*" Tit. ii. 14. Heb. ix. 14. 1 Pet. ii. 24.

" The law of the Spirit of life, in Christ Jesus," says the apostle, " hath made me free from the law of sin and death; for what the law could not do, in that it was weak through the flesh, God sending his own Son in the likeness of sinful flesh, and for sin, condemned sin in the flesh, that the righteousness of the law might be fulfilled in us *who walk not after the flesh, but after the Spirit.*" Rom. viii. 2, 3. Again, " For we ourselves also were sometimes foolish, disobedient, deceived, serving divers lusts and pleasures, living in malice and envy, hateful, and hating one another; but after that the kindness and love of God our Saviour toward man appeared: not by works of righteousness which we have done, but according to his mercy he saved us, *by the washing of regeneration, and renewing of the Holy Ghost:* which he shed on us abundantly, through Jesus Christ our Saviour." Tit. iii. 3—6. " I, indeed, baptize you with water," said John the Baptist to the Jews, " but he that cometh after me is mightier than I, whose shoes I am not worthy to bear: he shall baptize you *with the Holy Ghost and with fire.*" Matt. iii. 11. Compare John, xvi. 26. 1 John, ii. 27.

Lastly, we learn from the inspired writers that the same Mediator of the New Covenant, who was a propitiation for our sins, and who sheds forth on mankind the gifts and graces of the Holy Spirit, is mercifully engaged in pleading for his people before the throne of his Father. " My little children," said the apostle John, " these things write I unto you, that ye sin not. And if any man sin, we have an *advocate* with the Father, Jesus Christ the righteous." 1 John, ii. 1, 2. " Who is he that condemneth?" writes another apostle: " it is Christ that died, yea rather that is risen again, who also *maketh intercession* for us." Romans, viii. 34. " But this, (man,) because he continueth ever, hath an unchangeable priesthood. Wherefore he is able also to save them to the uttermost that come unto God by him, seeing he ever liveth to *make intercession* for them." Heb. vii. 24, 25.

Such are the powerful and harmonious statements presented to us by prophets and apostles, on the great subject of *Christian Redemption.*

Now to the inquiry already suggested—for what mighty and equivalent purpose the Son of God, by whom all things both in heaven and in earth were created, condescended to take our frail nature upon him, to dwell amongst us, and to die on the cross—these statements afford an intelligible and perfectly satisfactory answer. In his adorable mercy, in his almighty power, he came to *deliver* mankind; to *recover* them from their lost condition; to *save* them from the dominion of Satan, and from everlasting destruction; to supply all their spiritual need; to reconcile them through his own blood-shedding and mediation to the Father Almighty; to regenerate and sanctify them by his Holy Spirit; to provide for them both *indemnity* and *cure;* and thus to secure for them eternal life. Here are unfolded purposes worthy of the Son of God, and worthy of that peculiar display of his love and condescension revealed to us in the Bible—purposes fully adequate to his divine dignity, and capable of being carried into effect, *only* by him who, while he suffered in our suffering nature, was ONE with Jehovah—personally participating in the wisdom, power, and nature, of the only true God. Whether, indeed, we regard the human nature of Christ—in which he died for us, and is still " touched with the feeling of our infirmities"—or his divine nature, which imparts a mighty efficacy to the whole plan of our redemption;—we cannot but acknowledge, that between the spiritual wants of mankind, on the one hand, and the sure mercies of the MESSIAH OF GOD, on the other, there is a nice, an accurate, a perfect adaptation.

8. In order to avail ourselves of the means which God

in his unsearchable wisdom has thus ordained for our salvation, it is plainly necessary that we should *believe in Jesus Christ.* " These are written," says the apostle John, " that ye might believe that Jesus is the Christ, the Son of God: and that *believing* ye might have life through his name." John, xx. 31. " God so loved the world," said Jesus himself, " that he gave his only-begotten Son, that whosoever *believeth* in him should not perish, but have everlasting life." John, iii. 16. " I am the resurrection and the life: he that *believeth* in me, though he were dead, yet shall he live; and whosoever liveth and *believeth* in me shall never die." John, xi. 25, 26. Paul has declared that " a man is not justified by the works of the law, but by *the faith of Jesus Christ;*" (Gal. ii. 16.) and John the Baptist, when he bore witness to the power and excellency of the Lord Jesus, plainly stated the consequences both of believing and of *not* believing on the Son of God: " *He that believeth on the Son, hath everlasting life: and he that believeth not the Son, shall not see life: but the wrath of God abideth on him.*" John, iii. 36.

Now, the faith in Christ which is thus frequently declared to be the means of our salvation, is not a mere assent of the understanding to the history and doctrines of the Gospel. Such a faith is of itself a " dead faith," and we read that the " devils also believe and tremble." Jas. ii. 19. Saving faith is that living and active principle in our minds, by which, under the softening and purifying impressions of the love of God, we accept the Lord Jesus Christ as our only Saviour; spiritually feed upon him as upon the bread of life; place a humble yet sure reliance upon his mercy and power; and, *with full purpose and devotion of heart, submit our whole selves to his spiritual government.* This is " the faith which worketh by love." Gal. v. 6. This is the faith which enables us to bring forth the pure and lovely fruits of holiness, charity, gentleness, patience, joy, and peace. And thus " if any man be in Christ, he is a new creature: old things are passed away; behold all things are become new." 2 Cor. v. 17.

Mortally diseased as we are,—the fatal malady of sin rankling within us,—how are we to experience *recovery,* if we refuse to accept the appointed remedy? Then let us endeavour to lay aside the " evil heart of unbelief;"

let us no longer amuse ourselves with sceptical speculations on the theory of religion; but rather let us lay hold of its substance and flee from the wrath to come. Let us listen to the words of love and tenderness with which our compassionate Redeemer continues to invite us: "*Come unto me*, all ye that labour and are heavy laden, and I will give you rest: take my yoke upon you and learn of me; for I am meek and lowly in heart, and ye shall find rest unto your souls: for my yoke is easy and my burden is light." Matt. xi. 28—30. Yes, we must take upon us the *yoke of Christ*. " To obey is better than sacrifice, and to hearken than the fat of rams." 1 Sam. xv. 22. As we obtain reconciliation with the Father through the sacrifice of Christ, let us ever remember that we can be brought into a state of true holiness, and *avail ourselves of that reconciliation*, only by a *full submission* to the influence and guidance of his Spirit. It is by his Spirit that our all-sufficient Redeemer changes our vile hearts, mortifies our sinful affections, imparts to us his own holy nature, enables us to walk before him in purity and love, and thus prepares us for the enjoyment of that heavenly inheritance which he has meritoriously procured for us by his own perfect obedience, and by the sacrifice of himself. "*If we walk in the light, as he (God) is in the light*," says the apostle John, " we have fellowship one with another, and the blood of Jesus Christ his Son cleanseth us from all sin." 1 John, i. 7.

Nothing, indeed, can be more futile than even the most correct system of religious opinions, if our faith has no influence on the *heart*, and fails, therefore, to produce its legitimate consequence—*a godly life and conversation.*— Every thing in christianity is directed to *practical* purposes; and in the day of righteous retribution, it will only aggravate our condemnation to have heard, understood, and approved the word of the Lord, if we shall have persisted in refusing to follow its dictates. " Not every one that saith unto me, Lord, Lord, shall enter into the kingdom of heaven; but he that *doeth the will* of my Father which is in heaven." " Every one that heareth these sayings of mine and doeth them not, shall be likened unto a foolish man, which built his house upon the sand: and the rain descended and the floods came, and the winds blew and beat upon that house : and it fell, and *great was the fall of it.*" Matt. vii. 21. 26, 27.

Before I conclude, allow me briefly to recapitulate my whole argument.

Christianity is a religion which rests on the authority of God himself. 1. It is proved, by a greater variety and quantity of evidence than has ever been brought to bear on a similar subject, that the writings of which the New Testament is composed are *genuine.* 2. That the history recorded in those writings is true, we conclude from the testimony of several honest and independent witnesses; and that testimony is so confirmed by a number of remarkable and indisputable facts, as fully to meet the peculiarities of the case, and to establish the reality of the christian *miracles.* Now miracles are interruptions of the order given to nature by an omnipotent God, and, like the creation itself, can justly be ascribed only to Him. Since, therefore, he has attested christianity by true miracles, it follows that christianity is a religion of divine authority. 3. The real foreknowledge of future events is an attribute which must also be deemed peculiar to the Almighty, and God has attested christianity by *true prophecies.* Jesus Christ exactly predicted several events which were future when he spake. More especially, the prophecies of the Old Testament, respecting the Messiah, correspond with the character and history of Jesus, just as a lock of complicated and absolutely peculiar structure corresponds with its key. Hence again it follows, that christianity is the religion of God. 4. The Deity is a being of moral perfections; and christianity is the instrument by which he so transforms unregenerate men, that they come to render unto him the fear, honour, and love, which are his due—to show forth his moral attributes in their own conduct—and to enjoy a substantial and enduring happiness—whence the conclusion is again safely deduced, that our religion is *divine.*

The Scriptures are a divinely inspired record of christian truth. The inspiration of the writers of the Old Testament is evinced by the clear declarations, on that subject, of the apostles and of Christ himself. The inspiration of the writers of the New Testament, and especially of the apostles, is plainly recorded in the Gospel history already proved to be true; and these historical testimonies to the divine origin of the Scriptures are abundantly confirmed by the internal evidences derived from their holy, wise, harmonious, and practically efficacious contents. The difficulties in Holy Writ are analogous to those to be observed in natural science; but to the simple-hearted, sincere, and devotional reader, and as far as relates to those things which appertain to our salvation, the inspired writings are *plain* and *intelligible*.

The Bible is replete with important information, respecting God, ourselves, and Jesus Christ. 1. The various attributes and perfections of the Deity are described in the sacred volume, with a force and precision which clearly indicate the divine origin of the book. More especially the Scriptures represent the Deity as perfectly pure and just; so that he utterly abhors all sin, and will assuredly punish those who continue under its influence. Without holiness none shall see God. 2. Respecting ourselves, the Scriptures declare, that we are endued with a body and a soul—that the soul lives after death—that the dead will be raised in a spiritual body—that, in the eternal world to come, we shall, *according to our works*, be rewarded or punished, and be happy or miserable for ever—that we are fallen from the image of God in which Adam was created—that we are naturally prone to sin, and universally sinners—and that *of ourselves*, therefore, we can entertain no hope of salvation. 3. Respecting Jesus Christ, we read in the Bible—that he is the *Son* or *Word* of God, who was with God from everlasting—that all things were made by him—that he is one with the Father, and *himself God or Jehovah*—that he became incarnate, and assumed the nature of man, tarried upon earth, died on the cross, rose from the dead, ascended into heaven, and will come again to the judgment of quick and dead.

To the question—for what purpose SUCH AN ONE should so marvellously humble himself, as to come into this world, assume our nature, and die on the cross—the answer has been given : " *To supply all our spiritual need ;—to bestow upon us not only information, precept, and example, but indemnity and cure.*" This answer is explicitly confirmed by a multitude of passages selected from Holy Writ—by the perfectly accordant declarations of the prophets, of the angel Gabriel, of John the Baptist, of Christ himself, and of his apostles. These passages unfold in a luminous manner the whole doctrine of redemption, fully account for the great facts of the Gospel, and show that between the *spiritual wants* of mankind, and the *mercies of God in Christ*, there is an entire congruity. Lastly, I have observed, that we cannot avail ourselves of the promises and blessings of the Gospel, otherwise than by that true and living faith in Jesus, by which we rely upon him as upon our only Saviour, and through the operation of which we are sanctified, and bring forth the fruits of obedience, holiness, love, and peace.

Allow me, my dear Reader, to express an earnest and affectionate desire that such may be thy happy experience! If the afflicting hand of divine chastisement has convinced thee of the utter instability of every earthly joy—if thou art made sensible, that in the fleeting scenes of this present state of existence, there is nothing which can satisfy the aspirations of an immortal spirit—if thou art prepared to acknowledge thyself to be unworthy of the love of God; wretched, and miserable, and blind, and poor, and naked—mayest thou find a sure refuge for a wounded and weary spirit, in the bosom of the Holy Jesus! May he be made unto thee of God, " wisdom, righteousness, sanctification, and redemption!" Then, whatsoever tribulations may be permitted to attend thy path during the remaining stages of thy mortal pilgrimage, all will be well. Thy portion will be a true peace with God even here, and in the world to come, *life everlasting*.

And now a single additional observation will bring this Tract to its conclusion. If we are taught to mourn over our sins, we shall mourn also over the sins of mankind: we shall be humbled before God with deep sorrow of heart, when we reflect on the forgetfulness of their Creator, the falsehood, lasciviousness, malice, cruelty, and bloodshed, which are still so fearfully prevalent among the sons of Adam. But every one who is brought to a right understanding of the Gospel of Christ knows, that in its doctrines, as they are humbly accepted and practically applied, by the renewing and sanctifying agency of the Holy Ghost, there is a *powerful remedial principle*, by which moral evil of every description may be counteracted and subdued. Let us then pray for the hastening of that day when the dominion of Jesus shall extend "from sea to sea, and from the river unto the ends of the earth;" (Ps. lxxii. 8.) for under its blessed influence a mighty change shall still be wrought in the character and condition of men. "They shall beat their swords into ploughshares, and their spears into pruning hooks: nation shall not lift up sword against nation, neither shall they learn war any more." Isa. ii. 4. "The wolf also shall dwell with the lamb, and the leopard shall lie down with the kid, and the calf, and the young lion, and the fatling together, and a little child shall lead them. They shall not hurt nor destroy in all my holy mountain, saith the Lord; for the earth shall be full of the knowledge of the Lord, as the waters cover the sea." Isa. xi. 6—9. *Then shall this moral wilderness become a fruitful field.* "The wilderness and the solitary place shall be glad for them; and the desert shall rejoice, and blossom as the rose. It shall blossom abundantly, and rejoice, even with joy and singing; the glory of Lebanon shall be given unto it, the excellency of Carmel and Sharon: they shall see the glory of the Lord and the excellency of our God. And a highway shall be there, and a way, and it shall be called the way of holiness; the unclean shall not pass over it, but it shall be for those: the wayfaring men, though fools, shall not err therein. No lion shall be there, nor any ravenous beast shall go up thereon; it shall not be found there: but the redeemed shall walk there. And the ransomed of the Lord shall return and come to Zion, with songs and everlasting joy upon their heads: they shall obtain joy and gladness, and sorrow and sighing shall flee away." Isa. xxxv. 1, 2, 8—10.

While then, my dear Reader, we experience in ourselves a redemption from sin, *through faith in the Son of God;* and look forward to the universal extension of the same purifying principle, let us prostrate ourselves in all humility before the everlasting Jehovah, and exclaim with the apostle, "Thanks be to God for his UNSPEAKABLE GIFT!"

HYMN.

Christ, Dying, Rising, and Reigning.

He dies!—the Friend of sinners dies!
Lo! Salem's daughters weep around!
A solemn darkness veils the skies!
A sudden trembling shakes the ground!

Come, saints, and drop a tear or two
For him who groan'd beneath your load;
He shed a thousand drops for you—
A thousand drops of richer blood.

Here's love and grief beyond degree—
The Lord of glory dies for men!
But, lo! what sudden joys we see!
Jesus the dead—revives again!

The rising God forsakes the tomb!
Up to his Father's court he flies!
Cherubic legions guard him home,
And shout him welcome to the skies!

Break off your tears, ye saints, and tell
How high our great Deliv'rer reigns;
Sing how he spoil'd the hosts of hell,
And led the tyrant death—in chains.

Say, "Live for ever, glorious King!
Born to redeem, and strong to save!"
Then ask—"O death, where is thy sting?
And where thy vict'ry, boasting grave?"

PUBLISHED BY THE

AMERICAN TRACT SOCIETY,

And sold at their Depository, No. 150 Nassau-street, near the City Hall, New-York; and by Agents of the Society, its Branches, and Auxiliaries, in the principal cities and towns in the United States.

Other Solid Ground Titles

In addition to the volume which you hold in your hand, Solid Ground is honored to offer many other uncovered treasure, many for the first time in more than a century:

THE CHILD AT HOME by John S.C. Abbott
THE KING'S HIGHWAY: *10 Commandments for the Young* by Richard Newton
HEROES OF THE REFORMATION by Richard Newton
FEED MY LAMBS: *Lectures to Children on Vital Subjects* by John Todd
LET THE CANNON BLAZE AWAY by Joseph P. Thompson
THE STILL HOUR: *Communion with God in Prayer* by Austin Phelps
COLLECTED WORKS of James Henley Thornwell (4 vols.)
CALVINISM IN HISTORY *by Nathaniel S. McFetridge*
OPENING SCRIPTURE: *Hermeneutical Manual by Patrick Fairbairn*
THE ASSURANCE OF FAITH *by Louis Berkhof*
THE PASTOR IN THE SICK ROOM *by John D. Wells*
THE BUNYAN OF BROOKLYN: *Life & Sermons of I.S. Spencer*
THE NATIONAL PREACHER: *Sermons from 2nd Great Awakening*
FIRST THINGS: *First Lessons God Taught Mankind* Gardiner Spring
BIBLICAL & THEOLOGICAL STUDIES *by 1912 Faculty of Princeton*
THE POWER OF GOD UNTO SALVATION *by B.B. Warfield*
THE LORD OF GLORY *by B.B. Warfield*
A GENTLEMAN & A SCHOLAR: *Memoir of J.P. Boyce by J. Broadus*
SERMONS TO THE NATURAL MAN *by W.G.T. Shedd*
SERMONS TO THE SPIRITUAL MAN *by W.G.T. Shedd*
HOMILETICS AND PASTORAL THEOLOGY *by W.G.T. Shedd*
A PASTOR'S SKETCHES 1 & 2 *by Ichabod S. Spencer*
THE PREACHER AND HIS MODELS *by James Stalker*
IMAGO CHRISTI: *The Example of Jesus Christ by James Stalker*
A HISTORY OF PREACHING *by Edwin C. Dargan*
LECTURES ON THE HISTORY OF PREACHING *by J. A. Broadus*
THE SCOTTISH PULPIT *by William Taylor*
THE SHORTER CATECHISM ILLUSTRATED *by John Whitecross*
THE CHURCH MEMBER'S GUIDE *by John Angell James*
THE SUNDAY SCHOOL TEACHER'S GUIDE *by John A. James*
CHRIST IN SONG: *Hymns of Immanuel from All Ages by Philip Schaff*
COME YE APART: *Daily Words from the Four Gospels by J.R. Miller*
DEVOTIONAL LIFE OF THE S.S. TEACHER *by J.R. Miller*

Call us Toll Free at 1-866-789-7423
Send us an e-mail at sgcb@charter.net
Visit us on line at solid-ground-books.com
Uncovering Buried Treasure to the Glory of God